American Documentary Film

D0218743

American Documentary Film

Projecting the Nation

Jeffrey Geiger

Edinburgh University Press

© Jeffrey Geiger, 2011

Edinburgh University Press Ltd
22 George Square, Edinburgh

www.euppublishing.com

Typeset in 11/13 Ehrhardt
by Servis Filmsetting Ltd, Stockport, Cheshire, and
printed and bound in Great Britain by
CPI Antony Rowe, Chippenham and Eastbourne

A CIP record for this book is available from the British Library

ISBN 978 0 7486 2147 7 (hardback)
ISBN 978 0 7486 2148 4 (paperback)

The right of Jeffrey Geiger
to be identified as author of this work
has been asserted in accordance with
the Copyright, Designs and Patents Act 1988.

Grateful acknowledgement is made for permission to reproduce material previously published elsewhere.
Every effort has been made to trace the copyright holders, but if any have been inadvertently overlooked,
the publisher will be pleased to make the necessary arrangements at the first opportunity.

Published with the support of the Edinburgh University Scholarly Publishing Initiatives Fund.

Contents

Acknowledgements

I am very grateful to the British Academy for awarding a grant during the early research stages, and to the University of Essex for a generous sabbatical (2008–9). I'm lucky to work in a congenial and stimulating environment, so must thank the members of the Department of Literature, Film, and Theatre Studies for their support. Many thanks, also, to the following for their generous feedback: Sanja Bahun, Shohini Chaudhuri, Ian Scott, Randy Rutsky, Eithne Quinn and John Haynes. Students in my documentary seminars have helped me to crystallize and challenge many ideas discussed here; I would thank especially Nic Blower, Lina Alhafez, Kirsten Jones, Mark Tasker, Chloe Wilson and Richard Craig. Daniel Rellstab, Christiane Schlote and Danièle Klapproth kindly invited me to the interdisciplinary 'Out of War' conference in Bern, which fueled ideas for Chapters 5 and 8. I also appreciated the help of staff at the following libraries and archives: the British Film Institute; the British Library; the UCLA Film and Television archives; the Margaret Herrick Library, Academy of Motion Picture Arts and Sciences; the George Eastman House; Cantor Center for Visual Arts, Stanford University; the Bancroft Library at the University of California, Berkeley; the Butler Library at Columbia University; and the University of Illinois at Chicago Library, Special Collections. Sarah Edwards at EUP deserves credit for pointing me in the right direction early on, while Esmé Watson and Vicki Donald have been the ideal editors, with Peter Williams helpfully working on the manuscript. Finally, thanks to Hal Gladfelder who, with our selfless cats, has kept me focused on life beyond the screen.

Part of Chapter 8, revised for inclusion here, was published as 'Taking Aim: New Documentary and War', in *ZAA: Language, Literature, and Culture*, 56.2 (2008): 153–74.

List of illustrations

List of abbreviations

ACL	Amateur Cinema League
BMP	Bureau of Motion Pictures
CIAA	Co-ordinator of Inter-American Affairs
CPI	Committee on Public Information
CPUSA	Communist Party USA
FBI	Federal Bureau of Investigation
FSA	Farm Security Administration
GE	General Electric
GPO	General Post Office
HUAC	House Committee on Un-American Activities
ITVS	Independent Television Service
MOMA	Museum of Modern Art (New York)
MPPDA	Motion Picture Producers and Distributors of America
NAACP	National Association for the Advancement of Colored People
NBPC	National Black Programming Consortium
NFB	National Film Board (of Canada)
NIRA	National Industrial Recovery Act 1933
OB	Overseas Bureau
OWI	Office of War Information
PBS	Public Broadcasting Service
RA	Resettlement Administration
TVA	Tennessee Valley Authority
USIA	United States Information Agency
USFS	United States Film Service
[W]FPL	[Workers'] Film and Photo League
WIR	Workers' International Relief
WPA	Works Progress Administration

Introduction

American Documentary Film explores key themes, moments and movements in US documentary over the course of more than a century of cinema. In spite of the ambitious title, this is not a survey or exhaustive history of documentary.[1] Rather, this is an effort to distil important aspects of the documentary idea while tracing the form's development over time, focusing on the ways documentaries have engaged with US national identity and perceptions of American belonging. Moreover, by tracing lineages of the documentary idea that might not be seen as 'typical' or wholly representative of the form, I hope to suggest documentary's open-endedness and fluidity. Documentary has long been a negotiated concept: a site of personal, social, intellectual and aesthetic investment keenly fought over and debated.

I'll start by briefly outlining some ideas behind – and limits of – the book's title, *American Documentary Film: Projecting the Nation*. First, though the term 'American' features prominently, I would stress that the idea of 'America' is a contested one, not only through questions of what constitutes 'American' identity, but in the ways that the term 'America' manages to elide the rest of the Americas in one fell swoop. With this in mind, critics like Malini Johar Schueller and Mary Renda employ the terms 'USAmerican' and 'U.S. American', respectively, in efforts to draw attention to the implicit hegemony of common usages of 'America' and 'American' (Schueller 1998; Renda 2001). Whenever possible, then, I use 'US' both as a noun and as an adjective in the text, though the noun 'American', referring to a resident/citizen of the United States, has been generally retained, indicating a powerful idea – and hegemonic construct, as discussed below – of national identity.

'Documentary' is also a less straightforward term than it might seem at first; as employed here, it refers to cinematic forms that haven't always fit comfortably within stricter definitions of the term. 'Film', similarly, serves as shorthand for motion picture technologies ranging from celluloid to video and digital technologies, though restrictions on space have meant I've been unable to devote as much attention to television and Internet documentaries as I would have liked. Other difficult decisions and elisions had to be made, given these limits, and important areas relating to documentary's development – including newsreels, ethnographic film, feminist film, 'PBS-style' educational films, home movies, post–Second World War experimental film and documentary animation – remain underexplored.[2]

As for the book's subtitle, the word 'projecting' is an effort to incorporate several interlinked associations, the most obvious being the projection of a film on to a screen. 'Projecting' further is meant to convey an idea of audiences projecting themselves into the film text – both imaginatively and sensibly. Finally, the term also attempts to highlight the image of a nation constantly projecting itself into an imagined, bigger, and better, future. The United States, as the name of the Chicago World's Fair of 1933 – 'A Century of Progress' – stressed, has tirelessly promoted itself as being in a constant state of moving forward, and documentary has been a key mode for charting this idea of progress – the forward movement through what Henry Luce once laid claim to as 'the American Century'. The obsession with progress carried on, unevenly but seemingly unstoppably, until the Vietnam War, when the imperial and industrial imaginings of the 'American Century' and the 'Century of Progress' were pushed to a breaking point. Yet the national rhetoric of perpetual reinvention, projecting into a bigger and better future, has never really faded, as the aspirational language of presidential campaign slogans always strives to remind us – from 'It's Morning Again in America' (Reagan, 1984) and 'Prosperity and Progress' (Gore, 2000) to 'Yes, America Can!' (Bush, 2004).

DOCUMENTARY AND THE NATION

As this book sets out to show, documentary films have been important to forming ideas of the US nation, both as an imagined space and as a real place. Yet it is worth considering what makes up the idea of the nation, and whose interests it serves. Concepts of the nation and of national identity are rooted in cultural practices and beliefs, so much so that they might seem beyond questioning. As Ernest Gellner contends, 'having a nation is not an inherent attribute of humanity, but it has now come to appear as such' (2006: 6). To be without a national identity – to be 'nationless' or 'stateless' – is to be powerless in modern western consciousness, an aberrant prospect to be pitied or feared. Yet, as Gellner suggests, nations are a 'contingency, not a universal necessity' (6); as a 'natural, God-given way of classifying men, as an inherent though long-delayed political destiny, [nations] are a myth' (47).

An essential component of the nation-state, Homi Bhabha contends, is the effort to create a unified national culture. The nation is a 'progressive meta-phor of modern social cohesion', a concept that posits 'the many as one' (1994: 204). National identities are based on a variety of factors – some foregrounded more than others – such as birthplace, historically determined borders and boundaries, language, ethnicity, and religious and political beliefs. In this sense, nations can be seen as constructed out of perceived affiliations.[3] Yet at the same time it's difficult to dismiss the transformational passions that national identities arouse. The nation becomes invested with psychic and emotional power, so much so that members are willing to sacrifice their lives for them. In this sense nations are not merely – or simplistically – 'artificial', in that they carry with them the force of individual and collective belief and experience, making real that which is 'imagined'.

In Benedict Anderson's much-cited view, nations might therefore be seen as 'imagined communities'; that is, though it is impossible to know every member of one's own nation, there is a sense of affiliation and a mutual sense of 'knowing' other members: 'in the minds of each [national member] lives the image of their communion' (1991: 6). Anderson sees national thinking and nationalism as chiefly arising towards the end of the eighteenth century, advanced through centralized communication and perceptions of democratic access, which encouraged the idea that citizens belonged to a distinct yet shared national unit. Crucial for Anderson are the underlying roles played by mass communication technologies such as the printing press, and with them the possibility of cultural homogenization through standardized vernacular language. These observations, as Núria Triana-Toribio suggests, begin to imply the role of other forms of mass communication, such as cinema, in framing the 'narration and representation of the nation to itself': reflecting and shaping national identities (2002: 4).

Films, with the discourses that surround them and the institutions that support them, are central means through which the idea of the national is articulated and culturally determined. As Susan Hayward has shown, more than simply influencing or reflecting ideas of the nation, films, filmic dis-courses and institutional formations form part of complex, negotiated national identities. Film reflects and refracts national consciousness – it can help create a sense of national belonging through the national narratives and myths it (re)produces. Like national affiliations themselves, films and filmic discourses are selective: they can mobilize, promote and also suppress key ideas and myths of the nation (Hayward 2005: 6–8, 15). In documentary contexts, this process might be seen in its extreme version in propaganda documentaries of the Second World War, which strategically vaunted concepts of their nations' moral and military superiority while suppressing any appearance of ideological division or dissent.

The idea of 'national cinema', in academic film studies, has been commonly linked to state-sponsored cinema movements which work to reinforce the 'truth' of national identity by supporting national film industries that combat external influences and powerful market forces – in particular, Hollywood. Yet, if the US has a national cinema, it would naturally appear to be Hollywood. Hollywood films, between the years 1930 and 1945, averaged 80 million admissions weekly, or more than half of the US population (Ray 1985: 25). In the darkened space of the theater, 'utopian stories, political fantasies, and mythic narratives were told' (Denzin 1995: 14). Arguably this 'classic' period of US cinema saw the consolidation of a national ideology – particularly in mainstream media – culminating in the dominant projection of clear-cut American values and beliefs during the Second World War.

The relationship between US documentary and the idea of national cinema, then, becomes complex and at times contradictory. Documentary filmmaking has, on and off, engaged with state sponsorship and counter-Hollywood strategies, as this book will show, yet documentaries have at different times been produced by and absorbed into Hollywood frameworks. Likewise, it would be difficult to prove that documentary as a cinematic form has consistently constructed an 'alternative America' to the Hollywood version, though political documentaries since Vietnam have made concerted efforts in this direction (see Chapters 7 and 8). Hayward highlights similar ambiguities in the idea of national cinema, noting that the dynamic relations between 'central' and 'peripheral' cinemas *within* national formations are sometimes mutually dependent, and not always oppositional (2005: 15). Still, some critics have seen US documentary as undermining the very precepts of a national cinema. For Patricia Zimmermann, documentary can resist the status quo and signal 'the dissolution of the universal nation and its narrational strategies through its location within contestatory newly emerging identities and social collectivities' (2000: 12). Such 'postnational' readings stress the potential of documentaries to effect social and political change, to generate debate about national identities and responsibilities. As this book will show, however, not all documentaries – or even all those considered 'social' or 'political' documentaries – have always worked to demystify the nation. The documentary idea has long been predicated on nationalist ideologies and national identities, ranging from the explicit national rhetoric of FDR's Resettlement Administration films to the implicit nationalist address of *Fahrenheit 9/11* (2004).

This book attempts, then, to delineate ways in which documentary has potently contributed to shifting conceptions of US national consciousness and belonging. I wouldn't, in the end, propose US documentary as a kind of national cinema, though I would stress that documentary has powerfully contributed to both the nation's making and its unmaking. For Jonathan Kahana, the impact of documentary lies in its ability to gesture towards worlds, experiences, emotions and structures of feeling beyond the 'evidence' it depicts.

Documentary representation can make visible 'the invisible or "phantom" realities that shape the experience of the ordinary Americans in whose name power is exercised and contested' (2008: 9). In this sense, documentary does not just reflect or engage with national consciousness, it helps us to imagine ideas and futures beyond its immediate framework and subject matter; it has the potential to transform the experience and comprehension of a national imaginary. To examine this process in more depth, it would be useful at this point to reflect further on how the documentary concept has been variously defined and debated.

DEFINITIONS

The term 'documentary', it is generally agreed, was coined in the 1920s and has been in common use since the 1930s, yet its definition often has been less than clear.[4] In 1954, almost thirty years after the term appeared, Cecil Starr of the *Saturday Review* complained that the lack of a ready definition remained 'an irritation among film-minded people; and the repeated demand for defini-tion, when none is easily forthcoming, is even more irritating' (1954: 44).

John Grierson's much-cited phrase, the 'creative treatment of actuality', has long served as a dominant description of what constitutes documentary (Hardy 1946: 11). The documentarist works to produce 'art' by passing from the realm of purely descriptive uses of 'natural material' into the realm of 'arrangements, rearrangements, and creative shapings of it' (Grierson 1946 [1932]: 79). Grierson's notion of 'creative treatment' has remained, at the very least, ambiguous enough to survive the test of time; it also usefully, for many, differentiates documentaries from other 'lower categories' of nonfiction films (78). Yet it is also seen as limited, based on a 'denigration' of earlier forms such as travelogues, newsreels and actualities, suppressing their key role in documentary's development (Rosen 1993: 73–4). Indeed, there remains 'little consensus' about documentary: as a concept it has long been a the center of numerous 'competing discourses' attempting to claim it as art, propaganda, education, science, human interest and so on (Roscoe and Hight 2001: 7). Many critics have worked towards more coherent and unified definitions, while others, such as Bill Nichols, have broken the form down into more manageable subgenres and subcategories.[5] Still, as Dai Vaughan suggests, there is a 'labyrinth of rules and exceptions, and exceptions to the exceptions, which awaits anyone who tries to identify documentary by generic or stylistic criteria' (1999: 84). The range of genres and styles popularly consumed as documentary – from PBS educational films and Discovery Channel adven-tures to *I'm a Celebrity Get Me Out of Here* and *Wife Swap* – testifies to the very malleability and instability of the term.

Documentary has been seen to bear a special relationship to the concrete, pro-filmic world, as the filmic opposite of fiction. This emphasis on facts, evidence and accountability – what Michael Renov calls a 'scientistic yearning' in documentary (1999: 85) – might be traced along at least one genealogical line to the Enlightenment era of the later eighteenth century – around the time, according to Gellner and Anderson, that the very idea of the nation itself was gaining currency. During this period, demands intensified for more precise technologies for reporting facts and presenting evidence that could advance scientific and social progress. The film documentary, in particular, continues to benefit from a widespread acceptance that it is a fact-based mode, echoing Enlightenment differentiations between factual or 'documentary' representation (such as 'documentary drawing' that discouraged distortion and emphasized on-the-spot, *plein-air* technique) and more fanciful representations (such as 'inventive drawing' or 'illustrative drawing') (Smith 1992: 54; Geiger 2007: 32–3).

Thus documentary images, though normally grounded in the unpredictable and disordered realms of experience, are afforded pedagogical value as authoritative evidence of real phenomena and historical events. Other practices that have fed into documentary approaches reflect this Enlightenment tradition: illustrated lectures, ethnological displays, scientific collecting and exhibiting, and so on. If these aren't precise antecedents of documentary film, perhaps they might be seen as traces – harbingers of what was to come. As Grierson's definition indicates, this scientistic yearning meets, to varying degrees, elements of 'creative treatment'. This 'expressive' component inheres in the poetic leanings of Robert Flaherty, in 'city symphonies' such as *Manhatta* (1921), in the work of Joris Ivens and in the influence of the avant-garde. As a result, documentary's aesthetic function 'can never be wholly divorced from the didactic one'; in all, documentary might be summed up as a form of 'pleasurable learning' (Renov 1993: 35).

Most documentaries draw on photography's 'indexical' properties, relying on the 'here and now' impact of photographic technology.[6] Of the photographic index, Gilberto Perez suggests that 'the photographic image is an index because it is an imprint taken directly from the things represented; and it is also an index because, like the pointing finger, it tells us to look at those things' (1998: 395). In related terms, Laura Marks likens film to a fossil: as an imprint of something it once touched, the fossil is 'powerfully descriptive of cinema's disturbing ability to recreate its object in the present' (2000: 22). Vaughan, however, stresses that the power of the photographic index also relies on social and cultural beliefs that circulate around the image. He offers another analogy – in this case the Shroud of Turin – which sustains its unique aura not merely because the image is seen as an imprint (a kind of fossilized remains) of a crucified figure. Its power, rather, comes from its associations with the image of Christ: if it were an anonymous figure it wouldn't carry the same weightiness and mystic authority (1999: 135). Likewise, documentary requires discourses and systems of belief – of authenticity, immediacy, authority and knowledge – circulating around its 'indexical' images, imparting a kind of aura of legitimacy to the likenesses 'captured' on film.

Of course, the indexical nature of film is not unique to documentary, though it is harnessed, arguably, in distinctive ways. Nichols points out that though both live-action fiction and nonfiction share indexical properties, importantly documentary incorporates a host of mechanisms that 'prepare us to expect a privileged status for the indexical link between sign and referent' (1991: 230). This 'privileged status' depends on qualities and attributes that extend beyond basic elements of genre and style. For example, a fiction film might have a documentary 'look', as in neorealism or *film noir*, but it would very rarely be taken for a documentary. At the same time, some documentaries are openly reconstructions, or even use animation techniques, in which case the lack of emphasis on the photographic index is usually balanced by foregrounding other documentary codes and conventions, such as the presentation of factual information and analysis. In this respect, a documentary establishes its status and distinctiveness more through its intents, uses and public reception. Nichols thus sees the form's integrity as coalescing around three interlinked areas: the filmmaker, the text and the viewer.

The documentary filmmaker works within a series of social and institutional frameworks relating to economics, ideological beliefs and professional practices. In terms of professional practice, there is a range of expectations relating to camerawork, editing and cinematic codes and conventions, as well as a certain amount of 'discipline and control' exerted over what documentarists can and can't do (for example, pressures against distorting actions and events that they are recording) (Nichols 1991: 14). The Australian documentarist Philip Tyndall, for example, sums up some of these restrictions primarily in ethical terms, highlighting the importance of an 'honest' relationship between the filmmaker and his subjects and viewers; the filmmaker's 'responsibility' for recording people, places and events so that this knowledge is not lost from memory; and the importance of 'accuracy' (as opposed to stricter notions of capturing the 'truth') in documentary (Tyndall 2003). Yet, Nichols stresses, in spite of these presumed restrictions, there is always an element of lack of control, and this lack comes down to the unpredictability and variability of experience and history themselves.

Since this lack of control potentially undermines the intentions of the documentarist, more important than intention, for Nichols, is documentary's 'status as an institutional formation'. Documentaries are texts that bear common and distinguishing features (such as working through an argument or thesis, 'evidentiary editing' that stresses logical or cause and effect relations, voiceover narration, interviews, testimony and so on), and thus are more or less formally recognized as belonging to a common category. Finally, the role of the audience – the 'constituency of viewers' – is key (Nichols 1991: 18–21, 24). Audiences assimilate previous experiences of watching different kinds of films with their immediate analytical, critical and physical reactions to the film text passing in front of them. Hence, among a range of approaches – from educational to expressive, didactic to poetic – a 'documentary identity' will generally 'hold together' (Corner 2002).

It is the convergence of these various indices, and what might be called the nonfiction 'contract' between a film's producers and consumers, that constitutes the collective 'faith' or 'trust' invested in documentary. Hence, Carl Plantinga suggests that while the audience's receptive role can make or break a documentary, documentary film should be seen more as a two-way phenomenon: a kind of speech act or communicative action. If fiction takes a 'fictive stance' towards the world and does not overtly assert an authoritative claim to obtaining the 'actual world', documentary is recognized through its 'assertive stance' towards the actual world and its adoption of certain prototypical stylistic and narrative features. It is also, very importantly, contextualized and promoted as documentary in practices such as exhibition and advertising (Plantinga 2009: 498).

DOCUMENTARY AND/VERSUS FICTION

Even with this range of arguments framing documentary's enunciatory and social particularity, many have contended there is little difference between documentary and fiction. Though as a cinematic form documentary is aligned to nonfiction and factuality, and therefore not viewed as 'fancy' or fantasy, it's easy enough to see that documentaries are constructs containing elements of subjective interpretation, selection, fictional techniques, narrative modes and so on. As early as 1938, Frank S. Nugent of the *New York Times* expressed concerns about the form's ambiguities and potential deceptions. Writing at a time when documentary advocates were asserting the form's unique value (and the New School for Social Research had just launched its first course in documentary film 'as history and journalism'), Nugent was concerned that documentaries could 'be made to serve whatever purpose their compiler intends them to serve'. 'With camera reportage and camera distortage hopelessly intermingled', it was almost impossible to 'sift for the authentic among the documentaries' (Nugent 1984 [1938]).

Perhaps the most sustained challenge to documentary's autonomous status came with the poststructuralist focus on breaking down neat oppositional categories such as fiction and nonfiction.[7] Following the rise of poststructuralism in theory and criticism, there was a steep increase in the academic study of documentary, reflecting sustained interests in investigating questions of truth and representation.[8] These critiques helped collapse categorical distinctions, stressing that convenient markers separating documentary and fiction were always under suspicion and liable to interrogation. Documentary 'truth' could be seen as a construct like any other, always intimately bound to issues of power, subject position and ideological influence.

At the same time there have been attempts to reframe these claims by re-examining differences between fiction and nonfiction from social, semiotic, philosophical and phenomenological perspectives. Vivian Sobchack sees cinemagoing as always embodied, suggesting that experiences of nonfiction images can be phenomenologically distinct from those of fiction. The vivified, visible presence of people and objects in cinema can uncannily overlap with the filmgoer's physical presence and ability to bring cultural and personal knowledge that can intimately, even physically, engage with and relate to figures projected on screen. Sobchack supports this idea by posing the example of a cinematic representation of a dog. If it happens to show *my* dog, she argues, 'I will not engage its image in the same way that I engage the image of "Lassie", a dog with which I have romped only cinematically, in a fiction' (1999: 242–3). The filmgoer will project a different range of responses, marked by recollections of touch, smell and physical proximity, on to the 'real' on-screen dog.

Further countering the 'denial' of differences between fiction and nonfiction, Noël Carroll has questioned any simplistic levelling of distinctions by examining the moving image's differing qualities of 'depiction', 'nominal portrayal' and 'physical portrayal' (1996: 224).[9] For example, a shot of Clark Gable in the film *Gone with the Wind* depicts a man (as a general category or type) and physically portrays Gable himself, but it nominally (and predominantly) portrays the character of Rhett Butler (Carroll 1996: 241). Documentary generally combines depiction with nominal and physical portrayals, just as dramatic fiction does, but these shared characteristics do not automatically collapse distinctions between the two. The contextualization and reception of images is crucial: for example, in a documentary about the behind-the-scenes lives of Hollywood actors, the very same shot taken from *Gone with the Wind* would signify to audiences a physical portrayal of Clark Gable – a kind of nonfiction artifact – rather than the fictional character of Rhett Butler.

In identifying fictional and nonfictional strategies, we should be aware that depiction, nominal and physical portrayals are employed in varying contexts, and that their signifying properties can be strategically brought forward or suppressed, to varying degrees, in processes of production, reception, exhibition and advertising. Fictions tend to foreground nominal portrayals, while documentaries frame their portrayals in ways that testify to and highlight their nonfictional status, even if they sometimes 'lie'. As Carroll suggests, the use of stock footage of factory workers in a film about strikebreaking, for example, would be an example of a documentary relying on nominal portrayal in a nonfiction context, in that the image might not show the actual strikebreakers in question. Yet audiences would still be expected to perceive these factory workers as representative of the subject at hand (or at worst, viewers would revert to accepting the images as generalized depictions). As long as the shot is not explicitly misidentified, audiences will not consider the film to be patently misleading or 'fake'. In such cases, a documentary doesn't automatically become a 'fiction' so long as it conforms to 'established standards of objectivity' (1996: 241–2). More important, in this case, than the 'truth' or 'lies' of what a documentary shows is whether it can stand up to questions and tests of authenticity and verifiability, questions to which fictions normally would not be subjected.

As Vaughan states, 'documentary, after all, can tell lies; and it can tell lies because it lays claim to a form of veracity which fiction doesn't' (1999: 154). I may be arguing that documentaries do operate and circulate, in important ways, differently from fiction films, but I would also suggest that much has to do with *perceptions* of difference, and that documentaries should be seen as situated more along a continuum with fictions than standing in absolute opposition to them. Documentary is not a static or homogeneous form. Nichols opens his *Introduction to Documentary* with the intentionally contentious statement: 'every film is a documentary'; elsewhere he calls documentary 'a fiction unlike any other' (2001a: 1; 1991: 109). Essentially documentary, while marking out a space in the popular imagination both alongside and against fiction, occupies 'no fixed territory' and might be seen as a site of 'contestation and change' (1991: 12).

DOCUMENTARY EXPERIENCE

Documentary is in a state of flux, marked by shifting aims and practices, changing perceptions of its forms and functions, as well as remediation – a process that sees the character of representations constantly evolving as media technologies reinvent themselves (Chanan 2007: 22). Over the years, at least in Anglo-American contexts, documentary has shifted focus from Griersonian observation and advocacy, to direct cinema immediacy (a rebellion against Griersonian approaches), to postmodern self-reflexivity and indeterminacy (a rebellion against direct cinema). In recent decades, this mutability has arguably intensified, as the lines once drawn by critics such as Grierson and Paul Rotha between actualities, simpler nonfiction films, sheer entertainments and 'serious' documentaries have been further blurred.

My use of the term documentary, then, is at times rather approximate. I am, however, less concerned with arriving at a precise definition of the term than in considering the ways that this broadly recognized form produces a kind of imagined public space and a kind of real place. Documentary, as Sobchack points out, is a term that designates more than just a cinematic '*object*'. As she suggests, 'along with the obvious nomination of a film genre characterized historically by objective textual features, the term also – and more radically – designates a certain *subjective relation* to an objective cinematic or televisual text. In other words, documentary is less a *thing* than an *experience*' (1999: 241). This experience is crucial to the production of what I would call documentary reality. Documentary reality, while not 'reality' itself, is a cinematic experience of reality that indexes – and points towards – real people, places and events. It is socially produced, and experienced through cognitive and bodily processes. At times this reality is marked by extreme difference from the familiar and everyday, at others by powerful impressions of recognition and closeness. Just as the smell and taste of Proust's madeleine 'triggers' memories and desires (Mavor 1996: 4), documentary reality can work on and with the spectator's memories, cultural investments, beliefs, sympathies, emotions and senses. In this sense, documentaries are not detached replicas of the world, but might be seen as corollaries of lived experience.

Importantly, the documentary experience doesn't stand in isolation from the world but speaks to broader affiliations and collectives. As Kahana suggests, a documentary 'collects the evidence of experience in the most far-flung precincts, in coal mines, cornfields, cell blocks, convention halls, corporate boardrooms, and city slums. Then it delivers these social facts to a broader public, where they can be used for a variety of ideological ends.' Documentary might thus be seen as forming part of the 'social imaginary', helping us 'envision the collective consequences of our thoughts and actions, no matter how ordinary or idiosyncratic' (Kahana 2008: 1–2).[10] The social imaginary gives shape to a common understanding, and 'makes possible common practices and a widely shared sense of legitimacy'. At the same time, this imaginary site isn't limited to establishing a consensus; it might form part of cultural critique and expectations of social change (2).

Conceiving documentary in these terms might help, in part, to explain the heightened social status that documentary has long enjoyed. Documentary can translate experience and makes it 'available for interpretation' in institutional, public and community forums (Kahana 2008: 2). Documentaries might, therefore, be seen as corresponding to a kind of public space, forming part of a social imaginary that can help to determine shared identities, values and goals, while also holding the potential to alter these conceptual frameworks and assert dissensus. This collective role might be seen most clearly in thesis-driven documentaries such as *Bowling for Columbine* (2002) or *Super Size Me* (2004), designed to generate public debate and action, but can also apply to seemingly socially indifferent nonfictions like television reality shows. My intent here is not to return to a version of Griersonian hierarchy, where some documentaries are determined to have 'more' or 'better' social value than others. It is simply to suggest that most documentaries, at some level, serve a public function and contribute to the public sphere: they can be flashpoints for discussion about who and what we are, and want to be.

Of course the very idea of the 'public' sphere in the US – and of 'public' identities and 'public' interests more generally – is, increasingly, riddled with problems and contested definitions. Traditionally, the public sphere is associated with hierarchical power structures, where 'official' ideologies and discursive practices strive to suppress alternatives and challenges to power. Others have stressed the public sphere's lack of homogeneity, citing the existence of 'counterpublics' as sites and affiliations that develop discourses that challenge the very idea of official, 'top-down' social controls.[11] Because documentary is essentially a public format, appealing to and depending on shifting public understandings and beliefs, it has never, in the US at least, provided a fully stable basis for projecting unified social and communal values and goals (though some have tried). US documentary has always been differential and diverse, and in this very diversity has reflected multiple and often competing discourses of different social and cultural groups. Even so, perhaps due to ongoing presumptions of documentary's orientation towards the public sphere, often seemingly 'counterpublic' documentaries can be found attempting to encode and appeal to a horizon of shared interests.

There is a moment in Michael Moore's *Fahrenheit 9/11* that reflects this tension between 'official' and 'counterpublic' discourses. Moore films the grieving Lila Lipscomb, who lost her son in the Iraq War, putting up her American flag; later, when interviewing her in her kitchen, he utters 'it's a great country' in perfunctory fashion. Lila – almost too quickly – agrees with him. This insistence on American 'greatness' seems to stand out awkwardly within a film that is condemning a US act of war. Yet the scene suggests that the very basis of a film like *Fahrenheit 9/11*, and the reason why its status as a documentary is so important, lies in documentary's presumed public role. It also reveals what is at stake when making and 'selling' political documentary in the US. From Moore's position, criticism of US war policies necessitates avoiding the appearance of anti- or un-Americanism; the voice with which the film tries to speak, though dissenting, aims for a broader consensus constructed around shared ideals and values presumed embedded in an 'American way of life'.

Documentaries are not always as self-conscious about their public function as Moore's, but they do almost always maintain a presumption of some form of public address – even seemingly apolitical documentaries such as *Manhatta* (1921) or highly personal statements such as *Silverlake Life* (1993). Looking at a history of US documentary, we encounter the perpetual subject of this address, sometimes explicitly but more often implicitly conceived of as the 'American nation'. In this respect perhaps, much US documentary bears at least traces of a 'national cinema'.

OVERVIEW

The eight chapters that follow sketch a rough chronology, but I don't wish to imply a strict linear development of US documentary. Each chapter examines a key set of themes or movements (historical, political, social, aesthetic), while also containing a 'case study' of a single film. In choosing films for the latter, I was very conscious of the risks of implying that one film might, somehow, stand in for a whole era, group or movement.[12] On the other hand I wanted to stress the value of close reading, suggesting how particular rhetorical, technical and stylistic elements of individual films might always be seen as operating in tension with, and speaking to, more general contexts and concerns. Documentaries are texts that seem to resist close analysis: often treated as informational, they tend to give rise to opinion and descriptions of content rather than sustained attempts to investigate and unpack deeper structures and meanings. Many students of documentary are initially uncomfortable with the imposition of theoretical, symbolic, thematic, narrative and aesthetic modes of interpretation on a form still commonly considered transparent, immediate and real. Yet it's important not only to outline the social contexts and overt 'messages' of documentaries, but to engage with how a documentary constructs its realities, works as an experience, functions as a cultural and technical production, reflects and reveals the world around us. This means bringing to bear all of the tools familiar to film analysis – examining the history, culture, ideology, technology, markets and aesthetics of cinema – while also identifying the 'voice' of documentary, recognizing its social currency and value, discovering the meanings and broader concepts and histories towards which the text gestures.

Chapter 1 looks at what I call authentic attractions, and at an era that Michael Chanan aptly refers to as 'documentary before documentary' (2007: 55). Here I argue that, though the documentary had not yet formally come into being, one might discern a documentary 'impulse' in the combination of edification, sensation and entertaining display encountered at sites such as the Midway Plaisance at the Chicago Exposition of 1893. This event, importantly, brought together efforts to invoke a distinct American national identity through an amalgam of technologies, commercial ventures, cultural expectations and ideological notions that fed into early cinema in the US and into a popular taste for nonfiction actualities. The chapter moves on to study films of the Edison Company, suggesting that rather than see these early films as 'documents' as opposed to fully fledged 'documentaries', we might consider how they lie at the heart of the documentary tradition – in no small part due to their interactions with a national imaginary.

Chapter 2 expands on the idea of the Chicago Exposition as 'the cheapest and most exhaustive journey over the earth that was ever made' (Reed 2000: xxvi), reflecting on cinema's capacity to serve as a vehicle for mobility, travel and tourism. Associations between cinema and travel were widespread: actualities and travelogues revealed faraway sights to Americans at home, while the sensation of travel was incorporated into film technology itself. This chapter examines how modes of entertainment ranging from illustrated lectures to phantom rides were foundational to later documentary approaches. These forms of virtual travel, 'possessing the world' in images, also fed into national and imperial consciousness. Establishing a spectatorial relationship to sights and scenes 'over there', these films helped define a sense of 'us' and 'here'.

Chapter 3 further suggests the mobility of the documentary idea by looking at movements conventionally viewed in opposition to each other: documentary and the avant-garde. Avant-garde cinema has been associated with aesthetic innovation, imagination and playfulness, while documentary has been seen as a 'sober' discursive mode. This chapter works to excavate significant intersections between the two, finally considering how the modernist aesthetics of documentaries such as *Manhatta* helped to vivify a widely adhered-to notion of American individuality and newness: a progressive, unabashedly urban vision of the nation, tinged with a cautious nostalgia for a pre-industrial past.

Chapter 4 ranges between the late 1920s and the Second World War, charting the 'invention' of documentary film as it commonly came to be known. The idea of documentary as a specific form, and as a professional practice, came into its own during this period. At the same time, ongoing reassessments of what it meant to be American and part of an evolving national entity were paramount. Significantly, this period also saw a concerted effort to establish a government-funded documentary program under Franklin Delano Roosevelt's New Deal policies. Though this era is often seen as a time of increasing conformity and assimilation to a narrow ideological consensus, this chapter takes into account the incredible political and social diversity of the period – diversity amply reflected in documentaries of the time.

Chapter 5 focuses on propaganda documentaries of the Second World War, partly because they form a fascinating component of US documentary history, when documentary took a dominant public role extending far beyond any it had played before, partly because this explicit marriage of propaganda and documentary speaks to elements of propaganda that haunt the documentaries of other eras. The Second World War saw a severe straitening of notions of American selfhood, not least in the forceful pronouncements that saturated the media. As the voices of soldiers in John Ford's *December 7th* (1943) state, 'we are all alike . . . we are all Americans'. In addition to addressing issues of ideology and representation, this chapter works to untangle the complicated web of intense documentary production and distribution during the time, which was spread among various government, corporate Hollywood and military interests.

In Chapter 6, I investigate a key 'revolution' in US documentary production, direct cinema. Direct cinema was not only a case of the form's remediation, but brought with it a whole system of beliefs – variously referred to as a 'philosophy', 'ideology' or 'set of rules' – that privileged notions of documentary spontaneity and immediacy. It also helped advance the idea of documentary as a form of democratic access and democratic action, at times reinforcing and at others critiquing a hegemonic national ideal through capturing the diversity and contradictions of the American scene. This chapter carefully examines key influences, practitioners and landmark texts of direct cinema, charting the rise, fall and ongoing influences of its practices and beliefs.

Chapter 7 outlines postmodern influences in documentary, a meeting of theory and praxis often characterized by self-reflexivity as well as formal and semantic instability in nonfiction film. The postmodern era saw a shift away from documentary certainty and immediacy, corresponding to a poststructuralist questioning of truth and the transparency of representation. Critics such as Linda Williams have convincingly shown that postmodern documentary, by insistently exposing its artifice while retaining key elements of its traditional forms and uses, constitutes a break with convention. Arguably and somewhat paradoxically, as this chapter shows, moves towards postmodern ambivalence actually reinvigorated the form, leading to rich meditations on the ambiguities of evidence, testimony and other kinds of documentation.

Finally, Chapter 8 looks at the idea of 'documentary dispersion', considering whether new markets, technologies and social challenges can be met through documentary's distinctive modes of address and filmmakers' ongoing efforts to engage with and influence the social imaginary. Given the ever-broadening range of documentary production and consumption, this chapter focuses more narrowly on a pressing issue taken up by recent documentary: the representation of US wars, and in particular the Iraq War.

'Cinematic identification is as fragile and unstable as identity itself', Judith Mayne asserts (1993: 27), and national identification might be seen as similarly fragile, relying on interlinked networks of signs, affiliations and cultural reinforcements (such as cinema). Recently, US national identity has been caught up in the varying pressures of globalization (interlinked global economies), denationalization (erosion of the traditional nation-state under globalized conditions), transnationalism (movements and flows within and between nations that break down national fixities) and supranationalism ('superstate' affiliations, such as the European Union). The last few decades also have seen a resurgence of articulations of more local and regional affiliations: identities that can impact upon and supersede the national. As these shifting negotiations at local, national and global levels attest, and as this book hopes to show, engagements between documentary and experiences of American identity testify to a fluid range of formations and relations: both 'documentary' and 'America' might be seen as social and historical accretions rather than as fixed or natural entities.

NOTES

1. See, for example, Barnouw (1983), Ellis and McLane (2005), Rotha (1952) and Barsam (1992).
2. For further study see, for example, Nichols (1980), Fielding (1972), Hockings (1993), Waldman and Walker (1999), Edgerton (2002), Zimmermann (1995a) and Brakhage (1989).
3. The term 'nation' remains contested. Debunking direct links between ethnicity and nationalism, for example, Valery Tishkov suggests that 'all attempts to develop terminological consensus around *nation* resulted in failure' (2000: 627).
4. John Grierson's anonymous review of *Moana* (1925) used 'documentary' as an adjective, stating that the film had 'documentary value' (1979 [1926]: 25–6). Brian Winston traces the term's use in English to Edward S. Curtis, writing of 'documentary work' in 1914 (1988a: 277–9).
5. Nichols provides useful frameworks for what he calls the expository, observational, interactive and reflexive 'modes' of documentary (1991: 32–75). He later recasts the interactive as the 'participatory' mode and includes poetic and performative modes, or 'voices' (2001a: 99–137).
6. The notion of the index comes from the work of nineteenth-century theorist Charles Sanders Peirce, who described different categories of signs. In Peirce's formulation, signs are classified into three main areas that indicate how they denote their object (or subject matter): these are the icon (which denotes likeness or semblance, as in a painting), the index (which bears a concrete, if often indirect, connection to its object) and the symbol (an indirect or general sign, in need of further interpretation). In the context of cinema, the second category, index, has been taken up to describe film's relationship to reality, which bears a special quality or direct connection to the objects it 'captures'.
7. See, for example, Ryan (1979).
8. According to the Modern Language Association Bibliography, in 1990–1 there were sixty-two major scholarly publications appearing on documentary film; by 2000–1 there were 295, and by 2006–7, 472.
9. Carroll adopts Monroe Beardsley's terminology.
10. On the 'social imaginary' Kahana cites political philosopher Charles Taylor.
11. See Fraser (1992).
12. See, for example, Martinez (1993).

CHAPTER I

Novelties, Spectacles and the Documentary Impulse

Chicago was the first expression of American thought and unity; one must start there. (Henry Adams, *The Education of Henry Adams*)

So where should a study of US documentary begin – with the first copyrighted film? The five-second *Edison Kinetoscopic Record of a Sneeze* was directed in January 1894 by William Kennedy Laurie Dickson in Edison's West Orange, New Jersey, laboratory, appearing over a year before the Lumière Brothers' *cinématographe* films.[1] *The Sneeze* has been called the first 'film of fact' – that is, the first motion picture record of a real event – and so might represent the 'very genesis of the documentary idea' (Jacobs 1979: 2).[2] For others, the Edison films are the earliest 'filmed recordings of actuality' (Ellis and McLane 2005: 6). Still, most agree it would be overly simplistic to see these films as prototypes for documentary, per se, due to varying ideas and histories of documentary film. Moreover, though labelled with the scientific-sounding prefix 'kinetoscopic record', *The Sneeze* could be closer to dramatic fiction than to nonfiction: a neat bit of acting by an Edison employee, Fred Ott.

The cinema developed as a collusion of technologies – photography, persistence of vision devices, projection – that were underwritten by legacies of intersecting and often competing inventions, social impulses, commercial imperatives, popular cultural phenomena and ways of seeing the world. Rather than trace documentary film's origins, then, I'd like to explore some contours of pre- and early cinema that might characterize a documentary *impulse* – a combination of enlightenment, engagement and spectacle that underlies the production and apprehension of documentary realities.

For Bill Nichols, the documentary impulse 'answers a need for evidence', for living proof and the potential to garner knowledge about worlds both aligned to and extending beyond our own experience (1991: 211). Such an impulse might be glimpsed in popular cultural phenomena that were parallel to, and often intertwined with, nonfiction film's emergence in the US, including circus displays, dime museums and fairground attractions. This chapter will chiefly focus on one of these phenomena poised on the transition from pre- to early cinema, the Chicago World's Columbian Exposition, an event which incorporated an amalgam of the technological, commercial, psychical and ideological currents that fed into early cinema and a popular taste for nonfiction film. In particular, I want to turn towards the Exposition's Midway Plaisance, an entertainment zone that took shape during the summer of 1893, several months before the appearance of Edison's *The Sneeze*.

DOCUMENTARY AND THE FAIRGROUND

The Midway Plaisance was a mile-long strip of land that housed the most popular attractions of the Chicago Exposition, a monumental spectacle staged to celebrate the 400th anniversary of Columbus's 'discovery' of the New World, which ran from 1 May to 9 October 1893.[3] Over this period there were nearly twenty-eight million admissions. Fairgoers came from across the continent, enduring twenty-nine hour journeys from Montreal, twenty-six hours from New York, thirty hours from Boston, and three-and-a-half days from San Francisco, all to take part in a monumental display of wealth, power and all-American know-how.

The Chicago Exposition wasn't merely a showcase for US innovation and industry or just an expensively mounted public entertainment, it was a conscious effort by government and business leaders to provide a rapidly expanding, diverse and recently urbanized population with a sense of cultural synthesis. It showed a collective desire, as Robert W. Rydell argues, to 'define social reality' for Americans, to crystallize cultural and national consciousness, just as the US was coming to terms with its newly acquired global status and wanting to flaunt it (1984: 39). Essentially, the fair signified the passing of empire from the 'old' European powers to the 'New World'. The Exposition didn't invent the concept of a unified American culture, but it did go a long way towards amalgamating and promoting an American cultural ideal within a single, sprawling location on the shores of Lake Michigan. It might be seen, then, as a celebration of the nation and of nationalism. But it was also, like any public event on this scale, a more complex mixture of encounters, sensations and ideas: far less ideologically unified and predictable than its organizers might have intended.

The Exposition occupied the 686-acre Jackson Park site south of the city, transformed by the renowned landscape designer Frederick Law Olmsted. It included an array of vast neoclassical structures, collectively known as the White City since all were painted brilliant white (for speedy completion as much as for aesthetic unity). Among the buildings were the 400,000-square-foot Agricultural Building, the Manufactures and Liberal Arts Building (with eleven acres of exhibition space, the largest building in the world), the Machinery Hall (full of deafening gas engines and turbines), the Transportation Building (with a stunning 'golden' doorway by Dankmar Adler and Louis Sullivan) and, lofted above them all, the gilded dome of Richard Morris Hunt's Administration Building, declared the 'crown of the exposition palaces' (Bancroft 1894: 129).

For Montgomery Schuyler, the buildings and overall scheme of the Exposition could be summed up by three words: unity, magnitude and illusion. 'In this country', noted Schuyler, 'mere bigness counts for more than anywhere else' (quoted in Badger 1979: 127). Boasting 65,000 different exhibits, the Chicago Exposition was designed to surpass the scale and opulence of the Paris Universal Exposition, staged four years earlier, and outdo the educational exhibits of the Philadelphia Centennial Exposition of 1876. The Chicago fair was to provide Americans with 'a veritable encyclopedia of civilization', underlining the prominent position the US occupied in the 'civilized' world (Rydell 2000). Still, whether the Agricultural Building's 22,000-pound monster cheese, a map of the US constructed entirely of pickles or the California exhibit's statue of a medieval knight made of prunes qualified as the crowning glory of 'civilization' would, even then, have been debatable.

In spite of the fair's idealized vision, controversies hung over the proceedings. Significantly, many noted that the White City's 'whiteness' went beyond its painted facades: not a single African American had been appointed to the fair's governing commissions. This lack of recognition of African American contributions to US culture led to the publication in 1893 of Ida B. Wells's protest pamphlet *The Reason Why the Colored American is Not in the World's Columbian Exposition*. Though it was finally agreed that a single fair day would be set aside as 'Colored People's Day', many viewed this as tokenism. Wells boycotted, while Frederick Douglass – then in his late seventies – arrived to launch a passionate speech against discrimination and the hypocrisy of the fair's organizers (Findling 1994: 28).

By the fair's end, it was clear that skewed racial messages had prevailed. One souvenir book declared: 'perhaps one of the most striking lessons which the Columbian Exposition taught was the fact that African slavery in America had not, after all, been an unmixed evil, for of a truth, the advanced social conditions of American Africans over that of their barbarous countrymen is most encouraging and wonderful' (quoted in Rydell 1984: 57). Racial stereotyping at the Exposition echoed other commercial amusements, such as vaudeville theaters and carnivals, providing heterogeneous white audiences with 'a unifying point of reference and visible and constant reminders of [their] privileged status' (Nasaw 1993: 47). As Anne Maxwell notes, the fair's illusions of US supremacy and imperial unity not only screened out the violence of the nation's past (the 1890 census had ascertained that over the previous forty years, half the American Indian population had been wiped out), but also encouraged people to ignore the most pressing social problems of the day (1999: 77).

Ultimately, the list of firsts that came out of the fair seems to define the highs, lows and complex in-betweens that would come to define American culture: George Ferris's massive wheel, meant to rival the Paris Exposition's Eiffel Tower, was the first of its kind; the very concept of the amusement park started here; Cracker Jacks, Cream of Wheat, carbonated soda, Juicy Fruit gum and hamburgers all were introduced; fifty-nine-year-old Chicago domestic worker Nancy Green appeared with her pancake mix as Aunt Jemima; and the US Postal Service offered some of the first mass-marketed picture postcards. Disposable amusements, fast food, commercialized stereotypes, aspirational dreams – all were readily found at the Exposition.

If the White City constructed a monumental fantasy of imperial order and national unity as a concrete (if stage-managed) reality, the Midway Plaisance was the site where other realities could be consumed in diverse, disordered and disruptive fashion. Geographically, the Midway occupied a marginal space, projecting like a westward-pointing finger from the main fairgrounds. Segregated at the edge of the White City, the Midway nonetheless became integral to the financial viability of the Exposition as a whole. The reasons for its immense popularity were at least twofold. First, the Midway, contrary to the organizers' original designs, became one of the fair's main entrances when a railway company dispute altered the plan for visitors to enter from the great railway terminal and pass into the Court of Honor, where they would face the uplifting grandeur of Hunt's golden dome. Instead, half entered through the Midway, where rather than the golden dome they confronted the huge Ferris wheel, 'the epitome of money-making entertainment' (Badger 1979: 120). A second reason for the Midway's success was that it housed the kinds of exhibits and distractions that people demanded. A visit to the Midway to ride the Ferris wheel became an obligatory part of the fairgoing experience: reputedly nine out of every ten visitors paid fifty cents to ride the wheel.

Crucial to the Midway's unique heterogeneous appeal were its ethnological displays, directly influenced by those featured at the 1889 Paris Universal Exposition. There the French government had enlisted prominent figures from the field of ethnology to create exhibits that transformed diverse peoples from France's colonial outposts in Africa and Asia into living displays that fairgoers could study at length, or simply gawk at before moving on. In Chicago, the planned Midway exhibits were initially placed under the auspicious direction of Frederic Ward Putnam, professor of anthropology and head of Harvard's Peabody Museum. Putnam had ambitions for a 'dignified and

Figure 1. Midway Plaisance with Ferris Wheel. Portfolio of photographs of the World's Fair, Household art series; no. 2. Chicago: Werner, 1893–4. Courtesy of the University of Illinois at Chicago Library, Special Collections.

decorous' educational zone that would provide visitors with a 'street of all nations' (Badger 1979: 107). The Midway was to become a premiere ethnological showcase that would, as in Paris, offer live displays of 'primitive' humanity (Rydell 1984: 55–64; Brown 1994: 155). It would introduce fairgoers to human exhibits that would be integrated into the universal, utopian aims of the fair as a whole, affording visitors 'the opportunity to measure the progress of humanity toward the ideal of civilization presented in the White City' (Rydell 1984: 57). In such a vision of the 'sliding scale of humanity', as the influential ethnologist Augustus Pitt Rivers once argued, 'the existing races, in their respective stages of progression, may be taken as the bona fide representatives of the races of antiquity', providing 'living illustrations' of the 'remote' origins of modern 'civilized' man (quoted in Chapman 1981).

Putnam's vision of the Midway was never realized. Fair organizers, lured by the promise of financial gains, began to allow entrepreneurs to bid for entertainment venues and food stalls along the linear route. Putnam was obliged to give way to the twenty-three-year-old showman Sol Bloom, who took over as the zone's manager. Construction delays also plagued the Exposition – clearly seen in the hulking, half-finished Ferris Wheel that greeted early fairgoers – and continued well beyond the fair's opening, leading many concessions to struggle or close altogether. These problems pressed organizers into quickly recouping investments through various moneymaking enterprises.

Thus the Midway became a tumultuous variety of consumable sights and sensations, a combination of the 'human zoo' and the carnival: a 'Dahomey village' (the Fon of Benin) opposite an ostrich farm, a Javanese Settlement and German Village set across from South Sea Islanders and Turkish Village exhibits, and (more or less jumbled together near the Midway's center) the Streets of Cairo, a Moorish Palace, Venice-Murano glass spinning, a model of the Eiffel Tower, an Indian bazaar, a Viennese cafe, an ice railway ride and finally the Ferris wheel, the commercial rival to the grand statues and domes of the White City. After construction was complete, the Midway was the fair's most popular area, giving birth to the concept of the amusement park that would soon sweep the country. David Nasaw emphasizes the segregationist tendencies of the two fair zones: the contrast between the 'districts' – one 'edifying' and the other 'entertaining' – was profound (1993: 47). Yet Reid Badger wonders if the messy presence of the Midway contrasting the lofty aims of the main Exposition might have engendered a kind of unexpected, dialectical encounter. The White City was a grandiose model of unity and order, but the tumult of the Midway showed up the White City's false facades of steel and plaster (1979: 120). Perhaps the elegant, stage-managed national fictions of the White City were undermined, as much as reinforced, by the fascinating realities along the Midway.

AUTHENTIC ATTRACTIONS

While the Chicago Exposition was just one of a range of public entertainments available to urban audiences, it was clearly unique in variety and scale. Fairgoers were given access to a myriad of unfamiliar worlds, captivated by mechanical entertainments, exposed first-hand to cultural and ethnic difference. The Midway was a jumbled combination of educational aims and tawdry distractions that brought together desires for gaining knowledge and engaging with reality-based spectacles. In this broad sense the Midway, like a demand for 'bona fides' in dime museums, provided not just public amusement or distraction, but engaged what might be called a documentary impulse.

Strictly speaking, 'documentary' film refers to an established, though always rather unstable, term for nonfiction cinema coined in the 1920s and popularized in the 1930s. But the documentary idea, along with documentary's social functions, has long cut across different kinds of texts and media occupying varying production and reception contexts. Hopefully without obliterating important historical differences, I would echo Ellen Strain's suggestion that 'cinema's ability to deliver the illusion of direct experience was not born with the invention of cinema, but was cultivated in other nineteenth-century entertainment forms, ranging from the world's fair exhibits to natural history museum displays and furthered through the invention of precinematic technologies' (2003: 6). Elizabeth Cowie uses the term 'spectacle of reality' to describe an impulse that links different popular pursuits, ranging from the circus to the European 'grand tour' to the actualities of early cinema. In this sense, the spectacle of reality evokes 'two distinct and apparently contradictory desires': desire for pleasurable entertainment and desire for knowledge (1999: 19). We experience in these spectacles 'an entertaining of the eye through form and light in showing, and an entertaining of the mind in the showing of something known either as familiar or in a new and spectacular way, as something not yet known that thereby becomes known' (27).

Tom Gunning has suggested that the early 'cinema of attractions' was grounded in the fascinations of the fairground and the amusement park (1990: 56). Midway attractions, like documentary films, grounded their allure in constantly referencing reality, engaging audiences as desiring as well as knowing subjects. On the Midway, there was a peculiar juxtaposition of sensation and knowledge-building through the consumption of reality-based displays, as the problematic idealism of Putnam's educational zone met, head on, with the crowd-pleasing and at times scandalous sights commissioned by Sol Bloom. Fairgoers could witness the Streets of Cairo, with its 'hootchy-kootchy' belly dancer, alongside displays of South Sea islanders, the wonders of a Moorish palace, or the architecture of a Bavarian village. To distinguish themselves from competitors and lure the crowds, Midway entertainments often emphasized strangeness, but they still commonly drew on verifiable phenomena, promoted as 'bona fide' or authentic. A few years later, the guide to the Buffalo Pan-American Exposition of 1901 promised 'dazzling, realistic' displays of 'bona fide natives' along its Midway (*Official Catalogue* 1901). Midway fairgoers would have been immersed in a locale that persistently referenced global travel, sightseeing and the otherness of worlds increasingly becoming objects of knowledge and curiosity, yet perhaps never before seen. These staged attractions were imbued with a sense of 'direct experience': like later motion picture travelogues they constituted 'the cheapest and most exhaustive journey over the earth that was ever made' (Reed 2000: xxvi).

Viewing unprecedented yet authenticated sights from a position of relative mastery – a 'god's eye' view of the world – spectators were able to discover, individually and collectively, both who they were and who they were not. Sampling the foods, smells, sensations and images of different ethnicities and cultures, fairgoers could form a clearer sense of personal and collective affinity with respect to the displays around them. As Strain suggests, forms of the 'tourist gaze' that emerged around this period offered means of testing the fragile boundaries between the self and the cultural and racial 'others' that, potentially, threatened (western) autonomy. Indeed in Chicago, racial and cultural hierarchies were reinforced in explicit ways: the 'World's Congress of Beauties', for example, featured '40 ladies from 40 nations', using the beauty contest format to assert western beliefs in racial superiority (Strain 2003: 17, 55). Such exhibits 'provided Americans with a shared set of myths about their common origins and their present status in the race for supremacy among western nations' (Maxwell 1999: 94). Among the heterogeneous crowds in Chicago were millions of recent immigrants, and many might not have had a precise sense of what it meant to be 'American', nor would they have felt closely attuned to growing US imperial ambitions. Yet they could link the idealized vision of American selfhood – the White City – to the consumption of the world and hierarchies of races and cultures on the Midway, asserting identities as 'modern', 'civilized', 'American' and even 'white' subjects. The Midway was a site not only for gleaning knowledge and entertainment, but for building cohesion and a sense of belonging to a dominant version of the nation.

Though the Exposition strove for a persuasive ideological vision of America, the tourist gaze on the Midway was not yet the well-oiled, largely one-sided experience that, Strain argues, solidified in later versions of the travelogue and package tour. Midway attractions would have both encouraged and at times disrupted the gaze at otherness. Though the experience was essentially mediated by the fair's structure and organization, fairgoers walked through and in a sense became part of the displays: the attractions were not paraded in front of them. The displays of 'native' bodies would have provided visual and even erotic interest, but there was always interactive potential. The Fon, Javanese or South Sea Islanders were not just objects to be looked at, but also looked back. They freely wandered the fairgrounds, reportedly with as much curiosity as other spectators. Christopher Robert Reed has argued, for example, that the African presence at the Exposition, typified by the much maligned Dahomey (Fon) village, actually led to 'multiple layers of ambiguities, paradoxes, and dilemmas' that have been clouded by subsequent interpretations of the event (2000: xvii). The African presence was not wholly a one-sided exercise in imperial power but led to unexpected links between peoples of diasporic back-

Figure 2. Javanese house builders. Portfolio of photographs of the World's Fair, Household art series; no. 2. Chicago: Werner, 1893–4. Courtesy of the University of Illinois at Chicago Library, Special Collections.

grounds. For example, Reed argues, African Americans and people from the African diaspora forged new friendships and relations that in many cases lasted long beyond the closing of the fair. That said, the exhibits on the Midway were hardly ideologically neutral, constituted as they were by commercial imperatives, racial and cultural stereotypes and the nationalist ideals of the White City. The 'human zoo' could be grossly inhumane: Inuits exhibited at Chicago had to wear heavy furs through the summer heat; Africans displayed in Buffalo in 1901 succumbed to illness and death.

The documentary experience fostered on the Midway isn't easily categorized; it offered an alchemical mixture of verisimilitude, immediacy, otherness, education and spectacle. The Midway was a public space that permitted audiences to see, learn about and (in a restricted manner) engage with forms of life different from their own. This arrangement of fact-based sights might suggest what Keith Beattie calls 'documentary display', forms of 'sensational knowledge' that extend beyond the narrower confines of documentary as it was later defined. Such displays can arouse pleasure in the spectator by combining elements of performance, visual allure, illusions of liveness or immediacy and the possibility of knowledge (2008: 19). Importantly, these spectacles of reality persistently index the real: a tacit contract is established between producers and consumers, anchored in a faith that the display is, at some level, authentic and verifiable.

The Midway experience further asserted its authenticity through juxtaposing different modes of apprehending reality. Midway attractions blurred lines between artificial or virtual reality and 'live' witnessing, between the automated and the animated. Exhibits like the panorama of the Hawaiian volcano Kilauea added to the smorgasbord of artificially reproduced real sights and sensations. This exhibit showed a simulated eruption with flowing lava lit up by more than 300 electric lights and was so realistic that one visitor remarked, 'observers could easily imagine they had been transported to that interesting but dreadful place' (quoted in Brown 1994: 103). The human displays, rather than undermine or give the lie to mechanical or virtual realities such as Kilauea volcano, served to reinforce these reality effects. If we consider what Sergei Eisenstein (influenced by the variety of compelling stage elements that featured in theater) called the 'montage of attractions' – a program of juxtaposing a series of discrete elements that solicit audience attention – the Midway might be seen as a kind of montage of authentic attractions. Here mechanical displays and direct or immediate real sights complemented each other, giving rise to perceptions of reality as consumable, spectacular and informational.

The montage of authentic attractions along the Midway thus might indicate emerging 'documentary' modes of apprehending reality that mix an idea of direct experience with technologized illusions of immediacy. There were yet other harbingers of documentary's coming technologies and functions. With moving pictures about to be unleashed on the public, Chicago featured the latest technologies for capturing life in motion.

THE ZOOPRAXOGRAPHICAL HALL

Though cinema, per se, did not quite make it to the Exposition, photography was everywhere. In the Manufactures and Liberal Arts Building alone, photography displayed as both science and art came together in dozens of exhibits. Amateur photography too came into its own. George Eastman Company had introduced the 'Kodak #1' camera in 1888: a basic, single-focus box camera already loaded with a 100-exposure roll of film. Keen to capitalize on the explosion in amateur photography that followed, the Kodak booth in the Manufactures and Liberal Arts Building strove to be the most sophisticated at the fair. Kodak also aggressively campaigned with the fair's organizers for the exclusive rights to rent and sell film cameras on the fairgrounds, even debuting the 'Kodak #4', or 'Kolumbus Kodak', in honor of the event (West 2000:

21). Because it was accessible in scale but also offered views on to sights both novel and spectacular, the Midway became, as Julie K. Brown suggests, the landscape where 'the photographer, especially the amateur photographer, was most clearly and intensely at home' (1994: 103). The invention of the 'snapshot' allowed the tumultuous, constantly moving global modernity crammed onto the Midway to be framed as a 'precise, bounded [. . .] instant in time' – captured and held as a souvenir (21).

As one devoted to transforming these discrete 'instants in time' into a continuous stream of images that could reflect movement and time's flow, Eadweard Muybridge had set up an exhibit not far from the Ferris wheel, between the Persian concession and the German village, rubbing shoulders with the popular Streets of Cairo exhibit. Born near London and transplanted to California, Muybridge was already well known as a chief architect behind a process called chronophotography, a stop-motion photographic technique that was a forerunner of modern cinema. Muybridge's Zoopraxographical lecture hall offered significant precursors of nonfiction motion pictures, and promoted their educational and scientific potential.

Muybridge was sixty-three when he opened his Midway exhibit; over twenty years earlier, he had begun work developing photographic processes for the transcontinental railroad magnate Leland Stanford. With keen interests in science and 'determined to unravel the mystery of motion' (quoted in Solnit 2003: 78), Stanford commissioned Muybridge in the spring of 1872 to photograph his favorite racehorse, Occident. He was eager to resolve a dispute about whether a running horse actually was capable of having all four legs off the ground at one time. The dilemma of the running horse wasn't quickly resolved, and Muybridge had other issues: after notoriously killing his wife's lover in 1874, he spent several years on projects in Central America, returning to Northern California in 1877 to photograph massive, multi-plate panoramic views. Records are vague about exactly when Muybridge finally photographed a horse with four legs off the ground, and he would not actually publish a photograph of a horse in motion until 1877. None of the photographs from this period remain, but a key turning point came with the first public demonstration of his techniques in June 1878. Having acquired improved lenses and an electrical shutter device, Muybridge placed twelve cameras, each twenty-one inches apart, to take twelve sequential views. Each camera was operated by tripping a wire buried beneath the track (for horses and carriages) or thin threads strung across it (for horses alone). The results were published as popular cabinet cards – a series called *The Horse in Motion* – that still serve as signature images for Muybridge, and chronophotography itself.[4]

Muybridge would forge a successful career improving his photographic inventions, lecturing and presenting public demonstrations. His work helped advance instantaneous photography – 'stopping time' – where motion could

Figure 3. Plate 188, 'Dancing [Fancy] woman draped [Miss Larrigan]' (1885–7). Eadweard Muybridge, *Animal Locomotion* (1887). Courtesy of the Iris and B. Gerald Cantor Center for Visual Arts, Stanford University.

be captured without blurring, a project pioneered by inventors such as Thomas Skaife. More generally, Muybridge contributed to visually documenting the relationship of time to continuous motion. The latter task brought him together with the physiologist Etienne-Jules Marey in Paris in late 1881. Afterwards, Marey developed a *fusil photographique*, or 'photographic gun', based on a *revolver photographique* invented by the astronomer Pierre Jules César Janssen. Muybridge would produce his own chronophotographic sequences with the 'gun', releasing the definitive version of his motion studies in 1887: *Animal Locomotion: An Electrophotographic Investigation of Consecutive Phases of Animal Movements, 1872–1885.*

By the mid-1880s, Muybridge had shifted his focus towards human motion studies. This work paralleled Marey's physiological photography, but was marked by Muybridge's distinctive visual sense and, occasionally, sense of humor (as in 'Jumping; running straight high jump [Mrs Coleman]' [1887], where a serious, conservatively dressed woman suddenly leaps over a chair). Working in Philadelphia with another follower of Marey, the painter Thomas Eakins, Muybridge photographed varieties of humans in motion: wrestlers, acrobats, women and men, both heavily dressed and fully undressed. He even photographed himself in motion, nude, under the title 'ex-athlete'. The detached, highly clinical nature of these studies is observed by Rebecca Solnit: 'Pretty Blanche Epler with thick fair hair down to her waist was an immeasurable distance away in her own thoughts, more a body than a person, not as women are bodies in pornography but as people are bodies in anatomical and medical texts. Unlike an actress, she was not emoting or expressing for the camera; she offered it only the motions of her body' (2003: 225). He also collaborated with physicians to photograph people with various disabilities;

in *Animal Locomotion* he included studies such as 'Arising from the Ground [Miss Cox]', which shows a very obese woman attempting to stand up. Some have found these studies disturbing, though they are symptomatic of the ways that photographic technology was appropriated into the medical and scientific obsessions of the late-nineteenth century (Solnit 2003: 221). Such studies strove to dissect, itemize and preserve human movements for future study; problematically, though, they suggest hierarchical and Darwinian readings of physiological differences.[5]

The moving picture machine that Muybridge brought to Chicago had been in development since 1879, when he performed the first private demonstrations of his zoopraxiscope (a neologism from Greek words meaning 'animal action viewing device') – a technology that would help lay the foundations for projected cinematography. The zoopraxiscope, very nearly, brought together the core technical elements that made up modern movies: the illusion of continuous motion, projection and photography. Muybridge combined his experience of making instantaneous sequential photographs with two much older technologies: the zoetrope or 'magic wheel' or 'wheel of life' – a device that exploits the illusions of persistence of vision – and the magic lantern. The zoetrope used a strip of paper depicting drawings of successive phases of movement, placed within a spinning drum. Viewed through slits on the drum's side, the changing images provided an illusion of continuous motion. A similar device called a Phenakistiscope, developed in the 1830s, used sequential images drawn on a spinning disc which, when viewed in a mirror through the slotted sides, also produced continuous motion. The magic lantern, still widely used for popular entertainments and lectures during Muybridge's time, is a projection device dating back through various permutations as far as the fifteenth century. Using bright light, glass slides and lenses, it both projects and amplifies images.[6] Where the zoopraxiscope fell short of the soon to arrive *cinématographe*, however, was surprisingly in the area in which Muybridge specialized – photography. Due to technical limitations, photographs had to be simulated through painted versions of the original chronophotographic studies. These were then transferred to circular glass plates that rotated at a steady pace in the zoopraxiscope and projected on to a screen.

In Chicago, Muybridge showed motion studies such as 'Woman Dancing [Miss Larrigan]' with its eye-catching swirling skirts, and 'Athlete; Running Long Jump'. Each was projected for a few seconds, after which he would move on to the next one. The crowd-pleasing effect of juxtaposing still and animated images (watching the still image 'come to life') was central to the presentation, as it later would be at the Lumières' demonstrations. At the front of the concession patrons could purchase paper versions of Muybridge's displays for their own (non-projecting) zoetropes. Both the painted transcriptions and the reliance on an invention that dated from years earlier meant that Muybridge's exhibit, based on fifteen years of lecture tours, might have appeared already somewhat conventional. As Phillip Prodger notes, Muybridge produced very little new work after the publication of *Animal Locomotion* in 1887 (2003: 7). Coupled with this, the ponderous content and tone, underscored by the exhibit's quasi-scientific name, the Zoopraxographical Hall, were not a hit with fairgoers.

Compounding problems, the early weeks of the fair were plagued by poor attendance due to construction delays. In the end, Muybridge's illustrated lectures couldn't compete with the array of strange, arresting, erotic draws on the Midway. The concession struggled in its first weeks, earning only $350, and soon closed. Replacing Muybridge's effort was more simulated authenticity: the eruption of Mount Vesuvius and subsequent destruction of Pompeii. More exciting, apparently, than animals and figures in motion, it ended up with receipts totaling $19,505 (Brown 1994: 104). Still, Muybridge's contribution to pre-cinema at the Chicago Exposition should not be dismissed. He not only displayed a cinematic forerunner like the zoopraxiscope, but embodied qualities of the motion picture showman and incorporated moving pictures into his illustrated lectures (also precursors of documentary, as seen in the next chapter). His decision to try his wares on the Midway, too, suggests an anticipation that motion pictures could be popular amusements affording 'wonder and astonishment' to mass audiences (Gunning 2003: 255). In Muybridge's work, we glimpse a meeting of education, enlightenment and spectacle found in later documentary forms. His experiments, according to Erik Barnouw, 'foreshadowed a crucial aspect of documentary film: its ability to open our eyes to worlds available to us but, for one reason or another, not perceived' (1983: 3).

THE MISSING KINETOSCOPES

Muybridge's stint at the fair was brief, though another 'father' of cinema, Thomas Edison, was an omnipresent figure in Chicago. The proceedings were effectively a pageant celebrating the wonders of electricity and, especially, Edison's fourteen-year-old invention, the light bulb. Paris had seen the first use of electricity at a World's Fair in 1889, but it didn't approach the scale of Chicago, where the extensive lighting displays would have been novel and awe-inspiring (Badger 1979: 92). Edison, a consummate entrepreneur, strove to make the most of the fair's publicity. With the help of his secretary, Alfred O. Tate, he contracted in 1892 to debut his revolutionary new motion picture machine, the kinetoscope, at the Exposition.

According to most sources, the development of the kinetoscope was spurred on when Edison and his employee, W. K. L. Dickson, attended a demonstration of Muybridge's zoopraxiscope on 25 February 1888. Two days later, Muybridge had a momentous meeting with Edison at his West Orange laboratory, which seems to have been the impetus behind Edison's interest in developing 'an instrument which does for the Eye what the phonograph does for the Ear, which is the recording and reproduction of things in motion' (quoted in Robinson 1996: 23). Dickson was put in charge of producing the prototype: a complex task greatly assisted by the invention of photographic celluloid by John Carbutt in 1888 and the commercial production of celluloid film in 50-foot rolls by the Eastman Company in 1889. Together, these innovations helped Dickson ultimately to produce seamless, continuous moving images.

As late as October 1892, the press was heralding the coming of Edison's groundbreaking machine, to be called the Kinetograph, a peep-show (not projecting) machine combining moving images with synchronized sound. The *Phonogram* announced: 'At the opening of the Columbian Exposition there will appear a dual instrument [. . .] The Edison Kinetograph is an instrument intended to produce motion and sound simultaneously' (quoted in Musser 1990a: 74). But in the end there were neither kinetographs nor kinetoscopes at the Chicago fair. Edison's laboratory failed to fill the order, though the promotion was so widespread that many sources still claim that the kinetoscope debuted at Chicago.[7] The failure seems to have come down to several factors, including Dickson suffering from a nervous breakdown and the serial drunkenness of the carpenter in charge of making kinetoscope cabinets. A leaflet for a subsequent London exhibit explained: 'Thousands of visitors to the [Chicago] Fair inquired daily at the Edison exhibits concerning the new machine [. . .] But great inventions take a long time, extended experiment, and large expense before reaching practical and practicable perfection, and thus it was that the Kinetoscope was not perfected in time for the great Fair' (quoted in Robinson 1996: 40).

Taken together, the closure of the Zoopraxigraphical Hall and the case of the missing kinetoscopes would suggest that Chicago 1893 was essentially a catalogue of cinematic might-have-beens. But the fair everywhere bore traces of the transition towards the 'birth' of the cinematic machine. Also on the Midway was the electro-Photographic Tachyscope, devised by Otto Anschütz, which 'reproduced [. . .] the natural motion of objects and animals [. . .] with a degree of truth and accuracy that is absolutely bewildering' (quoted in Nasaw 1993: 68). Thomas Armat, who by 1895 would be demonstrating his own Phantascope moving picture projector, later claimed that he had a moment of revelation when viewing the Tachyscope along the Midway. Peering into the machine, Armat watched an elephant walking in a 'foreign setting'; he later concluded, 'the idea of bringing scenes from far and interesting countries and projecting them on a screen before comfortably seated spectators, was an exciting thought' (Armat 1979 [1935]: 17). Watching fellow spectators paying to consume these technologized displays of foreignness no doubt added to Armat's excitement.

With the kinetoscope's debut in 1894, motion pictures – first as peep shows, then as projected images – finally came to the US public. The earliest films were concerned with showing off the wonders of a technology that could produce moving images that were no longer just lifelike, but *from life*. Edison's early subjects were mainly taken from real or familiar phenomena, usually in the form of re-enactments (*The Barber Shop* [1893]) and elaborate entertainments (*The Boxing Cats [Prof. Welton's]* [1894]). Still, it is the Lumière films, not Edison's, that are often cited as the first to exhibit a range of characteristics later associated with documentary. Barnouw stresses that 'it was Louis Lumière who made the *documentary* film a reality', and dismisses the 'show business' direction that Edison's films quickly took (1983: 5). Lumière actualities such as *Workers Leaving a Factory* (1895) and *Arrival of a Train at La Ciotat* (1895) drew their material from life without overt manipulation, and the use of natural light and real locations (recalling the *plein air* tradition) endows them with an impression of immediacy. They were also, importantly, projected films watched collectively, as opposed to Edison's individual peep shows. I would suggest, however, that to confine these very early films to categories like documentary or dramatic fiction is probably too restrictive; as Miriam Hansen notes, early cinema's diversity is difficult to pin down within the more precise categories that came later (1994: 30). The film industry developed unpredictably and rapidly, and technologies and public tastes kept changing.

Dickson, working for Edison, followed a path quite different to that of the Lumières. He developed a studio setup that allowed for the regulation of lighting, framing and action, and nicknamed it the 'Black Maria' because the cramped space was like a police paddy wagon. Many Black Maria productions recall the motion studies of Marey and Muybridge: *The Sneeze*, for example, is a basic re-enactment of a physiological event. Here, however, instead of impersonal studies of physiognomies in motion, the act of sneezing is addressed to the viewer, showing off technology's ability to capture a fleeting, seemingly spontaneous event. Edison's new invention, however, was all about generating business, and these early technical and physiological demonstrations soon gave way to commercial entertainments such as *Arab Knife Juggler* (1894) and *Bucking Bronco* (1894), where the foregrounding of entertainment over technology began the process of sublimating the viewer's awareness of the apparatus delivering the spectacle.

Films made by Dickson and his assistant William Heise from 1893 onwards – produced to advertise the kinetoscope – were largely drawn from carnivals, circuses and the vaudeville stage. Still, in spite of their 'show business' leanings, perhaps these films are no less documentary in nature than those of the Lumières. To most viewers, Lumière actualities would appear natural, while the Edison Company's staged re-enactments, strange sights and eye-catching performances might seem artificial. Yet we know that documentaries also still commonly employ performative elements and staged re-enactments. The next section attempts to draw out affinities between these early Edison films and later documentary, problematizing the tendency to read the Black Maria films as show-business fabrications versus actualities as proto-documentary revelations.

BLACKSMITH SCENE (1893), *BUFFALO DANCE* (1894) AND *MESS CALL* (1896)

Produced for the Edison Company, the films discussed in this section range from an early demonstration in the Black Maria to the kind of on-location actuality that would supplant Edison's studio-based productions. Rather than revisiting the 'staged versus spontaneous' and 'fictional versus factual' debates, I'll suggest that each indicates an approach to documenting reality that roughly corresponds to the varying, often overlapping 'modes' of documentary as defined by Bill Nichols. These modes range from observational and slight narrative techniques, seen in *Blacksmith Scene*, to interactive performativity, as suggested in *Buffalo Dance*, to the implied participatory stance of *Mess Call*. In many ways these films suggest a meeting point between the authentic attractions consumed along the Midway and the documentary attractions that would come later.

Blacksmith Scene is distinguished as the first motion picture publicly shown on the kinetoscope, appearing at the Brooklyn Institute of Arts and Sciences on 9 May 1893. It depicts three Edison employees in the Black Maria, dramatically lit against a black backdrop. The setup bestows an iconographic quality on the image, recalling the sharply lit aesthetics of chronophotographic studies (especially Muybridge's 'Blacksmiths, two models hammering on anvil' [1887]). The camera reveals the men's figures from head to toe, allowing an unobstructed view of their motions. The set is schematic rather than scrupulously realistic. An anvil lends compositional weight to the center of the frame while providing a focal point for the action. The camera is stationary, but the three men constantly move in their work, as if movement is itself on display. The men's actions and interactions all seem engineered to convey authenticity, and in this respect the strategies of reconstructing reality, imposing a skeletal story and maintaining the camera's relative anonymity might be seen to anticipate aspects of later documentaries. The illusion is hardly seamless, however: as the men pass around a bottle, there's a palpable impression of hurrying that shows up the film's artifice (they need to complete the process within the film's 50 feet (roughly 28 seconds) running time).

There are other anomalies on view: at one point one of the men slips out of frame, though perhaps more jarring is the silhouetted figure that momentarily appears, partially blocking the view. The appearance is a kind of accident, interrupting the staged actions, imbuing the film with an unexpected immediacy. Juxtaposing the planned and unplanned, the order and disorder of experience, *Blacksmith Scene* from the start displays the superiority of the cinematic apparatus for the task of 'capturing' spontaneous action. Yet this cutting-edge technology, Charles Musser suggests, is paradoxically used here 'to prop up and document a past that it is quickly making obsolete', betraying a modern nostalgia also visible in other films in the Edison catalogue (2004: 17).

This nostalgic impulse – indicating a nation perched between the advances and sins of its past, and a hastening modernity – is even more evident in Edison's *Buffalo Dance*. Like other Black Maria films, such as the macho display of *Sandow* (1894) or the racy skirt-lifting of *Carmencita* (1894), *Buffalo Dance* offers a re-enactment of a popular stage performance. These acts provided entertaining subjects that were in most cases (considering technical limitations) relatively straightforward and formally predictable. *Buffalo Dance* was shot along with *Sioux Ghost Dance*, both featuring Sioux dancers made famous through one of the era's most popular attractions, Buffalo Bill Cody's Wild West Show. *Buffalo Dance* 'stars' three warriors: Last Horse, Parts His Hair and Hair Coat.

Luring Buffalo Bill's attractions into the Black Maria might have been an attempt by Edison to redress the absent kinetoscopes at Chicago, while further riding the coat-tails of the Exposition's massive success. The Wild West Show had been an 'unofficial' draw in Chicago in 1893, stationed (not entirely to the fair organizers' liking) outside the Exposition's gates. *Buffalo Dance* was also a form of advertising: in its companion, *Sioux Ghost Dance*, Buffalo Bill's signature 'brand' is clearly displayed in the lower right corner. *Buffalo Dance*'s 'primitive' display both recalls the live ethnological attractions of the day and prefigures later ethnographic and expeditionary films, gesturing towards US popular culture's present and future consumption of ethnic and cultural 'types'. Here, ethnological displays like those on the Midway are seen entering the realms of the virtual: animation and automation seamlessly meld together.

Though staged, the film might be seen as carrying 'documentary' properties, inscribing 'live' actions and foregrounding (as discussed in the Introduction) physical depictions rather than nominal portrayals. As in *Blacksmith Scene*, the actions in *Buffalo Dance* appear monitored: the dancers circle around a carefully delineated area on a raised platform. The dance is offered without detailed context, as a sheer performance. As Strain notes of early ethnographic subjects featuring dance, they appear 'solely for the benefit of a US audience without forcing that audience to recognize the movements, postures, and music as components of a complex culture that may have been beyond audience understanding' (2003: 108–9). Indeed, the Buffalo Dance was traditionally a ritual for assuring a successful hunt. It had powerful implications for the Sioux, being closely tied to collective memories of famine and to ongoing struggles for the group's survival. Performed for Dickson's camera and destined for the peep show, the dance suggests a kind of *mise-en-abyme*: a re-enactment for the entertainment of post-frontier audiences, subsequently reconstructed for virtual posterity (Griffiths 2002: 176). The ritual dance would be exhibited alongside other authentic attractions in the kinetoscope, many lurid, and some even illegal: cock fights, boxing matches and indiscreetly lifted skirts.

Taken alongside other Wild West Show films such as *Annie Oakley* (1894), *Buffalo Dance* helped to market myths relating to the United States' recent frontier past. The consumption of the 'real' Native American complemented the production of an imagined past, of a nation that had tamed a rugged wilderness yet still was constituted by contact with it. These myths of the US frontier were also highly exportable, potently contributing to the 'Americanization of the world': *Buffalo Dance*, with other Buffalo Bill films, was distributed in Europe as advance publicity for the Wild West Show's upcoming engagements there (Rydell and Kroes 2005).

Still, it is worth noting that the dancers perform *to* the camera rather than simply being captured *by* it. The subjects of *Buffalo Dance*, arguably, aren't merely or simplistically trapped within the restrictive bounds of a burgeoning US imperial imagination. One of the dancers looks directly, challengingly, into the lens: a sustained and interactive stance. The look creates a palpable tension between modern technology poised to capture and preserve the 'bona fide native' and the subject's determination to fix his look directly back at that technology and at the spectral audience beyond it. Unlike the observational stance of *Blacksmith Scene*, the exhibitionism and performative nature of *Buffalo Dance* address the audience directly from another space and time. Highlighting this phenomenon, Tom Gunning and André Gaudreault coined the term 'cinema of attractions' to refer to a dominant strain in early cinema that *shows* something, that establishes contact with audiences. It 'directly solicits spectator attention, inciting visual curiosity, and supplying pleasure through an exciting spectacle [. . .] that is of interest in itself'. As part of this cinema of attractions, *Buffalo Dance* implies an 'exhibitionist confrontation rather than diegetic absorption'. Spectators are briefly drawn into the action and confronted by the subjects' looks, implicated in ongoing relations between performers and those who gaze at them, rather than simply being – in Filippo Marinetti's cutting words – 'stupid voyeurs' (Gunning 1990: 57–9).

If traces of documentary might be glimpsed in the Black Maria films, the illusion of immersion provided by actualities shot outside the bounds of the studio and the theater would, later, become more closely associated with the look and feel of documentary. Differing audience reactions to staged versus more spontaneous filmed attractions were obvious almost from the start, at the debut of Raff and Gammon's vitascope projection machine, presented by Thomas Armat on 23 April 1896 at Koster and Bial's Music Hall in New York. The screening signaled the shift in the US from the semi-private indiscretions of the peep show to the jolts of the large screen and the noisy proximity of the audience. Armat would recall that the most sensational reactions that night were not to Edison films such as *Umbrella Dance* (1895), which featured short skirts and a big umbrella, but to Birt Acres and R. W. Paul's modest *Rough Sea at Dover* (1895):

> All the scenes shown, with one exception, were what might be called vaudeville turns, or stage subjects. [. . .] The one exception to the stage scenes [. . .] was of storm-tossed waves breaking over a pier on the beach at Dover, England – a scene that was totally unlike anything an audience had ever before seen in a theater. When it was thrown upon the screen the house went wild. (quoted in Fielding 1972: 6)

Rough Sea at Dover's appeal was not just realism and spectacle – all films on show offered these to some degree – but its difference from studio productions that replicated scenes from vaudeville or the fairground. The film seemed to bridge more extreme displacements in space and time: in a darkened vaudeville house, this was a virtual voyage to a turbulent, dramatic seafront. The waves hurtling towards the camera threatened to break the fourth wall, bringing something and somewhere else into the here and now of the theater.

Mess Call, made for screen projection, was part of the Edison Company's shift away from the Black Maria towards an emphasis on cheaper, outdoor shooting. Paid performers gave way to 'found' or 'spontaneous' subjects. By May 1896, Edison had commissioned a portable camera, largely in anticipation of competition from foreign and domestic markets, and Heise used it to record local scenes around New York City (Musser 1990a: 118). Shot in July, *Mess Call*'s 50 feet of celluloid captures a somewhat raucous slice of life, featuring the state militia at their training camp in Peekskill, New York.

The film opens on a corner where a mess hall is doling out food. The stationary camera is positioned below shoulder height and captures the soldiers passing by. Some pause to gape at the camera, and soon a small group gathers, staring and laughing at the machine, seemingly delighted in being filmed. One man stands out from the rest, waving from the rear ground and then loping forward, taking exaggerated bites of food, pulling faces. Others stop to stare, open mouthed, while one man acknowledges the camera's phantom audience, taking off his hat and bending down in greeting, a gesture that helps to emphasize the camera's/spectator's low-angle (and perhaps by extension, vulnerable) position amid the posturing soldiers. In such moments, we see that 'the spec-

Figure 4. *Mess Call* (1896). Edison Company. Image capture, Kino International DVD.

tacle makers have themselves become a spectacle', as Tom Gunning notes of
another film from the same period (2006: 40). By the end of *Mess Call*, a crowd
is edging towards the camera, before the film runs out. The final seconds are
subtly menacing: this is an all-male world of bravado that might excite, challenge and inspire spectators to react all at once.

Like *Buffalo Dance*, *Mess Call* suggests a cinema of attractions, 'undertaken
with brio, establishing contact with the audience. [. . .] a cinema that displays
its visibility' (Gunning 1990: 57). The film's interactive and performative elements further underline how aware people already were of the camera, and
how difficult capturing offhand, unselfconscious moments – later hallmarks
of authenticity in documentary – would already have been. Beyond this overt
performativity, *Mess Call* encompasses certain features that the Black Maria
films commonly lack. There is no stage or safe distance between filmed subjects and filmmakers; the action appears to unfold spontaneously, catalyzed
by the presence of the camera. This already suggests what Nichols calls the
'participatory mode', which 'gives a sense of what it is like for the filmmaker to
be in a given situation and how that situation alters as a result'. The filmmaker
is positioned 'on the scene', perceived as a presence rather than an absence
(Nichols 2001a: 116). Though Russian *Kino Pravda* and French *cinéma vérité*
were a long way off, *Mess Call* is marked by similar elements of risk and play,

where, in Jane Gaines's terms, 'the frame is effectively taken by surprise' (2007a: 14). The film's lack of closure, cutting off mid-action, leaves unfinished business and suddenly draws attention to the film's status as a material, celluloid reproduction. The audience is drawn into the production of reality, imaginatively 'filling in' what extends beyond the film's duration.

By reproducing recognizable facsimiles of everyday experience, actualities like *Mess Call* testified to – and advertised – the power of the cinematic apparatus to capture a precise index of reality. Lacking a clear message or intent, *Mess Call*'s effects and meanings are more mobile than those of more controlled scenarios. The force of the film's attractions lies in its ability, through spontaneous interaction and direct address, to conjure up 'stolen moments' and a 'vivid sense of physical embodiment' (Gunning 2009: 331). As a moment distilled from the flow of time, *Mess Call* is both alluring and uncomfortable; the animated looks of the film's subjects stare back at the camera as if projected straight from the past.

Yet we must also be careful about privileging these 'stolen moments' as somehow 'closer' to reality as we consider the meanings, implications and uses of documentary film. The illusion of direct experience that *Mess Call* and other actualities produce lies in their ability to uncannily efface gaps in distance and time; yet they are not necessarily closer to the 'truth' of human experience, nor are they a more perfect indication of the range of documentary approaches and styles that would appear later. *Mess Call* does, rather, form part of a continuum of approaches to reproducing reality, ranging from re-enactments and careful restagings to more spontaneous 'uncontrolled' and 'direct' approaches.

In terms of Heise's choice of subject matter, *Mess Call*'s military setting and challenging machismo also imply a shift, observed by Musser, from the 'cosmopolitan vision' of the kinetoscope to the arrival of projected cinema in the US, which often 'provoked or constructed national rivalries'. In the Black Maria films we witness the multiple, somewhat chaotic varieties of the circus, vaudeville and fairground, where 'people of all cultures and races appeared on the same vaudeville stage, enjoying the same basic forms of compensation and attention' (Musser 2004: 26). Though the kinetoscope films were hardly innocent – with their erotic, violent themes and gender and ethnic stereotyping – Raff and Gammon's vitascope debut (mentioned above) noticeably and, Musser argues, quite consciously aimed to narrow the field of vision. More palpably 'American' in its emphasis on national and patriotic themes, the film program featured 'all [. . .] white, American performers' (Musser 2004: 26). *The Monroe Doctrine* (1896), two films down the program from *Rough Sea at Dover*, featured Uncle Sam protecting 'his' South American territory from European interference. The film's huge success (Musser notes, 'applause and cheers rang through the house' [27]) was prescient, signaling two years before the Spanish-American War the potent patriotic sentiments that the medium of cinema could mobilize. Film exhibition was already skillfully combining mass entertainment, attractions specifically coded as 'American' and jingoistic, nationalistic spectacles.

By late 1897, actualities had become so prominent that Edison and other studios were devoting the majority of their production time to them. With their dynamic images of travel, railways, boats at sea, famous monuments and cityscapes, actualities transformed the far away and the everyday into compact and seemingly direct experiences of the world. The far flung corners of the globe, distilled into images projected on the wall, were suddenly, tantalizingly, within reach.

As the next chapter outlines, actualities that featured travel and tourist views were foundational to the evolution of nonfiction film. John Grierson once referred to travel films as the groundwork of documentary, stating: 'I always think of documentary as having certain fundamental chapters. The first chapter is, of course, the travelogue, that is, the discovery that the camera can go about – it's peripatetic' (quoted in Sussex 1975: 206). Travel films were capable not only of reproducing and disseminating real sights, they could produce new perceptions of reality, providing a cinematic experience that paralleled modern modes of physical mobility and the expansion of global tourism. These virtual voyages were the inheritors of the documentary impulse found at locales such as the Midway; the grand tour afforded the intense pleasures of contact with the world's otherness, along with the satisfactions of knowing and mastering it.

NOTES

1. The *cinématographe* debuted in Paris in March 1895, and was first demonstrated in the US in June 1896.
2. Dickson's early camera tests (*Monkeyshines 1* and *2, c.*1889) or *Men Boxing* (1891) could fall under this category but were not made for the kinetoscope in its final form. Louis Le Prince's *Roundhay Garden Scene* (1888) also has been cited as the 'first' motion picture.
3. The Exposition missed the anniversary by a year due to Congress's late authorization of a host city. Sources include Findling (1994: 12–35), Rydell (1984: 38–71; 2000), Badger (1979: 43–112), Brown (1994), Bolotin and Laing (2002) and Schulman (1996).
4. For a more detailed account of this period see Prodger (2003: 141–52).
5. Muybridge's 'scientific' images weren't value free, as Linda Williams (1981) argues of his use of feminine and masculine props.
6. See Robinson (1996: 1–12), Solnit (2003: 200–3) and Musser (1990a: 15–38).
7. See, for example, Denzin (1995: 16), Applebaum (1980: 47) and Larson (2004: 247).

CHAPTER 2

Virtual Travels and the Tourist Gaze

The rise of motion pictures was closely tied to changing concepts and modes of travel. After the mid-nineteenth century, tourism saw unprecedented growth, and with it the distant corners of the world seemed to creep closer to established metropolitan centers. Tourism became such a fixture of modern life that, John Urry suggests, a 'tourist gaze' emerged as a 'socially organised and systematised' mass consumer phenomenon and dominant form of modern perception (1990: 1). For Ellen Strain, the tourist gaze was, and is, 'mobile, portable, and even culturally promiscuous': the gaze itself traveled, and was transported into other media that themselves referenced acts of traveling. The mobility and portability of the tourist gaze could therefore extend from actual tourism to perusing issues of *National Geographic*, or to the armchair tourism of watching a film travelogue (2003: 2).

As the tourist gaze took hold and solidified, people arguably began interacting more intimately with images of the world than with the world itself. Motion picture technology – like tourism, a growing leisure pursuit – kept pace with modern travel developments, mirroring and often exploiting them. The tourist and image-making industries were mutually dependent. Tom Gunning suggests that the production of images was essential to selling demands for travel: 'One wanted to travel partly because one had already seen images of distant places', while images of these places were often 'the end products of the journey, the proof one had been there' (2006: 28).

In cinema's early years, travel films became central to the roster of actualities produced at studios such as the Edison Company. Edison employee James White embarked on extensive filming tours in 1897 and 1898, taking in sights throughout the American West, Mexico and the Far East, bringing back actualities such as *Hong Kong Wharf Scene* (1898) and *Theatre Road, Yokahama* (1898). This period, often said to mark the end of cinema's 'novelty period', saw the rise of travel views alongside other nonfiction actualities and ethnographic-themed material. Like popular panoramas, stereograph views and picture postcards, travel films carried with them a fetishistic and souvenir appeal – crucially distinguished by their astonishing ability to display movement. These were not static views, but animated 'postcards in motion' (Strain 2003: 111).[1] Film was a new medium for the consumption of foreign views, complementing and even upstaging entertainments such as Wild West shows and anthropological exhibits that fascinated viewers at World's Fairs.

Early travel films distributed in the US often emphasized not just an ability to show life in motion, but illusions of the cinemagoer's own mobility, altering the relationship between ordinary Americans' experiences of the world and the spaces and places they might never have hoped to encounter first-hand. As David Nasaw notes, travel films were designed to keep up the 'novelty' of the cinema product, providing cinemagoers with access to new views of varied places like Cairo, the Eiffel Tower, Jerusalem, Niagara Falls, India or Japan. The material existence of these sights was confirmed through technical accuracy and realism: scale and image quality allowed for an unprecedented degree of illusory immersion into the scene. Indeed, 'sharp and clear' was a common phrase advertising travel films in distributor catalogues (Nasaw 1993: 149).

Travel films could draw clearer lines between mobility and its opposite, stasis, between 'the haves and have nots, the mobile and the static, the tourists and the toured' (Strain 2003: 123); they contributed to the shoring up of emerging American, western and imperial identities. The possession of the world through images of 'native' displays, foreign sights and exotic views encouraged the vicarious appropriation of space, placing the American spectator both at the center and within arm's reach of the world. By the end of the nineteenth century, the US was a highly industrialized, technologized nation, with growing imperial aspirations. The sheer scale of the events that took place over an eighteen-month period between 1898 and 1899 – when the US government took possession of Hawai'i, the eastern islands of Samoa, Wake Island, Guam, the Philippines, Puerto Rico and Cuba (as an occupied country and protectorate) – testifies to a nation looking to 'take its rightful place among the great World-Powers, and assume the unselfish obligations and responsibilities demanded by the enlightened civilizations of the age' (Procter 1972 [1898]: 21). Cinema would become a key mass medium (with print, advertising and – after the 1920s – radio) for spurring on imperialist and mass tourist drives, and the US would become the powerhouse of international film production. As Giuliana Bruno suggests, the tourist gaze 'was not always a mere expression of curiosity, for it was also complicit with the aggressive desire of "discovery"' (2002: 77). This imaginative 'taking possession' of sites and their inhabitants often went hand in hand with the tourist gaze of the film spectator. As commercial amusements, they also gave currency to forms of commodified ethnocentrism, 'making faraway cultures into commodities that could be enjoyed for the price of admission' (Rabinovitz 1991: 85).

VIRTUAL MOBILITIES

The cinema experience might be described as a form of virtual mobility. For Anne Friedberg, film was key to the emergence of the 'mobilized virtual gaze': a manner of seeing – and consuming – the world, and a hallmark of modern life that has evolved over the pre-cinematic, cinematic, televisual and Internet eras. This gaze is 'virtual' rather than 'actual' because it is not a form of direct perception but posits a 'phenomenal body' where perception is mediated through modes of representation (1993: 143). As outlined in the previous chapter, World's Fairs expanded 'the regimes of the wandering eye'; as Gunning suggests, they were 'expert tutors in the delights (and possible perils) of this new mobile vision' (Gunning 2002). Friedberg's approach stresses important links between these mobile acts of looking, commodity fetishism and the emergence of cinema, arguing that the 'newly conjoined *mobilized and virtual* gaze of the cinema answered the desire [. . .] for temporal and spatial mobility'. In this sense, the film experience goes hand in hand with 'the pleasures of escaping [. . .] physically bound subjectivity', and allows, at the same time, other forms of escape: temporary transcendence not just of physical bounds but of certain social and cultural restrictions and expectations (Friedberg 1995: 65).

Because it developed out of an apparatus that combined the mobile and the virtual, cinema spectatorship changed 'concepts of the *present* and the *real*' in unprecedented ways (Friedberg 1993: 2–3). In other words 'over there' and 'then' is experienced as 'here' and 'now', a disruption of established spatial and temporal relations. The illusion of direct experience can engage with an exciting yet self-contained sense of immediacy. Virtual travelers are safely ensconced in the theater, at a distance from the foreign scene, yet all the while immersed in its vibrant textures and interesting landscapes. This is a kind of 'environmental bubble' that 'imposes spatial divisions while enabling vision' (Strain 2003: 34). As the *New York Times* declared after the premiere of *Nanook of the North*, the film's success lay precisely in the ways it transported 'life itself' from the frozen Hudson Bay in Northern Canada directly into the comfortable, well-heated environs of New York's Capitol Theatre ('The Screen' 1922: 16). In this sense new, imaginative relations to the world are forged in virtual space. The experience of travel images becomes a way of coming to terms with and 'possessing' the world's scale and diversity, perhaps even providing a virtual substitute for the instabilities of world experience itself (Gunning 2006: 27).

It was clear almost from the start that cinema could provide not just a medium of mimesis but of movement, furnishing spectators with new, previously unimagined forms of mobility. For the poet Vachel Lindsay, the cinematic apparatus could develop a mobilized viewpoint that was the technological equivalent of modern experience. Silent cinema's ability to capture the sensation of travel made it a new kind of 'noiseless electric vehicle, where you are looking out of the windows, going down the smooth boulevard of Wonderland' (quoted in Williams 2009: 348). Cinema, then, might simply be characterized as a 'machine for travel' (Ruoff 2006: 1), a concept embodied in the popular 'phantom ride'. By 1896–7, films were being contrived to enhance the immobile viewer's impressions of being a body in motion, mimicking increasingly fast modes of transportation. This can be seen in the Lumières' *Arrival by Train in Perrache* (1896) and Biograph's *Through the Haverstraw Tunnel* (1897), where cameras have been anchored on moving trains. *Haverstraw Tunnel* shows the front-mounted camera entering and then consumed by the tunnel (the very image itself dramatically swallowed by darkness), and proved so popular it was copied many times over. As the *New York Mail and Express* exclaimed of the phantom ride: 'one holds his breath instinctively as he is swept along in the rush of the phantom cars. His attention is held almost with the vise of fate' (quoted in Kirby 1997: 62).[2]

Starting in 1904–5, George C. Hale's touring cars, or 'Hale's Tours', extended the phantom ride tradition and were hugely successful at amusement parks such as Riverview Park in Chicago, Luna Parks in Cleveland and Pittsburgh, and New York's Coney Island (Fielding 1983: 124). Hale's Tours were possibly based on the idea of the Cinéorama, a 360-degree cinematic ride – though never fully workable – of a balloon trip that featured at the Paris Exposition in 1900. Here, they simulated a moving train car, complete with swaying, vibrations and train whistles forming a sound accompaniment to projected scenes of natural landscapes and cityscapes.[3] Some operators of the Tours included scenes of the San Francisco earthquake and from *The Great Train Robbery* (1903) – the latter of which also drew on the phantom ride with its train-mounted shots and projected moving scenery.[4] For Lauren Rabinovitz, Hale's Tours anticipated travel ride films – like Cinerama in the early 1950s and IMAX – that 'foreground the bodily pleasures of cinematic experience' through a careful coordination of 'the spectator's physical and cognitive sensations' (2006: 43). In so doing, they remind us of the crucial role that bodily senses, other than vision, play in apprehending and consuming cinema as virtual reality.

Along with phenomena such as the phantom ride, the improvement of panning camera movement around the turn of the century produced panoramic views that could place spectators in the midst of a highly realistic, virtual space. Camera movement, Strain observes, could trace out a complete, circular panorama of a locale, or more subtly imitate the movements of individuals moving their heads or eyes to look left or right, up or down, surveying a given scene (2003: 117–18). Such effects, from phantom rides and mounted traveling shots to panning and scanning, offered the illusion of the 'spectator put into motion'. As Strain elaborates: 'Instead of being placed in a position of stasis gazing out at a foreign world bustling with motion, the moviegoer was mobilized and transported across a globe whose minute motions are rendered insignificant in comparison to the limitless mobility of the armchair traveler' (2003: 119–20). In this sense, the cinema of travel and mobility began to perfect modes of illusory mastery over motion picture technology as well as over the world itself.

As cinema moved into the twentieth century, travel subjects remained popular draws. This was especially true of the railroad subgenre, which included phantom rides and scenery shot from railway cars. The latter became a reliable product for companies like Selig Polyscope, whose films *Panorama of Cog Railway* (1902) and *The California Limited of the Santa Fe Route* (1903) were subsidized by the railway industry and used to promote western states as tourist attractions (Musser 1990a: 334–5). Such was the popularity of the travel genre that in 1903, fully half of Vitagraph's 'catalogue of headline attractions' were films featuring travel subjects (Musser 1990b: 123).

While travel themes and imagery remained reliable draws, by 1903 to 1905 cinematic 'attractions' and actualities were moving 'underground' (Gunning 1990: 57). The influence of imports from Europe (such as the 'trick films' of Georges Méliès), along with the rise of American directors like Edwin S. Porter, heralded enormous changes in movie production. The year 1903 witnessed a resounding move towards films that told stories. Porter, working for the Edison Company, helped to pioneer complex, multiple-shot films based on familiar American stories and themes, such as *Uncle Tom's Cabin* (1903), which comprised fourteen separate shots edited together. As David Robinson notes, the coming of the story film 'transformed motion pictures from yesterday's faded novelty to the nation's universal pastime' (1996: 89). Porter's huge success, *The Great Train Robbery* (1903), skillfully brought mainly static, single-shot scenes together to construct a gripping fictional narrative, but also demonstrates the ongoing resilience of the travel genre, the railroad subgenre, and attractions addressed to the audience, which are synthesized into the robbery plot. Indeed the 'decline' of actualities and attractions after 1903 might be attributed to changes in formal approaches to filmmaking and exhibition rather than to diminishing tastes for reality-based subjects.

As *The Great Train Robbery* announced, nonfiction subjects largely were subsumed to storytelling after about 1903, but strong formal and imaginative connections between cinema and travel would endure through the 1900s and 1910s, in many ways problematizing easy distinctions between authentic or 'real' and imaginary cinema travels. The railway subgenre showed particular resilience, while imported films – such as *The Automobile Chase* (1905) and *An Impossible Voyage* (1904), both by Méliès – highlighted sensations of fast transport in other vehicles: here the motorcar and the rocket. Like *The Great Train Robbery*, Porter's *A Romance of the Rail* (1903) is a key example of the emerging nonfiction/fiction travel hybrid, intercutting images from a moving train with fictionalized scenes of a couple watching the scenery moving by as their romance develops. The technique of combining the railway subgenre with fiction persisted in Biograph's *Hold-up of the Rocky Mountain Express* (1906, with the Catskills standing in for the Rockies). Here what is primarily a 'travel programme of views' shot from the front of and inside a train skillfully incorporates a train robbery narrative (Musser 1990b: 131).

Musser notes that nonfiction in such films was becoming 'reoriented' around the emerging story film (1990a: 351), a move that began to revise the purpose, comprehension and reception of reality-based images themselves. Yet, as suggested below, there was always a degree of two-way traffic in this process, with fiction also 'reoriented' around presumptions of nonfiction, ranging from the common practice of 'fakes' and re-enactments in nonfiction shorts supporting the Spanish-American War (1898) to the later, more fully-fledged 'storytelling documentaries' of Edward S. Curtis (*In the Land of the Head-hunters*, 1914) and Robert Flaherty.

As cinema moved into its second decade, the theatrical screen was competitive, constantly evolving and highly commercialized. Magic, trickery and the world of fantasy had largely gained the upper hand over a film world drawn from reality, and longer multiple-shot films that relied on compositional and narrative continuities gained favor. During the nickelodeon era (roughly 1905 to 1914), mainstream film exhibition to a great degree – though by no means entirely – shifted away from amusement parks, converted shops and the vaudeville circuit. Cinema now had its own purpose-built facilities that targeted audiences interested in seeing films on their own, and not as part of mixed entertainment programs. Film viewing had evolved into a specialized entertainment. But cinema reflecting the documentary impulse was by no means dead and continued to travel, both embedded in nickelodeon entertainments and circulating beyond them.

'TO POSSESS THE WORLD': LECTURES, SCENICS AND TRAVELOGUES

One of these 'documentary' entertainments was the illustrated lecture, a form of touring performance that might be seen as a paradigm for later documentary approaches in film – particularly those that incorporate on-screen filmmakers/presenters, instructive intertitles or voiceover narration (Musser 1990a:

39). Lecturers were serious entertainers, presenting their topical themes and global scenes with a view to individual and social enlightenment. Travel material was the lecturer's mainstay: indeed Musser stresses important historical continuities between the lecture format, travel and the documentary impulse, contending that 'the travelogue has undoubtedly been the dominant form of nonfiction, documentary-like programming since photographic images were incorporated into illustrated lectures in the 1850s' (2006: 358).

Early lecturers were slideshow presenters, first using drawn or painted slides but increasingly incorporating photography and, later, moving images. After 1860, presentations drew on the stereopticon, a magic lantern device with complex editing abilities. The stereopticon allowed for quick shifts between slides, superimpositions and 'dissolving views' – all prefiguring cinematic cutting. In fact many showmen and audiences, when first exposed to projected films, viewed them essentially as more complex versions of the mechanical lantern (Robinson 1996: 70).[5] Many lecturers used hand-tinted photographic slides which provided a heightened realism, a practice that continued even after the invention of motion pictures, as some presenters preferred the magic lantern's familiarity and reliability (Musser 1990a: 221).

Along with current events and moral preachments, travel was a common topic. Speakers such as Henry Northrop, Alexander Black, Lyman H. Howe, John L. Stoddard (who retired in 1897) and Stoddard's chief successor, E. Burton Holmes, were lecture 'stars' who attained widespread success by documenting journeys to far away places. After about 1902, Holmes began to refer to his presentations as 'travelogues', popularizing the term. By 1897, Holmes and Howe were working short films into lectures, and the following year Oscar Depue, Holmes's lantern operator (who also worked with Howe), was gathering film material in Arizona's Grand Canyon and the Hawaiian Islands that would be integrated as 'motion picture interludes' into Holmes's lantern-slide presentations. These were not just travel lectures but 'refined educational entertainment' and 'sophisticated documentary presentations' (Krows 1936: 170; Musser 1990a: 223). Lectures offered 'highbrow' alternatives to the hubbub of the mass cinema industry – reflected in lecturers' fairly steep ticket prices. Lecturers such as Howe even reserved presentations for Sundays rather than Saturdays, to avoid associations with 'sinful, shameless' vaudeville and music hall entertainments (Krows 1936: 170). Eileen Bowser describes how lecture appearances coincided with demands for educational, morally uplifting topics in popular entertainments:

> In 1910 travel lecturer Burton Holmes could draw a crowd of 'fashionable people' to Carnegie Hall at prices of $2 and $2.50 ($1 in the gallery) [. . .]. A nickelodeon exhibitor complained because Holmes was showing the very same pictures that he, the exhibitor, had shown earlier at five

cents, yet the nickelodeon exhibitor could not get the exchange to stock the scenic pictures any more. (1990: 44)

Lecturers like Lyman Howe advertised their work as entertainments of 'merit, refinement, amusement, and educational value' (quoted in Griffiths 2002: 207), yet these elevated pronouncements gilded what were often more populist sentiments. Illustrated lectures played their part in reinforcing links between Americanization, imperial acquisition and a well-established missionary zeal for 'civilizing' the uncivilized. Holmes's material, for instance, included ideologically slanted reports such as 'The Hawaiian Islands' (1898–9), a pro-expansionist account of the annexation of Hawai'i, and 'Manila' (1899–1900), which lent support to the controversial US invasion of the Philippines (an occupation widely represented as an imperial 'civilizing mission') (Rafael 2000: 55).[6] To these he added ethnographic and 'primitive' subjects such as 'Moki Land (Hopi Land)' (1899–1900), a presentation on the Hopi Indians (formerly Moki or Moqui) of the Southwestern Pueblo. Working for Holmes, Oscar Depue documented the Snake Dance at Walpi as early as 1898–9 when he visited Arizona. Depue didn't just 'take' but disseminated motion pictures as well, presenting one of the first film shows in the area in 1900 (Rowe 2002). Holmes's lecture brochure that year referred to the Snake Dance as 'a spectacle unique in its impressive savagery' (quoted in Griffiths 2002: 176).

The lecturer's narration normally stressed the authority of the traveler-adventurer's eyewitnessed perspective. As Holmes famously stated, 'to travel is to possess the world'. For his presentation on Japan, he noted: 'The audience is taken to the heart of the Real Japan, far beyond the reach of foreign innovations. The experiences of three Americans on a tramp of over three hundred miles through the interior provinces, are vividly described and illustrated' (quoted in Musser 1990a: 43). Such an approach helped to ground images of distant places in a first-person (and 'American') point of view: viewers could identify with the western traveler/presenter while experiencing the vicarious pleasures of travel. Along with authoritative 'I was there' narration spoken from the podium and stills taken from Holmes's point of view, film clips featured point-of-view traveling shots, mounted on the front of a train or shot from a window – techniques still used in the first-person or 'celebrity' travelogue on PBS or the Discovery Channel.[7]

First-person visuals were only part of the show: Howe for example added mechanical sound effects to the travel experience. Howe's 'Lifeorama' film presentations included the sounds of clanging swords, blaring trumpets, railway noises and 'natives [. . .] heard chattering in their jargon' (quoted in Griffiths 2002: 222–3). As Musser sees it, these shows constructed a 'privileged' perspective in the system of visuals, sound and narration that

MIDDLE WEST COMPANY

22nd Semi-Annual Tour

Lyman H. Howe

—STILL PRESENTS—

The World's Greatest Exhibition of

Moving Pictures

Coming Again with a promise of unfailing entertainment sustained by 21 semi-annual tours of triumphant achievement in the highest fields of Moving Pictures.

Our offering this time will touch many fresh fields and unhackneyed themes to which the various nations of the world contribute their most interesting incidents.

An Entertainment

MERIT

of REFINEMENT

AMUSEMENT and

EDUCATIONAL VALUE

VALENTINE THEATRE,

TOLEDO, OHIO.

Matinee and Evening, Saturday, January 6, 1906

Prices 25c. to $1.50.

SPECIAL STUDENTS' MATINEE AT 2:30 P. M.

Figure 5. Flyer for Lyman H. Howe's '22nd Semi-Annual Tour' (1906).

suppressed obvious technological and human mediation while enhancing identification with, and immersion into, the traveler's experience – a 'touristic positioning', in Strain's terms (Musser 1990b: 127; Strain 2003: 114). The travel lecturer thus served as a kind of diegetic and centering force, suturing together essentially disparate images and sounds.

Film travelogues were close cousins to the illustrated travel lecture: rooted in actualities, they expanded, unevenly, to incorporate multiple shots, structured editing and expository intertitles (introduced in film during 1902–3) which served dramatic, interpretive and scene-setting functions similar to those of the lecturer. One branch of the travelogue – multiple-shot films known as 'scenics' – were used both as inserts in travel lectures and to pad out programs at nickelodeons. Many of these shorts were imports to the US, coming from Pathé Frères, for example, or Gaumont, the latter being something of a specialist in color-tinted scenics. Cinemagoers could journey through the Alps by train with *O'er Crag and Torrent* (1910), visit the new US possession Hawai'i in *Pineapple Industry* (1910) or witness exotic wildlife through *In the Land of Monkeys and Snakes* (1910). These kinds of films, lasting three to six minutes, would soon face rapid changes in the commercial landscape with the coming of multiple-reel production and distribution.

In 1911, Milano's *Dante's Inferno* appeared in the US, an epic of five reels (over sixty minutes). Longer format nonfictions were soon finding a niche in the market; indeed the US was on the verge of a 'boom in expedition and nature films' exhibited in longer formats (Altman 2006: 74). In May 1912, the *New York Times*' 'This Week's Playbills' section featured several multiple-reel adventure and travel films, including *Paul J. Rainey's African Hunt* (1912), running at five reels, and Captain Frank E. Kleinschmidt's six-reel *The Alaska-Siberian Expedition* (1912). A popular draw at Maxine Elliot's Theatre, Kleinschmidt's film gave New Yorkers an up-close view of 'Eskimo life and customs', the 'roping of a polar bear cub' and 'a walrus hunt close at hand'. Further uptown, *Paul J. Rainey's African Hunt* was attracting 'the largest and most fashionable crowds seen at the [Lyceum] theatre in more than a year' ('This Week's Playbills' 1912: X8). Made in Kenya with photographer John C. Hemment and a taxidermist from the Smithsonian, *Rainey's African Hunt* was a highbrow entertainment that brought together guns, cameras and hunting with dogs in wild Africa. While tapping into the popularity of exploitative films such as 'Colonel' Selig's *Hunting Big Game in Africa* (1909) – which showed a Theodore Roosevelt lookalike killing an aged lion in East Africa (actually, Selig's mocked up 'jungle' in California) – Rainey's hunt promised bona fide 'thrills' that placed the audience in the middle of an exotic, yet 'fully authentic', East African scene. It included exciting images of 'a leopard [actually a cheetah] hunt, a lion hunt', and informative shots of 'native African life' ('This Week's Playbills' 1912: X8). Initially accompanied by a lecture from

Hemment, additional intertitles later allowed *Rainey's African Hunt* to be screened independently.[8]

Nonfiction travel spectacles were establishing a 'fashionable' place in the longer format market. Also in May 1912, the *New York Times* reported the much-anticipated return of *The Delhi Durbar* (1912), which was shifting from Broadway to Coney Island's Luna Park. The Durbar ceremony in India was a grand, manufactured spectacle of empire dating from Queen Victoria's reign, which crowned the new British head of state 'Emperor of India' (McKernan 2009: 122). The 1911 proceedings were painstakingly recorded by the entre-preneur Charles Urban in Kinemacolor, a 'natural' (as opposed to tinted) two-color process developed by Urban's associate George Albert Smith. The two-and-a-half hour (16,000 feet) *Delhi Durbar* had been an enormous success at Urban's Scala Theatre in London, with a stage setting that represented the Taj Mahal accompanied by a forty-eight piece orchestra, a chorus of twenty-four, a fife-and-drum corps of twenty and three bagpipes. Its debut on Broadway prompted the *New York Telegraph* to praise the transport through time and space provided by scale, image quality and color: 'There is no need to seek the fabled East in the distant Orient. It may be found in Broadway at the New York Theatre where Kinemacolor is showing all the glorious color and movement of life in India [. . .]. They were not merely moving pictures – they pulsated with life, color and emotion' (quoted in McKernan 2006).[9] The intense 'here-and-now' realism of Kinemacolor could produce a distinctive, immediate affective response: a moving pageant of imperial mastery and unity (Brown 2009: 143).

Film's potentially enormous influence on the social and civic realms was not lost on Urban, an American who worked in Britain for much of his career. He argued that 'the cinematograph must be recognized as a national instrument by [. . .] every institution of training, teaching, demonstration and research' (quoted in Griffiths 2002: 230).[10] Urban's *The Making of the Panama Canal* (1912, by the Kinemacolor Company of America) was, at nine reels, certainly just this sort of 'national instrument': an imperial spectacle arising not out of the opulence of monarchy but out of American grit, industry and ingenu-ity. The Panama Canal had long been seen by established colonial powers as the linchpin to achieving dominance of Pacific trade routes. At the 1893 Exposition in Chicago, a working model of the canal brought this concept home to millions of Americans: the canal could do for US global expansion what the transcontinental railroad had done for the mastery of North America, yet on an even grander scale. The American achievement (the Canal opened in 1914) was widely figured as a triumphal tale of technological expertise 'in which nation is featured as hero' (Strain 2003: 79). Urban's film ran to plaudits in New York, earning a strong run at the Carnegie Lyceum.

Throughout the 1910s a number of travel films – many attached to high-profile explorers – entertained largely well-off urban audiences. Vilhjalmur Stefansson, whose quest for an 'unknown continent' and discovery of 'blonde Eskimos' in the Arctic had garnered reams of press attention, featured in *Rescue of the Stefansson Arctic Expedition* (1914), documenting the rescue of the exploration party, feared lost when their ship the *Karluk* was crushed by the Arctic ice.[11] The photographer Herbert G. Ponting could have had an even greater impact on the travelogue format, but the release of his extensive *cinématographe* footage of Captain Robert F. Scott's ill-fated exploration of the South Pole was hindered by Scott's death. Distributed in part by Gaumont in 1912, it was re-edited and released later as *At the South Pole* (1929), *90 Degrees South* (1933) and restored for a 2010 release.

Wildlife adventure films also enjoyed ongoing popularity. As in *Rainey's African Hunt*, animals were represented as 'game', hunted or caught for display in western zoos, again suggesting that imaginary possession of distant and exotic locales was a key draw for many audiences. Frank M. Buckland and J. F. Cleary explored Canada's wildlife in *American Game Trails* (1915), while filmmaker Albert Blinkhorn's travels to Mexico's Guadalupe Island yielded *Capture of a Sea Elephant and Hunting Wild Game in the South Pacific Islands* (1914). This was a period of transition, when travelogues were moving from being tied to personal appearances, lectures and independent distribution to becoming self-contained 'industrial products' available for mainstream distribution. The explorer Edward A. Salisbury's expeditionary films *On the Spanish Main*, *Pirate Haunts* and *The Footsteps of Capt. Kidd*, shown with only intertitles at New York's Rialto Theatre in 1917, signaled, as Rick Altman puts it, the 'wrenching of documentary films out of the live performance lecturing world' (2006: 75–6). The lecturer gradually entered and became a kind of ghost in the machine; the live presence was no longer essential to producing diegetic unity and a focalized point of view. Nonfiction films were in the process of becoming self-contained narrative vehicles, perfectly engineered virtual experiences of reality.

Two other films of the 1910s stand out as exemplary of the exploration and travelogue modes, as well as anticipating a film like *Nanook of the North* (1922), the commercial and artistic documentary breakthrough of the following decade. The first, Edward S. Curtis's *In the Land of the Head-hunters* (1914, a.k.a. *In the Land of the War Canoes*), mixes travelogue, staged re-enactments and ethnographic footage in attempting to construct a detailed portrait of Kwakiutl Indian life in the Pacific Northwest. Frank Hurley's extraordinary *South: Ernest Shackleton and the Endurance Expedition* (1919, a.k.a. *Endurance*) is an exemplary use of motion picture technology as documentation and as careful aesthetic composition, all done under extreme freezing conditions. In spite of this range of films, there has long been an assumption that during the 1910s nonfiction was a poor relation to fiction film, inferior in both its popular appeal and its ability to engage with emerging narrative modes. In fact, nonfiction films were establishing their own audiences, carving out specific functions as informative and enlightening entertainments, providing alternatives to a film industry that was churning out increasingly standardized products.

When the US, in spite of deeply divided public opinion, entered the First World War in 1917, nonfiction film exhibition became dominated by war footage and propaganda newsreels produced (under US government supervision) by powerful companies like Hearst-Selig News Pictorial and Pathé. Only two years later, the Versailles Treaty was signed to riotous celebrations – yet the European war had left behind a devastating legacy. The conflict's technological mass killing was unprecedented, and in its wake was a social climate of postwar malaise and profound uncertainty about the West's 'civilized' advancements over 'savagery'. As late as 1921, the war still haunted the public imagination: the magazine *Current Opinion* ran a cartoon that read, 'Getting the last boy out of the trenches', with a graphic image showing a lifeless body dangling from a crane.[12] By the early 1920s, the US public was anxious to rediscover the mobilities halted by war. Tourism, travel books and travel films returned with renewed vigor. There was also an increasing curiosity about other, seemingly more 'innocent' cultures around the world that might offer escape from memories of the savage war and from the sterile and mechanized routines of postwar modern life.

NANOOK OF THE NORTH (1922)

Often referred to as the 'father' of US documentary, Robert Flaherty was nearly thirty in 1913 when he began experimenting with film. Just two years earlier, a fateful meeting had occurred with Sir William Mackenzie, the industrialist responsible for the Canadian transcontinental railroad; Flaherty would later refer to him as 'the Cecil Rhodes of Canada' (Rotha 1983: 12). Flaherty worked for Mackenzie mapping and searching for iron ore in northern Canada. Though he had almost no experience of filmmaking, at Mackenzie's suggestion Flaherty purchased a camera and began making filmed records of his journeys along the sub-Arctic coast of Hudson Bay.

Flaherty's signature and most popular work came only after he decided to abandon the results of earlier efforts at filming (which were, in any case, destroyed by fire in 1916 when he dropped a cigarette on the nitrate negative). He decided that his early 'Eskimo film' lacked dynamic visuals or a fully coherent storyline – two formal aspects that would ultimately distinguish *Nanook of the North* from most non-fiction films of the time. Flaherty and his wife Frances tirelessly sought funding for a second attempt at a more crowd-pleasing film, finally achieving a breakthrough in 1920 when the French fur-

Figure 6. *Nanook of the North* (1922). Revillon Frères. Courtesy of the British Film Institute.

trading firm Revillon Frères agreed to sponsor a trek to the North with the sole purpose of making a film.

The location was determined by Revillon Frères: a trading post on the northeastern shore of Hudson Bay. Conditions could be extremely harsh. On one occasion when the thermometer read 35 degrees Fahrenheit below zero, the negative froze and shattered in the camera 'like so much wafer-glass' (Flaherty 1926: 87). Still, Flaherty held total production and post-production costs to only $53,000, meaning *Nanook* was relatively cheap to make; yet in its first three months of release it earned $251,000 at the box office (Murphy 1978: 10). It was the first feature-length documentary to achieve financial success on this scale through mainstream distribution channels, and it was also critically successful, with the *New York Times* exclaiming that 'beside this film the usual photoplay, the so-called "dramatic" work of the screen, becomes as thin and blank as the celluloid on which it is printed' ('The Screen' 1922: 16). But the film didn't receive universal acclaim: indeed, questions about its authenticity quickly arose. The explorer Vilhjalmur Stefansson noted that Inuits had for generations hunted with guns, though Flaherty portrayed them as only having primitive weapons (the intertitles stating that the Inuit still hunt with nothing more than harpoons). Stefansson also pointed out that Nanook's battle with the seal was obviously faked, since the animal pulled from the ice was, clearly, 'still and dead' (quoted in Murphy 1978: 57).

Questions about the ethics and documentary value of staged reconstructions still surround *Nanook*, though more forceful criticisms of Flaherty came with postcolonial investigations of the chauvinisms and fetishisms underlying traditional exploration and ethnographic representations. One example of divided opinion relates to Flaherty's practice of developing the negative on site and then screening the rushes to local Inuits, so that they could see the results and work with him, Flaherty noted, 'as partners' (Rotha 1983: 31). The practice has led Flaherty to be seen as a pioneer of the collaborative feedback method in documentary ethnographic film, later adopted by filmmakers such as Jean Rouch. Yet 'collaboration' also involved putting his native subjects to (often grueling) work, including Allakariallak ('Nanook') himself, who spent long hours, often through the night, washing and drying the negative. Such practices reveal the fine line that separates participatory filmmaking and subtle forms of indenture (Geiger 2005: 123).

Flaherty's background as an explorer and prospector has added to concerns about his relationship to imperialist ideologies and practices. While Flaherty saw himself as lobbying against blatant forms of cultural hegemony, his films nonetheless conjure up little-known worlds on the frontiers of civilization, helping feed US and European fantasies of the 'savage' existing uncorrupted in nature. For Brian Winston, Flaherty was 'a child of the last age of imperial expansion, and beneath the veneer of sympathy and understanding for the peoples he filmed there is nothing but the strong whiff of paternalism and prejudice' (1995: 20).

Nanook's reputation has not been helped by interpretations that place it alongside other, more brutal practices involving the display of native people. One notorious incident involved the explorer Robert Edwin Peary, who in 1897 took six Inuit from Greenland to New York as 'living specimens' for study and exhibition. Four quickly succumbed to tuberculosis and pneumonia. The body and possessions of one, Qisuk, were put on display at the American Museum of Natural History. His son, Minik, after being tricked by a sham funeral, pursued a lifelong battle for the right to claim his father's remains, without success (Garroutte 2003: 59).[13] Such incidents suggest the extreme ends of the desire for authentic representatives of racial and cultural difference – for evidence of the mysteries of the world at the fringes of western territories and perceptions. Though Allakariallak's display was virtual, his end was similarly tragic; he died of starvation just two years after *Nanook of the North*'s release.

Like the travelogues and illustrated lectures that came before, *Nanook* is haunted by a history of western attitudes towards 'other' lives and cultures. At the same time, the film speaks of western self-perceptions, registering anxieties about modernity and its creeping mechanization. With its sentimental and elegiac undertones, *Nanook* seems to highlight, albeit elliptically, the loss of natural and 'primitive' harmony in a technologized world. This was also an era when the US was coming to terms with increasingly popular concepts of cultural relativism emerging in anthropological circles, and widely affecting modern art and popular culture more generally. Cultural relativism, while problematic in its construction of cultural 'others' to the western 'self', helped to shatter a sense of western superiority in that it questioned the presumption that there were universal laws governing all cultures, or that a strictly hierarchical relationship existed between western and 'primitive' societies.

Of course, even as cultural relativism was exerting an influence, discourses of racial and cultural chauvinism in the US remained, as ever, extremely complex and fraught with division. While Flaherty was shooting his earliest films among the Inuit, D. W. Griffith's epic argument for racial segregation, *The Birth of a Nation* (1915), was breaking box-office records across the country. Griffith offered 'historical facsimiles' of racial hierarchy, while tracts such as Madison Grant's *The Passing of the Great Race* went even further, dividing races into different biological categories, positioning the Aryan and the idea of the noble Teuton against the inferiority of non-white peoples (Stocking 1968: 68).

This was the heated cultural and political climate into which Flaherty introduced his popular portrait of Inuit life, and these were some key debates with which his text would have collided. Flaherty himself always avoided attempts at any complex theorizing of his approach, and primarily expressed a sentimental affinity for his subjects. His mode of primitivism might best be seen as aligned to an idealization of the primitive that was becoming prevalent among his more liberal contemporaries. The sociologist Edward Sapir, for example, wrote an influential article, 'Culture, Genuine and Spurious' that circulated in the early 1920s and projected a vision of western cultural regeneration through an appeal to primitive types. Sapir sees the West as plagued by 'spiritual disharmony', particularly 'the case of America, where a chronic state of cultural maladjustment has for so long a period reduced much of our higher life to sterile externality' (1966 [1924]: 95–6). American culture, Sapir argues, needs the revitalization of a 'genuine culture' that is 'deeper and more satisfying':

> The Indian's salmon-spearing is a culturally higher type of activity than that of the telephone girl or mill hand simply because there is normally no sense of spiritual frustration during its prosecution, no feeling of subservience to tyrannous yet largely inchoate demands. (1966 [1924]: 93)

The nation's cultural sickness is revealed by invoking the spiritual health of the primitive ideal.

Flaherty's film, while never directly referencing the fragmentation and alienation of modern western life, posits primitive figures that are in key ways 'like us'. The family consists of patriarch Nanook, his wife Nyla (who at one point 'cleans her brand new ice window') and their children. Yet they are, importantly, also unlike us: 'noble savages' who exist at close quarters with nature's rhythms. *Nanook* evokes nostalgia for a seemingly more harmonious way of life – a way of life that perhaps never existed. Here an idealized western self is projected onto a cultural or racial other – partly real and partly imagined – familiarizing the subjects of difference while reducing the complexities of other cultures to a series of easily digestible tropes and themes.

The scene in which Nanook encounters a gramophone has often been cited as a key moment where the film infantilizes, while also distancing, its subjects. Here Nanook's ignorance of technology is underscored in the presence of the machine, the intertitles explaining that the trader, 'in deference to Nanook, the great hunter [. . .] entertains and attempts to explain the principle of the gramophone'. Apart from this scene, *Nanook* reinforces the contrast between civilized and primitive through suppressing the presence of the filmmaker and the trappings of western society. In this rare moment when technology is revealed, it paradoxically becomes a device to exclude Nanook from the modern era by showing his naivety. It also, unusually for the film, divorces us from Nanook's point of view, momentarily 'throwing us out' of the imaginary bond established between the audience and the 'great hunter'. Yet the scene might also serve another, more ambiguous function, as a means to estrange (western) viewers from any complacent sense of technologized modernity as the normal or 'natural' way of life. Nanook remains a primitive ideal, positioned out of time, out of the present, yet he reflects and projects the technologized West back to itself – now distorted, unnatural, at times (like the gramophone) even comical and bizarre.

Yet the film contains potentially darker undertones. The image of the 'happy-go-lucky Eskimo' can be seen shifting, ambiguously and unsettlingly, towards shades of savagery. Close-ups of the blood-smeared faces of Nanook, Nyla and Allegoo after the seal hunting sequence (the red appearing black due to the limited tonal range of orthochromatic film) reinforce a potentially derogatory meaning of 'Eskimo' as 'eaters of raw flesh'. Along these lines, Fatimah Tobing Rony sees *Nanook* as an extension of the colonial-era ethnographic spectacle, where images of cultural and racial otherness feed western curiosity, as in the displays along the Chicago Midway (1996: 105). Flaherty's follow-up, *Moana* (1925), shot in Western Samoa, perpetuated and extended these oppositions between civilized and primitive. Even more consistently than *Nanook*, *Moana* suppresses the filmmaker's presence and the trappings of modernity. Flaherty's Samoan film recreates a dream of a lost paradise in the South Pacific, a world out of time, where native participants act out a sensuous, largely carefree life, free from the harness of modern technology. Such films might be seen as expressions of western nostalgia, allegories of the loss of nature and fall from Eden, just as much, if not more, than they offer 'truths' about the cultures they represent.

Nanook focuses its gaze on an approximation of the past, though it does so through innovative approaches to nonfiction which borrow from narrative and montage strategies already successfully tested on mass audiences. The practice of interspersing staged sequences alongside candid scenes, while constructing a coherent episodic structure, was to become a Flaherty trademark evident in most of his major films. A key to appreciating Flaherty's style lies not in seeking out strands of unvarnished authenticity, but in observing his skill in bridging the gaps between on-site improvisation and diegetic continuity in the finished film. Moreover, Flaherty's approach mobilizes modes of audience investment and identification rarely employed in nonfiction film up to this point. As Richard Koszarski notes, early audiences coming to Flaherty's film were 'attuned to the usual Burton Holmes travelogue, a home-movie style ramble in which the Western adventurer situates himself in exotic climes' (1990: 243). *Nanook* broke out of this convention, focusing not on a traveler/narrator nor mainly on traveling views and landscapes. Flaherty wrote that he wanted to show 'the Innuit' and not lay the emphasis on 'where *I* had been and what *I* had done' (quoted in Koszarski 1990: 243). He created a fleshed-out 'native informant' character, a 'hero' with whom audiences could identify.

William Uricchio characterizes nonfiction cinema in the 1920s as undergoing a progression from imagistic description towards interpretation: a process of shifting the camera's role as 'a viewfinder on the world' towards a new conceptual orientation of nonfiction. Here, 'the construction of an elaborate artifice dependent upon sets, story, and psychologically credible characters, and the effacing of narrative agency, all contributed to a documentary form with far greater similarity to the classical Hollywood cinema than the preceding decades of nonfiction production' (1995: 291). Of course these similarities to classical cinema had limits; it was also the assertion of documentary's *dissimilarity* to Hollywood fiction that, crucially, set it apart from fantasy and invention. The ongoing belief that certain films bore a special, indexical relation to pro-filmic reality remained a key to their allure and market niche. This was provided not only via publicity and intertitles announcing the film's dcumentation of real people and places, but through other deviations from the Hollywood norm.

As Jeffrey Ruoff suggests, in the nonfiction travel genre one of these differences was the use of episodic structure over linear narrative (2006: 11). Indeed *Nanook* is episodic and ultimately open-ended, though it does not eschew all elements of plot. Rather, its scenes unfold within a 'slight narrative' frame of changing seasons and the search for food (Rotha 1999 [1935]: 149). Each vignette – walrus hunt, seal hunt, igloo building – is relatively self-contained, providing a focus for gleaning information or knowledge, while contributing to a framing narrative that holds the audience's attention. The film thus successfully integrates appeals to epistephilia (pleasure in knowledge) and scopophilia (pleasure in viewing) while providing narrative tension about what is pending or unresolved.

Nanook's popularity relied as much on the exhibitionistic and 'primitive' allure of its subject matter as it did on the successful integration of voyeuristic pleasure, identification and narrative storytelling in a nonfiction context. Yet Flaherty's film is also, many still agree, a work of art, containing moments of profound poetic and expressive imagery, especially in its opening and closing sequences.[14] In bringing these elements quite seamlessly together, Flaherty tapped into public demands for legitimate, enlightened entertainments: films that not only documented and displayed foreign places, but that seemed to create new, barely imagined worlds permitting immersion into cultural difference. In this sense, Flaherty's work forms part of what George Stocking calls the 'ethnographic sensibility' of the 1920s and early 1930s: a broad interest in producing more informed views of cultural diversity than the accounts and travelogues that came before, but that still lacked the precise rules and scientific trappings of emerging disciplines such as anthropology (1989: 212). This ethnographic sensibility ranged across different artistic and scientific endeavors, all of which took culture (as opposed to more fixed and oppositional notions, such as race) as the primary force determining how humans formed social networks and individual identities, how they shaped their public and private lives.

Nanook's ethnographic sensibility is thus subjective and undisciplined rather than rigorous, objective or precise. Flaherty never trained as an anthropologist, but did believe that his work could have some ethnographic value. As he recalled of *Nanook*, 'I had planned to depict an ethnoligical [*sic*] film of life covering the various phases of their hunting, travel, domestic life, and religion in as much of a narrative form as is possible' (quoted in Ruby 2000: 71). On this level, Flaherty projects a certain seriousness and interest in educational value that aligns his work more to the illustrated lecture tradition, or to Curtis's or Kleinschmidt's ethnographic studies, than to the manipulative sensations of films such as Selig's *Hunting Big Game in Africa*.

In 1922, travel programs made up of multiple shorts were still headlining at theaters, as this *New York Times* entry suggests:

Travelaughs: 'Such is Life', in 'Monte Carlo', 'Nice', 'Munich', and 'Amsterdam', among 'Alpine Shorts', and 'The Children of France', and

'Where Paris Shops'. In these works by Lily Mayer, in which motion pictures are skillfully and imaginatively combined with drawings, the travel film becomes delightful entertainment without losing its informative character. ('Screen: Pictures of 1922' 1922: 3)

While similarly 'delightful' and 'informative', *Nanook of the North*'s sophisticated approach to the feature format marks its distance from travel programs such as this one. But it should be stressed that Flaherty's film did not appear in a vacuum; it tapped into and extended a series of developing approaches to telling nonfictional stories on screen.

HARD TRAVELING: THE EXPEDITIONARY MODE

Flaherty's documentary practices might speak to a range of nonfiction approaches encompassing science, education and popular entertainment. Sitting closer to the 'scientific' end of things would be filmmaking that engaged the ethnographic sensibility: practices that included popular ethnography and more carefully systemized anthropological film work. Leaning more towards popular entertainment was the expeditionary mode: discovery and adventure films that were conceived and distributed on a larger scale than previously seen. Like *Nanook*, these features incorporated slight narrative, candid and staged footage, and tightly edited sequences. Yet they tended to eschew one of *Nanook*'s key features, the focus on a 'rounded' native character, preferring to stay closer to the format inherited from the illustrated travel lecture. Martin Johnson was one of these adventurer-filmmakers who retained the lecturer's function as mediator and primary point of view. Johnson's early presentations, such as *Jack London's Adventures in the South Sea Islands* (1913) – documenting a cruise through the South Pacific as assistant to London – had brought him modest success. With his wife and filming partner Osa, he pursued the lecture-on-film format, releasing *Among the Cannibal Isles of the South Pacific* (1918), made in Vanuatu and the Solomon Islands, *Jungle Adventures* (1921) and *Headhunters of the South Seas* (1922). Together the Johnsons would carve a specialist niche in safari and exotic wildlife films, as in *Trailing African Wild Animals* (1923), based on their expedition to Africa in 1921–2.

After garnering the support of important figures such as Carl Akeley of the American Museum of Natural History and Kodak's George Eastman, the Johnsons went on a major expedition to Kenya, which yielded the box office hit, *Simba, the King of the Beasts* (1928). *Simba*'s success lay in its thrills and technical virtuosity, but must at least in part be attributed to the *Nanook* effect, which had not only whetted popular tastes for exotic and travel subjects but had convinced studios and exhibitors that they could be highly lucrative.

Still, for Akeley, the power of the Johnsons' work lay not just in its popular appeal, but in the ways their pictures were 'true to the facts' and 'sound natural history'. Their animals were not 'borrowed from a zoo' but 'photographed in their native haunts'; the Johnsons' images were 'thrilling, not as they satisfy the blood lust of the savage within us, but because they portray the novel and fascinating truth ('Martin and Osa Johnson' 2002). Yet, while they aimed to capture what Martin rhapsodically called the 'beauties' of 'untouched Africa', *Simba* is also a colonizer spectacle, featuring not only exotic animals but their vanquishing at the hands of white adventurers (quoted in Pierce 1992). We see Osa shooting down a charging rhinoceros, elephant and lion, all in orderly succession.

The Johnsons' Fox Studios follow-up, *Congorilla* (1929), would take the travel adventure into similar though more openly exploitative territory. With its subtitle, 'Adventures among the Big Apes and Little People of Central Africa', the film distinguished itself as the first sound film shot entirely in Africa. In it, the Johnsons appear as adventurer-heroes, world famous for their 'thrilling expeditions' and 'renowned career with gun and camera'. Hard travel by boat, motor car and camel is interspersed with animal footage and 'comic' interludes that effectively infantilize the Africans appearing in the film.

Thomas Doherty neatly distinguishes earlier travelogues from the emergence of this more grandiose expeditionary approach:

A travelogue is the cinematic equivalent of the act of tourism, a film that provides a comfortable berth for seeing the sights and gawking at the natives. [. . .] In contrast, the expeditionary film demands hard traveling. No packaged tour but an adventure in cinema at feature length, it possesses the immediacy and intensity of on-location shooting and spontaneous action, a sense of wonder mixed with the adrenaline rush of fear. The expeditionary film promised a true voyage of discovery. (1999: 222–3)

The travel-adventure film is organized around a narrative of rugged journeying with cameras (and, usually, guns); at the same time it heightens the emotional peaks and dangers of these voyages, staging dramas when necessary. In Merian C. Cooper and Ernest Schoedsack's *Grass* (1925) and *Chang* (1927), viewers are encouraged to identify with the western voyager and storyteller who shows off the sights and peoples encountered. Narrative control, mobile camerawork and panoramic views all imbue the armchair traveler with a sense of voyeuristic mastery. Heightened events and the photographers' heroic efforts to capture them take center stage, such as the dramatic river crossing in *Grass* or the elephant ('chang') stampede in *Chang*. These are the 'sublime' moments of the travel narrative: highlighted encounters that help to embellish arduous, frequently dull journeys (Lamb 1994: 7).

Other than newsreels and what *Variety* called 'two-reel lecture stuff', the beginning of the sound era in the 1930s saw travel-adventure films dominating the non-fiction feature output of studios and smaller companies. Dana Benelli notes that in the four-year period from 1930 to 1933, of the sixty documentaries reviewed in the *New York Times*, most were related to the expeditionary mode (2006: 180). *Ingagi* (1930), made by the one-off Congo Pictures, took the genre to extremes in exploiting cultural projections, desires and fears of the foreign, conjuring up exotic dangers lurking just beyond the western horizon. *Ingagi* advertised itself as 'an authentic incontestable celluloid document showing the sacrifice of a living woman to mammoth gorillas!' Interestingly, though the film was banned by the Motion Picture Producers and Distributors of America (a.k.a. the Hays Office), it was not for its lurid content (which at first prompted an investigation for 'sexual perversion'). Instead it was lambasted for its deceptive presentation and its advertising that attempted, among other things, to pass off a Los Angeles zoo as Africa and an actor in a fur suit as a gorilla (Erish 2006: E6). *Ingagi*'s fakery was controversial (leading RKO to drop the picture), but the aggressive marketing of the film as nonfiction seemed to pay off: audiences and the independent exhibitors who picked up the film ignored accusations of deceit and official attempts at a ban. Andrew Erish estimates that the film made $4 million on independent release, making it one of the most successful films of the Depression era. The Hays Office had failed to stop the film, and even the new Advertising Code of Ethics adopted in the wake of the *Ingagi* scandal failed to stanch the flow of fakery in the expeditionary mode. *Ingagi*'s success shows the marketability and malleability of the documentary impulse, here engineered to shore up existing fears and fantasies of 'otherness'.

More 'legitimate' sensations came in the form of wild animal collector Frank Buck's *Bring 'Em Back Alive* (1932), shot in Malaysia and based on his best-selling book. W. S. Van Dyke's Academy Award-nominated *Trader Horn* (1931), set in Africa, was openly marketed as fiction, but grounded its appeal in its on-location scenes featuring wild animals and indigenous peoples. B. F. Zeidman's *Samarang* (1933), about South Pacific pearl divers, was a similar mixture of fictional conventions and non-fictional subjects. Contemporary reviewers were hardly troubled by the seeming contradictions of blending fact and fiction: the *New York Times* commended the film's 'melodramatic episodes [. . .] for the most part set forth with no little skill', yet at the same time maintained that it was 'a picture distinguished by the obvious authenticity of many of its scenes' (Hall 1933: 22). It seems Hollywood had hit on a winning formula: an 'ethnographic' context could permit displays of nudity and violence, while the insertion of documentary footage into fictional frameworks both heightened a film's realism and extended its marketability. Benelli suggests that this 'travel-incorporating hybrid film' could potentially appeal to 'multiple segments of the mass audience' through its presentation of varied elements, mixing education and adventure with romantic subplots. At the same time it could be marketed flexibly by exhibitors as satisfying a wide range of tastes (2006: 190).

Cooper and Schoedsack's *King Kong* (1933), set on a fictional Melanesian island (a character claims that the language spoken on Skull Island resembles that of Nias Islanders), further draws on core features of the expeditionary mode. The heroic explorer enters uncharted and 'savage' regions, returning to civilization with living physical specimens captured on his adventures. But the film, with its central character Carl Denham serving as chief adventurer, animal wrangler and voyeur (Denham was said to be based on Frank Buck), also pushed the boundaries of the expeditionary mode into the realms of self-reflexive ambivalence. *King Kong* might be seen to present a cautionary allegory of colonial and ethnographic mastery, revealing the hazards of the desire to capture spectacular images of 'unknown' places and peoples, and of the public's insatiable demand for them. Arguably, these desires have never really faded: twenty-first century celebrities like Bear Grylls or the 'crocodile hunter', the late Steve Irwin, might recall past rugged adventurers from fiction (Trader Horn) and fact (Frank Buck).

Along with the travel and expeditionary features of the 1920s and 1930s, the newsreel travelogue was becoming a familiar site not only for armchair adventures but for shoring up national and imperial identities. This might be glimpsed in films such as James Fitzpatrick's *Travel Talks* newsreels, distributed by MGM and screened in thousands of theaters across the US. *Travel Talks* provided 'a stock set of images and concepts about the world abroad at a time when hardly any international films were available to American audiences and when comparatively few Americans could travel to Ceylon, Argentina or Japan' (Ruoff 2006: 13). Fitzpatrick's series also interpreted these places, orienting American impressions of them.

As the 1920s moved into the 1930s, any notion of the US as a fledgling or isolationist state was firmly in the past: US expansionist politics, particularly in the Pacific region, were approaching their zenith. In this context, Fitzpatrick's *Fiji and Samoa: The Cannibal Isles* (1933) essentially served as an advertisement for joint British and US imperial control in the Pacific, giving an indication of how the US was portraying itself as the natural inheritor of established colonial networks and prepared to take up the mantle of the 'empire of the English speaking race' (Kachru et al. 2006: 296–7). As the voiceover stresses on approach to the Samoan islands, these are national possessions: an 'enchanting group of islands belonging to the United States and the British Empire'.

Fitzpatrick's film gives an indication of how cultural and racial chauvinism, masquerading as educational enlightenment, can be a by-product of the tourist gaze. *Fiji and Samoa* offers a hierarchical point of view: the voiceover authoritatively describes 'ravenous cannibals' and 'savage brown faces', while menacing music plays over shots of Fijians glancing towards the camera. Fitzpatrick argues that, 'as a race they have traveled far along the path of development during the fifty-nine years under British rule. Perhaps war, cannibalism, polygamy, and their attendant evils are but memories of the dark past from which they have emerged'. Similarly, over a shot of a Fijian policeman the voice intones: 'Perhaps the most remarkable achievement of the white countries that have colonized the earth is that manner in which they have utilized the military services of the natives, so that they can entrust them with the very guns which were formerly used to conquer them'. Fitzpatrick's voiceover offers one-sided messages referencing threats of savagery, but the images reveal 'native' figures that seem hardly dangerous or disturbing. Fitzpatrick's *Travel Talks* thus reflects the interdependency of the tourist gaze, racial chauvinism and forms of cultural and territorial possession, but also hints at conflicts and tensions that are always nascent in cinema viewing. The voice of the film strives to restrict the viewer's interpretations, but can never wholly eliminate other, potentially more complex or open-ended forms of reception and understanding.

The contours of travel and tourism in US nonfiction film – as a physical experience, concept, metaphor and theme – are certainly too broad to contain in a single chapter. My intent has been to highlight some modes and ideas of travel that moved across a range of early documentary approaches and that appealed to ideas of national solidarity through constructions of an 'American' tourist gaze. These approaches – travel short, travelogue, illustrated travel lecture, expeditionary feature – have never really disappeared, having branched into a wide spectrum of instructive media and popular diversions. Illustrated travel lectures continue to draw large audiences, while the format persists in the 'show and tell' approach of home-made travelogues as well as in the cavalcade of virtual tours on the Discovery Channel, the Travel Channel and elsewhere (Ruoff 2006: 235). IMAX releases are typically designed as virtual voyages, where cinemagoers might embark on 'an epic adventure to places unknown, seemingly unattainable and beyond imagination'; in *Antarctica* (1991), for example, you can 'vividly experience what life is really like on the planet's largest, driest desert' ('Antarctica' 2009).

At the other end of the spectrum, low-budget travelogues and actualities – souvenir postcards in motion – also persist. Short tourist views, shots from trains, planes, cars and ships, videos of family vacations and so on, have returned with a vengeance via YouTube and other sites. YouTube even streams an updated version of one of the earliest phantom rides, *Through the Haverstraw Tunnel*, remade as *Southbound at Haverstraw Tunnel* (2008).

Arguably, with the ease of shooting and sharing online, travel actualities again rank among the most widely consumed modes of filmmaking.

NOTES

1. Postcards widely featured at the 1893 Chicago Exposition; by 1908 circulation had reached 680 million in the US.
2. The first film of this type was shot by a Lumière camera from the back of a train leaving Jerusalem (1896); films shot from the front of a train were usually referred to as 'phantom rides'.
3. See Gomery (1992: 10), Fielding (1983: 118).
4. See Barnouw (1983: 30), Musser (1990a: 429–30, 1990b: 129).
5. Perhaps 'new' technologies are never quite as new as they seem, as they are experienced 'in relation to older and more familiar media, which they challenge and destabilize' (Renov and Suderburg 1996: xii).
6. As John Robert Procter wrote: 'From the blood of our [American] heroes, shed at Santiago and Manila, there shall rise a New Imperialism' (Procter 1972 [1898]: 26).
7. For further details, see Griffiths (2002: 203–13), Altman (2006: 61–76) and Barber (1993: 68–84).
8. See also Grau (1912: xvii), and 'Show Rainey's African Hunt' (1912). *Rainey's African Hunt* was re-released with intertitles in 1913, running at six reels.
9. See also McKernan (2009: 131) and 'The Delhi Durbar' (1912: X9). Urban was previously known for producing a series of 'Bioscope Expedition' films also featuring exotic sights.
10. Urban's representative in New York, George Kleine, offered thousands of film subjects, including Urban's films, to the New York City Board of Education in 1910. Though never fully taken up, the Board superintendent William H. Maxwell became known as a 'pioneer in visual education'. See Krows (1936: 170).
11. See 'Stefansson Off for Arctic Quest' (1913), 'Stefansson's Own Peril' (1914) and 'Stefansson Tells of White Eskimos' (1912).
12. *Current Opinion*, 70, June 1921, p. 735.
13. See also Harper (2001).
14. Many scenes and shots evoke Inuit drawings done on site (Barnouw 1983: 37).

CHAPTER 3

Serious Play: Documentary and the Avant-Garde

As the previous chapter showed, cinema embodied the idea and physical experience of the modern world in motion – from the legacies of moving crowds and exhibits at world fairs to the disorienting speed of fast travel. Emerging nonfiction genres such as the travelogue encapsulated film's ability to capture a god's eye view of the moving world: the tourist gaze helped to stabilize the blur of modern urban life, delivering views of far-flung sites and peoples as consumable spectacles. The virtual journeying provided by panoramic, first-person and mobile perspectives bolstered the viewer's belief in knowing the world through the accretion of images. Yet there are other strands in documentary's development that engaged more critically with modern spectacle – what Thomas Elsaesser calls the modern 'tyranny of the eye' – in particular, the modernist avant-garde (1996: 16).

Important links between avant-garde work and documentary remain relatively overlooked even as, in recent decades, clear boundaries between documentary and other cinematic forms have come into question. Indeed, documentary is often still viewed as the avant-garde's opposite. While the latter implies innovation, experimentation and playfulness in both content and form (traced to the traditions of fantastic and otherworldly 'trick films' of showmen like Méliès), documentary is seen as an established mode (usually traced to actualities and the Lumières) for revealing the 'real', if often hidden, worlds we inhabit. Valued for formal transparency and heuristic authority, documentary, Bill Nichols notes, has been known for its 'discourses of sobriety'. It is seen to 'speak directly about social and historical realities', engaging issues such as foreign policy, medicine, science, economics and education (2001a: 39).[1]

Yet, Nichols forcefully argues, established histories of documentary's development have obscured complex influences, propagating in particular the 'repression of the role of the 1920s avant-garde in the rise of documentary'

(2001b: 581–2).[2] Key proponents of the documentary form such as Grierson, for example, insisted that modernist innovation was a 'dangerous' model for documentary, and effectively erased the avant-garde from the documentary tradition (Beattie 2008: 20; Grierson 1946 [1932]: 85). Yet divisions between avant-garde and documentary – aligned, respectively, to opposing 'aesthetic' and 'scientistic' impulses – have not always been so strict. Early experiments with nonfiction and avant-garde techniques, such as Paul Strand's and Charles Sheeler's *Manhatta* (1921), discussed below, illuminate productive tensions between form and content that work to reveal the materiality of documentary images and draw attention to the technologies of representation themselves. This tradition might be traced right through landmark *cinépoem* and 'city symphony' films such as Dziga Vertov's *Man With a Movie Camera* (1929), Joris Ivens's *Rain* (1929), Chris Marker's *Sans Soleil* (1982) and Robert Gardner's *Forest of Bliss* (1986). Here, variously, the poetics and aesthetics of lived experience, rather than being suppressed in favor of 'sober' facts and information, are brought to the fore as contemplative, disruptive and even ecstatic (as in Vertov or Ivens) pleasures. As I hope to show, what the avant-garde bequeathed to documentary was an undercurrent of anti–illusionism: an element often sublimated after documentary became bound to projects of civic responsibility and social instruction. If documentary as a public institutional form came to be associated with a collective belief in a unified or agreed–upon 'truth', avant-garde influences always suggested the possibility of a more critical stance, where moving images and the modern technologies that produced them were met, as Elsaesser puts it, with 'skepticism and sarcasm' just as much as 'wonder and amazement' (1996: 18).

This chapter outlines alliances between avant-garde and documentary circles in the US even as, by the early 1930s, the concept of documentary was taking on more precise social and heuristic associations. In the decade that followed Grierson's 1926 review of *Moana* – where Grierson argued the film had 'documentary value' (1979 [1926]: 25) – documentary became delineated as a form, with a clearer set of objectives. Advocates for documentary like Grierson argued that cinema could promote national unities and civic-minded identities, and that nonfiction moving images in particular could and should be manipulated to political ends. As Chapter 4 shows, documentary in the US – and the authority bestowed on it as a mode for delivering social arguments to mass audiences – would become harnessed to the nation-building interests of government film projects of the 1930s. But these developments should not eclipse the crucial links between avant-garde and nonfiction traditions: a closer look reveals documentary's ongoing, dialectical relationship to innovative form, aesthetics and even elements of the fantastic. At the heart of this discussion, then, is my intention to stress documentary's historical diversity rather than its unity or linear progression. Documentary needs to be seen, I suggest,

more as the sum of a lengthy social and historical process than as a logical or
pre-given category.

UNSTABLE BOUNDARIES, DEFAMILIARIZED REALITIES

The work of several critics (for example Jan-Christopher Horak, Bruce Posner
and David E. James) has helped chart the emergence of the 'first' US cinematic
avant-garde that, approximately, coincided with a period of increasing self-
awareness of, and theoretical interest in, the documentary idea. Importantly,
this critical work defines certain key features of an 'American' avant-garde
and underscores the ways that early (pre-Second World War) US avant-garde
film might be distinguished from later movements in 'experimental film' (the
1940s and 1950s) and 'underground' or 'independent' film (the 1960s–1970s)
(Horak 1995: 3).

Of course the meaning of the term 'avant-garde' is widely contested. In this
chapter it refers, broadly, to experimental and often subversive artistic endeavors that spanned national boundaries and traditions. While there were always
key and often profound rivalries and shifting affiliations between members of
different avant-garde movements, we might also perceive a certain syncretism:
an overarching belief in 'vanguard' artistic and social practices that defied the
conventions of a bourgeois status quo. In film, the influence of the avant-garde
was firmly established after the First World War and became increasingly
widespread during the 1920s. Experimental dance featured prominently in
early avant-garde films: with its mixture of abstraction, fluid motion, compelling visuals and music, dance dispelled any need for linear narrative. Dudley
Murphy's *Soul of the Cypress* (1920) envisioned the seductions of a tree
nymph, using dramatic backlighting, color tinting and long shots to emphasize the cadences of music and gesture. Murphy's *Danse Macabre* (1922), a
filmed ballet made with photographer Francis Bruguière and dancer Adolph
Bolm, mixed techniques of animation and double exposure to develop a new,
largely unfamiliar film aesthetic. The Dada film *Ballet Mécanique* (1924) was
put together in Paris the following year by Murphy, with financial and artistic
input from Fernand Léger. Conceived to accompany a brutally mechanistic
musical piece by Georges Antheil, the film was intended to 'try the specators'
patience', transforming everyday machine parts (pistons, gears, pendulums,
eggbeaters) and physical labors into a looping, repetitive, frustrating choreog-
raphy (quoted in Freeman 1996: 32).

In the US, the first cinematic avant-garde – sometimes uncomfortably
– spanned the coming of the talkies. It emerged from a series of interlinked
movements that examined cinema's pervasive cultural role and interrogated
presumptions that motion pictures were just mindless mass entertainments.

Figure 7. *Ballet Mécanique* (1924). Fernand Léger-Dudley Murphy. Courtesy of the British Film Institute.

The US avant-garde exerted the force, albeit from the margins, of 'a dynamic and fractious sphere of production and exhibition in which the ontology of cinema could be investigated and expanded' (Donald 1998: 30). It developed in the context of, and in collaboration with, radical artistic endeavors from continental Europe, Russia and Ukraine such as Futurism, Constructivism, Expressionism, *Neue Sachlichkeit*, Dada and Surrealism. Indeed as the First World War raged in Europe, New York served as a hot spot for Dada activism, one of Surrealism's key precursors. Dada signified a radical, international art movement founded in Zürich by a group of artists, essayists, performers and poets disillusioned by war. Among its key figures were Tristan Tzara and Marcel Janco, the latter of whom recalled: 'we had lost confidence in our "culture". Everything had to be demolished'. Dada wanted to 'shock the bourgeoisie', to destroy the very idea of art, to 'attack common sense' (quoted in Plant 1992: 41). In fact Dada – perhaps testifying to modernist impulses at the heart of postmodernism – refuted the postulation of any sense whatsoever: the moment a meaning emerged, Dada would question it through practices based on a simultaneous unfolding of vastly different or opposite events/performances and through perpetual negation and questioning. Tzara's pronouncements in his Dada Manifesto sum this up:

I'm writing a manifesto [. . .], and in principle I am against manifestos, as I am against principles [. . .]. I'm writing this manifesto to show that you can perform contrary actions at the same time, in one single, fresh breath; I am against action; as for continual contradiction, and affirmation too, I am neither for nor against them, and I won't explain myself. (1987 [1918]: 45)

In New York, Alfred Stieglitz's gallery 291 hosted exhibits by Dada artists Francis Picabia and Marcel Duchamp. Duchamp is well-known for his seminal 'anti-art' from found objects such as 'Fountain', a urinal first submitted (though rejected) for exhibition in New York in 1917. Such Dada ready-mades were aimed at 'short-circuiting the means by which art objects acquire financial, social, and spiritual values' (Elsaesser 1996: 17). Also in New York, the artist Man Ray garnered his early avant-garde influences. Later, with his friend Duchamp, he would make *Anémic Cinéma* (1926), a kind of cinematic ready-made of found objects, aimed at critiquing the ways art was produced through an aestheticizing vision (Judovitz 1996: 47). Dada strove against 'retinal' or pure visual aesthetics, and cinema seemed well-suited to anti-art, as it relied on mechanized as opposed to 'natural' or 'raw' forms of seeing and was itself a kind of social machine.

After the First World War, the strategically eclectic Duchamp helped establish Surrealism (though he avoided adopting the term himself) with Paris-based artists and provocateurs such as André Breton, Salvador Dalí and Luis Buñuel. Loosely aligned to the ideologies of anarchism and communism, surrealists strove to unmask the cultural, artificial, sometimes alchemical process of transforming objects into 'art' in the social sphere. Some, such as René Magritte, were interested in estranging the relationship between words, images and the things they conventionally represent; others, like Dalí and Buñuel, used painting, cinema, costume and spontaneous performances/ events to explore the psychological terrains of cultural repressions and the subconscious. Surrealists continually revisited the world of dreams and images of what Freud called the uncanny, harnessing their potential to push the defamiliarization of conventional realities to extremes.

Constructivism was an avant-garde movement that gained a following after the war, with its international profile enhanced by pioneering artists and sculptors like Naum Gabo and his brother Antoine Pevsner. Concerned with hidden 'mathematical' and 'symphonic' properties of objects transformed into artworks, the movement's importance was noticed early on in the US. Curators from the New York Public Library even traveled to the newly formed Soviet Union in 1923 with the sole aim of acquiring constructivist prints and publications. Constructivism was strongly aligned to communist politics and radical Formalism; indeed Gabo saw the Soviet revolution as renewing human values and leveling embedded social hierarchies. As the formalist Victor Shklovsky argued: 'The purpose of art is to impart the sensation of things as they are perceived and not as they are known'. These strategies, Shklovsky continued, were designed 'to make objects "unfamiliar"', to invert the ideological lens that defined dominant ways of seeing the world and its social realities (1965 [1917]: 12). Constructivism and Formalism, in Bill Nichols's words, were intended to 'confront the habitual, render it strange, and open the door to new ways of perceiving and acting' (2005: 162). Constructivist strategies of inciting new forms of perception over delivering established 'truths' and 'facts' were keenly felt in Soviet cinema, and their influence soon extended around the world.

So where does documentary fit into all of this? At the level of practice, there were productive exchanges: the Russian artist Aleksander Rodchenko, for example, designed animated sequences and intertitles for documentary filmmaker Dziga Vertov; later Rodchenko – heavily influenced by Vertov – would himself move towards photomontage and documentary photography. This kind of cross-fertilization was repeated in the US, where an avant-garde emphasis on radical form and defamiliarized reality was incorporated into nonfiction films of the 1920s and 1930s. Indeed it is extremely difficult, Horak asserts, to separate avant-garde movements from documentary film production as it advanced during these years: nonfiction films drew widely from a range of radical aesthetic approaches (1993: 388). Highly influential figures included Vertov and the *Kino Pravda* movement (founded in 1922, the same year that *Nanook of the North* was released). Strongly dissatisfied with traditional narrative, *Kino Pravda* celebrated spontaneity and attempted to explode the ordinary, mundane realities witnessed by the naked eye. Vertov sought deeper truths in reality revealed by the 'superhuman' mechanical properties of the camera. Sergei Eisenstein, more closely aligned to narrative and theatrical illusionism, influenced US filmmakers with his theories of experimental montage, while the works of surrealists Jean Vigo (*À propos de Nice* [1930]) and Buñuel (*Las Hurdes* [1932]) offered pointed critiques of cinematic realism and its appeals to any socially accepted 'truth' of human experience.

Allegiances were forged among those who shared a common sense of purpose: even the romantic primitivist Flaherty was impressed by Vertov's interests in dynamic and unplanned nonfiction scenarios. Writing to his wife Frances in 1930, Flaherty said she should immediately look up an article in the journal *The Realist* about 'a man in Russia [Vertov] [. . .] who has founded a new school of picture – pictures without plot or character' (Flaherty 1930). Flaherty was also instrumental in encouraging Eisenstein's documentary work in Mexico and his forays to Hollywood in the early 1930s. Willard Van Dyke, who shot the landmark documentary *The River* for Pare Lorentz in 1936, admitted the influence of German expressionist art, as filtered through films such as *The Cabinet of Dr Caligari* (1919). Van Dyke once mentioned that for two weeks in 1922 he watched *Caligari* 'almost every day' and was soon after enthralled by Eisenstein's *October: Ten Days that the Shook the World* (1928) and *Battleship Potemkin* (1925–6) (Engle 1979: 345–6). Van Dyke's first film, *An Automatic Flight of Tin Birds* (1932), was marked by expressionist and surrealist influences, and soon after he moved into social documentary projects.

In the 1920s and early 1930s, stylistic and ideological influences from aesthetic movements beyond US borders were transforming filmmaking at home, while avant-garde artists and photographers based in the US, as Horak has shown, were enhancing their repertoires with forays into cinema. Motion picture form and technology could inform artists working in other media who were 'intrigued by the rhythmic, kinetic, tonal, and dramatic possibilities' of film (Wolfe 1993: 353). Many would only 'dabble' in film, or use film as an extension of other artistic practices such as painting and photography (Horak 1995: 15). During the 1920s and 1930s, they came from various fields including music (Virgil Thomson, Aaron Copland, Marc Blitzstein), literature (Ernest Hemingway, John Dos Passos, Archibald MacLeish), dance (Adolph Bolm), painting and sculpture (Boris Deutsch, Stella Arledge), photography (Man Ray, Stella Simon, Paul Strand) and animation (Mary Ellen Bute). Many – such as Thomson, Hemingway and Dos Passos – would contribute to documentary projects (Wolfe 1993: 353).

Yet even with such an eclectic and mobile range of influences, it is important not to simply collapse different avant-garde movements and pursuits into each other – each had distinctive tendencies, specific ideas, and their followers did not necessarily always agree, aesthetically or politically, on the best ways to 'render strange' habitual aesthetic production and consumption. Still, for both Europeans and Americans engaging in avant-garde work, as Horak argues, there was a sense of sharing 'a broader, inclusionist rather than exclusionist view of independent cinema' (Horak 1995: 17). The boundaries of nations, institutions and media were being breached. Bold statements like *Potemkin* and *Man With a Movie Camera* were transforming ideas about delivering the truth of experience on screen, exerting an influence across national borders and across professional and non-professional practices. Radical journals devoted to seeing film as *the* new cultural medium were also springing up: for example, *Close Up* appeared in 1927 and *Experimental Cinema* in 1930, both exemplifying contemporary transnational tendencies. *Close Up* was published in English, edited in Switzerland, and included correspondents such as the communist-leaning American Harry A. Potamkin, Herman G. Weinberg, the poet H. D. and the British critic Ernest Betts, with contributors working out of London, Berlin, Moscow, Paris, Geneva, New York and Los Angeles. As this scope suggests, avant-garde really needs to be seen as an approximate label for varied and frequently quite different (if mutually influential) transnational approaches.

Certainly not everyone was happy with the term: speaking of the French avant-garde, Jacques Brunius argued that it was 'a rather meaningless name, with its military, would-be heroic ring that easily provoked smiles' (1948: 53). Terms such as pure cinema, integral cinema and absolute film – all operating within the parameters of avant-garde work – were attempts to distinguish and isolate qualities and styles unique to cinema as an art form, but in narrowing to 'film for film's sake' they also tended to constrain the very spirit of experimentation and boundary crossing that avant-garde artists set their sights on. James Donald suggests that avant-garde cinema is better seen as an open-ended, though not completely disparate, movement. Its purveyors shared 'the same concern with the power of the cinematic image to transform the objects it represents and to create a unique aesthetic experience for the film spectator' (1998: 31). Similarly, Horak stresses the ways in which US avant-garde critics and practitioners were cineastes: film lovers devoted to improving 'the quality of all films, whether personal or professional' (1993: 388).

A brief sketch of a few US experimental filmmakers might illustrate how eclectic their work was, moving across different media, across documentary and avant-garde circles. Ralph Steiner trained as a commercial photographer and worked on photographic plates for *Nanook of the North*, but later embarked on a series of films that meditate on the real or concrete world as abstract patterns and plays of light: *H2O* (1929), *Surf and Seaweed* (1930) and *Mechanical Principles* (1931). After joining the Film and Photo League, Steiner brought an avant-garde sensibility to pro-New Deal projects such as *Hands* (1934), which strings together artfully composed close-ups of hands to deliver a message about how leisure opportunities and everyday commodities rely on work, physical activity and, always, money. Soon after, Steiner joined the ultimately fractious crew of Pare Lorentz's *The Plow that Broke the Plains* (1936) and later made *The City* (1939), a 'city symphony' co-directed with Willard Van Dyke that became a major feature of the 1939 World's Fair in New York (Horak 1993: 388; Wolfe 1993: 354).

Lewis Jacobs also demonstrates the dovetailing of cutting-edge aesthetics and documentary, while revealing common links between critical, theoretical and practical work. A prominent purveyor of avant-garde experimentation, Jacobs's filmmaking legacy has effectively been eclipsed by later work as a film historian and theorist. But he never abandoned filmmaking: early projects included *Transition* (1927) and the psychological study *Mobile Composition* (1930), made as part of the amateur group the Cinema Crafters of Philadelphia. From 1930 to 1934 he was editor of *Experimental Cinema*, extolling the theories of Vsevolod Pudovkin, Eisenstein and Alexander Dovzhenko. His essay, 'Experimental Cinema in America, 1921–1947' (1947–8) is still considered a seminal piece of criticism on the topic (Posner 2005). Lewis's recently rediscovered film *Footnote to Fact* (1933) revisits Soviet montage techniques to highlight the tragic ironies of the Great Depression. Billboards for commodities are juxtaposed with down-and-outs sprawled on street corners and in gutters: the jobless veterans and 'forgotten men' relegated to the margins of US history's grand narrative. Later documentaries such as *Tree Trunk to Head* (1938) draw on experimental techniques (extreme close-ups, zooms, swish pans, blurred images) to create a time-lapse portrait of Chaim Gross producing a sculpture. Like many who came out of avant-garde circles in the 1920s, Lewis's range of interests and tastes was complex and at times seemingly contradictory. While closely identified with the experimental left, his *The Rise of American Film* (1939) was criticized for its appreciation of Hollywood and admiration (and tacit apologia) for the controversial *The Birth of a Nation* ('Lewis Jacobs' 1997: 28; Stokes 2008: 279).

The varied work of practitioners such as Steiner and Jacobs underscores Nichols's assertion that modernist elements of 'fragmentation, defamiliarization [. . .] collage, abstraction, relativity, anti-illusionism, and a general rejection of the transparency of realist representation all find their way into acts of documentary filmmaking' (2001: 593). Nichols's point is useful, even if his chief examples – Vertov, László Moholy-Nagy, Pudovkin, Ivens, Vigo and Walter Ruttmann – don't include work produced in the US. In the following section I want to turn to a key example of this work, made by two prominent figures linked to Stieglitz and the 291 gallery: Paul Strand and Charles Sheeler. Their *Manhatta*, if not the very first avant-garde film made in the US, is a quintessential work bridging modernist aesthetics and emerging documentary modes to encapsulate Manhattan's kaleidoscope of forms and movements. This marriage of modernist avant-garde strategies and nonfiction also helps to project an ambivalent image of US national identity, just as Americans were coming to terms with the imposing scale and anonymity of the modern metropolis.

MANHATTA (1921)

Strand and Sheeler's eleven-minute study has become one of the most influential motion pictures to explore intersections between avant-garde and nonfiction, using modernist abstraction to defamiliarize scenes of everyday life in New York – the quintessential ready-made urban landscape.[3] As proponents of Precisionism, Strand and Sheeler were invested in capturing the precise and sharply defined forms of an industrialized, modern American landscape. While influenced by European movements such as Futurism and Cubism, Precisionism aimed for a distinctly American aesthetic, fused to the newness and energy of urbanized New World spaces.

Reflecting its makers' backgrounds in painting and still photography,

Figure 8. *Manhatta* (1921). Paul Strand-Charles Sheeler (Film Arts Guild). Courtesy of the British Film Institute.

Manhatta appears almost modest as a cinematic statement, characterized by carefully framed shots that evoke more an impression of still photographs with movement than of dynamic moving images. Juan Suárez, however, sums up the diverse elements that contribute to the film's lasting value: 'It is at once a documentary, a critical statement about modernity, an aestheticist exploration of patterns, shapes, movements, and rhythms, and a visual counterpart of the descriptions of metropolitan modernity produced by contemporary sociologists, architects, and planners' (2002: 88). *Manhatta* is in many ways exemplary of the tensions and aspirations of the time and place of its making.

Suárez observes that cinema has been 'married to the city from birth'. Perhaps fittingly, then, *Manhatta* helped establish an international vogue for the 'city symphony' genre, resulting in films such as Ruttmann's *Berlin: Symphony of a Great City* (1927), Herman Weinberg's *A City Symphony* (1930 – now lost, but sections survive in *Autumn Fire* [1930–3]), and Jay Leyda's *A Bronx Morning* (1931). The 'city symphony' also betrays avant-garde roots going back to Dada: the ready-made cityscape is revealed not as the primary material out of which cinematic 'art' is produced, but as always already formed and transformed by mechanical processes.

But Strand's and Sheeler's film might be seen as more ambivalent about the mechanized cityscape than many 'city symphonies': it arrived at a juncture when the nation's self-image was in flux, perched between notions of an American identity steeped in agrarian and frontier traditions and those that recognized its advanced state of urban modernity. In October 1920, Frederick Jackson Turner's famous frontier thesis (premiered at the Chicago Exposition in 1893) arguing that American character was forged on the frontier through contact with the wilderness, was reprinted in *The Frontier in American History*, a well-received collection that reflected revitalized frontier interests. As David M. Wrobel sees it, the frontier image returned as an idyll that acted as a 'kind of solace' for Americans experiencing a newfound sense of technophobia and urban unrest during uncertain postwar years (1993: 98). In the 1920s, post-frontier anxieties were enhanced by Malthusian debates that projected overpopulation and limited resources for a nation now pressed, so it appeared, against its continental boundaries. Best-sellers such as Hal G. Evarts's *The Yellow Horde* (1921) and Edison Marshall's *The Voice of the Pack* (1920) celebrated the transformational powers of an unspoiled wilderness, providing the public with an imagined return to an American Eden.

Given this backdrop, Horak understandably discerns a tension in *Manhatta* between the manifest celebration of the urban and modern and a latent sense of nostalgia for passing rural and agrarian ways of life. He traces this tension in the elaborations on the work of Walt Whitman (drawn from 'A Broadway Pageant [1860], 'Mannahatta' [1860], and 'Crossing Brooklyn Ferry' [1856]), which express a 'yearning for a reunification [of the city] with nature, inscribing technology, urbanization, and industrialization in mass society with naturalistic metaphors' (Horak 1995: 280). Suárez attempts to move past what he sees as the limits of this interpretation by questioning the notion that *Manhatta*'s 'antimodern' tendencies are grounded in nostalgia for nature or desires for a holistic state that would reverse the trends of modernity. Suárez prefers to see modernity as itself marked by conflicting urges that move both backwards and forwards. A modernist text like *Manhatta* 'reveals instead a mongrel practice that combines traditionalism and innovation, abstraction and figurativeness, romanticism and antiromanticism, the cult of technology and that of nature' (2002: 90).

In both its prevailing themes and formal tensions between avant-garde and realist aesthetics, *Manhatta* sums up the contradictions of a nation steeped in the complexities of modernity: the buzzing, multicultural, constantly changing landscape of the city clearly serves as a kind of microcosm of the United States itself. As the opening titles tell us, New York is international yet distinctly American in its multi-ethnicity: it is a 'city of the world (for all races are here)'. It is a 'proud and passionate city', suggesting a diverse nation full of potential, with nearly limitless human and technological resources. Organic shapes and masses are fused with the man-made: the arrival of a ferry packed with commuters recalls a lumbering beast, introduced as 'million footed Manhattan unpent'. The anonymous crowd pressing against the ferry's gates also nods to the multicultural mass cinema audience, recalling Charlie Chaplin's bitter arrival at the 'land of liberty' in *The Immigrant* (1917), where America's new immigrants, expecting instant opportunity and abundance, are instead penned in and tagged like cattle. After the ferry crowds are discharged in *Manhatta*, a series of shots moves the viewer ever higher, soon losing any sense of the individual and instead stressing the anonymity of the human mass in a built landscape.

This image of the mass – its melding to the cycles of both natural and industrial production and consumption – is stressed two minutes into the film with a striking and somewhat jarring image of a church cemetery. The high-angle shot reveals people and gravestones practically indistinguishable from each other: the hard, dynamic visible city is linked to the invisible world below it. The tower of Trinity Church cuts a shadow across the yard, linking the shot to larger concerns: the memento mori, or traces of previous lives, which suggest that the city's temporality is not fixed or constant but marked by transition, change and movement. The image also indicates the return to the soil of all work and life, even in the midst of the oblivious concrete wilderness.

The same churchyard appears near the end of the film, book-ending the text with images that signify time's invisible passage. This later shot is, importantly, bisected down the middle, the sidewalk cutting the frame at an angle from top left to bottom right. As Eisenstein's work suggests, it is not just juxtapositions between different shots, but angles, divisions and complex 'overlapping of symbolic networks' created within the frame that can produce pressures and intensify tensions in form and meaning.[4] Above the line is the bustling street with its endless streams of traffic, the living world in constant motion, oblivious to fate. The lower left side of the screen is dominated by the cemetery, marked by tombstones and stillness, again a reminder that the built environment visible to the camera is mirrored by an invisible population lurking below ground. Here too, the neoclassical notion of 'et in Arcadia ego', a phrase that invokes Virgil, is referenced in an indirect way: 'even in Arcadia, death is to be found'.

Following the earlier shot of the cemetery, another shot near street level recalls Strand's photo 'Wall Street' (1915), emphasizing several huge windows – blank eyes that dwarf pedestrians and traffic passing beneath them. Strand's acute sensibility for the semiotic resonances of line, juxtaposition, visual weight, volume, lighting contrasts and framing in still photography is everywhere in evidence. As John Berger puts it, Strand's approach (influenced by his mentor Stieglitz) 'lets him choose ordinary subjects which in their ordinariness are extraordinarily representative'. Strand's photographs can 'enter so deeply into the particular that they reveal to us the stream of a culture or a history which is flowing through that particular subject like blood' (Berger

1980: 42–3). Strand's press release for the film stated his intent in more clearly Precisionist terms: 'The photographers have tried to register directly the living forms in front of them and to reduce through the most rigid selection, volumes, lines and masses, to their intensest terms of expressiveness. Through these does the spirit manifest itself' (quoted in Horak 1995: 272).

As the film develops, the volume, line and mass of the cityscape appear simultaneously as acutely defined, machine-made yet strangely organic. The city now exhibits a degree of anthropomorphized spirit: buildings are 'high growths of iron, slender, strong, splendidly uprising toward clear skies'. While recalling city panoramas such as Biograph's *Panorama from Times Building* (1905) and striking skyscraper images from the series *Ford Educational Weekly* (1916–24), Strand and Sheeler's long shots interrupt the established realism of urban photography by intently fetishizing the skyscraper's thrusting height and power. The camera tilts top to bottom, then again bottom to top, encouraging wonder at the sheer scale of these animal-like 'iron beauties'. Human silhouettes toil in landscapes of towers and cranes, hanging tentatively from rafters, melding and disappearing into the machine-made world.

Any impression of idealistic fusion of the city with nature, like the 'clear' sky itself, is soon obscured – by smoke. It pours from chimneys, the camera perched on roofs alongside smokestacks. On occasion the camera itself – aligned to the viewer's perspective – is engulfed by smoke (the film premiered in Paris in 1922 as *La Fumée de New York*). Smoke pours from train yards and from the stacks of ferries on the harbor: at times it gives the grand city a satanic and stained appearance (the theme would become a mainstay of the 'city symphony', as seen in *The City*'s industrial 'City of Smoke' sequence). These shots of smoke in the sky, on land and over water imply not just endless urban energy and industry, but contribute to a theme: rather than simply illustrating the poetic intertitles, Strand's and Sheeler's urban images lie in dialectical tension with the romantic, holistic ideals expressed by Whitman. Whitman's work, according to Horak, 'constructed [. . .] a romantic discourse that repressed the conflicts of nineteenth-century industrial and class relations in favor of a homogeneous melting pot of technology, art, science, nature, and man' (1995: 278–9). Again and again lines used in the film similarly combine man-made and natural imagery: 'city of hurried and sparkling waters, city nested in bays'. But the shot from one of the highest vantage points, giving a bird's eye view that aligns the spectator's mastery with the eye of camera, features the ziggurat chimney of the Banker's Trust Building releasing more smoke into the air. Such images work against Whitmanesque romanticism: decay, pollution and renewal are inextricably entwined in this fusion of nature and human industry.

The film's final few minutes are given over to the movements and flows of water: the river and traffic on the harbor. The Cunard Line's RMS *Aquitania*, a popular and luxurious cruise ship, takes star billing as several tug boats cluster around like eager fans. We then return to the streets, which now appear as deep ravines, traffic barely visible within their dark recesses. Shadows create disturbing angles and cut across the view, suggesting uncertainty and foreboding, while extreme camera angles contribute to a 'fragmentation of the [viewing] subject's perception' (Horak 1995: 275). This disorienting view recalls the constructivist canted perspective that aimed to challenge traditional perspectival order and coherence; it also draws attention to the filming apparatus as the instrument of vision. Yet it's also akin to other artistic practices that aimed to undermine the complacency of the here and now, like the anamorphic skull that cuts across and disturbs the balance of Hans Holbein's *The Ambassadors* (1533). This warning is reinforced by the stunning split image of bustling street above and cemetery below.

Finally, the titles command the sunset – the end of day – to 'drench with your splendor me or the men and women generations after me'. In the distance a tugboat crosses the frame, suggesting again that images captured by the 'timeless' medium of film are not wedded to particular instants in time, but are part of time's flow. Like smoke dissipating over water, urban humanity is transient, bound to cycles of life, death and renewal (or reconstruction and rebuilding). From the onrushing crowds of its opening scenes to this final coda, *Manhatta*'s imagery suggests that 'unnatural' city rhythms and flows are fused with nature. Horak suggests the film echoes Whitman's 'yearning for reunification with nature', and its tendencies towards visual and narrative closure 'violate' modernism's 'discontinuous and nonnarrative aesthetic strategies' (1995: 280–3). Yet rather than being saturated by nostalgia, qua Whitman, or expressing scepticism towards the coupling of nature and technology, the film stresses the complex fusion of presumed opposites: a fusion that leads to delirious growth and expansion of the nation, but also to the loss of individuality and specificity. The static aesthetic of the photograph fuses with the dynamism of the moving city; the precision of lines, angles and careful juxtaposition meets the unpredictable flows of nature; growth and progress are shadowed by spoliation and pollution.

Horak partly retreats from aligning Whitman and *Manhatta* too closely, finally suggesting that *Manhatta*'s heterogeneity reveals a text that is both modernist and antimodernist, that might be ultimately self-conflicted and unresolved. Similarly Suárez, extrapolating from Siegfried Kracauer, argues that the film's reassertion of nature would not, in any case, necessarily make it anti-modern – in fact modernist art is characterized by a flattening of oppositional categories that finds 'the natural back in the heart of the modern' (2002: 104).

Manhatta, Suárez continues, looks not only forwards but also backwards, recalling the popularity of actualities and the tradition of the panoramic view. Unlike the traditional panorama, however, which sought to produce a 'complete impression' of a scene or view via its expansive format, *Manhatta* reproduces the city as a 'fractured space' (2002: 99). This is not the conventional tourist gaze striving for visual mastery, but a fragmented journey that reflects constant disruptions experienced when moving through urban space. Persistent formal and thematic techniques reproduce this fracturing, as in the shot-counter-shot sequence first from, and then of, the ferry near the film's opening. Strategies of repetition such as the shots of Trinity Church cemetery early and late in the film disrupt any sense of organic progress, while the back-and-forth echoing of natural and built environments such as ravine/street, eye/window, beautiful beast/building suggests (like that quintessentially modernist film *King Kong*) that nature and technology lie in dialectical tension at the heart of modern experience.

Manhatta both reflects and refracts American urbanism, imaging the distinctiveness of US modernity and compelling viewers to look afresh at the familiar cityscape. It celebrates American newness, hybridity and dynamism while subtly marking this optimism with caution and the mementos of a common, inescapable fate.

CINEMA AT THE MARGINS

As the 1920s progressed, Hollywood's streamlined, highly standardized industrial approach dominated movie-making and distribution in the US, and commanded the world's markets. The studios had a stranglehold on US theater exhibition, though alternative screening spaces did exist in venues such as universities, rented halls and art galleries. Save for a few exceptional 'blockbusters', networks for distributing avant-garde/experimental and documentary films remained unreliable at best, nonexistent at worst. Small-scale experiments like *Manhatta* struggled to find audiences: after a brief distribution run as *New York the Magnificent*, the film was screened in art galleries and later acted as a scenic inserted into longer programs. Similarly Flaherty's *24 Dollar Island* (1926–7) – an elegant 'city symphony' that envisions New York as an intricate series of intersecting lines and graceful, abstract forms – was barely seen. Flaherty's film eventually could be glimpsed as a moving-image backdrop to a stage show at New York's Roxy Theatre, entitled 'The Sidewalks of New York'.

Still, there were production and distribution networks being established outside the burgeoning Hollywood system. These included, but were not limited to, amateur films, film clubs and 'little' cinemas – all of which were important to the development of documentary in the US.[5] Before the 1920s, various nonfiction subgenres such as travelogues, ethnographic films, industrials, scientific films, military films and (though more rare due to the expense) home movies had been produced outside of mainstream production networks, though, as Patricia Zimmermann reminds us, the precise definitions and functions of these films were not always completely clear (1995b: 147). The amateur movement of the 1920s, devoted chiefly to non-commercial filmmaking, offered direction, self-definition and a 'discursive umbrella' under which a variety of non-Hollywood practices could coexist (1995b: 140). Amateur filmmaking played a key role in constructing the idea and social location of nonfiction film as lying outside or beyond the constraints of Hollywood and the commercial market – a legacy it would carry into the 1930s, as the formal and social objectives of documentary also became further crystallized. Though the idea of amateur filmmaking was not new in the 1920s, it was around this time that amateurs, with the help of newly marketed hands-on technologies, developed into a widespread and well-organized group, replete with publications, ideals and dogmas.

A range of products – such as Kodak's 16 mm safety film and a streamlined Cine-Kodak 16 mm camera, first marketed in 1923 – helped to initiate massive changes in both the practice and idea of film. Hands-on access meant (keeping in mind the significant costs of much of this equipment) that 'every man and woman potentially [could] become a film artist' (Horak 1993: 389). This allowed individuals to control the finished product, bringing filming and viewing into everyday experience, into domestic and leisure activities. The idealization of amateur work sprung up via advocate organizations such as the Amateur Cinema League (ACL), founded in 1926, with its flagship journal *Movie Makers*, which stressed the value of doing creative work outside of institutional and professional circles.[6] The valorization of the amateur coincided neatly with the interests of outsiders like the cinematic avant-gardists, who 'rejected consumer culture through experimentation' and strove to define themselves as removed from the demands of capitalism and commercialism (Zimmermann 1995b: 141; Horak 1995: 28–9).

Avant-garde advocates tended to share in hostilities towards Hollywood's well-established assembly line and the 'mediocrity' it produced. Ernest Betts argued in *Heraclitus, or The Future of Films* (1928) that 'when the Future of Hell is written [. . .] a large number of pages will have to be reserved for the Americans who make films'. Hollywood had 'doped the world with rotten juices. By a strength of purpose which is staggering and its one superb virtue, it has flung at us, year by year, in unending deluge, its parcel of borrowed stories and flashy little moralities' (1928: 40–6). The critic Bryher quipped in *Close Up* that 'Hollywood can produce kitsch magnificently but it cannot produce art' (quoted in Donald 1998: 28).[7] Avant-garde filmmakers shared in this disaffection, critiquing Hollywood's crass commercialism and Fordist approach. Filmmakers snubbed Hollywood by making a virtue of cheapness:

the opening titles of Robert Florey and William Cameron Menzies's *The Love of Zero* (1928) flaunt the fact that 'this impressionistic picture' was made for $200. Florey and Slavko Vorkapić's *The Life and Death of 9413: A Hollywood Extra* (1927) was supposedly made for $97, and successfully ran at alternative movie houses.

Yet if avant-garde artists and groups like the ACL, initially, viewed amateurs and independents as opposed to Hollywood, it should be stressed that not everyone was interested in subverting mainstream cinema's commodification of art and culture. As Zimmermann argues, subtle connections and distinctions existed between professionals and non-professionals. Amateur filmmaking 'mapped out a discursive, production, and social space for experimentation' not only among individuals interested in making 'personally meaningful' political and avant-garde statements, but among professional cinematographers who tested and created new film effects using amateur equipment (1995b: 139). Cecil B. DeMille used Bell and Howell Filmo and Eyemo amateur cameras to shoot tight crowd scenes and obtain a spontaneous 'documentary' style for films like *The Ten Commandments* (1923) and *The Godless Girl* (1929). Florey was 'lionized' by amateur magazines as the ideal amateur to emulate, yet was an experienced assistant director who worked for major studios and directors such as von Sternberg (Zimmermann 1995a: 82, 1986: 63). Slavko Vorkapić anonymously contributed to the left-wing social documentary movement in the 1930s, yet was also an innovative montage specialist in Hollywood (a 'Vorkapich edit' became familiar Hollywood terminology). Dudley Murphy, pioneer of the American avant-garde, made short music films (screened between feature films) featuring major performers such as Bessie Smith and Duke Ellington, marked by both documentary and avant-garde flourishes. For David E. James, such 'hybrid' careers underline the ongoing transactions between non-Hollywood and Hollywood circles, between political and/or avant-garde outsiders and industry insiders, a process where 'experimentalism was industrialized in various ways' (2005: 42). The techniques and aesthetics of amateur, avant-garde and documentary movements all were in part influenced by, and found their way into, Hollywood films.

Indeed, as seen in the previous chapter, many nonfiction filmmakers actively sought mainstream distribution, accepting Hollywood funding and producing the consumer-friendly spectacles it demanded. Among them, Cooper and Shoedsack, Flaherty, and Osa and Martin Johnson, for example, showed little aversion to Hollywood and the lucrative careers that beckoned – at least not while their films remained popular draws. Cooper and Schoedsack found great success creating Hollywood fantasies, while Flaherty, after some aborted stints for the studios, would eventually develop a hardened attitude towards Hollywood and all it signified. By the mid to late 1920s, Flaherty was losing faith in the same studio machine that had provided carte blanche financing for his *Moana*, and was manifesting a stubborn preference for small-scale shooting methods while experimenting with visual composition and editing. A shift away from narrative and studio concerns was already demonstrated in films such as *24 Dollar Island* and *The Pottery Maker* (1925), the latter made with the Metropolitan Museum of Art. Perhaps Flaherty's gradual (in terms both of practice and attitude) migration towards the margins of Hollywood reflects a general trend in US documentary as it began to define itself in the late 1920s and early 1930s. Working alongside amateur and avant-garde movements and their advocates, many documentary filmmakers would view nonfiction as a form that, at its most meaningful and most ethical, was produced outside of the formal strictures and commercial imperatives of the studios.

The sense that there were viable options outside Hollywood extended to distribution and exhibition as well. The idea of the little cinema, an art and foreign language cinema movement, was first suggested by the National Board of Review in 1922, following interest in European films like Ernst Lubitsch's *Passion* (1919) and *The Cabinet of Dr Caligari*. By the late 1920s little cinemas, taking inspiration from the cine-clubs of Paris and London, were appearing in cities such as New York (including Michael Mindlin's 'subway circuit' of theaters), Washington, DC, Rochester, Boston, Baltimore, Philadelphia and Los Angeles (Gomery 1992: 173–4; Horak 1993: 390–5). Some, such as Rochester's 'Little Theatre', are still doing business and remain devoted to the distribution of lesser known and art-house films.

Most little cinemas were committed to developing mixed programs showing both US and European (especially German and Soviet) films. Hollywood films were bolstered by lavish marketing campaigns, mass circulation magazines and radio advertising, and screened in the picture palaces that were dominating the film-viewing landscape. Little cinemas were posed as more intimate alternatives to the Hollywood experience: spaces of 'civil exchange and polite engagement' (Wasson 2005: 39). The little cinemas' commitment to a range of motion pictures spanned foreign films, avant-garde and documentary, as confirmed by the Rochester Little Theatre's stated desire to screen 'unusual, entertaining, documentary, foreign-language, artistic, and musical pictures' ('History of the Reel World' 2008).

In the 1930s, expenses involved in the transition to sound and the hardships of the Depression saw many little cinemas struggle and close, delaying the spread of alternative movie houses until after the war, when 'art cinema' and 'art houses' were widely established. The 1930s did, however, see a boost for experimental and documentary film when, in 1935, New York's Museum of Modern Art set up a film library, screenings and circulation networks that helped establish art cinema as a social and institutional framework for thinking about film. MOMA would become an important 'institutional prop' for the documentary movement, sponsoring the premiere of *The Plow that Broke the*

Plains in 1936, acquiring eleven British documentaries in 1937 and becoming a depository for Joris Ivens's work during the Second World War (Waugh 1981: 226).[8]

The 1930s saw the establishment of the New York Film Society and the Film Forum, both private membership clubs formed to show 'motion pictures of excellence, not ordinarily to be seen in even the little playhouse, or forbidden for public performance by the censor' (quoted in Wasson 2005: 41). Alternative film was boosted, as Haidee Wasson observes, by writing about film: a range of texts – from the criticism of Terry Ramsaye, Eisenstein and Rudolph Arnheim (*Film als Kunst* [*Film as Art*] was published in German in 1932) to popular magazines and journals – began to 'apologize for movies' by extolling their social value (Wasson 2005: 14). Film viewing was encouraged among elite circles devoted to viewing cinema as art and education. As Wasson argues, 'attempts to define and shape the cultures of cinema during this period should also be understood as a set of social practices that included writing, arguing, and reading about films on a wide and public scale that was significant unto itself' (2005: 15). As many bemoaned the banal state of popular Hollywood fare, the notion of a sophisticated 'film culture' was taking root.

The 1920s was a decade of unprecedented industrial expansion for American movies, with US films comprising 95 percent of those shown in Britain and Canada, 80 percent in South America and 70 percent in France: 'The sun, it now appears, never sets on the British empire and the American motion picture' is how one magazine described the situation (quoted in Rosenberg 1982: 103). With such prominence on the national and international scene, film was under intense scrutiny, with demands for careful investigation into the medium's pervasive cultural, moral and ideological roles in everyday life. As Barbara Low wrote in *Close Up* in 1927: 'Can we be satisfied that the Cinema is a method of promoting mind growth rather than one of mechanizing mentality?' (1998 [1927]: 250). Discourses springing up around issues of film culture and its links to social betterment or degeneration reflected awareness of cinema's inherent 'publicness'[9] – and this idea of publicness, of cinema as a kind of social machine, would underlie documentary's enhanced profile over the coming decades.

The emphasis on cinema's social and heuristic potential was framed as a challenge to Hollywood's established methods. The cinematic apparatus, rather than simply entertain crowds and turn a profit, should produce socially transformative texts, even feed radical social change. Coming from the political left, the denser socially and ideologically persuasive possibilities of cinema were being investigated, while on the right, film was being tested as a force for morality, 'Americanization' and uplift. Hollywood was the conventional target in these debates, but other non-Hollywood modes were becoming sites of intense ideological contestation and appropriation as well. Documentary, as it became more closely associated with social enlightenment and anti-illusionism, would be singled out by many who saw it as key to mass media intervention in the nation's social ills.

As William Stott has suggested, as the devastating effects of the Depression set in, economic crisis and political upheaval coincided with the unprecedented expansion of mass information: movies, radio, magazines and newspapers assailed and captivated the American public. At the same time, documentary material across these media seemed to take on a heightened status, as 'reliable witnesses' were sought to uncover the hidden facts and the 'awful truths of a broken economy'. The documentary approach was finding favor as the dispossessed sought 'the presentation of actual facts in a way that [made] them credible and telling to people' (1973: 72–3). Documentary would play a major role in the increasingly radicalized popular imaginary of the 1930s, though its enhanced profile was probably not merely the result of economic crisis – rather it came out of a series of overlapping developments that positioned it as a unique vehicle for representing and mobilizing America's disenfranchised masses and 'forgotten men'. Documentary, with roots in avant-garde and low-budget nonfictions, could be seen as operating outside elite corporate and capitalist interests. As the 1930s progressed, this sense of documentary's relative immunity from crass commercial imperatives would see it raised to a unique public status.

The next chapter tracks some of the trends in documentary through to the start of the Second World War. It maps the uneven yet persistent shifts in the mid-1930s towards the assimilation of radical photography and film movements into public projects and government-backed information units aimed at raising social awareness. This was also a period when the term 'documentary film' would become common parlance, seen as a distinct approach with specific aims and functions relating to promoting public responsibility and national unity.

NOTES

1. Michael Renov argues that the association of documentary with 'sober discourses' misrepresents the historical complexity and play of documentary signifiers (as in the work of Vigo, Ivens or Franju). See Renov (2004: 100).
2. Film histories cited as inadequate by Nichols include Rotha (1952 [1935]), Ellis (1989) and Barnouw (1983).
3. In 2008 Posner supervised a digital restoration which runs for twelve minutes.
4. See, for example, Aumont (1987: 87–8) and Nilsen (1935: 116–19).
5. Other movements, especially the African American 'race picture' business, are highly significant in terms of the history of independent production and distribution.

6. By the 1930s, however, the ACL was emphasizing the need for higher professional standards.
7. Bryher was the nom-de-plume of Annie Winifred Ellerman, the daughter and heiress of Britain's wealthiest man.
8. After the Second World War, art cinema revived with the help of popular European imports. Influential film clubs like Cinema 16, founded in New York by Amos Vogel in 1947 and inspired by Maya Deren's work, signaled the 'second wave' of avant-garde filmmaking in the US. See MacDonald (2003).
9. For more detailed discussion see Wasson (2005: 15), who glosses Hansen (1995: 365–6).

CHAPTER 4

Activism and Advocacy: The Depression Era

In 1936, an article in the *Mid-Week Pictorial* took some sideswipes at avant-garde films like *Rain* (1929) and *Lot in Sodom* (1932) while praising the varied, low-budget efforts being made for politically active projects:

> Not all the films that are made are the product of Hollywood. [. . .] There are little fadistic art movies – studies in light and shade of a box of matches, or a prolonged camera attack on an afternoon of rain. There are films made obscurely without box-office appeal, by serious craftsmen who wish to experiment with the medium of pictures; wealthy amateurs who do symbolic stories out of the Bible; and amateur rookies who try their hand at direction with the Brooklyn Bridge as the cast. But the really important films, made outside the iron confines of Hollywood, are those produced by genuine film artists, seriously experimenting with the young technique of the camera, and the producers of the scattered films that attempt to portray American Labor Problems. ('Dignity of Toil' 1936)

As this overview attests, the 1930s was marked by beliefs that the 'really important' work was not taking place in major studios nor in the aesthetic experiments and armchair travels of wealthy cineastes, but in street-level political films. *The Mid-Week Pictorial* singles out here the American Labor Productions' union activist film *Millions of Us* (1936). There is, however, a more complicated story behind this opposition of art and politics in that the anonymous group that called itself American Labor Productions was actually made up of just those 'fadistic' art movie-makers and Hollywood professionals dismissed here as superficial, such as the avant-garde montage specialist Slavko Vorkapić. Indeed, much political documentary of the 1930s was indebted to an ongoing film culture of experimentation and to crossovers between professional and non-professional circuits established during the previous decade.

Though it might seem logical to see the rise of politically active filmmaking in the 1930s as directly resulting from the social and financial pressures of the Great Depression, the seeds of dissent were actually sown at the height of 1920s economic hedonism. As left-wing filmmakers Leo Hurwitz and Ralph Steiner recalled:

> During the twenties we grew disgusted with the philistinism of the commercial film product, its superficial approach, trivial themes, and its standardization of film treatment: the straight-line story progressing from event to event on a pure suspense basis, unmarred by any imaginative use of the camera, unmarred by any freshness in editing or any human or formal sensitivity. Our reaction, which we shared with the young generation of experimental filmmakers, was a more or less aesthetic revolt from the current manner of film production. (quoted in Alexander 1981: 19)

This stress on form and aesthetics as a means to contest mainstream practices underlines the ways in which film art and increasing access to hands-on film-making and exhibition (evidenced by avant-garde and amateur movements) underpinned a cultural politics that fed into the radical documentary projects of the 1930s.

The heated political climate of the Depression era would overlap with the distillation of documentary form and practice; many of the generic elements we now commonly recognize in documentary were established during these years. As Charles Wolfe observes: 'In 1930, [Harry] Potamkin projected a future cinema born of experimentation with the filmic image as document; by the end of the decade, [Lewis] Jacobs was able to speak confidently of a full-fledged genre, the maturation and social relevance of which seemed amply evident' (1993: 351). Paul Rotha's landmark study *Documentary Film* appeared in the mid-1930s, though even then, critics believed the majority of cinemagoers probably still didn't know what a 'documentary film' was (C. N. 1936: 763; Anon. 1936: 47). This state of affairs was quickly changing. During these years, identities as working 'documentarists' and 'documentarians' were forged, while documentary emerged as a 'conceptual category through which discussions concerning the history, aesthetics, and social value of cinema advanced' (Wolfe 1993: 351–2). As such, documentary was being claimed as a mode in urgent need of defining, categorizing and theorizing.

Documentary's increasingly prominent social status in the 1930s came within the context of unique convergences between politics and mass culture in the US, among them the 'cultural front' that resulted from 'the encounter between a powerful social movement – the Popular Front – and the modern cultural apparatus of mass entertainment and education' (Denning 1997: xviii). Amid the political upheavals of hunger marches, labor protests, rioting, intense left-wing demonstrations, right-wing reprisals and the growing threat of fascism were ongoing reassessments aimed at stabilizing 'American' identity and the disruptively evolving nation: at creating 'an official mass culture' from 'competing aesthetic and political tendencies' (Kahana 2008: 67). Writers, intellectuals, historians, journalists, artists and filmmakers were grappling with questions of what constituted an American 'public' or 'popular' culture, and how its attendant cultural expressions might mobilize Americans and promote a collective national good. Moving images, for many, seemed to hold the promise of raising public awareness of social ills and instigating reforms.

This chapter looks at the escalating ambitions for documentary in the 1930s, focusing on how the documentary idea became tied to political radicalism, to demands for authenticity and transparency in the media, and finally to government photography and film projects. We see here growing tensions, identified by Jonathan Kahana, between documentary as a mode of expression 'in which radicals and progressive intellectuals grappled with the problem of how cultural form and social action could be related', and documentary as a mode for organizing audiences 'in a hegemonic capacity, announcing crises and managing them on behalf of the state' (Kahana 2008: 68). In this latter sense, documentary can be seen serving as a kind of 'state apparatus' operating in the name of national interests.

SOCIAL DOCUMENTARY: EARLIER TRACES

The reformist roots of social documentary film in the United States precede photography, but in many histories the early use of photographic images to document, highlight and publicize social ills is often linked to the Danish immigrant and police reporter Jacob A. Riis. In 1888, using the advent of flash photography, Riis developed a stereopticon presentation called 'The Other Half: How it Lives and Dies in New York', and soon published the illustrated book, *How the Other Half Lives: Studies Among the Tenements of New York* (1890). Riis's photos remain classic documentary exposés of social inequities and divisions. As Musser puts it, Riis's exhibitions 'almost single-handedly launched the social-issue screen documentary, which prospers, primarily now on television, to this day' (1990: 40). While there are gaps – historically and ideologically – between Riis and the social documentary turn of the 1930s, Riis's lectures and publications were among the few in the late-nineteenth century to document the abject poverty of immigrants' slum dwellings and dark tenement interiors; the cellars and back alleys removed from the hubbub of middle- and upper-class life. Riis helped to uncover 'the dislocations between the private and public spheres that were symptomatic of the daily life of the poor' (Musser 1990a: 40).

At the same time, Riis's views gave the educated middle classes a glimpse into the 'dangerous, the fantastic, the grotesque, the impossible, at a close but safe remove' – as Robert Sklar describes the popular draw of lurid early cinema attractions (1994: 21). Contemporaries described Riis's mercury flash images of the private worlds of the poor as 'pictures of reeking, murder-stained, god-forsaken alleys and poverty-stricken tenements'. Such 'sensational language', Maren Stange argues, speaks to wider questions not only regarding the motives and public functions of Riis's work, but of the mixture of entertainment and ideology that lies at the heart the documentary tradition itself (1989: 1).[1] Indeed, Riis's presentations might be seen as implicitly conjuring a kind of tourist gaze: the lecture tour of the urban slum suggests associations with the touristic 'excursion', where the 'respectable half' could be assured of their elevated social position and domination (Stange 1989: 5–6).

In her careful unpicking of the Riis legacy, Stange shows that he was not the first to use photography to document the conditions of the poor (some point to John Thompson's photographs in *Street Life in London* [1877]). Riis probably didn't even photograph some of his best-known images, nor was he the first to use magic lantern technology to put across socially conscious messages. Moreover, the solutions to poverty he presented were grounded in an enduring faith in late-nineteenth-century bourgeois ideals and private interests in the form of sponsorship, patronage and charity (Stange 1989: 5). Still, Riis's focus on the New York poor and on tenement reform was distinctive and influential beyond its local contexts. With hindsight, this combination of photographic projection, public presentation and moral philosophizing (Riis's lectures were sometimes preceded by scripture reading and a prayer) – and even Riis's reliance on sensation, spectacle, staged pathos and the guiding force of the lecturer/voiceover and music to create a mood – can be seen to point the way towards later strategies in social documentary.

Perhaps closer to social documentary – and particularly to the institutional functions of 1930s documentary – was the photographic work of Lewis Hine and the Pittsburgh Survey, which appeared in 1908–9. The survey intended to use new methodologies for collecting and analyzing data about social conditions to construct an 'objective' representation of industrial workers that would 'substantially contribute to organizing and stabilizing the reform coalition's influence on corporate and government policy making' (Stange 1989: 49). Hine's work demonstrates the meeting of the increasingly formalized practice of sociology with advancing visual technologies such as photography, which, it was thought, could more accurately document social conditions. Hine was primarily a still photographer, working after cinema had already come to prominence; as a result many documentary histories skip over his role in the use of photographic records as social documents.[2] But photographer Arthur Siegel suggested that Hine 'defined very simply the documentary attitude when he said "I wanted to show things that had to be corrected. I wanted to show things that had to be appreciated"' (quoted in Stott 1973: 21). Hine himself underlined the importance of the 'social photographer' to 'social uplift':

> Curtis, Burton Holmes, Stoddard and others have done much along special lines of social photography. The greatest advance in social work is to be made by the popularizing of camera work, so these records may be made by those who are in the thick of the battle [. . .] [W]hat a field for photographic art lies untouched in the industrial world. There is urgent need for the intelligent interpretation of the world's workers, not only for the people of today, but for future ages. (Hine 1980 [1909]: 112–13)

Hine's invocation of illustrated lecturers such as Burton Holmes and Stoddard and an ethnographic photographer and filmmaker such as Curtis suggests a keen understanding of the diverse social uses and political potential of photography and film. The work of Riis and Hine shows a passion not just for social documentation and revelation, but for defining a participatory public role through documentary images.

Hine had other influences on documentary's future: Paul Strand was a student of Hine's at the progressive Ethical Culture Fieldston School, and it was while on a fieldtrip in Hine's class that Strand first visited Alfred Stieglitz's and Edward Steichen's 291 gallery, motivating Strand to take photography seriously. Hine was also close to Roy Stryker, who, we will see, was to become a central managerial figure in the photography initiatives of Roosevelt's New Deal. In 1924, Stryker published the reformist economics study *American Economic Life and the Means of Its Improvement*, drawing on his mentor Hine's photographs of rural and industrial working conditions.

Also echoing the work of Riis and Hine were films aimed at social education and uplift made by commercial interests, such as Edison projects dealing with welfare institutions: *Children Who Labor* (1912) and *Public and Private Care of Infants* (1912). The latter's high moral stance saw it become one of earliest movies to be screened on Sundays in conservative, Sabbath-observing cities in the South. *Public and Private Care* is a dramatization of a working widow struggling to look after two children, one of which dies in a public care home (thus advocating for better funded and individualized care). The film, sometimes referred to as a documentary, uses what we'd now call 'shock doc' strategies (also seen in sex hygiene films of the First World War), showing stark images of starving infants that are unsettling and explicit. In addition to these social welfare films, later dramatic films made by activist groups such as Labor Film Services, shown at labor film festivals in major cities in the early

1920s, were significant uses of cinema as social intervention before the 1930s and demonstrated alternative media practices that served as challenges to the censors. Some labor agitators were considered so dangerous that J. Edgar Hoover arranged for spies to monitor their film productions (Ross 1998: 171).

'A WORKING CLASS CINEMA FOR AMERICA'

The early years of the Depression are often typified by a hapless government, headed by Herbert Hoover, turning its back on the dispossessed poor and unemployed who were passively waiting for handouts in Hoovervilles and breadlines. Yet, Roy Rosenzweig reminds us, this was actually a period of mass unrest and intense political action: 'sit-ins at relief stations, national and state hunger marches, demonstrations at City Halls, and direct resistance to evictions' (1980: 5). On 6 March 1930, communist organizers oversaw one of the largest protests of unemployed workers yet staged: nearly one million came out for what became known as 'Red Thursday'. But media coverage was limited, and newsreel footage was censored by the New York police. Sam Brody, a founding member of the Film and Photo League, wrote in the *Daily Worker*: 'If the capitalist class fears pictures and prevents us from seeing records of events like the March 6 unemployment demonstration [. . .] we will equip our own cameramen and make our own films' (quoted in James 2005: 105; 'Tear Gas Routs Reds' 1930: 1–2).

As William Alexander describes it, the establishment of the Workers' Film and Photo League (WFPL) of New York in 1930 was an effort to bring together 'a scattered, but ideologically united, *left-wing* kino-group' (1981: 4). The WFPL's roots went back to communist and socialist organizations of the early 1920s, specifically to the Workers' International Relief (WIR), a communist front that was set up, at Lenin's request, in 1921 by the political impresario Willi Münzenberg in Berlin to coordinate famine and drought relief efforts for Russia. Despite providing cultural and ideological directives, the Berlin-based WIR was relatively decentralized, and would affiliate with a range of left-wing cultural organizations in the US, such as the Workers' Laboratory Theatre. It also became a key force during the 1920s for extending film production and distribution towards radical ends, focusing on industrial labor and class politics (Campbell 1984: 69–71).[3] The WFPL inherited the WIR's interest in socialist politics and cinema theory and an interest in film's mass audience potential (during the 1920s, the WIR largely handled the non-theatrical distribution of Soviet features and political newsreels in the US). The WFPL would extend this role, calling for radical changes in US film practice and distribution (Campbell 1984: 70). The coming of the Depression reinforced efforts to forge links between communist, socialist and labor union-based activism, and to further develop a systematized approach to producing and distributing political films that could address a mass public.

The WFPL included the journalist Seymour Stern in Hollywood, Lewis Jacobs in Philadelphia and Samuel Brody, Leo Seltzer, Robert Del Duca, Lester Balog, David Platt and the group's 'unofficial spokesman' Harry Potamkin in New York. As Stern wrote in *The Left*: 'A working class cinema for America? . . . A cinema, in a word, that offers the exploited class of America precisely the opposite, in spirit, technique, and ideology, to the Hollywood movie – the advertisement for American Money? . . . What a possibility! What a vision! . . . Films in the name of the American Revolutionary Proletariat!' (quoted in Alexander 1981: 3–4). The New York branch of the (W)FPL ('Workers' was dropped after 1933) would list among its associates Leo Hurwitz, Jay Leyda, Margaret Bourke-White and Ralph Steiner, all of whom would, to a greater or lesser extent, blur lines between avant-garde aesthetics, politics and documentary. As Brody put it: 'Ours is a gigantic task, challenging the most institutionalized of all the bourgeois arts [US cinema] with its monster monopolies and gigantic network for mass distribution' (quoted in Alexander 1981: 30–1). At its peak in the early 1930s, the FPL numbered nearly one hundred associate members and had affiliates in cities across the US.

The work of the FPL really can't be judged according to the standards of a substantial body of polished or professional filmmaking. As Russell Campbell observes, the FPL generally shot 'footage' rather than films: coverage of political events such as workers' strikes was usually taken on the run, developed and screened as quickly as possible for the greatest public impact – often for the strikers themselves, to boost morale. Seltzer suggested that challenging Hollywood's mass production and distribution system on its own terms was neither realistic nor attractive; FPL films were explicitly aimed at workers, the unemployed and left-wing political activists (Campbell 1985: 126–7).[4] The FPL footage would often be re-edited after showings – in town halls, workers' centers, tents, private houses, even roller-skating rinks – into compilation documentaries that operated as alternative newsreels. Films like *The Ford Massacre (Detroit Workers News Special)* (1932) documented the chaos of industrial actions; here, 4,000 unemployed workers stormed the Ford plant in Dearborn, Michigan – four were killed. Joseph Hudyma (a jobless Ford worker) recorded the events as part of the Detroit FPL.

Some of the best-known FPL newsreels documented mass demonstrations. *Bonus March* (1932) covered the march on Washington by war veterans protesting government neglect and showed the police and government-backed military brutality that met them: beatings on the street, burning of their ramshackle shelters. *Hunger* (1932/3), which dealt with hunger marches organized by the Unemployed Councils, was similarly ad hoc. Hurwitz recalled: '[The cameramen] stood with the marchers on a hill above Washington, knowing that before dawn they might need to wield their cameras as clubs' (Alexander 1981: 28).[5] This largely sums up the FPL approach: to film from the perspective of struggling workers, raising public awareness – to, in Brody's words, employ 'worker cameramen' to film 'the viewpoint of the marchers themselves' (quoted in Campbell 1984: 76).

FPL compilation films weren't simply 'expository', however; George Steinmetz sees Hurwitz's camerawork as saturated with 'poetic' and aesthetic associations (2006: 498). In editing, they further worked with Soviet montage techniques to enhance the impact of rough footage. As in Eisenstein's work, they often manipulated mass, line and directional movement to create intellectual involvement and emotional dynamism, juxtaposing seemingly dissimilar images as part of a 'montage of attractions'. The prologue of *Bonus March* suggests such an effort to intervene in the consumption of cinematic illusion as implicit truth or transparent world view. It invites audiences to become critically involved, sceptical viewers, intercutting signs proclaiming 'Go places with the US Army' with images of exploding shells and dead soldiers on the battlefield, then of the unemployed and their Hooverville shacks. This 'model of savage political comment' (Campbell 1984: 76) was echoed by Busby Berkeley's almost surreal interpretation of the same event in the 'Remember My Forgotten Man' number from *Gold Diggers of 1933* (1933). Campbell contends, additionally, for a consideration of FPL cinematography as well as montage: '*cinéma vérité* has dulled our appreciation of participant camerawork, but in the thirties the hand-held, close-range cinematography of the street actions which the League footage offered must have struck spectators with great novelty and force' (1984: 75).

Throughout the mid-1930s the FPL, while sporadically producing newsreels, sponsored programs of Soviet and German features that were screened, often alongside FPL productions, in rented auditoriums, union halls, migrant camps, schools and occasionally purpose-built cinemas. As Wolfe stresses, the 'only modest success' of FPL film production and distribution was enhanced by the League's active devotion to film criticism, published in new journals such as *Filmfront* and *Experimental Cinema* and radical publications like *New Masses*, *New Theatre* and the *Daily Worker* (Wolfe 1993: 358). The establishment of the Potamkin Film School soon after the death of Harry Potamkin in 1933 created a further pedagogical base for League members such as Brody, Hurwitz and Jacobs to spread their ideas.

Though much attention has focused on the New York FPL, the makeup of the League across the US was far more diverse. Leagues sprung up in Detroit, Philadelphia, Chicago, San Francisco and Los Angeles, and in smaller towns like Laredo, Texas. 'Rather than a single or unified group', Carla Leshne explains, 'the Workers' Film and Photo League was a movement' (2006: 361). Leshne fills out the historical record, offering a glimpse of the San Francisco branch and its key members Balog, Otto Hagel and Hansel (Johanna) Mieth (who became a photographer for *Life* magazine), traveling cross-country with Edward Royce, an organizer for the WIR. Along the way they screened League productions together with Pudovkin's *Mother*, arriving in San Francisco in 1933.

The San Francisco group produced newsreels of the agricultural strikes that were sweeping California in 1933 and also the more ambitious *A Century of Progress* (1934). The latter recalls Irving Browning's *City of Contrasts* (1931), in which the wealthy of Riverside Drive are ironically juxtaposed against the poor in shantytowns along the Hudson River. *Century of Progress* begins with shots of the spectacular Chicago 'Century of Progress' World's Fair of 1933, only to undercut any notion of progress by inserting shots of Hooverville shacks and a woman picking over garbage to find food. The San Francisco group lasted only until July 1934, when it was forced to cease production after the violent San Francisco General Strike, where workers' cultural centers throughout the city were destroyed by right-wing mobs. (The 1930s saw a series of quasi-secret vigilante groups, like the Black Legion in Detroit, dedicated to combatting labor activism [Denning 1997: 126].) Over the course of its short existence, the San Francisco League endured police harassment, repeated confiscation and destruction of its footage, arrests and finally a vigilante rampage through their darkroom and meeting space during the General Strike (Leshne 2006: 362–3).

Along with reconsidering the geographical distribution of political nonfiction filmmaking, the idea that 1930s documentary was the province of a monolithic group of elite, intellectual, white males also needs to be reconsidered (Musser 2006: 356). Richard Meran Barsam stresses that significant members of the New York FPL were the 'talented sons of immigrants', raised on the Lower East Side and Brooklyn, with family roots in left-wing causes (1992: 147). Many were part of the 'new Americans', as Louis Adamic called them in 1934, mainly working-class, 'the second generation of the second wave of immigration' (Denning 1997: 60). Significant women in the League, such as Nancy Naumburg and Hansel Mieth, also deserve further attention. Naumburg, another graduate of the Ethical Culture Fieldston School, produced with James Guy two of the earliest radical documentaries, *Sheriffed* (1934) and *Taxi* (1935). Both were shot by Naumburg on her amateur 16 mm camera; both have been lost. Irving Lerner devoted an entire column to Naumburg's first film in the *New Masses*, hailing it as 'the first to come out of the revolutionary movement' (Koszarski 2006: 374).

By 1934, the FPL was arguably at its peak with the establishment of the National Film and Photo League, but there were also signs of internal division. The group's emphasis on a workers' revolutionary politics was becoming diluted as Roosevelt's 'first' New Deal, initiated in 1933, began to take effect. Still, the most damaging rupture took place within the New York branch when Hurwitz, Steiner and several others broke away in the wake of disagreements that flared after the League's National Conference in 1934. Inconsistent production methods were an ongoing source of frustration. The National Conference had underlined the League's lack of interest in artistic innovation: instead it argued for the centrality of the 'simple newsreel document, photographing events as they appear to the lens'. While admitting the 'weaknesses of lighting, photography, [and] direction' of FPL productions, the National Conference expressed their hope to eventually match the skill and sophistication of Vertov's *Kino Pravda* 'newsreel' productions (Alexander 1981: 57).

A split emerged not only between FPL members' differing aspirations, but along questions of how best to produce a politically effective documentary 'truth'. While members shared in their admiration for Soviet ideas, they were split between advocating for moving pictures that were 'taken' and those that were 'made', a distinction emphasised by Seymour Stern that divided the revolutionary nonfictions of Vertov from the more fictive 'reconstructed reality' of Pudovkin, Eisenstein and Dovzhenko (Alexander 1981: 57). For Hurwitz, truly revolutionary filmmaking had to move 'beyond the document':

Because newsreels are fractional, atomic, and incomplete, the revolutionary movement has required a more synoptic form to present a fuller picture of the conditions and struggles of the working class. And so the synthetic documentary film has become an important form for film workers in the revolutionary movement – a form which allows for more inclusive and implicative comment on our class world than the discursive newsreel.

Hence, 'a mixed form of the synthetic document and the dramatic is the next proper concern of the revolutionary film movement' (Hurwitz 1979 [1934]: 91–3). Such interests echo efforts, such as Eisenstein's, to move film representation away from the stress on observation, shifting emphasis from a 'literal imitation to a metaphorical interpretation of reality' (Nichols 2005: 163). As accomplished filmmakers, Hurwitz and Steiner were stung by the League's apparent anti-aesthetic and anti-dramatic stance. They wanted, rather, to 'recreate events and emotions not revealable to the camera in the document' (Hurwitz 1979 [1934]: 92), to pursue experimental approaches that would blend radical aesthetics with politics, fictional strategies (in particular, acting) with fact.

Working with Lerner and the photographer Sidney Meyers, a splinter group formed during the autumn of 1934 calling itself Nykino – a statement of international solidarity, blending New York political activism with Soviet formalist experimentation. Nykino, linked with the Workers' Laboratory Theatre, went on to find a degree of stability and success, enlisting Elia Kazan and his wife the playwright Molly Day Thacher for their first publicly released production, *Pie in the Sky* (1934). The film was a declaration of intentions to move away from documentary sobriety and transparency. It lampoons what Karl Marx called the 'opiate' of the people, religion, which is seen as thwarting radical change and pragmatic solutions by proffering an imagined escape – heaven and the afterlife – from the real world of struggle and privation.

In spite of splitting from the FPL over their stress on 'taken' footage, Nykino did not wholly ignore the newsreel format. Aiming to 'revolutionize the method of dramatizing actual news events', they conceived *The World Today* (1936), a series (though only two were released) designed to counter the success – and political superficiality – of *The March of Time* (Alexander 1981: 126).[6] The group's influence spread. Willard Van Dyke and Strand joined in 1935, just after Strand had shot *Redes* (*The Wave*, 1937) in Mexico, with Mexican government backing. Widely admired when it came out for its stunning photography, *Redes* is a semi-fictional, political exposé based upon the personal and economic struggles of fishermen near Vera Cruz. The project nicely complemented Nykino's 'interpretive' documentary strategies, and showed Strand's affinity both for Flaherty's 'slight narrative' and the montage effects of Soviet films such as *Potemkin* and Pudovkin's *Storm Over Asia* (1928).

In the meantime the FPL, devoted to producing radical newsreels, began to struggle after 1935 with the weakening of the WIR's powers. The Nazi government had dissolved Willi Münzenberg's Soviet-backed front in Berlin and he was exiled in Paris. Without the 'organizational backing, financial support, and political direction' that existed under the WIR, as Campbell points out, the motion picture production of the League began to dissipate (1984: 79). By 1936 very little new work was appearing – only brief newsreels of marches, such as Maurice Bailen's *Chicago May Day* and *Peace Parade*, and (though a League project in name only) the first of a series of consumer rights films, *Getting Your Money's Worth* (Julian Roffman, with Del Duca, 1936) (Campbell and Alexander 1977: 35; Campbell 1984: 79). The mid-1930s era of the New Deal and the Popular Front saw a shift in emphasis away from revolutionary struggle towards a stress on the common needs of 'the people': ' "the people" became the central trope of left culture in this period, the imagined ground of political and cultural activity, the rhetorical stake in the ideological battle' (Denning 1997: 124). Popular Front beliefs in shoring up affinities across class and ethnic divisions were summed up at the end of the decade by Paul Robeson's classic anthem, 'Ballad for Americans'. 'Are you an American?' the chorus asks. The reply first embraces profession and class: 'I'm an engineer, musician, street cleaner, carpenter, teacher [. . .]', then ethnicity: 'I'm just an Irish, Negro, Jewish, Italian [. . .] Russian, Chinese, Polish [. . .] American' (quoted in Denning 1997: 128).

New Deal and Popular Front alignments, explained further below, saw key shifts in rhetorical strategies on the left. While the plights of American labor and unionism remained central to left-wing political ideals, the image of the neglected worker became more closely tied to 'the people' as a diverse yet unifying symbol of America. In this spirit the group of film professionals calling themselves American Labor Productions, as mentioned earlier, released the seventeen-minute sound film *Millions of Us* in 1936, a dramatic re-enactment of a day in an unemployed machinist's life. Testifying to the ongoing and deep ideological divisions of the time, at one cinema in New York the whistles and hisses of angry cinemagoers forced the film to be withdrawn by the management (Rosenzweig 1980: 8).

SELLING THE NEW DEAL

As shown above, the Soviet and other governments had long been interested in employing film for explicitly ideological purposes, helping to inspire the efforts of groups like the FPL. The US government, wary both of Hollywood's commercial power and any appearance of politically manipulating the public, was far less invested in using film as a persuasive medium. Still, the documentaries that would result from New Deal financing were not the first efforts at government filmmaking. By the time Pare Lorentz arrived in Washington in 1935 as consultant to the Resettlement Administration, film units already existed at the departments of Agriculture and the Interior (starting as early as 1911, advertising agricultural expansion to the west) and at the US Army Signal Corps (Wolfe 1993: 365).

The difference, as Bill Nichols argues, between earlier social interventions and the enhanced sense of identity and purpose that marked documentary work in the mid-1930s was a stricter disciplining of the form. Public advocates in the Soviet Union, Germany and Britain – to varying degrees – were emphasizing factual film's usefulness for disseminating a collective sense of national unity and social urgency. Here ideas of the 'social' and the 'public' were tied to national interests and documentary was seen as possessing persuasive power to 'serve the political and ideological agenda of the existing nation-state' (2001b: 583). In the US, even while scepticism of major government film projects had the upper hand, the stage was being set in other ways. Lawmakers were making their presence felt at almost all levels of the film industry.

Grounds for government intervention in movie-making were reinforced by the publication, between 1933 and 1935, of findings by the private foundation the Payne Fund, devoted to studying the effects of popular and 'low' media entertainments on children. As David Cook relates, the Payne findings 'confirmed the worst – the movies did seem to bring new ideas to children; did influence interpretations of the world and day-to-day conduct; did present moral standards' (2004: 237). Here was proof of the movies' widespread influence on education, behavior and development. The Payne Fund results not only fortified calls for a stronger Production Code, they indicated a need for government 'films of merit' (as Lorentz would call them) that might contribute to public education and responsible citizenship. By 1934, the Code and government powers of censorship had 'acquired teeth' with the formation of the Production Code Administration and its newly appointed head, the conservative Roman Catholic Joseph I. Breen (Doherty 1999: 6–10). New Deal government film projects should be viewed, then, in the context of both these growing state interventions into the film industry and the broader impact of 1930s radical filmmaking.

In revising policies established by Hoover's government, FDR's New Deal was wide ranging but hardly revolutionary. Rather, it aimed to reframe and re-appropriate the polarized extremes of US politics. Roosevelt 'saved capitalism in eight days', as one commentator said of the president's early days in office. Sidney J. Weinberg recalled the volatile political climate: 'We were on the verge of something. You could have had a rebellion. You could have had a civil war' (quoted in Doherty 1999: 337). Roosevelt's acceptance speech for the presidential nomination in 1932 directly addressed – and more or less dismissed – the revolutionary spirit that had fired up communist and trade union movements of the time. 'Wild radicalism has made few converts', he stated; 'to meet by reaction that danger of radicalism is to invite disaster. Reaction is no barrier to the radical. It is a challenge, a provocation. The way to meet that danger is to offer a workable program of reconstruction' (Roosevelt 1938 [1932]: 647). Roosevelt's ideal of 'reconstruction' was a far cry from socialism: it lay in reconstructing the US's capitalist dominance – even if this meant increasing use of public funds in the shorter term.

Major legislation known as the First New Deal was put into place soon after FDR took office, giving rise to the Unemployment Relief Act (31 March 1933), the Federal Emergency Relief Act (12 March 1933), the Social Security Act (14 August 1933) and the Agricultural Adjustment Act (12 May 1933), all of which gave the government sweeping powers to funnel public funds into social programs. Beginning in 1935, the Second New Deal incorporated support for labor unions – partially stabilizing a disruptive political faction – and programs to aid tenant farmers and migrant workers. The resulting 'Alphabet Agencies', such as the Resettlement Administration (RA) (reorganized as the Farm Security Administration (FSA) in 1937) and the Works Progress Administration (WPA) would become the key sponsors of photography and film projects.

Further political shifts taking place just as the New Deal was gathering strength would affect the character and rhetoric of the left. The Communist Party International's decision in 1935 to back a Popular Front against fascism, precipitated by Adolf Hitler's rise to power in 1933, paved the way for a broad international alliance of leftist parties and organizations. This included the Communist Party USA (CPUSA), which would drop its opposition of Roosevelt and the New Deal and join Roosevelt's efforts to organize and manage labor union issues. This official change of policy sent ripples across the political spectrum: broad-based Popular Front liberal–left coalitions would determine that the 'crucial struggle of the day was to be not socialism versus capitalism, but democracy versus fascism' (Waugh 1984: 107).

The 1930s, then, might be seen as a period when a range of highly disruptive factions were negotiated back towards working within the framework of a hegemonic capitalist system. Sacvan Bercovitch suggests this process of framing radicalism in his assessment of the centrifugal force of American ideology, which 'undertakes, above all, as a condition of its nurture, to absorb the spirit of protest for social ends'; it has 'accomplished this most effectively through its rhetoric of dissent'. This 'triumphant liberal hegemony' attests to 'capacities of the dominant culture to absorb alternative forms, to the point of making basic change seem virtually unthinkable' (1993: 367). The 1930s saw the Americanization of a range of 'foreign' or 'marginal' ideological movements: the Marxist readings of the American literary canon by Granville Hicks; V. F. Calverton's efforts to 'Americanize Marxism'; Edmund Wilson's history of socialism; Kenneth Burke's Marxist engagements with psychoanalysis and literary theory. More to the point, the Popular Front era saw a rhetorical fusion of presumed oppositions: 'Communism is Twentieth-Century Americanism', stated Earl Browder, Secretary General of the CPUSA, in his run for president in 1936 (quoted in Rabinowitz 1994: 101). Protest, dissent and debate were placed at the heart of achieving consensus: the aim became not the destruction of the old system, but the rebirth of the 'soul of America'.

New Deal documentaries, while part of this process of leveling political factionalism, were nonetheless viewed as aligned to the party politics of Roosevelt and the progressive Democrats. For many, such state-sponsored projects indicated the unthinkable: 'socialist' filmmaking – it was difficult to suppress obvious parallels to the Soviets. But the Soviet example was not the only one. In Britain, John Grierson had established a film unit at the Empire Marketing Board in 1930 and then at the General Post Office (GPO) in 1933. Grierson's activities were crucial precedents and provided a safer institutional model for US government interests. The Soviet example 'represented a form of excess for Grierson' and as such his funding models combined both state and corporate investment (Nichols 2001b: 599). In theory, the state could sponsor the popular culture industries while remaining relatively immune from the ideological extremism of Soviet-style controls. Still, Grierson continued to have great belief in the state's central role, arguing 'the State is the machinery by which the best interests of the people are secured'. The great dilemma of mass education, for Grierson, lay 'in the realm of the imaginative training for modern citizenship and not anywhere else' (quoted in Nichols 2001b: 602), and documentaries were considered the principal vehicles for this training. Grierson's grand plan for a state-sponsored documentary culture called for revitalizing nonfiction forms of address, transcending the 'lower categories' such as the lecture film, travelogues and nature shorts, all of which could 'describe, and even expose, but [. . .] only rarely reveal' (Grierson 1946 [1932]: 79).

In the US, the Griersonian approach, while influential, was not wholeheartedly endorsed. When Paul Rotha, just thirty years old at the time, came in 1937 to promote Grierson's 'documentary idea' on a trip sponsored by the Rockefeller Foundation, he was both welcomed and critiqued. Rotha was a strong advocate for social documentary, for fusing 'the cinematic with the citizen' (Wasson 2005: 145), and sternly criticized what he saw as 'escapist' films such as Flaherty's *Man of Aran* (1934). British newspapers enthusiastically reported that Rotha had almost single-handedly encouraged 'films of fact' to strike 'new roots abroad, notably in the United States' ('Documentary' 1939: 18; 'Documentary Films in America' 1939: 32). Some, such as Van Dyke and Steiner, were impressed with Rotha's ideas, and the establishment of the short-lived American Film Center at Rockefeller Center can be traced to his five-month visit. But figures like Lorentz were reportedly unhappy with Rotha's criticisms of how documentary was organized in the US (Wolfe 1993: 374; Wehberg 1938: 163–6). Leo Hurwitz thought the films produced by the Grierson unit were 'pale, passionless, restricted in range'. For many that had come through the FPL and Nykino, the Soviet example remained the more compelling (Alexander 1981: 246).[7]

The establishment of the film unit at the RA in 1935 might thus, to an extent, be seen as a 'Griersonian' move.[8] Responsible for this move was Rexford Guy Tugwell, an agricultural economist from Columbia University who came to the RA already equipped with a clear idea of the government's social role. Part of FDR's academic 'Brain Trust', Tugwell had formulated progressive economic theories in the 1920s based on the management concepts of F. W. Taylor – ideas rooted in a highly 'technocratic, pro-corporate ideology' (Stange 1989: xvi). Overviews of social and economic networks were by this time influenced by the scientific methods of disciplines like sociology. These concepts were married to 'Taylorized' management and Fordist mass production systems. Notions of the 'scientific management' of social diversity through orderly design, already embedded in the academic and industrial zeitgeist, were soon being felt in central government agencies (Stange 1989: 107). For Tugwell, the Information Division at the RA was crucial to explaining official policy to those participating in public works programs. At issue was not merely justifying the unprecedented scale and expense of the government intervention, but encouraging an ideological shift in attitudes towards central management of public affairs. The production of photographic materials was high on Tugwell's list of Information Division activities.

Tugwell's support for government photographic projects was effectively a continuation of collaborative work done with his former teaching assistant, Roy Stryker, who became his chief of photographic staff. By the 1930s, photojournalism had established itself as a primary medium of mass communication. According to Stange, 'newly founded mass circulation picture magazines worked successfully to establish a public view of corporate photojournalism as a mode of mass communication not only reliable and professional but also "artistic"' (1989: 107). The power of the image to relay information to the masses was hardly overlooked by a government seeking to 'sell' the New Deal. 'Not inconsequentially', Stange continues, 'the camera, with its image both realistic and mass reproducible, rose to become [as James Agee wrote] the "central instrument of its age."' Tugwell and Stryker would amass an impressive staff of thirteen photographers working for the Information Division, including Dorothea Lange, Walker Evans, Ben Shahn and Arthur Rothstein.

In June 1935, Pare Lorentz was brought in to serve as the RA's motion picture consultant. Leonard MacTaggart Lorentz ('Pare' was taken from his father) was a movie critic whose wife was 'vaguely related to the president' (Ellis and McLane 2005: 81), yet his political sensibility made him ideally suited to the New Deal post. He brought to Tugwell's office a mixture of Southern populism (he was raised in the small town of Clarksburg, West Virginia), a respect for nature rooted in his upbringing and concern about how government should intervene in popular culture (Lorentz 1992: 4). Having worked for a major corporation (General Electric), he was critical of what he saw as corporate philistinism and elitism, finding that its bottom-line ruthlessness could transform idealistic young people into victims of the 'bootlicking' and 'mean advancement' of big business practices (quoted in Alexander 1981: 94). His hatred of hierarchy and 'corporate behemoths' was projected onto figures like Will Hays, president of Motion Picture Producers and Distributors of America (MPPDA) and master of the 'Hays Code' (the 1930 Production Code), a 'conniving, sanctimonious Indiana Presbyterian elder', Lorenz called him, and 'chief magistrate' of the motion picture industry (Lorentz 1992: 20–1).

Before coming to the RA, Lorentz had no filming experience, though he had originally conceived his book *The Roosevelt Year* (1934) as a newsreel about 'the tragic events going on in our country' (Lorentz 1992: 28–9). He had also written *Censored: The Private Life of the Movie* (1930), with Morris L. Ernst, in which he lamented 'politicians of the lowest order' and the 'unlearned and stupid hecklings of the censors' (Lorentz and Ernst 1930: 2). As a critic for *Vanity Fair, Town and Country* and *The New York Evening Journal*, Lorentz had closely observed film technique, voicing strong opinions about the kinds of films he respected. His reviews often railed at Hollywood's 'standard, cheap, and unimaginative' products ruled by profit motives, and admired more independent and individualist work that seemed to challenge corporate control of the industry (Alexander 1981: 95–6). His writing was trenchant, satiric and deliberately confrontational. In a review of *Sunrise* (1927), Lorentz dismissed a whole history of assembly-line filmmaking:

> So far, most of the movies that have been made since Edison invented the moving picture have been a mongrel, illegitimate breed, a mechanical curiosity, with the less said about them the better. [. . .] [T]here are but two or three men who have felt the real possibilities of the motion picture as a medium for expressing human emotions with photography and musical accompaniment. (Lorentz 1975: 5)

Critical of Hollywood business as usual, Lorentz's politics were still far from radical in the mold of the FPL or Nykino. He remained suspicious of anything reminiscent of the Soviet school, since it uncannily mirrored the corporate behemoths with its didactic messages and centralized controls that, he argued, hindered freedoms of expression.

Lorentz was, many recalled, not easy to work with, and his lack of professional experience was cited as a persistent problem. But among his major contributions to the RA's output was the idea of government 'films of merit' that could meet the highest professional standards and share the bill with commercial productions (Snyder 1968: 25). Inspired by investigations into migrant camps by the economist Paul Taylor published in July 1935 along with Lange's photographs, Lorentz lobbied the government for a budget of $6,000 to make a film about 'overgrazing, overproduction, mechanized farming by absentee owners, etc., and the results thereof', since a motion picture would be 'one of the most effective, quick, and inexpensive means of explaining some of these problems of the Administration to its employees and to the employees of these agencies' (quoted in Snyder 1968: 202–3). Thus *The Plow that Broke the Plains* started as an RA training film: any expectations of publicly distributing a government film would have been highly controversial, probably killing the project before it even got off the ground.

The bid was approved in August 1935, and Lorentz immediately hired the experienced group of Ralph Steiner, Paul Strand and Leo Hurwitz as camera crew. Given that he was acting as government representative of the New Deal, Lorentz's choice of a crew with avant-garde and radical credentials would appear odd, but professionals schooled in studio production methods wouldn't have offered the flexibility and innovation he needed for a small, on-location shoot. At the same time, Lorentz managed to steer clear of associations with the Hollywood mediocrity he often criticized in his writing.

Though holding only a 'sketchy' outline script, the group began shooting in Montana in September (Snyder 1968: 30) but ideological and practical differences between Lorentz and the crew became untenable. The Nykino group wanted the script to underscore 'capitalism's anarchic rape of the land', but Lorentz was geared more towards the 'metaphor of natural disaster' (Denning 1997: 265). *Variety* reported that the camera crew was 'on strike' in Texas. After a brief reconciliation during which the dust storm sequences were completed, Lorentz decided to fire his crew and complete the film by intercutting stock footage with the existing shots (Snyder 1968: 30–1). He would later denounce the 'left-wing, self-conscious, social irony that so often defeats the purpose of creative workmen with a point of view' (quoted in Rabinowitz 1994: 97).

With few friends in Hollywood and at the helm of a government-sponsored film, Lorentz had enormous difficulties getting access to stock footage. The leftist critic Peter Ellis described the challenges Lorentz faced:

> In an effort to keep the screens of America safe for private investment, the motion picture industry not only attempted to block the progress of *The Plow* during production by refusing to sell the government stock shots necessary to round out the narrative, but on completion of this, the first important American documentary film, summarily refused to distribute it. (Ellis 1936: 18)

The story of *The Plow* has become a textbook example of the ambitions, compromises and pitfalls underlying state-sponsored filmmaking in the US, and of the pressures that powerful Hollywood studios and private interests could exert, even against the US government itself.

THE PLOW THAT BROKE THE PLAINS (1936)

In his assessment of *The Plow that Broke the Plains*, Lorentz called it 'a melodrama of nature, the tragedy of turning grass into dust, a melodrama that only Carl Sandburg or Willa Cather perhaps could tell as it should be told' (quoted in Barsam 1992: 153). In many ways the film does play out as melodrama, with its strong narrative line, surging musical score and at times heavy-handed voiceover, suggesting that the complex dynamics that led to the Dust Bowl were rather aggressively pared down for the sake of emotional storytelling. The film exhibits a romantic streak, invoking America's once-virgin land and appealing to simpler agrarian ideals, even while self-consciously attempting to avoid overt didacticism. *The Plow* is also, as many have observed, a work of propaganda designed to publicize a cause, and it successfully did so for numerous RA staff. One of these, the documentary filmmaker George Stoney, recalled using it in workshops, town meetings and seminars designed to 'convert' the public to New Deal policies (Stoney 2007).

As Charlie Keil argues, of the four broad functions that Michael Renov discerns in the documentary mode (preservation, analysis, persuasion and expression), Lorentz's film is symptomatic of a 1930s emphasis on the latter two: social persuasiveness and poetic expressiveness (1998: 119). The film persuades on one level by echoing the 'preachment yarn', a form invoked in many post-Crash era films, such as Michael Curtiz's *Cabin in the Cotton* (1932).[9] Thomas Doherty notes that the Hollywood preachment yarn contains at least two distinctive features: the exculpatory preface and the Jazz Age prelude. The exculpatory preface is a text that 'gainsays in print what the images proceed to affirm', thus providing 'plausible deniability' to a film's political statements that might be deemed partisan or controversial. The Jazz Age prelude marks the 'shameful sins committed in the previous decade' of rampant consumer excess (Doherty 1999: 50). We see both employed in *The Plow*.

Exculpatory prefaces were no stranger to mainstream films dealing with the politics of the Depression: one was tacked on to the opening of John Ford's *The Grapes of Wrath* (1940), a screen treatment of Steinbeck's searing portrait of Okie exile and the politicization of the laboring underclass. 20th Century-Fox prefaced Ford's film by stating it was 'about a limited place called the Dust Bowl, and about people displaced by economic circumstances that were beyond anybody's control'. In *The Plow*, the preface informs us that the film is a 'record of land . . . of soil, rather than people' – the sort of natural disaster scenario that so incensed the Nykino crew.

The Plow's Jazz Age flashback comes later, in the juxtaposition of the endless harvesting of wheat (even – to spectacular visual effect – under artificial lights) with a ticker tape machine spitting out a seemingly endless stream of stock quotes. This is intercut with a jazz band wildly playing. The ticker tape (signifying the flimsy dream of endless profits) finally runs out, pulling the machine to earth with a quite literal 'crash'. Such overt visual and montage tactics are tempered by the film's poetic expressiveness, which produces more subtle effects in delivering the film's message. The lyrical voiceover draws on aural and mnemonic devices of repetition and alliteration, while evocative images – captured by the Nykino crew – connote a land of plenty followed by utter loss and spoliation.

The film's structure is roughly chronological, providing a snapshot history of Great Plains land use from settler times to the present day. A title crawl comes first, describing the region as 'a high, treeless continent, without rivers, without streams . . . a country of high winds and sun . . . and of little rain'. These lines are repeated several times in the film – a warning, yet one that obviously was not heeded. A map of the Great Plains area and then the screen itself fill up with undulating grass, which initiates the second section, 'Grass'. Lorentz's script outlines nine sections in all, from the prologue through 'dev-astation'. An epilogue – often characterized as a bureaucratic addition that detracts from the film's poetic expressiveness – spells out government solu-tions. Cut some time after the first distribution run, the epilogue is rarely seen now, though it remains useful for contextualizing the film's public functions and situating its broader ideological aims.

The 'Grass' section meditates on what Lorentz called the 'heroine' of the film, grass (quoted in Barsam 1992: 153), and suggests a virgin land waiting to be settled, though the Prologue briefly mentions that 'the Indian' and 'buffalo' had been 'cleared from the Great Plains'. Finally the voiceover intones, 'first came the cattle', initiating the third section. Panoramic scenes emphasize wide open spaces, recalling the sublime of American landscape painting and photog-raphy, and the powerful psychic links between landscape representations and national identity. The vast views also reference the Hollywood western, a genre coming into its own in the 1930s as on-location visual spectacle. Continuing the western theme, the voiceover introduces section four, 'Homesteader': 'The railroad brought the world into the Plains. New populations. New needs crowded the last frontier.' Images of cattle overrun the frame in ever tighter close-ups. The cattle are funneled into a pen, pushing at its sides, encapsu-lating Malthusian fears of overpopulation and renewed anxieties about the loss of the frontier. The next image usurps the previous one, supported by a command: 'Make way for the plowman!' Commotion fills the frame, with shots of wagons on the move, and close-ups of fence posts being driven into the ground, cutting up and enclosing the land. A series of dynamic shots show fieldworkers harvesting grain, and the farm equipment creates abstract pat-terns of mechanical motion. The editing here recalls the avant-garde – particu-larly the Soviet tradition – marrying American western imagery to didactic, experimental (but now well-established) montage techniques, reminding us of the close contacts between the nationalist documentary traditions of the US and the Soviet Union. As the sequence ends, a train in silhouette traverses the frame, suggesting the coast-to-coast crossing of the transcontinental railroad: the open plain/frame has been spanned and compressed by new settlers, new mobilities, new technologies. As the Plains witness the arrival of modernity, the shot fades to black.

The first indication of the desolation to come introduces the fifth section, 'Warning': 'the rains failed and the sun baked the light soil . . . the rains failed them'. The finale of this section shows a return to activity with the declaration of the First World War and newspaper headlines shouting about the rise of wheat prices. War dominates the sixth section, and with it the juxtaposition of conflict overseas and agricultural (over)productivity at home. The next juxtaposition of shots – tanks rolling overseas and brigades of tractors moving across the land – has generated much critical discussion, and again suggests the influence of Soviet montage. Indeed, the importance of montage for producing visual impact and complex meaning in Lorentz's film cannot be overstated – having fired his Nykino crew, Lorentz was impelled to make the most of stock footage. The message is clear: as plows break up the land and tanks defend national interests, the dust and frenzy of war begin to obscure the view. The monoculture of wheat is fated to exhaust the fragile integrity of the soil, halting the progress of the nation itself.

The next section shows the 1920s: the Jazz Age flashback. These were the 'golden harvest' years, though the section is called 'Blues'. The voiceover recalls optimism: 'We had the manpower, we invented new machinery, the world was our market', but the use of the past tense indicates nostalgia for something lost that only briefly existed. The blues-inflected score plays out over flyers for cheap land, conjoining comic and tragic – 'a few dollars now means a farm for your old age' – pipe dreams that will end in bitter regrets. The section concludes with the ticker tape running out.

A fade-up on a skull against cracked earth is accompanied by the lines, 'a country without rivers, without streams, and with little rain . . . and the sun baked the earth'. This eighth section, 'Drought', contains a spectacular dust storm sequence; it approaches the surreal as a child runs towards the camera and dust blankets broken homes. In an almost ironical touch, we hear a wordless doxology ('praise God from whom all blessings flow [. . .]') played on an invisible pump organ, as if at a funeral. The families are 'baked out – blown out – and broke': lines drawn from interviews with displaced farmers that had captioned Lange's photos in *US Camera*. As the film gathers towards closure, section nine, 'Devastation', envisages the great Okie exodus.

Closing shots of twisted trees in a dead landscape recall the ghostly transients of the previous scenes. Interestingly, there is only fleeting nostalgia for an idealized rural past up to this point in *The Plow* – the history of settlement is retold as one of ongoing struggle and opportunism. The forward movement from occupying the land towards industrialized farming is presented almost as an inevitability. Though it would seem the opposite of an urban film like *Manhatta*, *The Plow* also deals with tensions between the built environment and nature, though here the environment constructed via human labor and industry is an agricultural space. The final shots mark the irrevocable distance of this industrial agricultural space from any image of nature's originary fecundity. The solutions to the killing of the land, one is left to infer, rest only in further human ingenuity and better management, not in going back to nature per se.

The epilogue returns to the strategies of the prologue, with maps of the region, projected improvements and 'model farmsteads for resettled farmers'. It ends with an image of grass, a 'bookend' to the film's opening shots, though this grass is no longer an image of nature's bounty but of calculated effort and strategic, centralized management. Keil's reading focuses on the narrative drive produced by these 'solutions', but the epilogue's absence in later versions (its excision, Keil contends, perhaps due to fears that the film was being overly identified with government propaganda) lends a different impression of the film's structure and overall impact. Without clear-cut solutions, cause-and-effect linearity is less pronounced, leaving the viewer suspended in the midst of an unresolved crisis – probably a useful tool for encouraging the group discussions and debates that often followed screenings. The absence of solutions also allows for meditation on the expressiveness of the images that close the ninth section: dead trees, parched earth, unforgiving sky. Minor chords on the soundtrack barely resolve beneath the final shot, reinforcing an iconography of the costs to the nation of gaining power and international prestige on the back of the profit motive.

In *The Plow*, the soundtrack might be seen to compete with, as much as it completes, the images. Many praised Virgil Thomson's score as 'the finest [. . .] of any American film' (Ellis 1936: 19). The emotive music, while non-diegetic, does more than simply shadow or reinforce the diegesis: Keil suggests that the music expresses and 'possesses' the same degree of knowledge as the narrator (1998: 127). In many ways the music, in its emotional intensity, contributes more to the film than the spoken text. Lorentz referred to *The Plow* as a 'documentary musical picture' and was so impressed with the results that he employed Thomson again for his next government feature, *The River* (1937) (Lorentz 1975: 135).

'Voice of god' narration, which also features prominently, is often derided for instructing audiences about how to think and feel about images. The meaning of documentary images (in publications, illustrated lectures, museum exhibits and so on) is often shaped, as Stange asserts, by 'a particular rhetorical framework created by its interaction with caption, text, or agency' (1989: xvi). *The Plow*'s written text and voiceover, too, come within the context of a government-sponsored film, which lends a problematic state authority to any directives or meanings that the written and spoken material invokes. Still, Stoney defends the voiceover, originally performed by Thomas Chalmers, as 'the narrative style of the day'. He points out that it was influenced by the pervasive popularity of the newsreel format and radio (the dramatized *March of Time* for radio began in 1932–3), and was necessary due the difficulty of employing sync-sound equipment on a relatively cheap, on-location shoot (Stoney 2007). Lorentz said he had hoped to subordinate the text to the image, influenced by Murnau's minimal, 'reiterated' and 'repeated' text in *Sunrise* (Lorentz 1992: 42).

The term 'voice of god' might itself be misleading, as Wolfe notes, in that the voice in many of these films is often not central or omniscient; rather it

Figure 9. *The Plow that Broke the Plains* (1936). US Resettlement Administration. Courtesy of the Academy of Motion Picture Arts and Sciences.

tends to occupy an indefinite, undefined space, related in a relative rather than hierarchal manner to the images (Wolfe 1997: 150). The voiceover in *The Plow* further appeals to a collective rather than individuated subject. When it shifts from third-person overview to first-person commands, the voice conveys an urgency that might sway viewers' opinions but, as Keil contends, never quite usurps the image. Sound and image in films of the period, rather, tended to be integrated in 'a state of ongoing negotiation' as they struggled to attain the proper 'voice' that could modulate the tensions between the realms of the visual and aural, of poetic expressiveness and didactic persuasion (Keil 1998: 122). The spoken text aims to echo image and music through its poetic stylings, hypnotic alliterations and repetitions: 'high winds and sun, high winds and sun, without rivers, without streams, and with little rain . . .' In any case, audiences in the 1930s were probably as attuned to the hazards and manipulations of voiceover as they are today. 'Those film commentaries!' stated an exasperated critic in 1936: 'We all know the film commentator – that bodiless voice which speaks from the back of the screen to explain what is self-evident, generally with an accent that suggests an origin in Oxford or Chicago' (C. N. 1936: 763).

Lorentz hoped that the film's 'pictures' might 'tell their story' on their own terms, reflecting the RA's emphasis on striking photographic aesthetics – some thought to the detriment of their political impact (Snyder 1968: 28). As in much RA photography, the image in *The Plow* is displayed as icon: making use of sharp focus, an emphasis on line, contrasts of intense light and shadow, and the power of human faces and poses of resilience or resignation that might move viewers to action. Iconographic motifs are persistent and religious connotations are constantly invoked: sacred land, plenty, sacrifice, drought, famine, plague, exodus. The film's social realism, inflected by the modernist expressiveness of its Nykino crew, exhibits precise aesthetic strategies that work to restrict and direct our interpretations of the images. At times this aesthetic is so exacting that the use of motion picture technology in *The Plow* seems almost incidental. Images of people in the film, which are few, are characterized not by dynamism but by their iconic stillness and silence. Irving Lerner recalled *Variety*'s sarcastic observation: '[People] aren't called upon for any histrionics other than staring at the sky or whittling sticks to indicate complete resignation to fate' (quoted in Campbell 1982: 223). Walking figures are shown only occasionally; at their most animated, people gaze into the distance warily. These Dust Bowl icons signify the profound failures of politics and history, larger and more complex than the people themselves, requiring solutions over and above the powers of the individual.

So, it needs to be asked, did Lorentz's 'melodrama of nature' succeed in its aims? On the level of historical accuracy, the film takes liberties and oversimplifies numerous points. Its melodramatic tendencies might seem to undermine the power of images to speak for themselves and its artifice to negate its political messages. But Jane Gaines reminds us too of the power of melodrama, particularly in documentary images. Gaines suggests:

> Since recently film studies has been asked to understand what realism does for melodrama, we would want, reciprocally, to ask what melodramatization does for the political aspirations of photographic realism. The short answer to this question is that, contrary to all assumptions about emotion as engendering powerlessless and immobility, in the history of the American melodrama, 'sentiment enables action'. (2007a: 8)

Arguably *The Plow* served its aims: to raise awareness of the displacement and havoc taking place in the Dust Bowl, to arouse public sympathies and support for the social welfare programs of the New Deal. Beyond this, the film provides a portrait of US documentary in the process of coming to terms with the legacies of radicalism and the contemporary climate of financial desperation, and stands as a testament to the skills of its Nykino crew and the tenacity of Lorentz himself.

CONSENSUS, DISSENSUS AND THE POPULAR FRONT

Lorentz's budget for *The Plow* had ballooned from $6,000 to nearly $20,000. In a time of economic pressure, wasteful government expenditure would be carefully scrutinized. At the same time Lorentz failed to find a distributor, as Hollywood studios froze the film out of their theaters. Curiously, this probably had little to do with New Deal scepticism, nor even with studio fears of propaganda. As Doherty points out, with the notable exceptions of MPPDA president Will Hays and MGM chief Louis B. Mayer, Hollywood was essentially pro-Democrat and had supported Roosevelt. Within days of FDR's inauguration, movie theaters were offering slides, trailers and lobby cards urging cinemagoers to 'stand by your president', since this was the man who was 'paving the way for prosperity'. A national committee was formed of film industry executives to organize the preparation of 'propaganda pictures' that would help to get the nation behind the New Deal, and by autumn 1933 all five studios had produced shorts that endorsed FDR's policies (Doherty 1999: 83–4).[10] Yet by 1936 the tone had changed, and with *The Plow*'s appearance on the scene, perhaps Hollywood executives truly feared that the government was going 'into the picture business in earnest' (Ellis 1936: 18).

Lorentz faced an uphill battle to get the film screened, in spite of a landmark debut at the White House in March 1936, after which FDR was 'brimming over with enthusiasm' (Anon. 1936: 47). A premiere at the Mayflower Hotel in

Washington, DC, sponsored by the Museum of Modern Art, was attended by Hollywood figures, RA officials, congressional representatives and diplomats. On the bill was an excerpt from Leni Riefenstahl's *Triumph of the Will* (1935), Lucien Backman's 'city symphony' *Midi* (1929), a Russian short, the GPO unit's landmark animation *A Colour Box* (Len Lye, 1935) and Paul Rotha's *The Face of Britain* (1935). The grouping caused *Time* magazine to quip: 'When made by governments, as most documentary films are, they are usually interlarded with propaganda', though it found *The Plow* to be an exception (Anon. 1936: 47–8).

Still, accusations of propaganda and government manipulation continued to follow Lorentz's film. One distributor (backed by the condemnation of the Washington screening by Will Hays) argued that, 'if any private company or individual made this picture, it would be a documentary film. When the government makes it, it automatically becomes a propaganda picture' (quoted in Snyder 1968: 46). Lorentz cannily circumvented the studio blockade by appealing directly to individuals, social groups, reviewers and theater operators. Ultimately the cooperation of independent cinemas meant that *The Plow* was screened and generated income, but, more importantly, it garnered excellent reviews. When it opened at the Rialto on Times Square on 28 May, legendary theater manager Arthur Mayer cleverly played on the film's maverick status, declaring in advertising that, '*The New York Times* said: "It is unusual, timely, entertaining." [. . .] Yet Hollywood has turned its manicured thumb down!' (Snyder 1968: 46). Even with this support, the experience of marketing *The Plow* left Lorentz on the verge of resigning his RA position. As he recalled, within two hours of seeing Tugwell to offer his resignation, he was given a green light by FDR himself, and a $50,000 budget, to produce a second documentary (Lorentz 1992: 51).

This was to become *The River*, about water management and the Tennessee Valley Authority (TVA). Similar in style and approach to *The Plow* (and also filmed by a Nykino member, Willard Van Dyke) it is sweeping in its techniques of mass persuasion. Peter C. Rollins observes that 'every rhetorical device in the lexicon of film is employed to force upon the viewer a realization of the folly of our industrial exploitation' (1998: 47). *The River* forms a neat companion to *The Plow*: land management to combat desertification followed by water management for one of the nation's most impoverished regions. Also similar, as Stoney describes it, is the fundamental form of an evangelical sermon, and this remained key to *The River*'s success. Its components echo the preachment yarn, and the problem/solution structure of religious narrative: 'Eden, man's sins, we know what we did, repent, heaven, and the TVA' (Stoney 2007).

The film's opening emphasizes water's motion and fluidity, stressing correlations between America's waterways and the nation itself. 'Down the Yellowstone, the Milk, the White and Cheyenne', the voiceover intones,

'carrying every rivulet and brook, creek and rill, carrying all the rivers [. . .]'
Here the 'melting pot' metaphor weighs upon the narrative: a nation of rivers
in flow and flux, gathering together, constantly moving forwards, collapsing
and containing recent histories of political, cultural, ethnic and racial division.
The narration recalls mellifluous verse, invoking Whitman and his hyperbolic
views of the growing nation; like Whitman, Lorentz had succeeded 'in imagining the nation as landscape and language' (Rabinowitz 1994: 101).

Lorentz's films thus imagined national management solutions forged out of
land, water and celluloid, and helped establish the wider critical and popular
cachet of documentary in the US. Yet these efforts were not alone. Even as
Lorentz was beginning work at the RA, debates presisted over how to advance
the form. By 1935–6, while the FPL was 'on its last legs', groups like Nykino
were actively engaged in diversifying their production and distribution strategies (Waugh 1984: 107). Still, among independent filmmakers, uncertainty
lingered about how to achieve widespread and lasting collective organization
and ideological coalition. There was great excitement, then, when Joris Ivens
– respected, connected, admired on the left for both his politics and filmic
expertise – arrived in the US in January 1936 to lecture and host film screenings. Appearing at the invitation of the Popular Front organization New Film
Alliance, Ivens signified 'a turning point [. . .] a shot in the arm [. . .] [that]
confirmed the theories of Nykino' (Waugh 1984: 112). While *The Plow* helped
advance government involvement and a public taste for documentary, Ivens
would have a 'galvanizing impact', as Wolfe puts it, on the ideological and
formal directions that political documentary would take in the US (1993: 354).
In the Netherlands, Ivens had been closely aligned with Amsterdam's Film
League, founded in 1927 to promote avant-garde experimentation, and which
associated mainstream cinema with the masses, with 'the commercial regime,
America, kitsch' (Stufkens 1999: 46). Ivens had already built a reputation
working in nonfiction avant-garde through carefully composed shorts such as
The Bridge (1928) and the water-soaked 'city symphony' *Rain*.

In 1931 Ivens wrote: 'Documentary film is the only positive means left the
avant-garde *cinéaste* who wishes to commit himself fully to labor, insofar as
he represents the expression of the masses or popular expression in his work'
(Ivens 1988 [1931]: 79). Drawing on staged and unstaged footage in *New
Earth* (1933–4) about grain overproduction, and *Misère au Borinage* (1934,
with Henri Storck) which covers a miners' strike in Belgium, Ivens revitalized his radical and collaborative aims through an undecorated style, avoiding
too many 'agreeable photographic effects' that could 'distract' audiences from
'the unpleasant truths we were showing' (Ivens 1969: 87). In the autumn of
1936, he enlisted Archibald MacLeish, Ernest Hemingway, Dorothy Parker,
Lillian Hellman and Hellman's producer, Herman Shumlin, to back a film
that would generate American support for the Loyalist cause against Franco

Figure 10. *The Spanish Earth* (1937). Contemporary Historians Inc. Courtesy of the Kobal Collection.

in the Spanish Civil War. Calling themselves Contemporary Historians, the collective formed the network behind Ivens's first US production, *The Spanish Earth* (1937).

The Spanish Earth sees Ivens in a palpably didactic mode, using carefully constructed narrative and aesthetic framings to heighten the intensity of the brutal wartime footage shown in the film. His earlier emphasis on the composition of shots and on the juxtaposition of movements, shot scales and camera angles is still on display in certain sequences, but modernist extremes are scaled down (see also Waugh 1984: 116). The lyrical, idealized sequence that introduces the village of Fuentidueña de Tajo, where whitewashed walls are eloquently furrowed and cracked, bread is prepared in shadowy interiors and women sweep streets in dramatic long shots, is typical of a less obtrusive but still markedly self-conscious aesthetic strategy. Edited by Helen van Dongen, who also worked on *New Earth* and *Borinage*, the film reveals an occasional affinity with the montage techniques of Eisenstein, whom Ivens met (along with Vertov) while working with the Film League. But disruptive attractions are usually given over to integrated transitions. Even when shifting from dramatized scenes to newsreel footage, the film works towards narrative clarity rather than formal virtuosity.

This is not, however, the case in the war footage – war is revealed as a series of interruptions, discontinuities, dead ends. Though the scenes of battle and siege are always legible, war's shock effects aren't smoothed over. *The Spanish Earth* relies, to a great extent, on what Waugh calls the 'spontaneous' mode of filming – over half of the film captures intense conflict and its aftermath. Shots of long lines of civilians attempting to get food would have struck a chord with those who witnessed US breadlines, the narration driving this home: 'You stand in line all day to buy food [. . .] sometimes the food runs out before you reach the door, sometimes a shell falls near the line, and at home they wait and wait, and no one brings anything back for supper'. Images of bodies loaded into coffins, dead children face down amid the rubble, are presented with matter-of-fact directness. As the stark images of the dead and wounded escalate, the film becomes a documentary counterpart to Picasso's classic portrait of Spain's suffering, *Guernica* (1937).

The film's success underlined support in the US for the Spanish cause. The premiere in Los Angeles on 19 July 1937 was one of the Loyalists' largest fundraisers and the film was an unqualified critical, if not mainstream, success. When screened at the White House for FDR, it featured the 'slick' narration of Orson Welles rather than the 'frank, low-key roughness' of the Ernest Hemingway version screened in theaters (Waugh 1984: 124). In contrast to a traditional 'voice of god', as Bernard F. Dick contends, 'the greatness of *The Spanish Earth* lies in Hemingway's ability to subordinate his narrative to Ivens's images, enclosing them within a text that is never in competition' (1985: 124). Though Ivens was optimistic about a wide release, the film ended up in 'traditional marginalized distribution' channels, doing well in art houses and political venues but creating a 'mere ripple' elsewhere (Waugh 1984: 127). Denning confirms that whereas Popular Front ideas were making strong inroads in publishing and journalism, in the more corporate and monopolized film and broadcasting industries there were few means of competing with 'the majors' (1997: 95).

As *The Spanish Earth* was being shot in early 1937, the Nykino group, encouraged by the support of figures like Ivens, established Frontier Films: a not-for-profit organization devoted to producing professional-grade sound films. Inspired by Alexander Dovzhenko's *Frontier* (1935), the name also gestured towards, and perhaps strove to reframe, a powerful American metaphor and myth. Frontier would ultimately produce very few films based in the US, though its *People of the Cumberland* (1937) was probably the most successful independent Popular Front film of the period (Denning 1997: 72). It focuses on the Highlander Folk School in Tennessee, an experiment in fusing vernacular roots of local miners and farmworkers with leftist aesthetic projects. Filmed after the kidnapping and murder of local political organizers, the film drew on the combined talents of Kazan, Meyers, Leyda, Steiner, Erskine

Caldwell and van Dongen to present the Highlander School as a proactive force for American advancement, a natural fusion of local US traditions and union activism.

True to the internationalism of the Popular Front, Frontier supported anti-fascist and anti-imperialist causes abroad – the Spanish Loyalists, Chinese solidarity in the face of Japanese invasion – featuring the work of Herbert Kline, Henri Cartier-Bresson, Harry Dunham and others. *Heart of Spain* and *China Strikes Back* appeared in 1937, and Frontier released an English-language version of another pro-Loyalist film, *Return to Life*, the following year. *United Action* (1939) returned Frontier to core concerns in trade union activism. Combining 'home-movie' footage shot by United Auto Workers' cameramen at Detroit's General Motors strike with professional editing and a soundtrack produced by Frontier, the film works to convey a powerful Popular Front message: that 'labor militancy is the highest form of Americanism' (Rosenzweig 1980: 10).

In 1938, Steiner and Van Dyke created a rift at Frontier when they formed American Documentary Films, Inc., and embarked on making *The City*, which would become a key attraction at the 1939 New York World's Fair.[11] Though depleted, Frontier still had sufficient political and cultural connections to make what would be their last release: the Strand and Hurwitz collaboration *Native Land* (1942). The film was inspired by the Senate's La Follette Civil Liberties Committee (1936–41) findings on espionage, private police systems and other illegal strikebreaking methods used by employers' associations against industrial and farm workers' union organizing. Through a mixture of 'spontaneous' footage and dramatized sequences, it knits together stories of civil rights violations against workers and a history of American rebellion, ultimately drawing on patriotic sentiments grounded in Jeffersonian idealism. Just as the name Frontier assimilated Soviet and American ideals, the title of *Native Land* attempted to synthesize seemingly conflicting ideas: the concept of native includes both the diverse immigrants who adopted the land and those 'natives' displaced and subjected to nation-building policies that amounted to genocide. Campbell sees the film as persistently posing oppositions – light and dark, advance and setback – with an aim at dialectical synthesis: 'a Marxist aesthetic bridging Stanislavsky and Brecht' that was the result of years of theoretical debate and discussion (Campbell 1985: 83–4).

The opening titles state: 'Since the founding of our country the American people have had to fight for their freedom in every generation', and invokes the 'democratic strength' of the American people over the 'fascist minded' vigilantes and spies that threaten liberties. The first sequence portrays a series of industrial workers laid off and blacklisted – some for 'insubordination' and others for seemingly no reason at all. One by one they are denied their 'rights as Americans': rights to organize and protest guaranteed under the Constitution.

Figure 11. *Native Land* (1942). Frontier Films. Courtesy of the British Film Institute.

As it progresses, the film mixes melodramatic scenes with viscerally disturbing newsreel footage: women being pushed and harassed at a union march; brutal attacks on striking steelworkers in Ambridge, Pennsylvania. The film's climax responds to the suppression of newsreel footage of the Chicago Memorial Day Massacre of 1937, where police fired on protestors, killing ten.

Underlining links between dissent and Americanism, *Time* found the film to be at the same time 'unashamedly pro-labor propaganda' and 'as vitally American as Carl Sandburg' (Anon. 1979 [1942]: 200–1). As Wolfe sees it, it is 'Popular Front historiography writ large', with the FPL's working-class constituency reconceived as ' "we, the people," a democratic, classless force' (1993: 363). In this sense we begin to see the ideological blurring and interactions between the Popular Front and liberal Hollywood productions of the period. *Native Land*'s emphasis on the resurgence of 'millions of little people' recalls the studio ending to Ford's *The Grapes of Wrath*, where Ma Joad images the Depression's dispossessed as pioneers clinging to traditional frontier aspirations. This national dynamic pervades *Native Land*: 'little people' posed against potent forces of home-grown fascism (corporate spies, vigilante strike breakers, the Ku Klux Klan, corrupt police). In defending the 'innocent ones', the Roosevelt government becomes a key part of the solution. 'The state is now also viewed as a potential ally', Campbell notes; 'the La Follette Committee is extolled, and the film is awash with patriotic imagery' (1985: 83–4).

Native Land's vision is not one of sheer national homogenization, however, as it does emphasize ethnic and cultural diversity within a Popular Front 'pan-ethnic Americanism' – this during an era that saw some of the most severe limits on immigration, including racial quotas and exclusions (such as the 'Asiatic Barred Zone', established in 1917).[12] The first dismissed worker is Latino, called Antonio Machado, perhaps a reference to fascism in Spain by invoking the name of the Spanish poet who died in exile in 1939 having fled after Franco's *coup d'état*. The next two workers dismissed are Arthur Perkins (white) and William Grossman (Jewish). As Barsam notes, for some at Frontier, perhaps *Native Land* reflected a sense of being 'outsiders': 'outside of mainstream American culture as the sons of Jewish immigrants, and outside the mainstream of American film production' (1992: 149). Paul Robeson, an active supporter of the Spanish Republicans and civil rights campaigner, was a key endorser and fundraiser. Already experienced in documentary projects undertaken with his wife Eslanda, he provided resonant narration that, along with Marc Blitzstein's score, anchors and unifies the film.[13]

The events portrayed in *Native Land* were based in fact, but for all the power of its dramatic retellings the Popular Front's political acuity and highly regional impact at times gets lost amid a desire to assert an overarching, 'truer' vision of America and its people. Moreover, the timing of the release made any message of protest or dissent that much more difficult to deliver. Hurwitz reportedly received the answer print for the film on the day Pearl Harbor was bombed; not even the communist party would help promote a film which could potentially disrupt national unity (Campbell 1982: 248). In all, *Native Land*'s – and the Popular Front's – attempted synthesis of left-wing dissent, civil liberties issues and keen patriotic sentiments suggests a pattern of political critique in US documentary – dissensus as power, leading to a stronger and 'truer' America, more closely in touch with its 'national story' and its roots. This reformist pattern is still visible in the political documentaries of – to name a few – Barbara Kopple, Michael Moore, Robert Greenwald and Eugene Jarecki.

As the Second World War loomed, the radicalism of the early 1930s and even the liberal messages of the New Deal were subsumed beneath responses to the pressing threats of fascism. FSA (formerly known as RA) photographers were beset by demands for images that demonstrated national unity and spirit. Gordon Parks's now-famous 'American Gothic, Washington, D.C.', showing African American cleaner Ella Watson posed in front of an American flag with her mop and broom, led Stryker to comment that such controversial images would 'get us [FSA photographers] all fired' (Parks 2005: 66). Photographers were called upon to capture 'pictures of men, women, and children who appear as if they really believed in the US'. FSA photographer John Vachon lamented that government images were looking essentially 'like those from the Soviet Union' (quoted in Stange 1989: 133). Signaling the shift from social documentation and persuasion towards the demands of war propaganda, FSA photography was moved into the Office of War Information (OWI) in 1943. The latter was abolished in 1945, absorbed into the top-down management structures of the State Department.

Frontier's membership fractured after *Native Land*, while Lorentz's government role at the FSA – supported by FDR but embattled within congressional and Hollywood industry circles – had in 1938 been transferred to a new organization, the United States Film Service (USFS). Under this umbrella Lorentz made *The Fight for Life* (1940), a dramatized work dealing with medical care for the poor in Chicago, focusing on mortality during childbirth. Negotiating between the budgetary strictures of the USFS and various branches of the Department of Agriculture, he also managed to draft Joris Ivens to direct (with van Dongen again editing) *The Power and the Land* (1940). Distributed by RKO, the film became one of Lorentz's most successful projects, screening in 5,000 theaters (Ellis and McLane 2005: 87). One of his final government projects was working with Robert Flaherty on *The Land* (1942), a problematic production which aimed to criticize intensive farming but was hampered by the confusion caused by war in Europe and government policy shifts towards maximizing agricultural production. The film's costs ballooned to $80,000 of public money, and though it premiered at the Museum of Modern Art in 1942 it was never publicly released. Indeed, films like *The Plow*, *The River* and *The Land* would be withdrawn from circulation during wartime, 'lest in the wrong hands they should be used as anti-American propaganda' (Murphy 1978: 36). When Lorentz resigned his government position in 1940, it was a case of jumping before being pushed. Perpetually under threat, the USFS was never far from Hollywood criticisms of government 'contamination' of the film business, while Congress expressed fears that Lorentz's projects had expanded federal filmmaking 'beyond reasonable limits' (Snyder 1968: 91–2, 166). There were some positive, if short-lived, efforts: in 1939 Mary Losey, with the support of Grierson, spearheaded a study by the American Library Association on the use of educational films and the viability of film libraries for educational purposes, leading to the Educational Film Library Association's establishment in 1943. Losey's parallel project was the Association of Documentary Film Producers, meant to help organize US documentary 'after the Grierson pattern', though the coming of war meant the organization was dispersed (Griffith 1952: 309). Publicly sponsored documentary and educational films gave way to wartime propaganda.

The 1930s witnessed the coalescence of personal and organizational links between practitioners and theorists, radical politics and aesthetic experimentation. Though the war and immediate postwar periods saw political and formal experimentation in documentary curtailed, in many respects the foundations had been laid for future 'political docs' and alternative media that would persist in the belief that political contestation and critique lay at the heart of American values, beliefs and national identity. Comparing Kopple's *Harlan County USA* (1976) to the FPL work, Belinda Baldwin and Robert Bahar argue that *Harlan County* 'demonstrates why it and other films like it are vital to the democratic process' (2004: 13). Indeed, 1930s documentary experienced something of a revival during the politically heated years of George W. Bush, Hurricane Katrina and the Iraq War, with events such as the IDA's Pare Lorentz Festival in 2007 – the first time all the major Lorentz films were screened in Los Angeles. Betsy McLane thus compares *The River* to Spike Lee's *When the Levees Broke* (2006), suggesting: 'Massive technological changes, which in turn affect the funding, distribution, and aesthetics of documentaries, have made the 2000s a very different time than the 1930s, but despite the passing of decades, important continuities in the documentary ethos remain' (McLane 2007: 81). Documentary still envisions sites of collective social engagement; indeed the 'social change potential' of documentary, one critic argues, might be seen 'as approaching the miraculous' (Gaines 2007a: 18).

NOTES

1. See also Rabinowitz (1994: 5–6).
2. Some overviews that do not mention Hine include Ellis and McLane (2005), Barnouw (1983) and Jacobs (1979).
3. Campbell's (1982) remains one of the most complete studies of the topic.
4. See also Seltzer (1980: 18).
5. The New York FPL produced a number of films based on Hunger Marches, including *Albany Hunger March* (1931) and *National Hunger March* (1931, filmed during the first national march), in addition to *Hunger 1932*. See Campbell and Alexander (1977: 33–8).
6. Working for *The March of Time*, filmmaker Mary Losey recalled being labeled a 'dangerous radical', with limits placed on political expression (Fielding 1978: 127–9).
7. Already by the late 1930s, however, Soviet filmmakers' creative freedoms (including Vertov's) were being severely repressed by state controls.
8. See Ellis and McLane (2005: 80).
9. This film was so critical of capitalist exploitation that it was the first Hollywood talkie given permission to be screened in the Soviet Union.
10. Perhaps these pro-New Deal moves were partly self-interested, in that the National Industrial Recovery Act (NIRA) of 1933 provided the government with powers to restrict and regulate trade practices in industry, including the motion picture industry. The NIRA was declared unconstitutional in 1935.
11. For a more complete account see Barsam (1992: 166–8).

12. See Denning (1997: 130). Chinese exclusion was repealed in 1943, though with a yearly immigration figure set at only 105.
13. For further details on Robeson, see Musser (2006: 359).

CHAPTER 5

Idea-Weapons: Documentary Propaganda

In 1941, the first Academy Award for best documentary went to the Canadian short *Churchill's Island* (1941), which chronicled Britain's defence against the Nazis. The following year, the documentary winners all reflected the United States' and its new military allies' escalating involvement in the propaganda war: John Ford's rousing color combat film *The Battle of Midway*, the Australian newsreel *Kokoda Front Line!*, the Soviet military orientation film *Moscow Strikes Back* and Frank Capra's *Prelude to War*. By 1945, all the documentary winners had been war films, and in 1946, after the war's end, there were no nominees for documentary feature (though the category reappeared the following year). Given these beginnings, arguably the best documentary Oscar – designed to celebrate works where 'the emphasis is on fact' ('Rule Twelve' 2010) – was based in one of motion pictures' key ideological functions: rallying popular opinion and patriotic sentiments during times of national crisis and war.

But the invention of the Academy's documentary category, some suggest, was about more than just endorsing film's role in the war effort. Patrick Stockstill, a coordinator for the awards, has seen it as part of a more widespread 'recognition of the fact that documentary was becoming a bigger part of the theatrical experience' (quoted in Mertes 1998: 7). The social functions of documentary in the US had coalesced during the 1930s and the form's stature continued to rise, significantly, after Pearl Harbor. Addressing and bridging demands for information, education and entertainment, the wartime documentary became a key mode for swaying public opinion and reinforcing ideas of citizenship, patriotism and national duty.

Still, many commentators and policymakers continued to view documentary's authority with suspicion. The lines between persuasive instruction – the need to convey national unity in times of crisis – and the 'lies' of propaganda were too often far from clearly drawn. Propaganda, according to David

Culbert, 'involves the exaggeration of ideas already present in a given culture [. . .] [It] extracts and elevates selected themes to a dominant norm, in the process allowing exaggeration to become the norm' (Culbert 1990b: xv). As seen in the 1930s work of Pare Lorentz, Frontier Films and others, an amount of selectivity and exaggeration was permissible without destroying public perceptions that a film might be truthful or genuine. Yet this fragile foundation of trust – the informal contract between documentary producers and consumers – was pushed to its limits during wartime. Many propaganda films passed muster only because they mirrored and encouraged passionate wartime sentiments already very much in the air.

Philip Dunne once commented that 'most documentaries have one thing in common: each springs from a definite need, each is conceived as an idea-weapon to strike a blow for whatever cause the originator has in mind. In the broadest sense, the documentary is almost always, therefore, an instrument of propaganda' (quoted in Barsam 1974: 2). During the war Dunne worked for the Office of War Information, promoting documentary as a means for shaping public opinion at home and forging positive images of the US abroad. Dunne's 'idea-weapon' captures the basic perceptions and purposes of documentaries during the war: to serve as ideological tools that could help defeat the nation's enemies. But Dunne's metaphor also recognizes something often suppressed by claims that documentary maintains a special relationship with transparency and truth: in spite of appearances, documentaries produced both during and outside of wartime have been steeped in ideology. Ultimately, wartime documentaries raise the question of how closely aligned propaganda and documentary can be before the 'documentary idea' itself is pushed to its limits: how far can documentaries blur the lines between bias and fact and still be seen as documentaries? The task, then, is to unpack the manufacturing of truth in documentary while keeping in mind that not all documentaries, even those designed as propaganda, simply 'lie'. As we sift through texts designed to resist our interrogations, we might also begin to discern nuggets of historical fact and experience embedded in them.

WAR AND CINEMA

Wars have played a crucial role in the ebb and flow of global power dynamics and have shaped the societies that wage them. Whether revolutionary, civil or 'small' – as in the Philippines, Korea, Vietnam, Afghanistan, Kuwait and Iraq – wars have been fundamental to the construction of American identity and culture at key junctures in the nation's history.[1] As Tarak Barkawi has suggested, 'wars are shaped by the societies that wage them and [. . .] societies are shaped by the wars they wage. [. . .] War reacts back on its social context'

(2004: 125). Entwined in this process have been the cultural mediations of war: print media, film, television and the Internet, all of which reflect and impact upon the global power dynamics, ideologies, rivalries and nationalisms that give rise to military conflict. War and popular culture are closely related: 'citizens' subjectivities become sites of strategic significance' and the domain of the national-popular has been a 'key battleground' fought over by national interests promoting militarism to achieve political objectives (Barkawi 2004: 115). J. David Slocum argues that militarization was 'the process by which war and national security became consuming anxieties and provided the memories, models, and metaphors that shaped broad areas of national life', and concludes that 'American cinema has played an ongoing and privileged role in that process' (2006: 1).[2]

Rudyard Kipling famously observed, 'the first victim of war is the truth'. An early sign of nonfiction cinema's potential for enflaming nationalistic passions occurred during the run-up to the Spanish-American War in 1898. On 15 February, the US battleship *Maine* was bombed in Havana Harbor, sinking along with 263 sailors on board. The incident yielded numerous patriotic, anti-Spanish films, with public excitement fueled by the pro-war rhetoric and 'yellow journalism' of newspapers run by magnates like William Randolph Hearst. Pro-war nonfiction films often combined real and staged footage, and many relied on sheer fakery. In an infamous case, the Biograph Company, which a few months before the *Maine* explosion had released *Battleships 'Iowa' and 'Massachusetts'* (1897), re-released the same film after the event, now advertised as *Battleships 'Maine' and 'Iowa'*. The film was exhibited to great public approval: in Chicago, 'the audience arose, cheered and cheered again' at the appearance of what they believed, or wanted to believe, was the *Maine* (quoted in Musser 1990a: 241). A host of other films followed, such as Edison's *Old Glory and Cuban Flag* and *Campaign in Cuba* (shot not in Cuba, but in New Jersey), boosting support for war and helping to feed imperialist sentiments around the country. As Erik Barnouw notes, war-related images were not only a financial bonanza for companies like Biograph and Vitagraph, but helped advance the political careers of individuals like Teddy Roosevelt. It was said Roosevelt halted his march up Cuba's San Juan Hill in 1898 to strike a pose for a Vitagraph camera (Barnouw 1983: 23).

More pressing than any demand for verifiable facts in these films was the need to capture the drama of current events. Projected on screen, symbols of national pride tapped into powerful emotional undercurrents; allies could be cheered and enemies booed en masse. Indeed, whether it was the *Massachusetts* or the *Maine* was fairly irrelevant: audiences were seeking verisimilitude, not indisputable authenticity, to bolster their beliefs. Of course, the Spanish-American War film didn't rouse these sentiments on its own; it worked alongside other media, such as advertising and newspaper accounts, to further define a common sense of here and there, us and them (Kaplan 2002: 154). But war and cinema do seem to share a particularly intimate bond. Paul Virilio, for example, emphasizes how imbricated war and cinematography have been since the First World War, arguing that 'war is cinema and cinema is war': there is in particular a 'deadly harmony' that 'always establishes itself between the functions of eye and weapon' (Virilio 1989: 26, 69). These connections have manifested themselves in scientific and aesthetic concerns in the field of optics and the demand in combat for increasingly sophisticated technologies of magnification and sighting: for ever-expanding spatial mastery and accurate targeting. The multiple meanings of the term 'to shoot', then, speak to a larger truth, as connoted in pre-cinematic inventions such as Thomas Skaife's 'pistolgraph' or Étienne-Jules Marey's chronophotographic *fusil* (gun/rifle), the latter of which drew its inspiration from the machine gun and multi-chambered Colt revolver (see Kittler 1999: 124). Reinforcing this point, James Castonguay observes that early cinematic apparatuses were 'literally transformed into signifying war machines': Edison even renamed his projecting kinetoscope the 'Wargraph', so closely did he identify film with capturing war imagery (2006: 99).

The US government didn't take long to recognize the potential benefits and hazards of using film to disseminate ideas and images of war to the public. During the First World War, the Committee on Public Information (CPI) was involved in producing, monitoring and censoring war newsreels and features. Headed by the tireless muckraker George Creel, the CPI (known as the Creel Committee) aimed to project a unified image of the nation to its citizens and to the world, especially to European countries that remained neutral. Creel's promotion of America was little short of messianic: his job, as he saw it, was to transmit 'the gospel of Americanism to every corner of the globe' (Doherty 1993: 88). Official CPI films such as *Pershing's Crusaders* (1918) and *America's Answer (to the Hun)* (1918) drew on military and civilian footage, underlined by dramatic intertitles such as 'German arrogance casts its shadow on America when Deutschland rises like a serpent in our harbors' (quoted in Doherty 1993: 89). The CPI aimed to project an unwavering sense of US military and industrial power, and its films were marketed to theater exhibitors as essential to their patriotic duties. 'Hurrah for America' trumpeted advertisements for *Pershing's Crusaders*: 'Uncle Sam photographed it – Uncle Sam would like you to show it in your theater' (Culbert et al. 1990: 214–15).

Among the CPI's productions was the *Official War Review*, a propaganda newsreel distributed by the Pathé Company that drew on footage shot by the US Signal Corps and various British, French and Italian military sources – footage routinely censored by the Creel Committee. Indeed, the practice of censoring factual footage was institutionalized during the First World War. Censorship has always existed as propaganda's 'Siamese twin'; it was and still is justified by the reasoning that 'information which may be of value to the enemy must be prevented from flowing outside the battle zone and that the feelings of the relatives of dead or injured combat personnel must be protected' (Taylor 1994: 21). Closely related motives for censorship include suppressing public awareness of the grim realities of death, destruction and killing of civilians, and stopping the spread of potentially damaging information such as military or governmental mismanagement or corruption. All of this is believed to protect the interests of a nation at war.

The CPI encouraged the film industry to follow its lead – a rallying cry that many in the commercial sector were eager to take up: 'Let us show what the screen can do for patriotism!' enthused the President of the National Association of the Motion Picture Industry, William A. Brady (Culbert et al. 1990: 200). A persistent theme of the Hollywood 'hate' film was the German invasion of Belgium, and popular shorts represented the German 'monster' or 'evil Hun' as an oversized marauding ape that indiscriminately kidnapped and slaughtered Belgian women and children. These images circulated alongside an increasingly virulent anti-German press, and popular songs such as 'Let's Bury the Hatchet (in the Kaiser's Head)' and 'Hunting the Hun' strove to make a game of war's brutality.

The propaganda machine of the First World War resulted from government perceptions that pro-war rhetoric had to target the public aggressively, though a large proportion of the US population was made up of recent immigrants, and many retained ties to the European nations involved on both sides of the conflict. Public opinion about US participation in the war was far from unified. Many considered neutrality as the best way forward for an increasingly prosperous and multi-ethnic nation. European wars were not America's affair, and the Spanish-American War, and even the bloody battles of the Civil War, lingered in the memories of many. Shortly after Armistice was signed in November 1918, 'hate' films ceased to be relevant. As the facts of unprecedented destruction and the many millions of casualties in Europe sunk in, there ensued a backlash against the saturation of media propaganda and the censorship practiced by the US government.

After the war, anti-war narratives such as King Vidor's *The Big Parade* (1925) and Raoul Walsh's *What Price Glory?* (1926) underlined America's desire to distance itself from wartime's fevered sentiments. James Whale directed a film version of the anti-war play *Journey's End* (1930), while the vivid realism of Lewis Milestone's *All Quiet on the Western Front* (1930) drew on military and newsreel images of the first war to be so extensively captured on film, constructing a powerful anti-war message that led to a mini-boom in the early 1930s of films critiquing war's legacy. The brutality conjured up by Milestone's 'stark, awful drama' so affected its star, Lew Ayres, that he became a conscientious objector in the Second World War at the expense of his career (Chambers 1996: 25). The impact of the Great War and the intrusive role of the government in producing propaganda and regulating media coverage still haunted the public imagination twenty years later, as the next war approached.

PICTURES TO WIN THE WAR

As fascism was gaining the upper hand in Europe during the 1930s, US commentators were noting with awe and alarm the ways that state-sponsored mass communications – enabled by efficient, top-down governmental controls – could arouse the passions of the masses. Fascist spectacles such as Leni Riefenstahl's *Triumph of the Will* (1935), an ode to Hitler's displays of Nazi unity, had generated interest among cineastes for their intense aesthetic and emotional impact (scenes from *Triumph* were shown alongside *The Plow that Broke the Plains* at the latter's Washington, DC debut). Yet as war broke out in Europe, admiration afforded by the sheer scale of nationalist visions like Riefenstahl's gave way to concerns about replicating fascist aesthetics or imposing extensive regulations on the media. Even though the Soviet Union was an ally, 'Red Scare' suspicions persisted and few wanted to duplicate its state-run media networks.

Moreover, the US government's excesses during the First World War still overshadowed calls for greater centralized controls over print, radio and motion pictures. As Harold L. Elsten argued in 1941:

The present fear of government interference in politics, of interference with the rights of free speech, press, and the like, can be traced to the period of the First World War. [. . .] More recently, this distrust has been confirmed by the spectacle of government monopoly of mass communications in the authoritarian nations. (Elsten 1942: 7)

Even after the US joined the war, scepticism about propaganda and regulating information disseminated on the 'home front' never quite faded. Fears about protecting First Amendment rights were reflected in battles within and between Congress and the executive branch. As Ernst Kris saw it, the distrust of propaganda could be traced to a wider distrust, namely

the disappointment in government and the inflation of persuasion. Both developed fully after the last war [. . .] The first, the disappointment in government, is related to the feeling that the world has grown out of control. It is a phenomenon apparently typical of industrialized mass society under the impact of war and postwar conflicts. [. . .] The economic crisis in all countries, though at different times and with different intensity, has heightened the disappointment in government into a feeling of general insecurity. (Kris 1943: 383)

Such concerns continued to hang over the Roosevelt administration, even as the Office of War Information (OWI) was created by presidential decree in June 1942.

The bombing of Pearl Harbor on 7 December 1941 and the declaration of war to a great extent freed Roosevelt from hesitancies that reigned over government involvement in the media. Controls over the politics and morality of American movies were seen as crucial to the project of establishing national unity, but 'chaos' continued to prevail over various overlapping government information divisions which together lacked a unified war vision (Koppes 1997: 269). The OWI was meant to streamline the management of wartime propaganda, while controversial censorship duties were carefully segregated off into the Office of Censorship. Headed by the radio commentator Elmer Davis, the OWI was supposed to 'enhance public understanding of the war at home and abroad' through overseeing the production of pamphlets, posters, radio transmissions and films (Winkler 1978: 33). Davis approached his task from the position of a journalist defending freedom and democracy, insisting that his agency's goal was not to spread convenient lies but 'to tell the truth'. The OWI was to avoid the 'witch hunt' and 'anti-Hun' rhetoric of the First World War (Koppes and Black, 1988: 59). Propaganda might be an inevitable side effect of war, but Davis still preferred to take the high road, stressing American political openness rather than forcing measures that could appear to mirror fascist rhetoric. In spite of popular support for Davis, the OWI's propaganda operations – still suspiciously viewed in Congress as the machinations of 'New Dealers' – remained decidedly controversial (Koppes and Black 1988: 137–8).

It didn't help that the organization failed to streamline all agencies involved in war propaganda. The Office of the Co-ordinator of Inter-American Affairs (CIAA, devoted to Latin American operations), for example, retained its independence from the OWI when its head, Nelson D. Rockefeller – 'always jealous of incursions into his territory' – threatened to resign if he had to work within another agency (Winkler 1978: 26; Koppes and Black 1988: 58–9). The work of the OWI quickly devolved into separate branches – domestic and overseas – each responsible for their own film activities. The domestic branch oversaw the Bureau of Motion Pictures (BMP), directed by the newspaper editor and Roosevelt acolyte Lowell Mellett, based in Washington. Mellett planned for the domestic branch to follow a 'three-point' strategy: to coordinate the film activities of government agencies, to work with industry to assure the maximum distribution of government films, and to aid the industry in producing films that might assist 'the prosecution of the war' (Dyer 1943:

22). The BMP's 'Manual for the Motion Picture Industry' exhorted studios to ask themselves: 'Will this picture help to win the war?' (quoted in Koppes 1997: 269).

The domestic branch's Hollywood office, headed by Nelson Poynter (another pro–New Deal journalist who, as it happened, 'did not follow movies') was set up in April 1942 to work with powerful studio interests (Koppes and Black 1988: 58). The OWI intended it to serve a number of interrelated functions, including monitoring Hollywood scripts to ensure that they contained nothing that might undermine the war effort and that they guarded public perceptions of the US and its policies. This latter task, many industry figures complained, amounted to government 'surveillance' of Hollywood. There was resistance to the OWI's 'intrusive presence' and the 'pushy cues' handed down in memos from Poynter's office (disparagingly nicknamed 'poynters' by Hollywood insiders) (Doherty 1993: 46–7). Mellett intervened, contending that previewing and editing scripts was favorable to having completed films deemed inappropriate and yanked from distribution later on. Eventually a compromise was reached, and reading and approving scripts became a regular OWI function.

While the Overseas Bureau attained a degree of autonomy (see below), the OWI's domestic branch struggled with anti-New Dealers in Congress, the public, and industry power brokers suspicious of its functions. Congress blocked its budget in 1943–4, only reinstating it after strict restrictions were imposed – including the abolition of the Bureau of Motion Pictures' domestic operations. Though never far from scrutiny, the organization did create a number of straightforward public information and instructional films, like *Wartime Nutrition* (1943), which proffered messages of reassurance during a time of instability and confusion. Samuel Spewack's *The World at War* (1942), a compilation documentary broadly similar to Capra's forthcoming *Prelude to War*, was the government's first orientation film released to civilian audiences. Testifying to the OWI's nervousness regarding public perceptions of propaganda, *The World at War* affirms that 'nothing has been staged' and defensively draws attention to its own complicated ideological position: 'The editors are Americans', it notes, 'and therefore partisan, but every effort has been made to let the facts speak for themselves'. Yet even with its dramatic images of Pearl Harbor's flaming wreckage, the film failed to make a broad impact. It was met with resistance from exhibitors and lukewarm responses from audiences, reflecting the difficulties of releasing government propaganda on commercial screens.

Other films were directly targeted at domestic tensions and morale. *Campus on the March* (1942) showed the mobilization of US universities, where subjects such as agricultural management, chemical weaponry and aviation were being geared towards the war effort. *Manpower* (1942) dealt with the

War Manpower Commission and labor shortages, including the transition of African American and women workers from 'menial' and 'domestic' duties into more skilled work such as machine operation. But encouraging the public to re-imagine the social roles of traditionally marginalized or underrepresented groups was an uphill struggle. As Michael Renov notes, one wartime training manual designed for community-led indoctrination suggested: 'The ultimate goal [. . .] is to associate in the minds of the public the words "woman" and "work" just as firmly as the words "man" and "fight" are associated'. Such directives suggest the government clearly saw the need for a 'vigorous and repetitive public campaign' that could ensure extensive 'behavior modification' (Renov 1988: 85). The recasting of traditional sex roles, the radical rethinking of ingrained racial prejudices and hierarchies – these were crucial to rallying the whole nation around the war. The need to mobilize women war workers, in particular, resulted in government-led campaigns and popular icons like 'Rosie the Riveter' (initiated by the popular song of the same name). The reformation of social roles and ideological expectations attempted during the Second World War would have a long-term social impact.[3]

During the war, ongoing social divisions came up against urgent calls for unity. Events like the 'Red Summer' riots of 1919, precipitated in part by African American veterans still experiencing social exclusion after serving in the First World War, had threatened both the substance and the popular image of national harmony. As the US entered world war for the second time, unity was still hampered by widespread racial discrimination. In Detroit, for example, realtors had urged that 'negro workers be removed from certain large sections of the community [to] make their homes available for white war workers' (Culbert and Suid 1991: 1702).[4] Resentment prevailed throughout the African American community; even feel-good OWI films appeared to perpetuate an image of a 'white war' waged by a 'white man's country' (Garrett 1994: 71). This idea seemed reinforced by America's racist stance towards the Japanese, which at times threatened to mirror the racism of America's other enemy: the Nazi regime. At the Ford Motor Company in Detroit, some African American workers tore down a poster of a 'Jap soldier' menacing a white woman with a bayonet. As reported to Elmer Davis at the OWI, the workers argued that 'the Japs are colored people, so are we. We are not fighting colored people. We are fighting for democracy' (Culbert and Suid 1991: 1702). The quote suggests that the protest was aimed against the racism of the poster and not against the war effort per se, but the government was aware it needed to act on reports of racial discord. Though groups like the Army still were officially committed to existing policies of segregation, a rhetorical battle was set in motion.

The OWI responded to the 'Negro problem' with films like *Negro Colleges in Wartime* (1944), which characterizes war as an opportunity that can help level racial inequalities. Featuring training at African American institutions such as Howard University and the Hampton Institute, the overriding message is of African American self-determination, social progress and enlightenment. While several scenes depict black students being taught by white instructors, there are no references to the realities of discrimination and racial segregation, such as the Jim Crow laws that forbade these very students from entering mainstream educational institutions. Another 'patronizing' film addressed to African Americans was the Department of Agriculture's *Henry Browne, Farmer* (1942) (Cripps and Culbert 1998: 112). The film follows a black farmer working his forty acres, showing the rhythms of family, social and laboring life. Anchored by the voice of actor and civil rights activist Canada Lee, it depicts African American rural life as basically stable and comfortable. Still, Browne's rough-hewn cabin and under-equipped farm were meant to resemble reality just enough to engage black audiences, rather than alienating them through blatantly false images. At the film's core is the idea that, 'at a time when every American has an important job to do', there are crucial if often invisible links between African Americans laboring on farms and the war going on overseas. It was nominated for an Oscar, though Thomas Cripps calls it a 'second-rate' film that barely approaches the sophistication of the well-known Army indoctrination film *The Negro Soldier* (1944), discussed below (Cripps and Culbert 1998: 112).

If many of these films seem reasonably subtle vehicles for propaganda, others did invoke the racism of First World War 'hate' films. While racial slurs against Germans were usually kept to a minimum (Germans made up one of the largest immigrant groups in the US), the Japanese were openly reviled: portrayed as 'vermin' to be 'exterminated'. 'They live like rats, breed like rats, and act like rats', stated the governor of Idaho, while the *Los Angeles Times* referred to 'vipers' hatched from eggs (Lindqvist 2001: sec. 221). The most vitriolic anti-Japanese films released through the BMP were made for military indoctrination. In *Our Enemy – the Japanese* (1943), the former US ambassador to Japan, Joseph C. Grew, characterizes the Japanese as a nation of 'fanatics' guided by a 'primitive moral code'.[5] Grew argues the Japanese are 'as different from ourselves as any people on this planet: the real difference is in their minds. [. . .] Their weapons are modern, their thinking is 2,000 years out of date'. The dehumanizing spectacle of the Japanese in *Our Enemy* was restricted to military screenings, but similar sentiments were echoed in Hollywood exploitation films that were saturating the US market. RKO's advertisements for *Behind the Rising Sun* (1943) trumpeted that the 'villainous Japs have simply got to be exterminated! They sell their own daughters! They manhandle captive women! They make war even on babies! They torture helpless men and women! [. . .] and more, and more, and more!'[6] Fox's *Guadalcanal Diary* (1943) presented Japanese fighters as 'apes and monkeys'; killing them was likened to a 'turkey shoot'. OWI script reviewers praised this film as the 'most realistic and outstanding' motion picture yet made about war in the Pacific (Koppes and Black 1988: 260).

Perhaps most indicative of the OWI's fraught domestic role is *Japanese Relocation* (1942), which betrays the ideological instability of wartime propaganda. Taken alongside the bombastic claims of films such as *Behind the Rising Sun*, the film effectively works to repackage 'Yellow Peril' hysteria as prudent wartime behavior. *Japanese Relocation* was charged with the task of selling to the public the forced migration and internment of over 100,000 Japanese immigrants and Japanese-American citizens (*nisei*). Dominated by the defensive narration of Milton S. Eisenhower of the War Relocation Authority, the film exemplifies how home-grown propaganda strove to manipulate public opinion and fiercely protect the nation's image. The displaced *nisei* are misleadingly referred to as 'evacuees'. Bussed away from boarded up homes and businesses – 'quick disposal of property often involved financial sacrifice for the evacuees', the voiceover states – they arrive in remote areas of California, Utah, Arkansas, Colorado and Arizona. D. S. Meyer, director of the War Relocation Authority, would assure Elmer Davis at the OWI that the film was 'an accurate record of the early stages of the evacuation' (Culbert and Suid 1991: 1393).[7]

The relocation camps appear hospitable and open but in reality were patrolled by armed military personnel and enclosed by barbed wire. The film's upbeat narration is buoyed by patriotic tunes and even claims that forced internment offers an opportunity to establish 'new pioneer communities'. The 'evacuees' (technically, prisoners of war) now have the chance to embody the spirit of American expansionism. Over the image of visibly exhausted and bewildered Japanese-Americans filing towards a processing center, the narrator invokes Frederick Jackson Turner's frontier thesis and the cliché of the redemptive wilderness: 'Naturally the newcomers looked about with some curiosity – they were in a new area, on land that was raw, untamed, but full of opportunity'. They can now 'reclaim the desert'. Images of children focus audience attention away from war's brutalities and injustices towards a 'new world' led by America. But the paternalistic edifice of *Japanese Relocation* threatens to come tumbling down when the narrator admits that two-thirds of the displaced people are American citizens and the rest are 'aliens'. The Japanese are divided into two groups: 'loyal' citizens who might eventually hope to 'once again enjoy the freedoms that we in this country cherish', and 'disloyal' others who soon will have 'left this country for good'. In spite of its closing invocations of American decency and humane values, the film effectively endorses segregation and ethnic exclusion (already in force through the Asian Exclusion Act of 1924). These images and practices would long haunt the Japanese-American experience.

The OWI domestic branch was constantly under fire from Congress. In addition to fears over domestic propaganda, many Southern conservatives were outraged by the OWI's emphasis on rethinking race relations. The organization's operating budget for the fiscal year beginning 1 July 1943 was practically eliminated. Lowell Mellett resigned and returned to his job as administrative assistant to Roosevelt. Expressing barely suppressed relief at the demise of the BMP, the industry mouthpiece *Boxoffice* reported that its total production had amounted to less than a hundred films totaling 110 reels, which included theatrical releases, newsreels, 16 mm non-theatrical short subjects, numerous three-minute films for 'local campaigns' and the sponsored releases of other government agencies (Dyer 1943: 25). The OWI was reorganized by Ulric Bell, who had virulently campaigned for US intervention before Pearl Harbor, and domestic activities became more closely tied to the Office of Censorship.

The production of propaganda for overseas use encountered less resistance, helped by those who saw it as an essential 'attack weapon' (Koppes and Black 1988: 54).[8] The Overseas Bureau (OB), headed by Robert Riskin in New York, was devoted to psychological warfare and circulating pro-American propaganda in allied, neutral and key embattled regions such as North Africa. Riskin's bureau soon became 'a huge operation', asserting its autonomy from the domestic direction and control of the BMP (Scott 2006: 349). As Ian Scott contends, Riskin was committed to promoting documentary as a tool for persuading audiences around the world to endorse the American cause. His ambitious 'Projections of America' films, aimed at challenging preconceived notions of the United States in foreign territories, would become (alongside the well-known Allied 'Victory' films) one of the most 'influential and substantive collections of propaganda made during the war' (Scott 2006: 347).

Riskin made use of experienced documentarists who had come to prominence during the 1930s. Willard Van Dyke made *Northwest USA* (1945), which focused on the Northwest as the 'crossroads of the air': a gateway to international trade routes with Russia, Latin America and East Asia. Imaged from high above the earth's surface, the world suggests a paradox: globalized, yet intensely conflicted, in need of unification to restore the flow of goods and capital. The film then straightforwardly documents the Northwest region's industries, agriculture and growing urban centers. Working for the CIAA with Ben Maddow (who had worked on *Native Land*), Van Dyke also made *The Bridge* (1944), which again invokes an aerial perspective in examining air transport links between dispersed Latin and North American countries.

Other documentarists working with Riskin included Irving Lerner, who received an Oscar nomination for his first OWI film, *Swedes in America* (1943), an uplifting short about assimilation and ethnic tolerance which featured that most beloved of Swedish-Americans, Ingrid Bergman. Lerner's jovial *The Autobiography of a Jeep* (1943) joined a legion of films that anthropomorphized the machinery of war. In this seamless first-person tale, the Jeep becomes a kind of pop icon: we see its fabrication, its functions in the war, its growing celebrity status. War is a serious game, where the Jeep cuts a swath of American liberation and good cheer through the most forbidding terrains. Lerner also produced, with Alexander Hammid, the internationally distributed *Hymn of the Nations* (a.k.a. *Toscanini*, 1944), a compelling film that documented Arturo Toscanini conducting Verdi's music in New York as part of celebrations to mark the overthrow of Mussolini. Another Nykino veteran, Sidney Meyers, contributed to Larry Madison's and Helen Grayson's *The Cummington Story* (1945), a dramatized tale of Eastern European war refugees resettled in Cummington, Massachusetts (known as the hometown of William Cullen Bryant, an early promoter of American cultural nationalism). Often cited for its affecting 'melting pot' theme of neighborly cooperation, *The Cummington Story* is perhaps best remembered for its stirring Aaron Copland score (Pollack 1999: 408).

Riskin's overseas work came under the control of General Dwight D. Eisenhower's Supreme Headquarters Allied Expeditionary Forces, and received broad support in executive and congressional circles. Philip Dunne was chief of film production, sharing Riskin's belief in documentary's potential to shape attitudes about the nation. For Riskin and Dunne, the idea-weapon was subtly persuasive rather than aggressive ('soft' rather than 'hard' propaganda) and needed to project the American scene as open, inclusive and harmonious. OB films like *The Cummington Story* therefore avoided ethnic stereotyping of the enemy and aimed instead to generate sympathy for the 'American way' characterized by enterprise, free speech and equal opportunities.

The Town (1945) is exemplary of this strategy. Filmed in Madison, Indiana, by Josef von Sternberg, it conjures up an idealized and generic (as its title suggests) image of Middle America: clean-cut, industrious, family-oriented, churchgoing. Von Sternberg was himself the son of Austrian immigrants, and his film stresses multi-ethnic European influences – France, Greece, Italy, Norway, Austria, Germany, Czechoslovakia – embedded in US culture and identity. 'The United States was created by men who came from the four corners of the earth', the narrator states as a ferry (suggesting perhaps both transport and an untroubled, revisionist history of migration) slowly makes its way down a quiet river. Further images – harvesting grapes, gathering eggs, stalls on the market square, varied architectural styles dotted around town – evoke Europe before the eruption of war. Indeed, the US appears nostalgically to mirror prewar Europe, and notably absent are any explicit references to African American, Mexican, Chinese, Japanese or other non-European American groups.[9] The film invokes a distinctly 'white' American vernacular grounded in Disneyesque homilies and Norman Rockwell fantasy, yet manages to promote an inclusive (if eurocentric) multiculturalism that speaks to broader tensions – Europe's broken, war-torn societies would want nothing other than to emulate this American idyll. As Scott suggests, films like *The Town* presented American society as 'to a degree, Edenic', but most OWI films were cautious about preaching an ideal 'that might appear overtly false to foreign audiences' (2006: 358). Only the final images of *The Town* gesture towards the specter of war, as the sons of immigrants travel 'back across the seas' to 'fight for freedom' and restore order to a Europe now torn asunder.

More openly didactic, Alexander Hammid's richly photographed *Valley of the Tennessee* (1944) dramatizes themes explored in *The River* (and borrows its footage): drought, flooding and New Deal solutions brought about by the TVA. Hammid had worked on documentaries like *Crisis* (1939), about the German occupation of Czechoslovakia, but perhaps is best remembered for collaborating with his wife, Maya Deren, on the avant-garde *Meshes of the Afternoon* (1943). *Valley of the Tennessee* opens with a striking shot taken through a water-drenched lens: the camera perched on a seaplane taking off from San Francisco Bay. As in many OWI films, an aerial perspective surveys the American scene; the film then returns to earth with images of rural life: wide-eyed, impoverished children crowding a shabby schoolhouse. Individual characters are introduced, each embodying a distinctive political angle, and the audience is encouraged to establish imaginary affinities. The apathetic farmer Horace Higgins seems straight out of *The Grapes of Wrath*, contrasting with the open-minded (and classically handsome) farmer Henry Clark, who is 'descended of pioneers'. A boy, inspired by the epic scale of dam building, signifies 'inquisitive youth' and (again) the 'pioneer spirit'. Also making appearances are some heroes of civil management – Senators George W. Norris and James Polk, Harcourt A. Morgan (president of the University of Tennessee) and other architects of the TVA.

Avoiding controversies relating to dam building such as ecological impacts or population displacement, the film stresses how American ingenuity and the collective pioneer spirit have translated into social progress and personal empowerment. Even the sceptical Horace Higgins sees the light. Government initiatives, the film insists, are performed for and by the people: 'The development of people is the first concern of democracy'. An animated graphic showing a bird's-eye view of dams built along the Tennessee Valley encapsulates the role of the aerial shot in visioning a 'Taylorized', industrially efficient nation. The river and tributaries, branching out like veins and capillaries, are managed by human ingenuity and collective labor, 'by and for the people', indicating the social body of the American nation. For Scott, *Valley of the Tennessee* reflects Riskin's desire to highlight 'communal harmony and organizational logic within the grass-roots populace' (2006: 358). Hammid's 'soft' propaganda film conforms to contemporary views claiming that propaganda might actually serve as a constructive social tool. Propaganda, if 'intelligently' understood, could 'identify difficulties in our society', helping people become 'aware of the beliefs and aspirations of various groups'; it also could be 'a useful source in which to seek possible solutions [. . .] and some kind of unity of social action' (Tyler 1942: 155). Hammid's final, sweeping zoom towards the face of a young girl – her expression shifting from innocent awe to determination – brings the film full circle, resolving the images of poverty-stricken children that opened the film. As in many OWI films, references to Roosevelt's famous 'Four Freedoms' speech of 1941 dominate the narration, projecting a new world led by the US and characterized by freedoms of speech, of religion, and of freedom from want and fear. Collective American perseverance and knowledge can lead the world out of war towards a 'new and better world'.

Overall, Riskin oversaw twenty-six documentaries in the OB's 'Projections of America' series. His efforts during the final months of the war to extend government involvement in overseas distribution of films with a positive American outlook were, however, never seriously heard, and the OWI's functions ceased in August 1945 (Scott 2006: 363).

HOLLYWOOD RECRUITS

Aside from filming for strategic purposes (such as aerial camerawork for bombing and reconnaissance), nonfiction filmmaking during the war might be broken down into several broad areas. These include: training and industrial films for officers, medical personnel, troops going into battle and workers at home; indoctrination (or 'orientation') films providing historical and cultural background as well as justification for US intervention; records of battle or combat films; and propaganda dealing with social and cultural themes aimed at building a collective sense of purpose and boosting morale. There was an overlap between these different areas (combat footage was incorporated into indoctrination and training films, for example, as well as into Hollywood combat dramatizations), but in general these categories suggest the uses to which documentaries were being put during the war and indicate the contexts in which they were produced and screened.

Films came from units linked to the Army Signal Corps, the Army Air Force, the Navy and other military groups. The Signal Corps was relatively new to filmmaking when the war began, but when faced with the task of training millions of troops in a short time, it quickly started turning out films (Culbert 1990a: 267). Lacking experienced filmmaking personnel, the Signal Corps recognized that Hollywood had a major role to play and enlisted many of the industry's producers, technicians and writers. Over the course of the war, the Signal Corps produced over 2,500 films for a variety of purposes, over 1,500 of which were translated for screening in allied countries (Betts 2004:

28). In addition, Hollywood studios were commissioned to make training films that were sold directly (and, it would emerge, controversially) to military and government agencies.[10] Far from glamorous, these films served specific functions: *Ignition and the Spark Plug, Tanks, The 240mm Howitzer,* and *Care and Maintenance of Tapered Roller Bearings* are just a few of the thousands of titles. One of the most widely screened items was the War Department's no. 8-154, *Sex Hygiene* (1942), made under the auspices of John Ford and 20th Century-Fox.

A prominent example of Hollywood and military collaboration was Lieutenant Colonel Frank Capra's *Why We Fight* series: seven films made for the Signal Corps that compiled newsreel footage, Axis propaganda films, staged scenes and numerous animated maps and charts – all designed to provide irrefutable evidence of the need to go to war. When Capra – known for populist films celebrating small-town American life – was enlisted by General George C. Marshall to produce documentaries for the Army, he famously protested, 'I have never before made a single documentary film. I've never even been near anybody that's made one' (Doherty 1993: 24). Whether Capra's films were in fact documentaries at all would later be questioned by Philip Dunne, who saw them as essentially 'factual films' that were 'not the realm of the true documentarian' (quoted in Scott 2006: 352).

Whether seen as factual film or documentary, the *Why We Fight* series, beginning with the first installment *Prelude to War* (1942), is steeped in the traditions both of the newsreel and of the persuasive, thesis-driven documentary that came of age in the 1930s. The opening titles ground its authority in fact, stating unequivocally that 'the purpose of these films is to give factual information'. Through the use of hortatory voiceover, stirring music and ominous images of Axis power, the *Why We Fight* films intensify the argumentative and emotional strategies laid down in Depression-era documentaries. Driven forward by a historical narrative, seamless cause and effect and rapid-fire editing (few shots are held for more than two seconds), *Prelude to War* commands our attention. Capra's format leaves little room for contemplation; it disallows questioning of the images and their assigned interpretation. It presents audiences with a simple, divided world view: two globes, one white and one black. One is a world of free Allies, the other an enslaved Axis. For Bernard F. Dick, the film doesn't produce a broader 'historical awareness', it only gives an impression of learning through the recitation of verifiable facts and dates. *Prelude to War* served as a 'summary lecture' and a 'crash course' for those largely uneducated about the causes of war (1985: 4, 7).

The *Why We Fight* series was initially conceived for indoctrination of armed forces' personnel. When the Army, with the War Activities Committee and the OWI's OB, exerted pressure to 'force' the films into commercial cinemas, they tested the limits of the public's – and the film industry's – tolerance for government propaganda (Hoorn 1990 [1942]: 377). Moreover, the Army was faced with resistance from within the government itself in the form of Mellett and the BMP, who were opposed to other government organizations exhibiting films on domestic screens. This would have constituted 'an unwarranted incursion into their civilian franchise' (Doherty 1993: 79). The industry also protested: when in May 1943 it was announced that some 150 prints of Capra's *Prelude to War* would be distributed free of charge to exhibitors, *Boxoffice* complained of an 'overdose' of war films being imposed by the government. Even at no cost, the 53-minute film would add to the war-related newsreels and the 20-minute OWI and industry-produced 'Victory' films that exhibitors had already pledged to show. This would mean that the majority of valuable screen time would be devoted to war. Exhibitors claimed to be receiving hundreds of complaints every week, mainly from women already under stress with 'sons or sweethearts' going overseas, who wanted escapist fare to help 'get away from it all' or were seeking suitable entertainment for children ('Murmurs Against Overdose' 1943: 19).

After *Prelude to War*'s civilian premiere, the *New York Times* ignored pressures towards war boosterism to complain that Capra's film 'hammers the single thesis' that the war was 'between free states and those which would enslave the world' ('*Prelude*' 1943: 16). As part of a series, three of which – *The Nazis Strike*, *Divide and Conquer* and *The Battle of Britain* – were already being screened to US troops, the film's usefulness as a single release was also questionable. Finally, the *Times* took a swipe at *Prelude to War*'s oversimplifications and infantilization of its viewers: '[The film's] generalizations are vague and it leans heavily on patriotic symbolism to convey a sense of America. It leaves many obvious "why" questions completely unanswered' (16). All told, Capra's important documentary flopped as a commercial release, though it fared far better in the military sphere where, as of May 1943, it had been screened to over six million troops.

Capra's Special Services Branch unit also would produce *The Negro Soldier*, a film designed to address perceptions, such those of the African American soldier James C. Austin, that the nation was fighting a 'white war'. As Austin wrote to Elmer Davis: 'There are no colored bomber crews [. . .] there is no need for any machinists, electricians, machine-gunsmiths, welders, or aircraft technicians *if they are colored*' (Culbert and Suid 1991: 1704). A somewhat absurd memo sent to Capra from the War Department's expert on race relations, Donald Young, laid out the need to combat such thinking by producing an image of African Americans marketable to the broader public. In a lengthy list of 'typical subjects to be avoided', Young forbade showing any work that might require 'a strong back but no brain', the 'singing of spirituals', tap dancing, crap shooting and 'Negro dialect', and suggested playing down 'colored soldiers most Negroid in appearance'. He concluded:

'In short, avoid strictly any scene which shows Negroes in any role which may become stereotyped as characteristically Negro' (Culbert and Suid 1991: 1706–7).[11]

In spite of such egregious origins, the finished film was well received and went on to become mandatory military viewing. Capra had little hands-on involvement, leaving the directing to the relatively untested Stuart Heisler, director of *The Glass Key* (1942), and the writing to African American author Carlton Moss. Framed by the dramatic device of a preacher (Moss) delivering a sermon to a rapt congregation, *The Negro Soldier* lays out a history of American military heroism that foregrounds the roles of African Americans. In scene after scene, African Americans are represented as 'neat, clean, orderly, responsible, patriotic'; the black community is pervasively 'middle class' and aspiring chiefly to the status quo (Cripps and Culbert 1998: 118). For a brief, controversial period, the film was withheld from public viewing and limited to military screenings. The *Los Angeles Sentinel* was incensed, calling it 'not only one of the best pictures of its kind but [. . .] a powerful and telling refutation of racism' (Hardwicke 1944: 13). Through endorsements from the NAACP and celebrities like Lena Horne, *The Negro Soldier* gained wider distribution, though mainstream success eluded it. For Cripps and Culbert, the long-term influence of the film should not be underestimated; it was a 'watershed in the use of film to promote racial tolerance', indicating the role film could play in civil rights activism and initiating the development of the racial 'message' film (1998: 130).

Other prominent Hollywood figures such as John Ford, John Huston and William Wyler, well-versed in Hollywood's populist strategies, were turning out taut combat records that strove to rally the public to root for 'our boys'. During the war there was extensive overlap between documentary and the strategies of dramatic fiction; as Thomas Doherty suggests, combat documentaries in particular had 'an implied contract' with homefront spectators. This arrangement effectively stated that

> though a documentary, we will use the familiar conventions of the Hollywood feature film to accentuate the experience, but as a documentary we want you to remember that what you behold is really real. Thus, though the combat reports used the identifiable voices of Hollywood actors for narration and dramatic readings, heavenly choirs and musical soundtracks to modulate emotion, and transparently staged scenes for expository or polemical purposes, they also insisted on their special status as authentic records of wartime action and hence cinema that warranted special credence and respect. Wartime audiences and War Department filmmakers engaged in a mutual agreement to switch between Hollywood convenience and documentary rigor. (Doherty 1993: 252)

Of course standards of 'documentary rigor' were hardly, at this stage, set in stone, and much nonfiction work coming *both* from Hollywood veterans and those previously trained in documentary filmmaking continued to draw on a mixture of factual and staged footage, featuring professional actors and manipulating emotions via musical scores, just as documentaries had through the Depression years.

In Ford's work, combat documentary clearly received the benefits of Hollywood professionalism. His *The Battle of Midway* (1942) was the first US combat film, documenting the Japanese attack on the US Navy at Midway Atoll in the Pacific. Ford was well positioned to make films that stressed the urgency of America's mission against fascism. Before the war, he had directed intelligent, liberal dramas such as *Stagecoach* (1939) and *The Grapes of Wrath* (1940), subtly critiquing social prejudice, hierarchy and bloated corporate bureaucracy. *The Battle of Midway* takes up the anti-fascist cause with messianic fervor. Reflecting both military standards and Ford's innovative style, it was shot with handheld cameras on 16 mm color stock. Color also reinforces the film's ideological function, producing a powerful aesthetic response while conveying the feel of an amateur home movie (16 mm color stock was first marketed to amateurs in the 1930s).[12] The result is an intimate, visceral experience of battle.

Patriotic feelings are provoked through arresting color images of fighting, framed by shots of waving flags and marching soldiers. Drawing from a stock of Ford regulars (Henry Fonda and Jane Darwell added homespun touches to the narration, Alfred Newman contributed a rousing score), the 18-minute film laid down a standard for the combat documentary's intense immediacy. Hereafter combat films – both documentary and fiction – would aim to create a palpable sense of being in the midst of the fighting. Filmmakers became 'embedded' reporters: the body holding the camera was clearly in as much danger as the soldiers being filmed. Indeed, Ford sustained an eye injury at Midway, and as a result the film earned its director not only an Oscar but a Purple Heart.

John Huston's *The Battle of San Pietro* (1945) introduced elements of gritty realism that surpassed even *The Battle of Midway*'s arresting footage. Huston's first combat film, the technicolor *Report from the Aleutians* (1943), had mitigated any negative impressions of battle by positing a redemptive politics of the 'fight for freedom'. *The Battle of San Pietro* instead suspends redemptive messages until its very end. Made with hand-held Eyemo newsreel cameras on 35 mm black and white stock, *San Pietro* documents fighting at the Italian village of San Pietro Infine during December 1943: the first time that Italian forces joined the Allies against the Germans. Unusually, the film opens not with patriotic flag waving and marching troops but with San Pietro in ruins. The commentator reads from a guidebook describing sights such as the fifteenth-century church of St Peter: 'Note interesting treatment of chancel', he states, over an image of a bombed out shell of a building. A dead woman lies on the ground where she fell, photographed from two angles. One open eye stares blankly upwards, perhaps mirroring our own conflicting desires both to see and to shut our eyes to the tragedy of war. Like other combat records, the film matter-of-factly plots the progress of the battle through numerous maps and charts, but Huston's work is anything but matter of fact, showing war truly as hell on earth, to such an extent that the film can be read as condemning acts of war.

While never precisely unpatriotic, with implicit figurations of 'us' versus 'them', the film's very brutality invites ambivalence and the possibility of pacifist critique. The spectator him/herself becomes a vulnerable body aligned to the camera. During the battle scenes, the sound of bullets (added in postproduction) can be heard whizzing past the cameraman's ears. The results are clear: soldiers are shown bundled into body bags, their faces grotesquely disfigured. At first, the liberation of San Pietro seems to reveal little more than destroyed buildings and a handful of broken people. Notable are images of women emerging from the ruins, figures of resistance and resilience. Not soldiers, but simply survivors, they work amid the destruction, carrying baggage and heavy furniture – one woman balances a coffin on her head. While 'heavenly choirs' on the soundtrack threaten to dissolve the film's cumulative impact, the images of destruction and suffering recall other powerful statements of wartime carnage such as *The Spanish Earth*.

Indeed, the film was considered too strong for public release without extensive cuts. Army officials reportedly walked out during a preview, calling it 'antiwar', though the military eventually would come around, deeming it suitable for training troops (Huston 1980: 119). Years later, Huston called this and his subsequent film, *Let There Be Light* (1946), 'incendiary pacifist documents', as opposed to his jingoistic *Report from the Aleutians*, which he labeled a 'tainted' propaganda film full of 'patriotic cheerleading' (quoted in Mackenzie 2000: 23).[13] After the war, Huston passionately lobbied to make the ill-fated war critique *The Red Badge of Courage* (1951), choosing to feature as the deserter-turned-hero at the story's center the Second World War's most decorated soldier, Audie Murphy.

THE MEMPHIS BELLE (A STORY OF A FLYING FORTRESS) (1944)

One of the most successful (critically and commercially) combat films was William Wyler's *The Memphis Belle*, a prominent example of documentary and propaganda merging almost seamlessly. The term propaganda would seem to exclude documentary truth, conjuring up forms of address where excessive bias and selectivity are employed to promote a specific ideological position – but the US documentary tradition up to this point hardly carried with it assumptions of pure objectivity. Wartime films like *The Memphis Belle* intensified documentary's existing affinities with propaganda. Wyler's film presents itself as axiomatically the 'right' perspective, while evading any obvious appearances of bias. It does this largely by setting careful limits on its focus in terms of narrative, point of view and engagement with social and historical contexts.

As part of what Jeanine Basinger calls the 'second wave' of combat films, Wyler's 'visual shorthand' compactly gestures to issues already covered in films like *Prelude to War*. By 1944, audiences were well-versed in the justifications for going to war (Basinger 2003: 110). The strategy behind *The Memphis Belle* was instead to put a human face on the conflict, placing the spectator in the middle of the action while giving every indication of being an accurate record of wartime experience.

Combat films are a form of war documentary that might almost escape more obvious signs of bias by narrowing their frames of reference to the urgency and immediacy of battle. If *The Memphis Belle* appears free from artifice, it is precisely because it successfully constructs a 'here and now' simultaneity that limits other points of view. Taking a cue from filmmakers like Flaherty, Wyler engages the filmgoer in following a self-contained event or process unfolding, seemingly in real time, in front of the camera. At the same time the film minimizes evidence of overt manipulation and strips down (while not wholly eliminating) effects such as voiceover and music, achieving a purer impression of unreconstructed reality. In this sense, the film turns away from the more theatrical style of 1930s documentary towards the compressed 'slice of life' storytelling that would further develop in the 1950s.

The Memphis Belle unfolds in linear fashion, documenting a single mission on a single day, 17 May 1943, flying along with the crew of a Boeing B-17F 'Flying Fortress'. Heightening the drama is the fact that the *Memphis Belle* is set to be the first B-17 to complete twenty-five bombing missions over Europe. This is the crew's final mission, after which they can return home. The journey is both actual and metaphorical: a journey into enemy territory and a spiritual, cathartic flirtation with death in the name of freedom, the home and the nation. The film's intimate connection with the audience further draws on anthropomorphizing the hardware of war: the B-17 was named for the pilot Robert K. Morgan's girlfriend, Margaret Polk, who lived in Tennessee. Hence, in a film that shows no women other than the Queen, the 'star' is both a plane and (indirectly) a woman.

Much of what is shown was manipulated for dramatic effect. Wyler's finished film drew from over 19,000 feet of film exposed during five missions flown with the 91st Bomb Group based in Bassingbourn, Cambridgeshire. Much of the color footage was taken aboard the B-17 *Invasion II*, until that plane failed to return from a mission. Wyler shifted to the *Memphis Belle*, and a good deal of the action seen on screen actually occurred during the crew's second-to-last, and not final, mission. The *Memphis Belle*'s twenty-fifth and final mission was, in fact, flown over Lorient, France, not Wilhelmshaven. Indeed, the *Memphis Belle* wasn't the first B-17 to complete twenty-five missions, an honor that went to 'Hell's Angels', a combat group that would go on to complete more missions – 300 – than any other. To enhance the film's seamless realism, some scenes were restaged in California.[14]

This is not to underplay the dangers faced by Wyler and the crew. On earlier missions, four crewmembers had been killed and the *Memphis Belle* once suffered more than fifty holes in its fuselage and wings. By the war's end, 20 percent of the 91st Bomb Group would be dead. The radio operator Robert Hanson recalled once being saved by leaning over to sneeze, just before a shell went flying through the space where his head had been ('Robert Hanson' 2005: 66). Wyler himself nearly died at one point when his oxygen was cut off. Wyler was, in many ways, very well suited to combat filming. Born into a Jewish family, he had witnessed war as a child in German-occupied Mulhouse, France; over the years he had earned respect in Hollywood for skillfully directing tense action scenes. After finishing the highly successful anti-Nazi picture *Mrs. Miniver* (1942) ('propaganda worth a hundred battleships' according to Winston Churchill [quoted in Kozloff 2008: 459]), Wyler became one of the first high-profile figures to give up a Hollywood career and enlist full-time in the military.

Though *The Memphis Belle* avoids openly fictional touches, it unfolds with a formal and technical precision that on closer examination betrays its director's Hollywood roots. The combat genre was increasingly blurring the boundaries between fact and fiction: documentaries inspired popular Hollywood accounts, while Hollywood stars were becoming real-life heroes. Like a fiction film, *The Memphis Belle* has a strong narrative drive and carefully mounted scenes of suspense and action. Unlike many combat films, it is sparing in its use of non-diegetic voiceover and music, which enhances its mesmerizing effect. It also benefits from accomplished and often stunning camera work. Shot on 16 mm color (a German U-boat had sunk the ship transporting Wyler's 35 mm cameras to Europe), much of the combat cinematography was by professional camera operators William Clothier and William V. Skall, as well as by Wyler and First Lieutenant Harold J. Tannenbaum, who would not survive to see the film completed.[15] Filming conditions were extreme, and not only when the B-17 came under fire. As the film shows, the planes were not pressurized and sub-zero conditions meant that cameras would freeze; reloading film magazines could end in frostbite. The B-17 was 'tortuously cramped', with conditions considered among the toughest of the war with the possible exception of submarine duty (Miller 2006: 82, 122).

My intention is not to undermine *The Memphis Belle*'s impact: many with experience of bombing missions have praised it over the years for its verisimilitude and accuracy. Yet to draw an analogy to the 'Flying Fortress' itself – where a powerful steel frame bolstered what was in other ways a fragile craft covered in thin aluminium skin that was vulnerable to puncture – the film gives an appearance of unassailable formal and narrative integrity but is in fact 'riddled with cracks' (Comolli and Narboni 1976: 27). For all its realism, Wyler's film is expert propaganda. As Dana Polan suggests, we often think of propaganda as 'an art of the cheap and easy blunt effect'. Wartime propagandists, however, had to work hard 'to secure their propaganda effects and, as we look closely at the strategies they employed, we find both a relative success and relative limits to what they could achieve' (2004: 39–40). *The Memphis Belle* was only part of a larger propaganda network which included the widespread publicity produced for the Eighth Air Force – a 'high octane outfit', according to the reporter Harrison Salisbury, supported by an extensive public relations contingent. The Eighth also included a number of high-profile celebrities, including (then) Major Jimmy Stewart and Captain Clark Gable. This was not just a fighting unit but a successful propaganda machine, and the air war was seen as key to generating press attention that could capture the public's imagination and support.

The Memphis Belle derives its force from constructing a highly unified ideological and subject position. This is produced by a range of effects, from the closely observed faces of the crew members intercut with images of the skies they survey to the direct address of the narrator who draws 'you', the viewer, into the action. This marks an important shift in the combat genre, moving the audience from observer to participant (Basinger 2003: 114). Subjectivity can be variously constructed in documentary, as David MacDougall has shown: 'A film can involve the subjectivity of its subjects, the viewer, and the institutional or individual filmmaker in compound ways. From a textual point of view, each of these perspectives can become an "I" from which the other two are redefined as "you" or "they"' (1995: 223). Glossing Nick Brown, MacDougall recalls the overlapping elements that construct the 'spectator-in-the-text', which can include codes of position, narrative, metaphor and moral attitude. It should be said that not all spectators, of course, will be automatically drawn into this web of cinematic devices, since much depends on 'who we are and what we bring to the film' (1995: 223). Still *The Memphis Belle* strives, at multiple levels, to knit spectators into the frame so they might occupy a virtual place alongside the men of the 91st Bomb Group.

The film begins with evocative shots of middle England in summertime, establishing a *mise-en-scène* of rural order and tranquillity. A simple pan to the left, however, reveals an airfield, shifting from travelogue fancy to urgent reality, as the commentary by Eugene Kern breaks in: 'This is a battle front, a battle front like no other' – not a traditional front based on ground war, but an 'air front'. The stress on the air war recalls a persistent theme in Second World War documentary: the prominence of the airplane and the bombing raid, captured by the motion picture camera and the aerial shot. Just as the gun and camera shared a special relationship in pre- and early cinema, so the airplane, bomb and camera shared symbiotic relations in Second World War cinematography.

As mentioned above, Paul Virilio, who himself witnessed the aerial bombardment of Nantes during the Second World War, has surveyed the complex ways in which film technology and aerial warfare have coexisted over time, and how they have combined – from the First World War to the Gulf War – to make wartime destruction a potent visual spectacle. In *The Memphis Belle*, as the gaze of the camera lines up with the crosshairs of the machine gun, we witness what Virilio has called the 'deadly harmony' between camera and weapon: 'a war of pictures and sounds is replacing the war of objects (projectiles and missiles)' (1989: 4). *The Memphis Belle* is not merely a straightforward documentary representation of the aerial war. It is, rather, a complex technical and cultural artifact that engages with broader, multimedia processes of producing an aerial gaze over the war itself. *The Memphis Belle* is closely linked to an emerging *aerial perception* of war: a form of perception characterized by distance and remoteness from conflict (while simultaneously 'witnessing' from above). This results in a collective sense of mastery created by a process of overlooking. Designated bombing sites are described as 'pinpoints on the map of Europe – targets, to be destroyed'.

During the 1930s and 1940s, the development of what Virilio calls 'global vision' was rapidly being perfected through innovations both in photography and flight (1989: 1). In the pages of *US Camera*, one could witness aerial views over the earth never before seen: in one shot, a 'global panorama' of the Black Hills of North Dakota, taken from somewhere near 'the division between the troposphere and the stratosphere' also reveals 'the actual curvature of the earth – photographed from an elevation of 72,395 feet, the highest point ever reached by man' (Maloney 1936: 188–9). As the emphasis on aerial perspectives in documentaries ranging from *Northwest USA* and *The Bridge* to *The Memphis Belle* attests, the abstract concept of a shrinking globe was being authenticated through photographic evidence, even as the world was experiencing that most radical experience of divided perception – global warfare. Aboard the *Memphis Belle* we experience vulnerability, but it is difficult to deny the simultaneous exhilaration derived from flight and the mastery of its view. *The Memphis Belle* encapsulates the marriage of ideology and aesthetics in aerial warfare: the sunlight glistening off planes

Figure 12. *The Memphis Belle* (1944). US Army Air Forces First Motion Picture Unit. Courtesy of the British Film Institute.

arrayed in neat formation, against a blue sky, affords an undeniable visual impact.

The first half of the film shows preparations, taking off and journeying towards Germany, and outlines the complex details of the mission. The planes rise from the runway in a series of mobile shots taken from below, alongside and mounted on wings and landing gear. As the pace increases, music and voiceover are suspended for dramatic effect and the noise of roaring engines intensifies. Once in the air each member of the crew is introduced and succinct background stories are sketched in. Importantly, each crewmember is ascribed a home town, encouraging local interest and viewer identification. Captain Robert Morgan (called a 'hard drinking hell-raiser' by Donald Miller [2006: 79]) is from Asheville, North Carolina; radio operator and gunner Sergeant Bob Hanson is a construction worker from Spokane, Washington; tail gunner Sergeant John Quinlan is from Yonkers, New York. The male, all-white crew is huddled in the plane, the latter implicitly sexualized as the absent girlfriend figure and glamorous 'star' – Betty Grable or Rita Hayworth, perhaps – indicated by the 'leggy redhead in a bathing suit' painted on its nose (which, later in the film, Morgan climbs up to kiss) (Miller 2006: 117–18). But the *Memphis Belle* is also a kind of mother figure, sheltering the men in its cramped belly.

The airborne journey is tense and hypnotic. Suspended in air along with the crew, we sense the icy stillness of the surroundings; close-ups of the crew's faces are intercut with point-of-view shots of the sky and the earth below. This is an intimate space within the mother ship, the sole vantage point from which we view the outside world. Alongside the plane, vapor trails extend from the wings of bombers arrayed in elegant formation. As the sky's intense blueness ('at once luminous and laden with gloom' [Virilio 1989: 10]) fades to white, the soundtrack withdraws to sparing voiceover and the humming of engines. Aligned with the sights of the crew, guns and cameras 'cover the sky [. . .] in every direction'. The pace is eerily calm as the planes rise towards the stratosphere. The narrator's direct address continues to draw the viewer in: 'you plot your course, check your equipment, wait [. . .] and think'.

The incantatory role of poetic narration (written by Jerome Chodorov, Lester Koenig and Wyler) comes to the fore here, underscored by the steady humming of engines: 'You look out at the strange world beyond, reflections in plexiglass [. . .] like nothing you ever saw before outside of a dream'. But there is a gap between calm appearance and stark reality: the sublime vision combines beauty and danger. The vapor trails that 'stream the heavens' are 'far from beautiful' since they point 'like signposts in the sky for the enemy to spot us'. As if aware that the film is on the verge of imparting too much beauty in the midst of war, Wyler cuts to a very unbeautiful sequence lasting just over three minutes, where animated maps and charts reveal the plans behind the mission and enhance the sense of authority and factuality of the film itself.[16]

The 'here and now' is restored as anti-aircraft flak begins to burst near the plane. The sight of these 'harmless looking silent puffs of smoke' is at first almost pleasing, but as an explosion erupts nearby, sedate camera movement suddenly yields to violent shaking and an awkward loss of framing. Apparently Wyler, scurrying around the plane, was so anxious to capture dramatic flak shots that he 'begged Morgan to steer the bomber into the thick of the shrapnel field' (Miller 2006: 118). We now physically sense the menace in the air. Enemy fighters appear on the horizon, and tense scenes of battle ensue. Seemingly out of nowhere, monotonous suspense turns to jittery, dramatic action. The camera shakes and swoops, struggling to keep the enemy planes in frame just as the gunners struggle to keep aim. The narration now begins to betray an anger and bias that was, until now, largely suppressed. We are told that 'the Hun' lurks below and that the Germans 'lust for conquest'. The landscape may appear like any other from above, but this is the land that brought 'torment and anguish into countless American homes'.

As the target, Wilhelmshaven, comes into the *Memphis Belle*'s sights, the narrator utters 'bombs away' with little dramatic intonation. The bombs float down as if in slow motion, slipping alongside and below the plane. The voiceover gives way to the drone of engines as several shots linger over the smoke rising below, though the destruction remains distant and remote. The understatement of 'mission accomplished' might seem surprising, as this would appear to be the climax the film has been building towards. But the overall tone is consistent with the businesslike detachment of the aerial war. Bombs are 'delivered' to their 'targets'. No mention is made of houses or people, just 'factories', 'rail junctions', 'docks' and 'submarine pens'. The narrator argues that the bombing runs will help save the lives of Allied soldiers.

History would make clearer much of what was not fully visible from the air. The year 1943 saw Europe in the midst of a total war of mutual annihilation. Wilhelmshaven contained a subcamp of the notorious Neuengamme concentration camp; two-thirds of Wilhelmshaven's buildings were destroyed by Allied bombs. In one civil damage report after a USAAF bombing raid of 26 February 1943, bombs fell heavily on civilian areas; two schools and two police stations were damaged and nineteen civilians were reported dead (Hamilton 1999: 97). According to one Air Force publicist, the intent of *The Memphis Belle* was to show 'the ultimate destruction of Germany from the air' (quoted in Miller 2006: 119), but the human costs of bombing are carefully underplayed. Around the time the *Memphis Belle* was running its daylight raids, residential and urban centers were being targeted by massive Allied night-time campaigns. By the war's end, millions of civilians on both sides had been killed.

The novelist W. G. Sebald reconstructed the effects of some of these raids, recalling in particular the intensive bombing on 27 July 1943 of Hamburg (dubbed 'Operation Gomorrah' by the Allies), 120 kilometers from Wilhelmshaven. In the firestorms that ensued, 45,000 civilians are thought to have died. Sebald writes:

> [A]n hour after the first bombs had dropped the whole airspace was a sea of flames as far as the eye could see [. . .] the fire, now rising 2,000 metres into the sky, snatched oxygen to itself so violently that the air currents reached hurricane force [. . .] Those who had fled from their air-raid shelters sank, with grotesque contortions, in the thick bubbles thrown up by the melting asphalt [. . .] horribly disfigured corpses lay everywhere. (Sebald 2003: 27–8)

Aerial perception depends upon a detached, mediatized perspective that can suppress the details of death and destruction. In this 'sanitized' view, Patricia Zimmermann suggests, 'the physical and psychic horrors of war, its micro-practices and dismemberments, its fragmentations and disruptions, must be repressed' (2000: 51).

In *The Memphis Belle*, as smoke rises from the explosions below, the narrator prevents contemplation of the destruction by sustaining the airborne point of view, focusing attention on dangers still lurking in the skies. A dramatic

Figure 13. Ruins of Wendenstrasse, Hamburg ('Operation Gomorrha', July 1943).
Photograph: Hugo Schmidt-Luchs. Courtesy of Ullstein Bild.

battle with German fighters ensues and the voiceover track is taken over by
the voices of the crewmembers, seemingly captured on intercom during the
heat of battle (though recorded in Los Angeles when they were on a War
Bonds tour). We hear the waist gunner Clarence Winchell muttering, 'I see
him, I'm on 'em. C'mon you son of a . . .' – only to be drowned out by the
sound of firing. Even in the midst of war, 'bad language' was forbidden by the
Production Code. The sound here helps to intensify immersion in the action:
as a damaged B-17 careens out of control, the calls of 'c'mon you guys get out
of that plane' add urgency to the images. As another damaged plane careens
away from the formation, the images fade to black, leaving the fate of the
Memphis Belle and her crew suspended in the air.

The film breaks from its here and now intensity to return to the base in
England, where the ground crew 'sweat out the mission'. Parallel editing – a
standard technique for creating tension – briefly takes over until spatial unity
is restored as planes are heard in the distance. Planes begin to land one by one,
unloading their exhausted, sometimes mangled, passengers. The *Memphis
Belle*, the 'ship everyone has been pulling for', is, in dramatic fashion, the last
to touch down. To guarantee Wyler his grand Hollywood finale, group com-
mander Colonel Wray had radioed the other planes to land before the *Memphis*

Belle, and Morgan added his own flourish by buzzing the field (Miller 2006: 120–1). Having completed twenty-five missions, the American heroes can finally go home.

The Memphis Belle shows that documentary can, perhaps counter-intuitively, be at once propagandistic and also ring true for countless Americans. Wyler's film was highly popular for a wartime documentary: 500 prints were distributed by Paramount to over 10,000 theaters. It received glowing reviews, one appearing in unprecedented fashion on the front page of the *New York Times*. Wyler's 'fact film', exclaimed Bosley Crowther, had 'visioned the whole course of a bombing mission in all its real and exciting detail' (Crowther 1944: 1). The story of the *Memphis Belle* would become the stuff of legend, spawning imitations such as *Twelve O'Clock High* (1950) and lending immortality to yet another piece of fondly remembered military hardware.

The Memphis Belle intertwines aesthetics and ideology: the captivating visuals of the airborne camera work together with the technologies of war under the auspices of documentary truth. A close examination suggests questions pertinent to documentary more generally. For instance, are the truths produced by documentaries always subjective, or can they be universal? What is at stake when subjective views are presented as universals? In this sense the questions raised by *The Memphis Belle* are not unique to wartime propaganda.

The Memphis Belle is, in short, an idea-weapon: its ideological messages are constituted as much by what the film suppresses as what it chooses to show. Indeed, its impact is grounded in this 'less is more' strategy, which constructs a highly restricted point of view. Less overtly didactic than the *Why We Fight* series, it nonetheless joins these Second World War propaganda documentaries in projecting the 'truth' of the American nation's moral rightness and collective mission. The documentaries of the Second World War helped determine this sense of military and moral superiority for a generation; at the same time they solidified the image of a nation with unified goals and desires. As the voices of soldiers in John Ford's *December 7th* (1943) state, 'we are all alike . . . we are all Americans'.

The Second World War reinforced not only the nation's superpower status, but confirmed a pervasive sense of American ideological superiority: it was acclaimed as a moral war, battling against evil fascists. Photographic evidence – both still and motion picture – taken by horrified Allied troops during the liberation of concentration camps such as Bergen-Belsen easily reinforced these notions. The extreme nature of this atrocity footage, showing piles of anonymous dead bodies and shockingly emaciated survivors, meant that its appropriateness for domestic screenings was (and still is) debated, but it was officially, and very widely, screened to German civilians as part of efforts to indoctrinate a collective sense of culpability (Haggith 2005: 33–5).

Yet the end of war also saw political polarizations at home, tentatively kept in check by wartime patriotism, break into open hostilities. Though as recently as 1942 *Time Magazine* had selected Joseph Stalin as its 'Man of the Year' and Hollywood films like *Mission to Moscow* (1943) had flattered the Soviets, after the war, powerful anti-Soviet and anti-communist sentiments gained the upper hand. The FBI and its long-standing director, J. Edgar Hoover, were highly paranoid about communist infiltration of labor and government posts, and even during the war (with Roosevelt's consent) had been systematically investigating individuals and organizations, compiling extensive lists. Still reeling from the left-wing political organizing of the 1930s, Hoover and the FBI remained convinced that the nation would be destabilized if it dropped its guard during its alliance with the Soviet Union, and that the Allied coalition had in fact made the nation more vulnerable than ever to communist 'subterfuge' (Sbardellati 2008: 416). The House Committee on Un-American Activities (HCUA or HUAC), established as a special investigating committee in 1938, prepared documents listing 'Communist front organizations' that could be 'characterized by [. . .] the rigid conformity of these organizations to the Communist pattern, their interlocking personnel, and their methods generally used to deceive the American public' (the term 'front' transformed from meaning 'coalition' into a facade or conspiracy) (Committee on Un-American Activities 1948: 141). Hoover would single out the potentially dangerous role of motion pictures in mass culture, fearing the appearance of 'more films having a propaganda effect [that would be] favorable to the Communist ideology' (quoted in Sbardellati 2008: 412). When the Soviets tested their first atomic bomb in 1949, four years after the US destroyed Hiroshima and Nagasaki, the Cold War escalated further. For more than fifty years the world would live under the sword of Damocles known as MAD: Mutually Assured Destruction.

By the early 1950s, the nation was witnessing the severe repressions of Senator Joseph McCarthy's 'purges' of 'Communists and spies', with particular focus on the media industries (Barnouw 1983: 222). To the shock of many who had come of age in the era of the Film and Photo League, once-idealistic visions of ideological coalition and secure civil liberties were thrown into disarray: anti-fascist organizations formed before the Second World War in support of Spanish Republicans or against Japanese imperialism were labeled by HUAC and the FBI as 'Communist sympathizers' and 'fronts'. The 1950 publication of the pamphlet 'Red Channels: The Report of Communist Influence in Radio and Television' by the right-wing news journal *Counterattack* exemplified the impact of Red Scare tactics on the media. It placed leading figures such as Aaron Copland, Dashiell Hammett, Lena Horne, Langston Hughes, Orson Welles and pioneers from the documentary movement such as Leo Hurwitz under the category of communist 'subversives'. Others, such as

Irving Lerner, Lester Koenig and Ben Maddow (who had established a successful career as a screenwriter) found themselves facing the blacklist; some, like Maddow, finally cracked under the pressures of social and professional exclusion and 'named names' before HUAC (Burns 1998).

In March and April of 1954, a now-legendary series of exposés showing an increasingly volatile McCarthy were broadcast on Edward R. Murrow's influential *See It Now*, damaging McCarthy's reputation while establishing television news as the new frontier for political documentary. Cinema documentary, on the other hand, was not faring particularly well, and was notably absent from commercial theaters. At the end of the war, documentary film had seemed poised to serve as a dominant force in shaping the nation's and world's vision of America. More than fifty million dollars had been spent annually on documentaries during the Second World War (Basinger 2003: 113). Robert Riskin's concept of a Hollywood–Washington liaison that would fund and distribute pro-US documentaries after the war, however, never came to pass, though the Marshall Plan and later the United States Information Agency (USIA) did distribute postwar documentaries on a smaller scale (Scott 2006: 363). Hollywood reclaimed the theatrical screen time it had nobly sacrificed in support of the war, while appropriating aspects of documentary as a style in nostalgic war films and major trends such as *film noir*.

A few large-scale documentary projects lingered that had been conceived during the war, such as Huston's *Let There Be Light*, a frank treatment of combat-related post-traumatic disorders made for the US Signal Corps. Huston's film was potentially a vehicle for representing peaceful reparations: care and gentle attention to traumatized soldiers replacing the jingoism of the war years. Still, the status of *Let There Be Light*'s stark revelations as factual made it seem that much more dangerous to military officials as a critique of the 'warrior myth'.[17] More complexly, it unsettlingly images a postwar sense of what is not fully representable, of what Michael Chanan calls the 'inner space of the invisible wound we call the experience of trauma' (2007: 150). The film was banned from public view by the War Department.[18]

Taking a cue from influential figures like Grierson in Britain, much US documentary came to depend on corporate sponsorship, often with implicit ties to government interests. With lavish funding from Standard Oil, Flaherty made *Louisiana Story* (1948), drawing on the contributions of editor Helen van Dongen and cameraman Richard Leacock. Flaherty's elegant, highly wrought study at times seems to question the place of oil drilling in the remote Louisiana bayou, but as a 'subtle piece of public relations' it concludes with a message that accepts the need for 'progress' (Anon. 1948: 96). Such theatrical successes, however, were few. By 1952, Richard Griffith was sending out a cautionary message: 'Since few people now have real faith in the causes which documentary customarily promoted, it is hardly strange that they are indifferent to the documentaries themselves', he complained; 'this is the background against which American documentary makers have had to work. It is a story of sporadic endeavor, with nearly as many styles and purposes as individuals' (Griffith 1952: 315).

Griffith noted that, with the exception of films such as *Louisiana Story* and *The Quiet One* (1948), few postwar documentaries were 'breaking down the barriers' and having a wider impact (1952: 315). Indeed *The Quiet One*, made by Frontier Films' veteran Sidney Meyers, was essentially a piece of fiction scripted by James Agee, Janice Loeb and Helen Levitt (who also shot it), and even made use of Meyers himself on screen, playing a psychiatrist. Like Flaherty's film, *The Quiet One* used a young boy to create a protagonist who, like (it was presumed) the camera, faced the world with an 'innocent' eye. Meyers's film was made in Harlem on a small budget, but its focus on a troubled African American child touched a nerve with urban audiences; the nation was on the verge of revolutionary developments in the Civil Rights Movement.

In an effort to turn around notions that American documentary was on its last legs, in 1954 Griffith curated a major retrospective at the New York Museum of Modern Art, 'The American Scene: 1945–1953'. This included works by established filmmakers such as Van Dyke, Hammid, Meyers, Maddow, Fred Zinnemann and Henwar Rodakiewicz, along with names that were relatively new to US documentary circles such as Levitt, Loeb, Nicholas Read and Herbert Matter (Starr 1954: 44). Some significant films, however, were left out, including George Stoney's highly acclaimed *All My Babies* (1953), an intimate and sensitive study of childbirth and the work of black midwives in the South, commissioned by the Georgia State Health Department. The film's sponsors had restricted its distribution to medical uses only, deeming its graphic birth sequences 'not yet appropriate for general viewing' (Starr 1954: 45). Griffith's eight-week MOMA series made its mark, but couldn't reverse documentary's migration from the big to the small screen.

By the mid-1950s, the most widely seen US nonfiction film work was being produced for television news and educational programs like *See It Now* and *Omnibus*. Newsreels were on the wane, thanks to television's ascendancy, and by the end of the 1950s *Paramount News*, *Pathé News* and *The March of Time* had all ceased production, with Hearst's *News of the Day* and *Fox Movietone* soon to follow. Corporate sponsorship in most areas of documentary, from the occasional theatrical film to television, was the norm, and concerns about 'public service versus profit motives' dominated the debates of producers and directors.[19] As Erik Barnouw argues, 'closely watched by top executives, documentaries became institutional, depersonalized' (1983: 227).

NOTES

1. The term 'small' war refers to overseas war, waged at a distance.
2. Slocum glosses Michael S. Sherry.
3. See especially Renov (1988: 69–115) and Connie Field's film *The Life and Times of Rosie the Riveter* (1980).
4. Letter to Elmer Davis, 19 September 1942. See also James C. Austin to Davis, 1 August 1943, in Culbert and Suid (1991: 1704).
5. Grew had for a short time, after the attack on Pearl Harbor, been held by the Japanese government.
6. Advertisement for RKO's *Behind the Rising Sun*, *Boxoffice*, 17 July 1943, p. 28.
7. Letter to Elmer Davis, 27 October 1942.
8. These included William Donovan, who was in the process of setting up the Office of Strategic Services (forerunner of the CIA).
9. There is only one very brief shot of an African American in the film.
10. The organization responsible for funneling War Department requests to studios – the Research Council of the Academy of Motion Picture Arts and Sciences, headed by Fox's Darryl F. Zanuck – was investigated for favoritism in awarding contracts and even suspected of using instructional filmmaking as a means for keeping relatives of studio executives out of frontline duties. The four-month investigation resulted in no hard evidence of profiteering. See Culbert (1990a: xvii).
11. Memo to Frank Capra, Spring 1942.
12. Color was the film stock of choice for the military, since black and white couldn't register enemy camouflage. Hand-held color techniques were perfected by amateurs during the 1930s.
13. See also Mathews (1985: 6).
14. See Friedman and Simons (2008) and Miller (2006).
15. Tannenbaum was killed during a mission over France on 16 April 1943. See Kozloff (2008: 459).
16. Though the military favored color stock, many commentators were concerned that it might make 'war too pretty a picture' (Doherty 1993: 264).
17. According to Huston: 'it boils down to the fact that [the army] wanted to maintain the "warrior" myth, which said that our American soldiers went to war and came back all the stronger' (Huston 1980: 125).
18. The War Department's official reason for limiting screenings to military audiences was that the 'privacy of patients was invaded' (Pennington 1980: 1). *Let There Be Light* was finally released to the public in December 1980 with an edited soundtrack that omitted the names of subjects who were still living.
19. Paul Rotha was particularly vocal about this issue. See, for example, 'Documentary Film in Danger' (1947).

CHAPTER 6

'Uncontrolled' Situations: Direct Cinema

Since the term appeared in the 1960s, 'direct cinema' has been a source of confusion for some, frustration for others. Not only is the 'directness' of direct cinema questionable, but the term is often used as the Anglo-American equivalent of *cinéma vérité* (the latter coined by Jean Rouch and Edgar Morin in France in 1960 to describe their experiments in interactive documentary). For example, in 1971, Alan Rosenthal observed that the terms direct cinema and *cinéma vérité* were being 'used interchangeably [in the US] in accordance with general practice' (Rosenthal 1971: 2). Outlining precise divisions between the two approaches can be tricky, as they tended to overlap in many ways – especially as, over the course of the 1960s and 1970s, proponents of both direct cinema and *cinéma vérité* started to question and adjust their assumptions and practices.

Direct cinema and *cinéma vérité*, however, both have distinct origins and features; in particular I want to look at US direct cinema's narrative traditions, style and audience expectations. William Rothman dismisses the term, since 'direct' implies 'unmediated' (1996: 7), but this is actually a reason I want to maintain it here, since as a movement the idea of sidestepping or minimizing mediation was paramount. With its shaky, hand-held visuals ('wobblyscope') and on-location sync sound (or 'direct' sound, usually supplemented by on-location 'wild' sound) direct cinema can deliver an impression of disordered immediacy and tactility that stands in sharp contrast to the deliberate scenes and soundscapes of more traditional documentary. Mobile tracking shots, on-the-spot interviews, integrated close-ups and cutaways home in on marginal, telling details: physical gestures, facial expressions, unexpected or awkward reactions. These techniques place viewers 'in the position of vicarious witnesses' (Corner 1996: 2), creating a sense of 'being there' while producing an imagined, intimate connection between viewers and on-screen subjects. Direct cinema thus has been seen as appealing more to emotional rather than logical or analytical viewer responses.

Moreover, the approach tends to present subjects as characters, focusing on individuals' lives and struggles while embedding hand-held and direct sound effects within the storytelling conventions of popular film. This focus on individual personalities and lack of forthright interpretation has led critics to argue that direct cinema usually fails as trenchant social analysis. Jonathan Kahana asks whether much direct cinema simply 'serves to reify individual personality as the site of social truth' (2008: 153). Others have stressed that the approach is vulnerable to manipulation, disguising the artificiality of its dramatic structures beneath an overriding impression of unmediated access to the people and situations it represents. Still, with varying levels of effectiveness, many direct cinema documentaries manifested the 1960s mantra 'the personal is the political', striving to articulate social issues through a focus on highly personal accounts (Vogels 2005: 154).

For Rothman, direct cinema is also 'the fullest inheritor of the concerns of America's "classical" cinema': the closest thing documentary has to Hollywood. Direct cinema has helped uncover the complexities of the mosaic nation, showing 'the coarseness and ugliness of America', but also 'flashes of beauty, tenderness, compassion' (Rothman 1996: 80). The filmmaker Albert Maysles saw in it the potential to revivify US democratic ideals, leveling hierarchies through direct access to people's lives and bolstering shared national consciousness by letting citizens 'know' each other. 'We had this possibility', Maysles stated, 'with this equipment and this philosophy, to transfer one person's experience to another, so that the country could be transformed from a geographical entity into a nation' (Maysles 2001). Known both for the ideals of its practitioners and for controversies over misleading claims to immediacy, direct cinema nonetheless came to define the look and feel of US documentary for a generation of filmmakers.

'DON'T BE AFRAID, IT'S A MICROPHONE!'

The lure of direct cinema lies in the impression of intimate knowing, allowing viewers to feel part of the action, observing the unplanned and instantaneous, constructing a vicarious experience of 'other' lives. While facilitated by improvements to lightweight camera and sound technologies during the 1950s, its key inventors have continued to stress that the 'revolution' of direct cinema was not so much about the technological advances that became its hallmarks but involved a whole philosophy of filming. They were determined to 'ditch the tripod' and reproduce the spontaneity of real life (Leacock 2008 [2000]).

Keith Beattie cautions against the 'crude technological determinism' of some accounts of direct cinema's early years, stressing the social and professional pressures that always underpin new technological developments (2004:

85).[1] In the US, an overriding factor supporting the emergence of lightweight, sync-sound equipment lay in demands coming from television journalism for flexible devices that could document news events with ease, on location and in real time. In France, through figures like Rouch (who trained as an anthropologist), the demand came more via the interests of ethnography and the need for portable and unobtrusive recording devices for anthropological fieldwork (Beattie 2004: 85). Both approaches sought what might be called a kind of camera pen: a means to employ the camera and sound recorder with the ease of note-taking, as in journalistic or ethnographic fieldwork.[2]

Also working against technologically determinist accounts of direct cinema and *vérité* is the history of non-fiction filmmaking itself, which shows us that both professionals and amateurs were always interested in recording everyday life using candid, unplanned scenarios, and that technology matched these demands. The Lumières' *cinématographe*, at five kilograms (a small fraction of the weight of an Edison camera), was designed to be transportable and uncomplicated in order to shoot actualities with minimal setup. Flaherty's Bell and Howell and Akeley cameras were chosen for durability and flexibility, so they could be taken on treks along the sub-Arctic coasts of Hudson Bay. Workers' Film and Photo League crews carried their cameras alongside unemployed marchers to capture the intensity of protest at street level. Amateur filmmakers too indicated a popular demand for lightweight cameras, for narrower gauges of film and, later, for video and digital technologies that could record, as cheaply as possible, everything from world travels to backyard adventures.

Direct cinema and *cinéma vérité* advanced these efforts by making it a professional priority to reproduce scenes from life with ease and efficiency. Photojournalism had been doing this for some time: candid scenes were regularly caught by the instantaneous flash of Weegee or the intuitive framing of William Eugene Smith, but moving pictures seemed only inconsistently to reproduce spontaneous, off-hand encounters. In particular, the later 1950s saw unprecedented efforts to unleash the heightened sense of realism that lightweight cameras and sync sound might provide, thus doing away with voiceovers and artificial post-syncing. Key challenges lay in developing quiet, portable cameras and lightweight sound technology to go with them. Richard Leacock recalled the frustrations of working with traditional equipment on *Toby and the Tall Corn* in 1954:

> [*Toby*] was to be my final attempt to make a documentary using classical film industry techniques. A 35 mm Mitchell NC camera weighing about 100 lbs with its massive tripod and power-supply, a Reeves 35 mm magnetic tape recorder and its attendant vacuum tube amplifier at about 80 lbs (it was said to be portable and had handles on the two cases, we called it the knuckle-buster), and a hand-held Eclair Cameflex for pickup shots,

plus a vast array of lights and cables, a dolly and tracks [. . .] a truck full.
(Leacock 1990: 4)

Leacock, in spite of this 'elephantine' equipment, did manage to retain a 'trace
of spontaneity' in the finished film. When screened as part of the CBS television series *Omnibus*, *Toby* caught the attention of Robert Drew, a picture editor
and journalist at *Life* magazine who at the time was exploring the use of candid
photography in motion pictures. Though Drew thought the narration in *Toby*
was 'idiotic', he was struck by the realist dynamics of a scene showing a tent
being put up (Drew 2008). Drew was interested in developing a documentary
approach beyond what he called the 'propagandist' methods of Grierson, yet
true to (and improving on) the 'naturalist' and dramatic methods of Flaherty
(quoted in Saunders 2007: 9). By 1960, Drew and Leacock had teamed up with
D. A. Pennebaker and Albert Maysles. The groundbreaking television documentary they made together, *Primary* (1960), is discussed in the next section.

The 1950s was a period of keen experimentation not only with film technology, but with conceptions of film's relationship to reality and its effects on
audiences. Filmmakers ranging across popular fiction, documentary, journalism and anthropology were seeking out less cumbersome methods that
could heighten impressions of immediacy and foreground film's 'indexical'
relationship to the pro-filmic. The Second World War had precipitated key
advances in lightweight cameras. The German Arriflex 35 was introduced in
1937 for newsreel photography and later adapted for military surveillance.
Arriflex cameras taken by American soldiers were copied by the US military to
produce its own camera for combat filming, the Cineflex PH-330, and Leacock
famously used the Arriflex when shooting Flaherty's *Louisiana Story* (1948).
Other conditions and movements were having an impact on practice. After
the war, social and economic pressures helped give rise to realist, minimalist
approaches such as neorealism in Italy, where actors, directors and writers
advocated stripped down aesthetics for telling everyday stories. The neorealist
Cesare Zavattini argued for films that could offer people 'a direct approach to
everyday reality' (1953: 64).

Starting in 1956 in Britain, the Free Cinema movement began to gain
widespread attention, spearheaded by six film programs shown over three
years at the National Film Theatre. The screenings aimed to be eclectic,
experimental and edgy. From the US came Lionel Rogosin's *On the Bowery*
(1956), an improvised drama-doc with a neo-realist feel, dealing with poverty
and alcoholism on Manhattan's 'skid row' (John Cassavetes called Rogosin
'probably the greatest documentary filmmaker of all time') (quoted in Thurber
2000: B6). From France was François Truffaut's uplifting short *Les Mistons*
(*The Brats*, 1957) and Georges Franju's searing, at times surreal documentary
about the abattoirs of Paris, *Blood of the Beasts* (1949). Wlodzimierz Borowik's

underground film *Paragraph Zero* (1957) offered an exposé of Poland's 'invisible' social problem, prostitution, against which there were no specific laws at the time. The camera and spotlight probe and examine the squalid alleys and back rooms inhabited by some of Warsaw's most destitute women. *Paragraph Zero* exemplifies the arresting visuals, marginal subject matter and sense of immediacy that Free Cinema encouraged.

Meanwhile in Canada, the National Film Board's (NFB) Unit B was using increasingly flexible technologies to capture life in the street while minimizing Griersonian didacticism. Wolf Koenig's *The Days Before Christmas* (1957/8) was a pilot for Unit B's flagship *Candid Eye* television series and used light-weight cameras and intermittent synchronized sound to offer a compressed 'city symphony' of Montreal in the run-up to the holidays. Koenig also produced *The Back-Breaking Leaf* (1959) with Terence Macartney-Filgate (an important creative force in the NFB), a film that revisits the theme of human struggle with the land, graphically depicting transient field workers harvesting tobacco at the height of summer. The actor William Greaves also made an impact at Unit B, working as an editor on Macartney-Filgate's *Blood and Fire* (1958), about the Salvation Army, while directing shorts such as *Putting It Straight* (1957), *Smoke and Weather* (1958) and *Emergency Ward* (1959). *Blood and Fire* generated debate in showing a destitute person weeping profusely – the shot's 'emotional nakedness' pushed the boundaries of ethical correctness but was kept in, heralding expectations of personal revelation and raw intimacy that would characterize direct cinema and *cinéma vérité* (Jones 1988: 143). Another NFB project, Michel Brault's *The Snowshoers* (1958) is a much-cited early example of dynamic hand-held camerawork, but also indicates direct cinema in its hands-off treatment of its subject (snowshoe races in Quebec) and its 'unprettified view of robust conviviality' (Ellis and McLane 2005: 211). Jean Rouch was impressed, and Brault would later act as cameraman on Rouch's own breakthrough *Chronicle of a Summer* (1961).

Rouch had first worked with direct sync sound in *La pyramide humaine* (*The Human Pyramid*) shot in 1958 and 1959 in Côte d'Ivoire, which led to pursuing similar technologies in *Chronicle of a Summer*, a film about his 'own tribe', Parisians. This was shot with sociologist Edgar Morin in the summer of 1960 with input from Brault on camerawork and remote sound. A few months earlier, Rouch and Morin had coined the term *cinéma-vérité* on returning from the first international ethnographic film festival in Florence, where *On the Bowery*, *The Hunters* (1958) and Free Cinema films like *We Are the Lambeth Boys* (1959) had made a deep impression. *Cinéma-vérité* was an homage to Vertov's *Kino Pravda* ('film truth'), but in fact Rouch and Morin employed the term more precisely, calling it '*nouveau* [new] *cinéma-vérité*'. It was in many ways the 'new' that they wanted to stress (Morin 2003 [1960]: 229–30). New *cinéma-vérité* retained a fidelity to *Kino Pravda*'s unplanned scenarios and determination to get close to the spontaneous feel of everyday life, but at the same time Rouch recognized that *Kino Pravda*'s ideals were not universal, and that they occupied a specific time, place and purpose. What Rouch shared with Vertov, he often stressed, was the idea that film truth was not 'pure truth' but a kind of truth created with the assistance of cinema technology. Cinema initiated new forms of visual and aural perception that could conjure up parallel truths – 'filmically understood' truths – that might be comprehended through a 'new kind of audiovisual language' (Rouch and Feld 2003 [1973]: 98). In this sense, truth was produced by the presence of the camera and the dynamics that arose between filmmaker, camera and subject. Barnouw calls the camera a 'catalyst' for events captured in the *cinéma-vérité* scenario and the *vérité* filmmaker becomes a kind of 'provocateur' (1983: 255).

Along with Vertov, Rouch was 'consciously synthesizing' Flaherty's methods in the creation of new *cinéma-vérité* (Rouch and Feld 2003 [1973]: 99). Like Flaherty, he sought to establish close affinities and working relationships with his subjects. Specifically he adopted Flaherty's 'participating camera', or subject feedback method, which could demystify the filmmaking process for subjects and generate spontaneous ideas during filming, suppressing the demand for predetermined outcomes. Rouch's experimental films such as *Jaguar* (1954–5, released 1967) and *Moi, un Noir* (*I, a Black*, 1958), shot in western Africa, made this participation process explicit by recording the feedback of subjects and incorporating it as voiceover commentary. In *Moi, un Noir* the main actor, Oumarou Ganda, partly acts and partly lives out his daily life for the camera; the performance is then self-reflexively narrated by Ganda in voiceover. At its best the effect produces a kind of *mise-en-abyme* of self-fashioned characters reflecting the cinematic fantasies of real subjects, disturbing presumptions of documentary transparency (Geiger 1998: 3–8).

An early scene in *Chronicle of a Summer*, shot on the street, offers a somewhat fetishistic display of the new filming methods and technologies. Rouch's and Morin's assistants/subjects, Marceline Loridan and Nadine Ballot, conduct interviews with the microphone and portable Nagra tape recorder clearly visible to the camera. They engage passers-by with the question 'are you happy?' and elicit responses ranging from curious and fearful (a young boy), to diffident and amused (a policeman), to pretentious (a student flashes a book of philosophy). The novelty of the technology is clear: at one point a seventy-nine-year-old man looks confused by the object Marceline waves in front of his face. She explains: 'Don't be afraid, it's a microphone!' But *Chronicle of a Summer* was not just a technical experiment, it was also a social experiment, a self-critical examination of what truths the camera might provoke into being. Near the project's end, Morin and Rouch discuss the difficulties of communicating their feelings and intents through film: though they were catalysts and key players, the film became something separate from them, producing essentially 'filmically understood' truths and audience reactions that didn't always correspond to their own impressions and opinions of subjects they believed they intimately knew. 'Nous sommes dans le bain', states Morin finally, a phrase (translated in the subtitles as 'we're in for trouble') that has since animated debates – such as Brian Winston's – about the veracity and honesty of *vérité* approaches.[3] Already, *Chronicle of a Summer* was pointing to both the compelling possibilities and the pitfalls of *cinéma vérité*. Audiences might take home an impression of direct collaboration and the distribution of control among filmmakers and subjects, but this apparent openness tells only a part of the story and in its own ways can disguise a film's artifice and manipulation of 'truth'.

Due to the ambiguities of truth in *cinéma-vérité*, Rouch would come to prefer the term *cinéma direct*, which seemed less constrained by implicit claims to absolute truth. In the US, direct cinema would never really aspire to the perceived openness and analytical self-awareness of Rouch's approach. Robert Drew would note that, even as he was helping to reinvent television documentary in 1960, 'Vertov had no influence on me, and I had never heard of Jean Rouch' (quoted in Saunders 2007: 9). For Albert Maysles, Vertov was essentially 'Soviet propaganda' that lacked the immediacy of sync sound (Zuber 2007: 17). James Blue summed up the situation in 1964: while the French 'probe, interview, provoke', he noted, the Americans 'are, for the most part, fundamentalists. They eschew intervention whatever its goal. They cultivate alert passivity. They seek self-effacement. They want the subject to forget that they are there' (Blue 1964: 23). Portable sound, lightweight cameras and perhaps, above all, editing would help filmmakers and the filming apparatus disappear behind the scenes, to become flies on the wall.

CRISIS AND INNOVATION

Though a handful of filmmakers – especially Drew, Leacock, Pennebaker, Albert and David Maysles and Frederick Wiseman – are usually cited as direct cinema's key innovators in the US,[4] it is important to remember that these figures did not work in isolation. Scholars such as Kahana have looked beyond the usual suspects towards, for example, the work of Michael Gray and the Chicago Film Group (which included Lars Hedman and Mike Shea). Gray's *Cicero March* (1966, not released commercially) documented Civil Rights protests against housing policies and real estate 'redlining' in the all-white suburb of Cicero (Kahana 2008: 156). An important retrospective at New York's Film Forum in 1997 highlighted other integral figures in direct cinema's advancement and diversification, including Allan King, Stephen Sbarge, William Greaves, Hope Ryden, Charlotte Zwerin and Joyce Chopra.

Direct cinema's roots go back to the interest in heightening the immediacy of documentary that grew during the 1950s. This came out of mixed demands – cultural, commercial, ideological, aesthetic and personal – to transform structural and practical relationships between documentary films, their source material and their audiences. As Kahana (citing Michael Curtin) stresses, direct cinema's 'seemingly autonomous innovators' in the US were working within larger cultural and technological frameworks. These included Cold War and nuclear fears, simmering political tensions at home (labor rights, the civil liberties abuses of the McCarthy investigations, Civil Rights, the recession of 1958), the rise of US commercial television (aimed at both domestic and overseas markets), and international developments in film technology and new conceptual approaches to film.

While often viewed nostalgically, the decade and a half following the end of the Second World War (Drew himself was a veteran, Leacock a combat photographer) was a highly disruptive period. The McCarthy 'witch hunts' had targeted the film and media industries, leaving a swath of fear but also simmering resentment that would further stoke desires for 'democratic' alternatives to conventional ways of negotiating and representing public and private life. The 1950s was a decade of profound paradoxes: Civil Rights protests were sparking violence and abuses of authority; media commentators were observing increasing cultural disaffection, particularly among younger people, giving the lie to the rose-tinted Norman Rockwell image of America long proffered in the pages of *The Saturday Evening Post*. Films like Rogosin's *On the Bowery* unveiled a scarcely hidden world of desperation and depravity at the heart of the nation's flagship city. When the film appeared, critics commented that it reflected the deep alienation felt in American society at mid-century (Thurber 2000: B6).

As for the media available to address these social pressures, the theatrical newsreel was a rapidly fading force and its reporting was usually superficially entertaining rather than insightful (Fielding 1972: 307–8). At the same time the new medium of the masses, television, was under fire for not meeting public service needs. Beyond the occasional spark of newscasters such as Edward R. Murrow, television was a 'vast wasteland' of 'formula' and 'totally unbelievable' entertainment, as Newton W. Minow's famous speech to the National Association of Broadcasters described it (Minow 1961). These concerns were later echoed in Lyndon B. Johnson's 'Great Society' speech (1964), calling on social institutions to rebuild an America 'where the demands of morality, and the needs of the spirit, can be realized in the life of the Nation' (Johnson 1964). Responsibility in television was seen as central to a project of national regeneration, and broadcasting reforms gathered strength among government policymakers and in the media industry itself.

Robert Drew, an editor at *Life*, was keenly interested in advancing the cultural currency of documentary, in particular television documentary. Richard Leacock was a professional filmmaker, born in the Canary Islands, who had worked as an editor on Frontier Films' *Native Land* and as cameraman on *Louisiana Story*. Both were questioning the fundamentals of documentary practice. When Drew obtained the sponsorship of Time-Life Broadcasting, they formed Drew Associates, producing several films over the next few years. *Bullfight at Malaga* (1958) shows evidence of their efforts to find freer filming techniques. Perhaps more significantly, it exemplifies a key documentary narrative device: the conflict or 'crisis' structure (here manifested in a duel between two rival bullfighters). Produced through the choice of material and especially through editing, the 'crisis' structure would lie at the center of much direct cinema work that followed.

Seeking to maximize maneuverability and with no suitable equipment on the market, Leacock painstakingly developed, with Pennebaker, a 16 mm Auricon camera linked to a portable sound recorder, synchronized through the timing mechanism of a Bulova watch (Saunders 2007: 10). Other devices appeared around the same time: wireless microphones, increasingly sensitive film stock that reduced the need for complex lighting set-ups and film magazines that allowed for quick reloading. In 1960 Drew began work with a crew that included Leacock, Albert Maysles, Macartney-Filgate and Pennebaker, producing *Primary* (1960), the first fully-fledged example of a direct cinema ethos.

Dave Saunders calls *Primary* 'an important film in the documentary canon, but [. . .] not an especially good one' (2007: 21). Perhaps this assessment is a bit harsh. The film provides a well-paced account of John F. Kennedy's and Hubert Humphrey's competition in Wisconsin for the Democratic Party nomination. It depicts much of the uncertainty, artifice and awkwardness of the campaign trail. It also exhibits Kennedy at close quarters and at the peak of his charisma. He arrives on the campaign like a seasoned pop star, with screaming girls demanding autographs, an image contrasted to Humphrey's folksy, down home persona. Just as importantly, the film offers a palpable record of direct cinema coming into its own, with self-conscious displays of innovative camera and sound work. The excitement of working with new technologies is visible in segments such as the shoulder-mounted tracking shot of Kennedy arriving at a Milwaukee rally (shown twice in the film), conceived by Maysles and Pennebaker using a wide-angle lens to capture a maximum amount of peripheral detail. The shot follows Kennedy through the adoring crowds, up a narrow flight of stairs and on to a stage. The podium and crowd fan out before him; the back of Kennedy's head is at times so close it seems you could touch it.

Still, as Saunders argues, the film is far from perfect. The home-made equipment often failed to work and there is a fair amount of 'cheating' on display, where the visuals fail to match the audio track. Leacock recalls the film's successes and its limits: 'For the first time we were able to walk in and out of buildings, up and down stairs, film in taxi cabs, all over the place, and get synchronous sound', but only, he claims, in the scenes he shot himself. Pennebaker and Maysles were still shooting with silent Arriflex cameras (Mamber 1974: 30, 36). The film also falls back on voiceover to plug gaps in the narrative. Beyond these technical considerations, there are shortcomings in the breadth of coverage: in spite of direct cinema's aspirations towards candor and previously unseen revelations, *Primary* reveals little beyond the prevailing image of Kennedy and Humphrey then available in the mainstream press. This is not quite the democratic dream of leveling hierarchies and intimately 'knowing' the nation's political leaders and the political machine. *Primary*'s scenes are essentially anecdotes and, as many have noted, it fails to provide a genuinely insightful study of the election process itself.

Moreover, in capturing a private glimpse of a public figure, as Saunders suggests, Drew was essentially caught in the middle. He was compromised in his ability to reveal complex truths about Kennedy and the campaign, wanting to 'court the favour of high-profile subjects' but at the same time needing to 'remain innocuous in his coverage for fear of being ostracised from a clique that was defending national interests' (2007: 23). This situation is aligned to what Stuart Hall calls the media 'double bind', where broadcasting implies 'open, democratic, controversial' reportage but in fact is constrained 'within an overall framework of assumptions about the distribution of political power' (1988: 359). This is the 'lie' of direct cinema's political and pop cultural exposés: on the one hand revealing the 'warts and all' lives of public figures, on the other needing to convey an illusion of observational objectivity and unbiased reporting while not damaging the filmmakers' personal and professional contacts. In the end, the approach maintains the status quo – a product of consensus packaged as unmediated direct access. To make things more complicated, some direct cinema filmmakers, such as Pennebaker and the Maysles brothers, would themselves edge closer to celebrity status.

Drew Associates produced nineteen films in all, most of them for network television. *The Children Were Watching* (1960), contrasting white segregationists with the experiences of a black family during the integration of New Orleans schools, was one of the first television programs to openly show the direct impact of racism. Themes of race and social division were revisited in *The Chair* (1962) and *Crisis: Behind a Presidential Commitment* (1963), which stand out as exemplary of the Drew group applying their signature approach to volatile social issues. *The Chair* follows the high-profile appeal process of Paul Crump, sentenced to death in the electric chair. Rather than focus on a miscarriage of justice or on Crump's emotional state as he faces death, the film features Crump's defence attorney, Donald Moore, following the case he makes for Crump's rehabilitation. The 'crisis' structure is clearly laid out: Crump faces execution in five days and Moore must save him. In a key scene, we witness Moore in his office, achieving a major step towards clemency by attaining support from the Catholic Church; he breaks into tears, a cathartic reaction that underlines the intensity of the crisis. The scene is intimate and discomforting at the same time, eliciting a complex mix of voyeuristic fascination and sympathetic connection. Though Crump is the fulcrum of the plot, he serves more as a referential figure around which the crisis develops: the site of tension and viewer identification lies in the challenge of Moore's rescue attempt. *The Chair* won critical plaudits but it also had its detractors, including Jean-Luc Godard, who claimed that, in its emotionalism and lack of analysis, it was no more insightful than Robert Wise's Hollywood foray into capital punishment, *I Want To Live* (1958) (Mamber 1974: 102).

The Chair reveals a paradox amid direct cinema innovation: while shooting strategies were rapidly changing, the temptation to structure the material along conventional story lines remained. The new observational style still largely held itself to the cardinal rule of shooting and editing: the trappings of the filming apparatus should remain invisible. The raw material of the direct cinema documentary remained essentially useless in the public realm until it was manipulated into dramatic stories, crises, character motivations, causes and effects. In the case of *The Chair*, this meant a shooting to finished film ratio of over 30 : 1, similar to Hollywood productions. In this sense Godard perhaps had a point.

Crisis: Behind a Presidential Commitment would similarly rely on classical narrative techniques such as parallel sequencing, used here to establish familiarity with two 'camps' – North and South – hurtling towards a critical encounter. Attorney General Robert Kennedy attempts to implement the court-ordered desegregation of the University of Alabama, while Governor George Wallace intends to stop it (the former boxer Wallace is shown in close-up staring at the camera near the beginning of the film, already very much the villain). As in *The Chair*, *Crisis* invests itself in a conflict/resolution narrative, creating suspense in the lead up to the crisis: the meeting between Kennedy's Deputy Attorney General, Nicholas Katzenbach, and Wallace in Tuscaloosa. Wallace plans to personally block the doorway to the university building, literally and symbolically barring African American entry.

Recalling, while ideologically countering, the North/South parallel sequencing of *The Birth of a Nation*, each 'camp' in *Crisis* is associated with contrasting family values. In the Alabama Governor's mansion, Wallace's tiny blonde daughter is watched over by an African American servant. Wallace is heard expressing beliefs in the separation of the races, and anachronistically defends the Confederate cause; an imposing portrait of a Civil War general stares over him. Wallace's opulent quarters suggest a plantation house, con-

Figure 14. *Crisis: Behind a Presidential Commitment* (1963). Drew Associates. Courtesy of the British Film Institute.

trasting with Robert Kennedy's chaotic, casual family setting (RFK already had seven children at the time). Throughout, cross-cutting constructs a privileged spectator position where the viewer knows more about the interlocked drama taking place in different locales than the characters do, creating heightened tensions.

A number of elements stray from the direct cinema ethos, not the least being the use of intrusive voiceover (*What's Happening!*, the Maysles' 1964 film about the Beatles, was the first direct cinema film without voiceover) and some scenes – particularly those in the Oval Office – appear 'stage-managed'. Though the oncoming confrontation creates simmering tensions, neither RFK nor Wallace has the compelling screen energy or accessible humanity of JFK and Humphrey in *Primary*, and the excitement of the campaign trail is replaced here with a series of protracted meetings and telephone conversations. But the fascination of *Crisis* at the time lay in the historical moment: the previous year riots had marred the entrance of African American student James Meredith to the University of Mississippi, leaving two dead and hundreds wounded (as briefly mentioned in voiceover). Except for short scenes with the students Vivian Malone and James Hood, the most notable figure is Katzenbach, intently strategizing as he drags on a dangerously burned down cigarette. A much-admired moment occurs when RFK's daughter Kerry takes the phone from her father and briefly chats with 'Nick' Katzenbach (the sheer luck, Leacock recalled, of the Southern and Northern teams working on each end of the conversation without being certain that the other was still filming). The scene not only underscores the informality of the Kennedy administration, but is a reminder of how children are often ideal direct cinema subjects: conveying naturalness and injecting spontaneity even into scenes that are 'a little bit flat' (Leacock 2010).

Crisis was a popular breakthrough for Drew: the September 1963 issue of *Show* magazine declared, 'A New Kind of Television Goes Backstage with History'. But the program was also criticized for dramatic manipulation. In the *New York Times*, Jack Gould accused key figures in the film of 'an incredible bit of play-acting' (Watson 1989: 40–1). Stephen Mamber, unusually, counters Drew's defence that 'the cameras did not, in anything that was seen in the film, influence people's reactions'. Mamber acknowledges that the camera's presence might 'influence' its subjects, and that those moments when this influence is most palpable can 'often be the most revealing' (1974: 102). In this sense direct cinema encounters the filming dynamics openly admitted in Rouch's *cinéma vérité*.

After 1963, Leacock and Pennebaker left Drew Associates. Reflecting in part the need for commercial sponsorship, direct cinema projects gravitated towards what Mamber calls 'personality oriented' films. Best known perhaps is Pennebaker's legendary *Dont Look Back* (1967), an exercise in direct cinema demystification that served only to enhance the mystique of Bob Dylan. Direct cinema observation was also the preferred approach for rockumentaries such as Pennebaker's *Monterey Pop* (1968) and Michael Wadleigh's *Woodstock* (1970) – films which helped elevate the rock music festival to the supreme filmic signifier of hippie communal ideals.[5] Leacock's first film after leaving Drew was *Happy Mother's Day* (1963), made with Chopra, and suggested direct cinema's potential for social observation and critique. The film deals with events in the lives of the Fishers, the nationally famous parents of quintuplets, and casts an ethnographic eye on their home town of Aberdeen, South Dakota. Leacock displays a fascination for social oddities and cultural curiosities, and spurned re-enactments in favor of patient long takes to capture seemingly offhand details. The film also subtly shows up interactions between camera, filmmaker and subjects (Mrs Fisher's glance and brief smile at the camera is a classic – if ambiguous – instance of this).[6]

Telling moments reveal the Fishers' unprecedented situation: confronted with so many children, and at the height of early 1960s consumerism and family values, their straitened circumstances are obvious. Their faded Model-T car is thirty years old; during a visit to a department store we are told that Mrs Fisher 'has not had a store-bought outfit since her marriage'. Sponsored by the family-friendly *Saturday Evening Post* and Beech-Nut baby foods, ABC would decide to broadcast a different version from Leacock's. The televised version included more shots of adorable babies, and fewer peculiar, critical and humorous observations of small-town America (Mamber 1974: 195). Indeed, Leacock's version went against Drew's formulas engineered for network broadcast. For Saunders, Leacock's film is 'a critique of the tendency of conventional journalism to invade, reduce, commoditise and exploit the province of those who have no possible redress or alternative, and a response to the formal demands of national television' (Saunders 2007: 33). As Erik Barnouw summed up the situation in 1964, television documentary was restricted by the hegemony of the 'big three' networks; filmmakers were usually 'more aware of inhibitions than breakthroughs', while sponsors, 'with logic from the point of view of the merchandiser, prefer to avoid programming that will exclude them from any major "market"' (Barnouw 1964: 16–17).

Despite commercial challenges to projects like *Happy Mother's Day*, direct cinema did find a place in the market. The combination of lightweight equipment and a philosophy of non-intervention meant that the shooting process was dynamic and hands-on – thus popular with filmmakers. Before long direct cinema was an established practice with a firm set of ideological, ethical and practical principles attached to it. Mamber offers a summary of the 'rules' that became a dominant – and, many would argue, privileged – approach to documentary. Documentary should capture 'uncontrolled situations' where actions and events unfold spontaneously. As Mamber puts it:

> *Uncontrolled* means that the filmmaker does not function as a 'director' nor, for that matter, as a screenwriter. [. . .] [N]o one is told what to say or how to act. A prepared script, however skimpy, is not permissible, nor are verbal suggestions, gestures, or any form of direct communication from the filmmaker to his subject. The filmmaker should in no way indicate that any action is preferred by him over any other. The filmmaker acts as an observer, attempting not to alter the situations he witnesses any more than he must simply by being there [. . .] Interviews are also not employed, since their use, in effect, is a form of directed behavior. (1974: 2)

Mamber's version of the rules basically outlines so-called fly-on-the-wall documentary, with its expectations of non-interference, neutrality and invisibility. In this respect, ethnographic film in the observational mode overlapped on many levels with direct cinema, and practical and theoretical film courses often stressed their affinities: it was not unusual to find *Primary* and an NFB Unit B production screened alongside John Marshall's *The Hunters* (1962) and Robert Gardner's *Dead Birds* (1965).

Direct cinema rules occupied an elevated status in documentary circles for many years. Mentors at major documentary teaching centers such as UCLA and the National Film and Television School in Britain encouraged the approach as *the* filmmaker's modus operandi. More traditional approaches were sidelined, 'drummed out', as James Blue noted, 'for having "used" life for the dissemination of a "selfish point of view"'. For direct cinema filmmakers, Blue stated, the 'only proper material is believed to be life itself – not as it is recreated, but as it happens. To these men, all else is heresy' (Blue 1964: 23). There was effectively a 'right' method of capturing reality, opposed to re-enactments, formal interviews ('talking heads') or directorial intervention. Of course an ideal of pure observation was always just that, an ideal, and direct cinema practitioners would find themselves, consciously and unconsciously, having to adjust these ideals.

By the 1970s and into the 1980s, critics such as Thomas Waugh (1976) and Brian Winston were articulating the disillusion that many felt with the 'philosophy of documentary purity' being promoted 'with the fervor of true believers' in film schools and on festival circuits (Winston 1988b [1978/9]: 23–4). Invoking Morin, Winston stressed important divergences between direct cinema and *cinéma vérité*, the latter characterized by self-analytical scenes and practitioners willing to put themselves on display alongside their subjects. Still, it should be said that direct cinema always betrayed a weakness in the facade of pure observation. Many filmmakers, such as Leacock, already had a healthy suspicion of documentary approaches that veered towards orthodoxy. As *Happy Mother's Day* showed, direct cinema could reveal striking and unforced insights, and the rules were less stable than many liked to admit. 'These are rules, not laws, and rules can be broken', Leacock later stated (Leacock 1997).

LIMITS OF PURE OBSERVATION

Direct cinema developed in opposition to what Bill Nichols calls the 'expository mode' of Grierson and the RA/FSA films – though Grierson did advocate for the 'special value' of 'spontaneous gesture' and the 'intimacy of knowledge' (Grierson 1946 [1932]: 80). Still, where a Griersonian approach stressed universals and interpretation for the greater good, direct cinema looked towards the particular, the individual, the minutiae. As such, direct cinema heightened impressions of immediate access to the private and personal, even (or especially) when its subjects were recognizable public figures. Professing to be unobtrusive observers, direct cinema practitioners strove for a sense of invisibly entering into the scene, a strategy that could produce a range of affects, from intimate viewer participation to invasive voyeurism. Long lenses caught candid behavior at a distance; zooms provided intense, revealing close-ups; cutaway shots homed in on awkward and nervous gestures; directional and remote microphones captured whispered, offhand remarks. Such a fetishization of total observation works, as Corner suggests, to cover for the presence of the camera, fusing the idea of the 'putative event' (what would have happened without the camera's presence) with the pro-filmic event (what actually happened with the camera present) (Corner 1996: 20).

This implied personal connection between audiences and viewed subjects also helps to explain direct cinema's dependency on – and appeal to – television. Beaming directly into homes, television rapidly usurped the role of radio and became a familiar part of American life. Here the renowned celebrity and the average man-on-the-street could, in equal measure, be scrutinized at close quarters. Kahana, citing Rhona J. Bernstein, suggests that due to its 'location, its size, and its integration into social ritual', television provided an impression of personal and democratic involvement in the activities and concerns of the nation. Grierson observed that television could penetrate 'private emotional spaces and extend them unreasonably, making us care about people we will never meet' (quoted in Kahana 2008: 292–3). *Primary* and *Crisis* offer examples of this illusory levelling process, where political leaders are shown as glamorous and elevated, and mundane and accessible, often concurrently. In *Primary* we see the stellar JFK addressing an adoring crowd, watched over by a fastidious, somewhat shy Jackie, while Hubert Humphrey is serenaded by a band of children playing 'Davy Crocket' on accordions, then tucks into a humble dinner of 'ham, mashed potatoes, and string beans'. At the same time the coupling of direct cinema and television could transform ordinary people living ordinary lives into celebrities – a familiar by-product of more recent reality television.

Promising to offer honest and unobstructed access, direct cinema attempted to perform a double gesture: to observe people with whom audiences might identify and empathize, while offering 'simulations of depth' – getting behind or below the surface of the events and personalities represented (Kahana 2008: 297). These impulses are indicative of what Nichols labels the 'observational mode', which closely parallels the strategies of fiction films. Both observational documentary and fiction aim to produce a sense of absolute realism that offers 'unmediated and unfettered access to the world' (Nichols 1991: 43). Direct cinema thus strives 'to eliminate as much as possible the barriers between subject and audience' (Mamber 1974: 4), and as result these 'barriers' – the limits of the filmmaker and equipment as physical and technical presences in a particular space and time – are not normally visible in the finished film. Direct cinema masks the filmmaking apparatus, like classic Hollywood fictions, encouraging identification with characters and producing dramatic tensions that repress the contingencies of the spectator's location and the actual, complex dynamics of filmmaker, filming technology, subjects and filming conditions.

Take for example *Crisis* and its narrative produced via parallel editing, which creates a spectator position that transcends the perspectives of both the filmmaker on the scene and the subjects in the scene. Kahana notes that continuity editing in documentary can help to privilege an 'individuated perception' where the spectator occupies a position in which 'he or she takes in the scene from the best possible vantage point' (Kahana 2008: 294). Because the filmmaker in the observational mode remains an absent presence, rarely revealing him/herself or showing the filmed subjects' awareness of the ongoing production, the camera/spectator becomes a sort of ideal observer, witnessing the hidden truths of everyday life. As Nichols acknowledges, the fact that the raw material is still based on real-time events does limit a film's ability to create fully omniscient observers: the film content will always be partly restricted by actual events taking place in front of the camera. Nonetheless, 'the expectation of transparent access remains'. The filmmaker's absence 'clears the way for the dynamics of empathetic identification, poetic immersion, or voyeuristic pleasure' (Nichols 1991: 43–4). Technological innovations were meant to allow filmmakers to dispense with preconceived notions, but didacticism effectively went underground: direct cinema films are often driven by an underlying thesis or argument. We might attribute this gap between ideals, intentions and results solely to the interventions of obtrusive editing (such as the 'crisis' structure or the problem/solution story) but the issue really runs deeper. The processes of planning and choosing material, matched with issues of audience expectations, commercial imperatives and sponsorship – all of these are just a few of the many limits on 'pure' or direct access (Kahana 2008: 294–5).

The limits and ultimate progression of direct cinema are visible in the work of the famous partnership of Albert and David Maysles. In early films such as *Showman* (1963) and *What's Happening! The Beatles in the USA*, the 'crisis' structure and heavier narrative elements were put to one side in order to stress what Drew called 'picture logic' – limiting context and background information to what the camera could 'show' or 'reveal'. The direct cinema film intended to be legible, as fully as possible, via observation: what Mamber calls 'revelation through situation' (1974: 142). The Maysles brothers worked in what many consider the ideal direct cinema partnership: the two-person crew consisting of cameraperson and soundperson (for Drew, this translated to the 'correspondent' on sound and engaged with the subjects, and the photographer on camera). The two-person team appealed to direct cinema's hands-on ethos and was small enough to be flexible and discreet. But even a two-person crew, meant to minimize interference, is hardly invisible. Filming in confined spaces and small rooms, Al and David no doubt often resembled, in Beattie's words, 'elephants on the table' more than flies on the wall (2004: 97).

After the celebrity studies *Meet Marlon Brando* (1965, with limited release due to Brando's objections) and *With Love From Truman: A Visit With Truman*

Capote (1966), the Maysles wanted to produce 'not just feature length [documentaries] but a feature with all the drama to compete with mainstream features in movie theaters'. The result, *Salesman* (1969, with Charlotte Zwerin), was hailed by the *Saturday Review* as 'one of the most important films ever made'. Still, Maysles recalled, 'PBS wasn't a bit interested, no one was interested, and cinema exhibitors weren't quite getting on to the notion that a documentary could be a feature' (Zuber 2007: 10). *Salesman* follows the hard and often seedy lives of door-to-door Bible salesmen, highlighting the dramatic potential of everyday encounters. In dramatizing quotidian experience, it shows an affinity to contemporary movements such as New Journalism, which Al often suggested paralleled the aims of direct cinema. Also like New Journalism, *Salesman*'s classical realist style and focus on plot and character development (in particular on the hangdog figure of Paul 'The Badger' Brennan) reflect efforts to break documentary into the theatrical mainstream. *Salesman*'s debts to narrative realism might be seen not only in its observational approach but in its use of parallel editing, the 'meanwhile' structure that unites disparate storytellers from D. W. Griffith to Capote.

David Davidson observes that, unlike Drew, the Maysles stressed 'psychology over sociology' (both Al and David had backgrounds in psychology), creating 'self-contained' character-centered worlds that underline direct cinema's reaction against an Anglo-American tradition that privileged documentary's role in 'advancing understanding' and 'bettering social conditions' (1981: 4–5). For Mamber, however, *Salesman* mixes brilliance with problematic backsliding: it is 'full of devices heretofore more the province of fiction film'; thus it is 'edging back into the kind of manipulation that American cinema verite was originally reacting against' (1974: 161, 167). Drama is indeed emphasized through the shooting and cutting choices. In one scene, as a Florida woman is 'badgered' by an increasingly desperate Brennan, the camera zooms in on her beleaguered face as she wrestles internally with the salesman's entreaties. The lingering shot involves us in her interest in the lavishly illustrated Bible; we also sense her embarrassment at expressing her financial troubles. Similar to fiction, absorption and voyeuristic fascination are mixed with identification and empathy. But other effects – the unusually long take, the persistent focus on the woman's face and gestures, Brennan's soft-sell monologue off-screen, the lowly state of the house, the harsh natural light, the slight shake of the camera – all work to create a claustrophobic and intensely psychological space drawn from and contextualized as spontaneous experience. *Salesman* creates a highly wrought documentary space but is not 'simply' mimetic fiction.

The Maysles brothers and Zwerin's more experimental and controversial *Gimme Shelter* (1970) further modified direct cinema's rules, drawing attention to the paradoxes of editing out or streamlining the rough patches and inconclusive fragments of documentary production. As Jonathan Vogels observes, while remaining direct cinema's most ardent 'purists', the Maysles brothers manifested 'a surprising inconsistency between rhetoric and practice', developing an essentially modernist aesthetic that was 'sometimes more pragmatic, sometimes more widely experimental' (2005: 149, 12). In this sense (though Al Maysles contended differently [Zuber 2007: 13]) we might notice similarities between the Maysles' and Frederick Wiseman's work. Both have suggested that their work parallels New Journalism, though Wiseman's stated attitudes towards documentary purity tend to be more ironic than doctrinal, referring to his own work as 'reality fictions' (Wiseman 1994: 4). Wiseman's films largely but not exclusively have dealt with institutions and institutional life, ranging from *Titicut Follies* (1967), *High School* (1968), *Law and Order* (1969) and *Welfare* (1975), to *Public Housing* (1997), *Domestic Violence* (2001) and *State Legislature* (2006). Most were made with the support of the Public Broadcasting Service (PBS), and from 1971 to 1981 Wiseman's contract offered him essentially carte blanche treatment – one film per year without constraints on the subject matter or running time. He thus has occupied a rare position for a documentarist, with reliable funding sources and broadcast outlets not wholly dependent on market economics.

Wiseman's early films are not openly reformist, but reveal the dynamics and abuses of power at the heart of public institutions. Part journalistic exposé, part experimental collage, the films raise questions about institutional efficacy, showing up flaws in the superstructure while homing in on individual lives caught up in rigid frameworks and managerial hierarchies. Rather than highlight public figures and celebrities, Saunders observes, Wiseman deals with what Michael Harrington called 'the other America': the nation 'populated by failures, by those driven from the land and bewildered by the city' (quoted in Saunders 2007: 145). In the tradition of Jacob Riis, Lewis Hine and social documentary more generally, the films probe both the mundane and horrific undersides of institutional life, examining the detached lawmakers and bureaucratic functionaries who enforce rules and those caught up in their web, unable to stage a protest.

Wiseman's films are largely realist with moments that verge on the surreal, and generally lack explicit analysis. They pay careful attention to visual and aural textures and to the allusive potency of formal and thematic continuities and juxtapositions. For the most part manifestly non-intrusive, their compact, sometimes amusing, sometimes shocking scenes are structured in a stream-of-consciousness, episodic manner. Nichols discerns a 'mosaic' pattern to the films, where the organizational links are motivated more by rhetorical or impressionistic means than by plot or chronology (Nichols 1981: 211). Saunders further links Wiseman's anti-narrative or 'anti-syntactical' sequencing to his scepticism of 'reductive' institutional schemes. Any illusions of easy continuity would simply reinscribe the generic institution's false sense of ordering and containing the world (2007: 167–8). To achieve these free-flowing mosaic patterns, however, Wiseman has been known to rely on a very high shooting ratio (for *Juvenile Court* [1973] sixty hours of footage was edited down to two).

With a background in law, Wiseman chose to document in his first film, *Titicut Follies*, the grim day-to-day life at the Massachusetts Correctional Institution at Bridgewater. A combination prison and hospital for the criminally insane, the facility was familiar, as Wiseman had taken his law students on public tours. He was encouraged to make a film by Bridgewater's superintendent and the lieutenant governor of Massachusetts in a public relations attempt to 'humanize' the troubled institution (Atkins 1976: 5).[7] The results so alarmed officials that they called for a ban on the film which the State Supreme Court ultimately upheld.

Many in favor of the ban argued the film was sheer voyeurism, documenting private lives in order to exploit them. Still, Wiseman insisted that the film actually 'uncovered' nothing: everything in the film would have been visible on the public tours that officials themselves encouraged (Wiseman 1976: 70). Of course these comments are slightly disingenuous, as *Titicut Follies* is anything but a purely observational 'tour' of the facility. Self-reflexively framed by the 'follies' performed by inmates to entertain the prison staff, the film underlines the blunt ironies of institutional life though careful camera and sound work and associative juxtapositions that often border on horror film. In an unforgiving early sequence, we are shown emaciated prisoners lining up, stripped for inspection: frankly recalling a concentration camp. In another long take, a grinning prisoner is filmed in a harshly lit close-up, singing rough counterpoint against a television screen featuring the Greek chanteuse Nana Mouskouri. For *Variety*, such scenes appeared 'merely gratuitous' without advancing a social argument 'one whit' (Byro. 1967: 12). This was, however, effectively their purpose, to 'prevent us from maintaining a unified point of view' (Grant 1998: 242), to defamiliarize and disorient, challenging seemingly transparent cinematic modes that feed voyeurism and offer easy moral solutions. As we watch staff enforcing rigid compliance through degrading acts, amid this extraordinary world is a bleak, routine-like banality. Some inmates appear eminently rational, while guards are in turn kindly, automaton-like or borderline sadistic. As Kahana succinctly states, the film reveals 'banal and continuous forms of repression inside a generic institutional structure' (2008: 224).

Titicut Follies recalls the grim ironies of Franju's work, which offered oblique commentary on institutionalized violence in films such as *Blood of the Beasts* and *Hôtel des Invalides* (1952). In Franju's hands, the world's explicit and implicit horrors (animal slaughter and the memorialization of war, respectively) are wedded to moments of unexpected lyricism, even dark humor. Similarly, in spite of *Titicut Follies'* harshness, Wiseman found glimpses of humanity: 'Even in *Titicut Follies*, the guards in their own way were more tuned to the needs of the inmates than the so-called "helping" professionals' (Peary 2004 [1998]). In one scene, as a prisoner removes his clothes to be searched, he appears compliant and passive, yet we learn that he has molested his own daughter, committed aggravated assault and arson, and attempted to hang himself. We see the guard lifting and turning over the nude prisoner's arms and hands, then briefly running a hand over his close-shaven head. While fleeting and incidental, the gestures are palpably tactile, perhaps reminding us of the lived presence and vulnerability of these bodies amid others in the film. Here the filmmakers (John Marshall working camera with Wiseman covering sound) (Benson and Anderson 2002: 28), while 'invisible', are nonetheless felt presences in the hand-held movements, deliberate shooting decisions and proximity of the camera to the bodies being filmed.

The scene is marked by subtle editorializing: as the prisoner is led to his cell, Marshall performs one of direct cinema's signature maneuvers, the traveling long take. In the midst of the shot, the camera unexpectedly tilts upwards to capture a television screen, where images of a body on a stretcher accompany news commentary referring to Vietnam. The camera movement explores spaces on the periphery; similar to a cutaway it encourages active associations, here in a single continuous motion. Its implications are various: indicating the symbolic interaction of 'live' and mediatized realities, reminding us that the world outside the prison walls is not necessarily safer, or saner, than the one inside. As the door closes behind the prisoner, the guard opens a peephole, taking a look inside before the camera zooms in to frame the man – naked, confined, alone – at the window. Such scenes remind us of direct cinema's tenet that pro-filmic reality – even when limiting context to the recorded event alone – produces complex metaphors and meanings that can parallel fictional constructs. As Colin Young saw it: 'A [documentary's] events will have the weight of general metaphor, but first and foremost they will have meaning within their own context' (Young 2003 [1974]: 108).

Compelling in its simplicity and completeness, even with its subtle editorializing, this sequence actually performs much of what direct cinema's advocates preached – an appearance of non-intervention, fidelity to subjects, narrative legibility without added contextual information, mobile camera, sync sound, natural lighting and settings, and so on – and it shows how involving this approach can be. Yet, as the tilt up to the television hints, there is no unified or 'unmediated' observational position, though there are meaningful engagements that can nonetheless speak through the film.

GREY GARDENS (1975)

As Beattie concisely puts it, while practitioners of direct cinema and *cinéma vérité* made strong claims for 'the efficacy of their respective methods', these claims were 'not necessarily borne out in practice'. Both movements contained elements of intervention and efforts towards 'pure' observation, and the films they produced often relied on overlapping techniques (2004: 84). The Maysles' *Grey Gardens* is a particularly interesting case of this fusion.[8] The film was made under conditions that would confound attempts at non-interference and thus offers a glimpse of filmmakers who seem both at home and off-balance, adjusting to the capricious and sometimes anarchic lives into which they've arrived with their cameras.

As Charles Reynolds stressed in a mid-1960s interview with Al Maysles: 'Maysles's passion for recording life "as it actually happens" is equalled only by his sensitivity to the people and situations he films [. . .] [Maysles's] rule is never to tamper, never to impose on what is before the camera, but to watch and wait and react freely, approaching the scene spontaneously without preconceived ideas' (Reynolds 1979 [1964]: 401). If there were efforts at making *Grey Gardens* adhere to these principles, they were short lived. The film's restless and demanding subjects – 'Big' Edie and 'Little' Edie Bouvier Beale – required a good deal of attention, engagement and negotiation. An example of this appears when Big Edie, who has arthritis and is unsteady on her feet, says, 'I'm going to need David's hand to get up'. David, holding the sound equipment, moves into the filmed space to help her, and Al's camera briefly catches him in frame but quickly shies away, never showing David's face, finally zooming into an awkward close-up on the fabric of Big Edie's dress. Shots like this suggest the kind of compromise Jay Ruby refers to as ' "accidental" reflexivity' (1988: 73). The Maysles are obliged to break observational rules (and Vogels reminds us that nearly every Maysles film violates these rules [Vogels 2005: 149]), but still avoid the more open stance of French *cinéma vérité*. Rouch stated that he was not interested in the 'cinema of truth, but the truth of cinema' (Rouch and Feld 2003: 14). *Grey Gardens* on the other hand seems committed to capturing more essential truths about the lives of its subjects that lie beyond contingent cinematic truths. Al claimed in numerous interviews that the camera's presence changed nothing about the Beales' behavior – we see the truth of their lives. But it is worth asking: do *Grey Gardens*' truths run any deeper than cinematic artifice itself?

The idea for *Grey Gardens* began in a project initiated by Lee (Bouvier) Radziwill, sister of Jacqueline Kennedy Onassis. Radziwill hoped to make a film about her childhood memories on Long Island. As Al Maysles recalled, Radziwill was suddenly contacted by her aunt and cousin, who were facing threats of eviction by the Suffolk County Health Department, and she asked

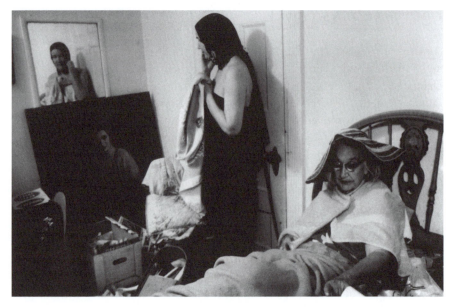

Figure 15. *Grey Gardens* (1975). Portrait Films. Courtesy of the Kobal Collection.

at that point if the Maysles brothers wanted to film at Grey Gardens. Little Edie would later describe the health inspectors' arrival in October 1971 as a 'raid' that traumatized her and 'almost killed' her mother through shock (Graham 2001 [1976]). At that time the brothers shot one and a half hours inside what newspapers would sensationally report as a 'garbage-ridden, filthy 28-room house with cats, fleas, cobwebs, and no running water'. Radziwill was reputedly so alarmed by the footage that she confiscated it. A clean-up and refurbishment took place in 1972, with Jackie O.'s financial and (much to the media's delight) on-site assistance. The filmmakers returned in September and October 1973, having agreed to pay the cash-strapped Beales $5,000 each and promising 20 percent of future profits from the film. The Maysles invested $50,000 in equipment and preparation for the shoot. In six weeks they had filmed '80 to 90 percent of the film', emerging with seventy hours of film and forty more of additional sound material (Graham 2001 [1976]).

What resulted is an observational documentary that seems always on the verge of breaking the bounds of cinema's narrative and perceptual frames, exemplifying the transitions and experiments going on in direct cinema. Indeed, as Al claimed, the aim behind *Grey Gardens* was always far less about creating a fly-on-the-wall exposé than about 'having a relationship' with the Beales (Froemke et al. 2001), perceivable through the off-camera banter that punctuates the film. Edie reveals her need for interaction: she is a restless interviewee, constantly pushing forward and stepping back (causing the camera to move forwards and backwards, struggling to maintain focus), running from well-lit rooms into dark corridors (forcing rapid adjustments to lighting – though Al recalled that the film stock, Kodak 7254, had a great 'tolerance for error' so that problems could be anticipated and later adjusted) (Froemke et al. 2001). From early on, Little Edie contrives much of the pro-filmic *mise-en-scène* and action, describing her 'revolutionary costume' and its rationale in detail, directing the crew to move through the garden and shoot from the top of the house. Highly conscious of the filming process, Edie urgently whispers 'the movie, the movie' to her mother when she threatens to take off her clothes in the sun.

At the same time the film reveals a meeting not just between observation and *vérité* interaction but between documentary – and its association with verifiable, factual discourses – and fiction. *Grey Gardens* is haunted by ghosts of gothic and romantic tales, and by Hollywood fantasy: the melodrama and the 'woman's film'. In the opening sequence, contrasting with its resplendent East Hampton neighbors, Grey Gardens exudes (even in its name) an overgrown, unkempt grandeur. A color shot of the house is intercut with a black-and-white photo, shifting to a sequence that outlines the Beales' ordeal with the Health Department; the contrast of color and black and white shrouds the house in mystery and isolates it in time. Grey Gardens easily recalls Billy Wilder's *Sunset Blvd.* (1950) where the character Joe Gillis encounters the faded glory of Norma Desmond's mansion, with its overgrown gardens and decrepit swimming pool. The house evokes the figure of an abandoned, aging woman: 'A neglected house gets an unhappy look; this one had it in spades', states Gillis; 'it was like that old woman in *Great Expectations*, that Miss Havisham in her rotting wedding dress and her torn veil, taking it out on the world because she'd been given the go by'. Norma is first glimpsed from behind a screen, sequestered and ominous (a similar image of Little Edie, speaking from behind a screen in an upstairs window, appears in Al Maysles's *The Beales of Grey Gardens* [2006], which features previously cut scenes).

Intertextual references abound: the gentle 1930s melody 'I See Your Face Before Me' plays beneath the opening sequence, helping to associate Grey Gardens with a bygone era. The sequence was developed, according to the filmmakers, to avoid using voiceover, but it also helps to underscore the sense of lost grandeur and the notion of the woman frozen in time as the world passes her by. The Beales' aristocratic connections are also emphasized, and 'real' royalty in the form of Jackie O. appears fleetingly in a photo where she is shown in the house assisting the clean-up. The fascination with celebrity extends to referencing the Maysles brothers' own: the sequence ends with a news article about the two descending on Grey Gardens to make a film.

The film's themes coalesce around the symbolic figure of the 'vanishing woman': in this case the aging woman deluded about her ongoing relevance while actually signifying a 'pathetic spectacle of loss'. Writing on *Sunset Blvd.*, Lucy Fischer suggests that the 'aging woman [. . .] was viewed by man only as a site of profound loss. And her sunset years stretched out as bleakly as the desolate Hollywood boulevard that presciently opens the film' (Fischer 1988: 112). For John David Rhodes, there are embedded social and symbolic connections between the Beales and the house they inhabit:

> Grey Gardens materializes very concretely the horizon of possibility for the Edies' interaction with and intervention in the world, and it is hardly incidental that *Grey Gardens* is a film about a mother and daughter living together in the family home; no accident that Little Edie's brothers are nowhere in sight [. . .]. Given the limits – both historically and contemporarily – placed on women's autonomy, the female child, much more than the male, will be subject to the rule of the house and the domestic sphere which tend to define, limit, and circumscribe her range of actions within the world. (2006: 86)

Complementing the idea of the women's close, entrapped relationship to the home is the ghost of the faded belle in Southern gothic literature and drama. The Maysles refer to themselves as 'gentlemen callers', a term that evokes, as in Tennessee Williams's *The Glass Menagerie*, empty promises of escape, faded youth, the pain of impossible romance and always the specter of madness (also associated with the feminine, as in the medical tradition of 'female hysteria'). Invoking one of Williams's most tragic heroines, the theatrical trailer quotes a critic from the *East Hampton Star*: 'The film promises to give Big and Little Edie as much a place in the life of our arts as Blanche DuBois has attained.' Little Edie herself underlines the comparisons when she comments, 'It's very difficult to keep the line between the past and the present, you know what I mean? It's awfully difficult'.

The filmmakers, who included co-directors/co-editors Muffie Meyer and Ellen Hovde and associate producer/co-editor Susan Froemke, were aware of these impressions and keen to make use of them. They recalled being struck by the overtones of 'aristocracy in decay [. . .] we kept talking about, "it's like Tennessee Williams, it's like Eugene O'Neill"' (Froemke et al. 2001). Even so, their dominant conceptions of the Beales were essentially the opposite of fading women isolated from the world. The Beales were 'not recluses' at all, and Hovde expressed an admiration for Big Edie, calling her 'strong and tough and willful and confident' and a dominant force in a tight-knit mother–daughter relationship. The Beales were 'nonconformists, they had made a stand' against suffocating cultural expectations and norms, they were 'courageous and inspirational'. For the filmmakers, *Grey Gardens* deals with 'feminist concerns', documenting what Little Edie refers to in the film as 'staunch' women who remained fiercely independent in the face of social, marital and financial difficulties, and who refused to cave in to paternal and other social expectations (Froemke et al. 2001).

There is evidence of these ideas in the finished film, and understanding the pressures of gender, class and social demands in the postwar era certainly underlies any fuller comprehension of how and why the Beales lived as they did. Always in tension with the invocation of the feminine figure marked by entrapment and loss are the simultaneous pressures that the subjects themselves – in particular Little Edie – exert against these narrative frames. Little Edie is not simply a curiosity in a sideshow: she constantly violates the presumed safe space that separates on-screen character and camera, disrupting the delicate balance between filmmaker and filmed, audience and screen, voyeur and object of the gaze. She might be seen as 'the director of her own show' (Vogels 2005: 136). As she pushes her face into the lens, we might perceive the weight of her embodied presence and the hesitancy and disorientation of the body behind the camera.

In Little Edie's 'revolutionary' costumes, and in observing the fine line drawn between performed and real life, the film partly resembles other celebrity documentaries such as *Dont Look Back* or *Gimme Shelter*. But the Beales' performances also offer profound elements of excess and even of camp (as borne out, subsequently, by Little Edie's appeal to drag performers). Camp, as exemplified so flamboyantly in the early films of John Waters, is based on 'the great discovery that the sensibility of high culture has no monopoly upon refinement [. . .] camp taste supervenes upon good taste as a daring and witty hedonism' (Sontag 1991 [1964]: 109). These ideas in many ways reflect the dynamics of excess and the disruption of 'good taste' seen in the film, as well as suggesting a shared camp aesthetic that brings together the film's still increasing army of fans.

A politics of camp excess is hinted at in the scene acted out to Norman Vincent Peale's 'try really try' radio sermon. Little Edie mimics Peale's hortatory speech while at the same time offhandedly inspecting her white high-heeled shoe. Through her flattened delivery and disinterested stare, she seems to undermine the rhetorical and masculine force of the sermon, ignoring Peale's demands for attention. When Peale states that his listeners have to 'get on top and stay there', Big Edie intones, 'does that mean women too?' In the end, they both agree that the sermon was 'very good', adding perfunctorily that it was 'very long'. In the much-admired 'staunch' scene that follows, Little Edie's costume of the day appears to be battle fatigues. As she describes her defiance against social and family pressures, she pushes her face and body forward into the lens, threatening the presumed autonomy of the camera.

So why did audiences and critics often take away a different impression of the Beales? Why would people argue, as Al recollected, that 'Edie Beale, she's senile, and the other one is demented; they're incompetent, so they can't be filmed' (Pryluck 1976: 12)? As Vogels outlines, ethical concerns have long dominated discussions of the direct cinema approach (2005: 152–3) and many critics found *Grey Gardens* particularly exploitative. Relating it to a circus side-show, one stated: 'we are in the position of those crowds who came and paid to look at the Wolf Boy in his cage' (Haskell 1976: 118). When recalling these reactions, the filmmakers have always dismissed them as opinions of conventional people taken aback by the Beales' 'unconventional' and 'nonconformist' lives (Froemke et al. 2001). But perhaps the idea of celebrating the Beales, as emphasized by Al in interviews (and even by Little Edie herself, who often expressed delight in the film, stating, 'thank god I met the Maysles') (Graham 2001 [1976]),[9] came up against *Grey Gardens*' narrative frame, cultural allusions and marketing tactics that together worked to produce a rather different range of effects. As Jack Kroll stated in *Newsweek*, the Beales seemed to inhabit 'a time warp of their own'. Indeed, the luridly fascinating spectacle of women trapped in time and the Beales' uncanny similarity to classic American gothic fictions were among the film's key selling points: both the Kroll quote and the Blanche DuBois reference appeared in a promotional trailer for the film.

As Al Maysles's camera roves across Big Edie lying on her stained, bare mattress amid the refuse of bags, tissues and dirty dishes, 'inspirational' is probably not a word that immediately comes to mind. Yet Big Edie's words suggest a challenge to any pigeonholing of her as a victim: 'I love that smell', she states; 'I thrive on it. It makes me feel good. I'm not ashamed of anything. Where my body is is a very precious place'. Such comments imply a challenge to conformist beliefs about social and domestic order, gender, the body, age. They might even encourage readings that pose the Beales' 'savage' lives as a subversion of antiseptic, bourgeois norms, their closeness to animals, both through association and lifestyle, being a case in point. Yet whether the film successfully empowers or celebrates the Beales remains an open question. Films always elicit competing reactions from audiences, but the negative and pitying responses generated by *Grey Gardens* cannot solely be pinned on narrow-minded audiences.

In examining *Grey Gardens*' connotations, it is worth looking more closely at the film's structure and how it was produced. As in many observational documentaries, *Grey Gardens* draws a 'slight narrative' out of the disarray and disorder of real life that was captured in dozens of hours of rushes. The editing process, in particular, was both painstaking and interpretive. Hovde recalled:

> When the material came in we just let it wash over us. [. . .] You almost couldn't tell if you had anything until you cut it, because it was so free flowing. Very repetitive. It didn't have a structure. There were no events.

There was nothing around which a conversation was going to wheel. It was all kind of the same in a gross way, and you had to dig into it, try to find motivations, condense the material to bring out psychological tones. (quoted in Rosenthal 2007: 282)

Indeed, while edited into a certain coherence, Little and Big Edie seem to be free-associating much of the time, and certainly an interesting paradox suggested by the film is that of characters obsessed with lost time who actually seem to have nothing but time on their hands. For Davidson, this sense of repetitive or static temporality reflects the 'modernist' nature of the film, where 'one scene follows the next without respect for orderly temporal sequencing' (Davidson 1981: 8).

Amid a free-flowing, modernist rhythm, the film does develop a forward momentum: a sense of mystery or gathering conspiracy (Jerry and the 'Marble Faun') and a specific set of themes. As Meyer noted: 'In documentary one is taking reality and trying to squeeze it into a fictional form, a form that has a middle, climax, and end; certainly not one that life actually has' (Froemke et al. 2001). The 'slight narrative' of *Grey Gardens* thus mirrors impulses in representation to discipline, via rhetorical and narrative means, the unpredictable and disordered nature of experience. Moreover, as the film was geared towards theatrical release, there was a commercial imperative to appeal to audiences. With a final investment of close to half a million dollars, the Maysles needed to deliver a film with characters, tensions and experiences with which audiences could strongly connect.

Thus, though the narrative is hardly linear, there are tensions underlying *Grey Gardens* arising from framing strategies that seem to restrict rather than enhance the range of connotations that characters and events might generate. This tension is palpable in what the filmmakers referred to as the 'Pink Room' scene, which serves as the film's climax of sorts. So far, *Grey Gardens* has indicated Little Edie's lasting regrets and a simmering, long-term dispute between mother and daughter that here flares into open argumentation. Little Edie sings a song that dramatizes her infatuation with David, 'People Will Say We're in Love' (from the musical *Oklahoma!*), much to her mother's consternation. Edie's insistent, weird rendition has 'ruined breakfast', left Big Edie irritated and out of sorts and even precipitated a moment in which Big Edie's bathing-suit top falls off on camera. After calming down on the terrace, Little Edie re-enters the room and glances left at a portrait of herself as a girl (already shown in the bedroom when she recounted her days as a model and debutante). In the scene just before the 'Pink Room', Little Edie remarks that she sees herself 'as a little girl, Mother's little girl' living in Grey Gardens. Her glance at the portrait seems to trigger another, more violent bout of regret. A proposal of marriage, Little Edie claims, was ruined by her mother's intervention, even though it had been her 'last chance' to get away from Grey Gardens' grip and an increasingly smothering mother–daughter relationship. She openly weeps at the Maysles: 'She wouldn't give me a chance. [. . .] I'm bored with these awful people'.

The scene hinges on the cutaway to the portrait. Michael Rabiger describes what he calls the 'legitimate' use of cutaways in the documentary context: 'Many times you will use eyeline shifts to "motivate" cutaways. [. . .] Frequently a person will show a picture, refer to an object in the room, or look offscreen at someone, and in each case he directs our attention to a legitimate cutaway' (2004: 366). In this sense, the cutaway here is legitimate, as it appears motivated by Edie's glance. But it is also an associative cut, what Eisenstein called 'a reconstruction of the laws of the thought process' (1949: 106). The effect is melodramatic and encourages speculation as to Edie's private thoughts while highlighting the persistent themes of loss and regret that encircle her. Though employing a fictional eye-line match the shot is actually poorly lined up: other shots in the scene suggest the portrait would have been hanging in front of Edie as she entered the room, and not to the left where she glances (although the zoom in to the picture from the left disguises this somewhat). The shot sums up some of the problems of transposing the techniques of fictional realism into nonfiction material: Edie's regret has already been potently portrayed, so the cutaway simply underlines our sense of gaining 'true' insights into her private life and past. On the other hand, the cut's lack of seamlessness might spark an awareness of our own capacities for belief in representation: how viewers participate in constructing myths as reality and fictions as truth.

The 'Pink Room' scene, situated as a climax to the film, offers further clues about how central the editing process can become in direct cinema. As Hovde recalled, though the scene comes near the end, it was actually one of the first the editors cut. They considered it to be the point where things 'came to a head emotionally [. . .] once you had that, you then began to understand how you were going to get to it' (Froemke et al. 2001). Elsewhere, Froemke notes: 'If we're lucky, one scene might suggest a strong ending, and that's what we cut first. Then you know what you're working towards' (Froemke 2003: 8). Essentially, then, much of the editing process involved constructing a comprehensible story around the 'Pink Room' scene, which could serve as an emotional climax. The raw footage would have been pared down to support the conflicts suggested here, with its themes of spurned proposals and Little Edie's sense of suffocated potential.

The film's final shot shows Edie dancing in the foyer, shot from behind a balustrade. The instrumental version of the song that opens the film, 'I See Your Face Before Me' ('crowding my every dream', the unheard lyrics would continue), accompanies the dance. 'She's inside her dreams', Al stated, noting that he was aware even while filming that the balustrade seemed to evoke a prison, or a birdcage from which Edie could not 'fly away' (Froemke et al. 2001). A similar shot of Big Edie behind a balustrade opens the film. Again the final scene engages with intertextual references: Norma Desmond lost in her dream world as she dramatically descends her staircase; Baby Jane dancing on the beach, lost in reverie as the world watches in horror. Little Edie is dressed in black: she dances off screen into black space and silence as the music stops.

In spite of these framing devices, it is possible to see the Beales exerting certain pressures against any definitive reading of their lives and motivations. There is a mixture of exuberance and ironic awareness in their words and behavior, and clearly their 'actual' lives could never have been contained in a ninety-four minute portrait in any event. Indeed, much material that was left out – accessible in DVD special features and in *The Beales of Grey Gardens* – arguably better supports the filmmakers' conceptions of the Beales as independent and inspirational figures than does the original film. In one outtake, we see Big Edie tenderly entreat Little Edie to make a costume change (we discover that she made Little Edie change costumes as often as ten times per day). The scene captures the exceptional dynamics of a relationship based on mutual consent, familial devotion, fantasy and constant role-playing. We see how accustomed the Beales were to performing and dressing up for each other, and how they might have adapted this performance element for the camera. In the outtakes, the Beales' long-term financial difficulties are also clearer. (In the original, one of the few references to money appears in a scene where Big Edie is writing checks, conveying an impression that their shabby surroundings have more to do with eccentricity than financial need.)

Perhaps the 'real' Grey Gardens lies beyond the confines of the original film, and beyond demands to pare down the subjects of representation into a range of accessible themes, storylines and tropes. An open dialogue has developed between the film and an archive of outtakes, recollections, ephemera and other extra-filmic material that, via DVDs and the Internet, have become integrated into the *Grey Gardens* viewing experience. In this sense, *Grey Gardens* is an example of how a documentary – or any cultural production – forms part of processes of making meanings that are never static but constantly subjected to changing interpretations, audiences and viewing/distribution technologies. The two women have entered into cultural myth, attaining cult status through the film and, after Little Edie's death (in Florida in 2002), through a whole *Grey Gardens* industry that has included fashion lines, a Broadway musical (reputedly the first ever adapted from a documentary) and an HBO dramatization. *Grey Gardens* dolls, t-shirts, coloring books and holiday cards are available for purchase online, while Little Edie imitators draw thousands of Internet hits and enthusiastic comments from new fans around the world.

For Albert Maysles, direct cinema practitioners were idealists: 'The most important revolution in documentary was the one I took part in', he argued (Iseli 1998: 15). Yet one of the great chroniclers of the American scene, Arthur Miller, felt differently about direct cinema. After seeing the Maysles brothers' *Salesman*, the author of *Death of a Salesman* expressed reservations about an approach that lacked insight, context and history: 'you are stopped at the wall of skin', he said (Canby 1969: C1). Perhaps a problem with an idealist version of direct cinema lies in a conflict between illusions of present-tense immediacy and the 'authentic' and intimate revelations it strove to convey. In retaining the explanatory functions of narrative and the sense of 'seeing but not being seen' that underlies the pleasures of voyeurism, the democratic ideals of direct cinema frequently broke down, essentially replicating the hierarchies, desires and demands for entertaining spectacle found in more traditional cinematic forms. But neither could the 'pure presence' of direct cinema really compete with the imaginative function of realism and suspension of disbelief in fiction, precisely because the pro-filmic stuff of documentary is always 'real' – contingent, interconnected, temporally displaced – far more complex and disorienting than shots, angles, zooms and even performance can relay. This sense of what is absent always haunts the documentary image, and in part defines its uncanny fascination; to suppress it is to initiate, even at the level of the subconscious, an impression of falseness.

In moving in this chapter from early experiments in direct cinema to *Grey Gardens* and its 'modernist' intertextual and cultural resonances, I wanted to suggest how direct cinema's ideals of truthful immediacy came into productive interplay with the multiplicities and contingencies of truth that would begin to define postmodern documentary approaches. Noël Carroll suggests that accusations about direct cinema being interpretive – even fictive – came to widely 'stigmatize' all nonfiction films' claims to truth (Carroll 1996: 225). Critiques of documentary truth intensified, accelerated by a backlash against 'exploitative' direct cinema that came with television series such as *An American Family* in 1973. For Jean Baudrillard, the Loud family in the series confirmed the collapse of public and private space: 'the entire universe comes to unfold arbitrarily on your domestic screen' like an 'all-too-visible [. . .] obscenity' (Baudrillard 1983: 130–1).

Still, direct cinema's influence has persisted: in the US, Charles Burnett, Barbara Kopple, Jennie Livingston and Rex Bloomstein are just a few directors who have perpetuated and expanded the approach. Direct cinema stylizations still largely dominate the 'look' and structures of belief that define documentary: sync sound, rough continuity editing littered with jump cuts, the wobblyscope of handheld cameras – all constitute a key strand of documentary's generic signature. As Dai Vaughan suggests, 'after *Primary*, documentary was able to redefine its mission as the entrainment of the unrehearsed into the process of signification; and from that point, the markers of spontaneity began to be understood as the markers of documentary per se' (Vaughan 1999: 147). As a result, mockumentaries also tend to favor direct cinema stylings: Jim McBride's *David Holzman's Diary* (1967), Mitchell Block's *No Lies* (1974) and rockumentary spoofs such as *This is Spinal Tap* (1984) copy its 'look' and key narrative strategies such as the crisis structure. *Spinal Tap* even references famous moments such as *Primary*'s traveling shot at Kennedy's campaign rally: in Rob Reiner's parody the shoulder-mounted camera doggedly follows the heavy metal band as they get lost in a series of corridors and stairways. Direct cinema's technical and stylistic keynotes have been widely adapted to mainstream industry practices, honed into 'real-life' news programming and innumerable reality shows. As Corner succinctly notes: 'Verité has been a central strand informing the newer styles of "infotainment"' (Corner 1996: 33), though primarily as a stylistic signifier of immediacy rather than as a comprehensive philosophy or mindset.

NOTES

1. Beattie references Winston's concept of 'supervening necessities' (Winston 1986, 1998) and Allen and Gomery's notion of historical and contextual 'generative mechanisms' (Allen and Gomery 1985).
2. Stephen Mamber states: 'the filmmaker is a reporter with a camera instead of a notebook' (1974: 3).
3. The phrase means literally 'we are in the bath' (or perhaps 'in hot water') and is translated in Rouch and Feld as 'we are in the know' (2003: 328). It might also imply 'we are implicated' or 'we are in the midst of things'.
4. See, for example, Mamber (1974), Barnouw (1983: 240–55), O'Connell (1992), Beattie (2004: 85–8), Ellis and McLane (2005: 208–26), Saunders (2007).
5. See Saunders (2007: 102).
6. See Saunders (2007: 34).
7. See also Kahana (2008: 222–5), Benson and Anderson (2002: 10–24).
8. The filmmakers have, in a general sense, referred to *Grey Gardens* as 'a *cinéma vérité* film' (Froemke et al. 2001).
9. Little Edie, never wholly consistent, could easily reverse her opinion, stating in 1998: 'I was so disappointed in *Grey Gardens*! It upset me terribly [. . .] I thought we were going to make some money, and we didn't make a thing' (Crain 1998: 43). The Beales were never paid their 20 percent since, Al argued, the film never turned a profit.

CHAPTER 7

Relative Truths: Documentary and Postmodernity

As the Vietnam War shuddered to an end, dominant images of a nation underpinned by universal aspirations were undergoing a crisis of containment. Fault lines had become visible through issues such as the war, demands for civil rights and legal protections for marginalized peoples. Voices displaced or ignored by aggressively marketed versions of 'average' and 'typical' American values were asserting presence and influence. The US was always already irreducibly diverse, multicultural and multi-ethnic, but the idea of America was, as this book has stressed, also subject to complex negotiations among different social strata and competing ideological influences. During the 1960s and 1970s, hegemonic concepts of US cultural and national identity came under renewed pressures, particularly in the media. If, for much of the 1960s, media outlets had suppressed controversial political content, by the decade's end they were reflecting widespread public disillusion. Americans could hardly avoid the barrage of photographic and moving images revealing the brutalities of military actions overseas and unrest at home.

As US troops were withdrawing from Vietnam, Peter Davis's *Hearts and Minds* (1974), which concludes with Vietnam veteran Randy Floyd declaiming the 'criminality' of US policymakers, won an Academy Award. Emile de Antonio criticized the film's 'political emptiness', lack of historical rigor and 'japing, middle class superiority' (de Antonio 2000 [1974]: 359); still Davis's film and its reception seemed to underline a period of collective national contrition known as the 'Vietnam syndrome'. Producer Bert Schneider's acceptance speech at the Oscars included reading a telegram from the Viet Cong delegation at the Paris Peace Talks; this was countered by Frank Sinatra's and Bob Hope's apology for Schneider's words later in the show, in effect summing up the nation's broader ideological – and generational – rifts (McEnteer 2006: 19). And if the periodization of US history into pre- and post-Vietnam eras – American 'innocence' and 'loss of innocence' – has become something of a cliché, still the fallout from this particular protest era across the political and cultural landscape should not be underestimated. The legacies of Vietnam-era cultural shifts are palpable in documentaries produced during the Vietnam syndrome years, through the rise of Reagan-era neo-conservatism and into the Bill Clinton presidency.

As this chapter outlines, documentary was redefined and rejuvenated as a popular form and mode of self-expression during this period, reflecting a range of pertinent issues: political debates, multicultural views and the profound effects of the postmodern turn in cultural theory and the arts. Moreover, the broad 'democratization' of filmmaking advanced, with cheaper technologies such as video newly marketed to the public. Revaluations and vigorous critiques of documentary conventions and assumptions meant that by the 1990s, documentary as a popular term and concept arguably no longer resembled what it had twenty years earlier.

LEANER TIMES

During the 1970s, what *Variety* calls 'nonperformance' documentaries were having scant impact at the box office. Indeed it would have been easy to conclude that theatrical documentary was a thing of the past. Karen Cooper, director of New York's Film Forum, recalled that, 'in 1972, we had zero competition for documentaries' (Harmetz 1986: C21). It didn't help that documentary was aligned in the popular imagination to discourses of sobriety, or that direct cinema had become integral to the conventions of television journalism, thereby associating documentary's most prominent style with information-gathering and the grim realities shown on daily newscasts. Perceptions of documentary reliability also had been undermined by controversial military propaganda films such as *Why Vietnam?* (1965), shown widely in schools. The film evoked Capra's *Why We Fight* series in painting communism in Southeast Asia as equivalent to the global security threats posed by Nazism (Springer 1986: 161). By the war's end, such 'voice of god' pronouncements seemed only to further underline the evasive machinations of government policymakers.

With a few notable exceptions (for example, *The Sorrow and the Pity* [1972] and *The Ra Expeditions* [1972]), 'nonperformance' documentaries were difficult to sell on the big screen, and by the late 1970s and early 1980s audiences were still by and large staying away (Cohn 1992: 22). With the re-ascendancy of Hollywood's blockbuster mentality after *Jaws* (1975) and *Star Wars* (1977), competition for screen time was fierce. The highest grossing nonfiction releases were, by far, rockumentary and comedy films such as Martin Scorsese's *The Last Waltz* (1978), the Led Zeppelin concert film *The Song Remains the Same* (1976) and several Richard Pryor 'live' films which lampooned the politics of race and class through explicit, subversive stand-up comedy sketches. There were a few surprises: the relative financial success of Barbara Kopple's *Harlan County USA* (1976) was driven by rave reviews and word of mouth. The film followed the events of a bitterly fought miners' strike in Harlan County, Kentucky, recalling the activist traditions of 1930s documentary. Perhaps fittingly, the best documentary Oscar was presented to Kopple by the formerly blacklisted playwright and Nykino supporter, Lillian Hellman. Still, such films earned only a fraction of what the performance films were making (Cohn 1992: 22).

At less conspicuous levels, documentary form and practice was continually evolving, with the help of technological and distribution developments. As discussions of movements such as the FPL and direct cinema have shown, not only the practice but the very idea of documentary has been continually reshaped by remediation. Throughout the 1970s, video technology was becoming cheaper and alternative media and community access groups were taking advantage. In the late 1960s, the Challenge for Change program at the National Film Board of Canada had been a landmark experiment in using video to encourage local, small-scale filmmaking about social issues. George Stoney, who headed the program until 1970, set up the Alternate Media Center at New York University in 1972, and the same year Jon Alpert and Keiko Tsuno established the Downtown Community Television Center, also in New York (Barnouw 1983: 290–1). Their video features included *Health Care: Your Money or Your Life* (1977) and *Vietnam: Picking Up the Pieces* (1977): riveting, critically lauded works that gained attention through screenings on public television. (*Health Care* in particular makes Michael Moore's *Sicko* [2007] seem almost tame.) Half-inch portable video was introduced in the US in 1968 and became the medium of choice for various 'guerrilla' movements such as Videofreex (founded in 1969), Ant Farm (1968) and People's Video Theater (1969). Influenced by the media theory of Marshall McLuhan and marked by a 'pronounced strain of technological euphoria and utopianism', Michael Shamberg and the Raindance Corporation published *Guerrilla Television* in 1971 (Boddy 1990: 92–3). The book offered a manifesto for underground video collectives to break the stranglehold of mainstream television networks and reach out to mass audiences.

Other projects, some working with video, others 16 mm film, strove towards wider access that could alter the monotone landscape of US television. The influential African American political affairs series *Black Journal*, produced by William Greaves, appeared on PBS in 1968. It covered current concerns of the black community, examined controversial issues such as racial discrimination in the media and provided air time to black leaders such as Angela Davis and Bobby Seale (Lott 1999). The innovative video project *Detroit Black Journal* premiered on Detroit's public station WTVS the same year, lampooning racial stereotypes and promoting African American activism and cultural production.

By the early 1980s, Sony Betacam brought video camera and sound together, eliminating awkward cables and initiating the video 'revolution'. With the marketing of portable camcorders in the mid-1980s, independent video groups gained a foothold around the country (Fuller 1994; Halleck 2002). If, in general, the political left was 'slow to engage with public access', key collectives such as Paper Tiger Television, established in 1981 by DeeDee Halleck, were driven by the ideals of reinvigorating, through widespread access, the nation's faith in participatory democracy. Paper Tiger aimed to 'demystify the information industry' and still defines itself in opposition to corporatized mass media (quoted in Boddy 1990: 96–7). Independent and small-scale documentary was increasingly viewed as aligned to left-wing politics, partly due to practical links between documentary activism, demands for access and alternative media outlets, partly because of many filmmakers' alliances with political and aesthetic movements such as feminist counter-cinema and Third Cinema. Certainly the form's heuristic and muckraking potential seemed uniquely suited to bringing 'unrepresented or underrepresented' social issues to light (Bullert 1997: xv). 'Documentary is a battleground of social and historical truth', notes Michael Chanan, 'and this is one of the main reasons why people make them' (2007: 22–3).

For much of the 1970s and 1980s, major television networks presented few opportunities to independent producers, so low-budget film and video documentaries were generally found on public television, self-distributed or distributed through organizations such as Kino and California Newsreel to universities, schools and film festivals. Though on the surface they would hardly seem to pose a threat to large corporate and political interests, independent documentaries became targets for right-wing attacks. The Reagan and Bush administrations (1980–92) polarized the political climate, intensifying a conservative agenda well beyond previous administrations. The Reagan years saw steep funding increases to the military industries, endorsed the proliferation of nuclear arms, reinvigorated Cold War rhetoric and spearheaded a renewed emphasis on heterosexual 'family values' and traditional sexual attitudes (hence the administration's retrograde response to the AIDS crisis). As Norman Denzin describes it: 'Throughout the 1980s the New Right constructed conceptions of who the ideal subjects were and how they personified the sacred values of religion, hard work, health, and self-reliance. This ideological movement redefined the meaning of an "ordinary, normal, commonplace" individual', and 'played on common sense and ordinary American values' (Denzin 1991: 6). Battles about national character and the 'true' definitions of 'America' and 'American' were waged with renewed force in the media and at all levels of government.

Small-scale production was under pressure: the federal Cable Franchise Policy and Communications Act of 1984 took away the power of local authorities to regulate cable access, meaning that 'underused' public channels could be appropriated by powerful business interests (Boddy 1990: 96). Added to this, the presumed threat from liberal and left-wing filmmaking was addressed by new, Reagan administration guidelines for government funding. The *New York Times* predicted 'leaner times for documentaries', citing ongoing problems with fundraising and in particular federal directives declaring that any project advocating 'a particular program of social action or change' was ineligible for National Endowment for the Humanities grant money – at that point a mainstay of independent documentary, having awarded $4.4 million to various projects in 1983 alone (Stein 1984: 25). Filmmakers found themselves caught up in political rows enthusiastically followed, and often fanned, by the media. There were attempts to block broadcasts of films such as *Dark Circle* (1982), about the nuclear weapons industry; *Days of Rage: The Young Palestinians* (1989), which dealt with the Palestinian Intifada and with calls for a Palestinian state; *Stop the Church* (1990), a vigorous critique of the Catholic Church's views on contraception and safe sex; and most controversially, Marlon T. Riggs's *Tongues Untied* (1989), discussed below. Bette Jean Bullert explains: 'These battles raised questions about which views of reality would be allowed to contend on the public television airwaves, and which would predominate' (Bullert 1997: 2).

Declamations against documentary 'propaganda' gained renewed force. The Oscar-winning short *If You Love This Planet* (1982), a filmed lecture about the dangers of nuclear weapons, was officially designated by the US Department of Justice as 'foreign political propaganda' and public screenings were suppressed (Guenette 1987: S-26). As for PBS, once seen as the exemplar of the 'Great Society' ideals advanced in the 1960s, interrogations of its relevance were rife. PBS's stated mission to 'give voice to the voiceless' was re-examined, and its role in a 'heterogeneous and changing society' was being redefined along strict ideological lines (Bullert 1997: 91). A long-term 'political tug-of-war' ensued which saw PBS programmers on the front line, negotiating tensions between the new conservatism and politically motivated funding policies, and filmmakers demanding opportunities to air viewpoints on social realities they believed were being hidden from the public by corporate media interests (Bullert 1997: 2).

THE *RASHOMON* EFFECT

Yet less than two years after the *New York Times* predicted 'leaner times' for documentaries, an unexpected, parallel phenomenon was emerging: theatrical documentary was undergoing a revival. The *Times* suddenly headlined: 'Nonfiction is Surging in Movies'. Films such as Claude Lanzmann's *Shoah* (1985) and Martin Bell's *Streetwise* (1985) were, as one distributor put it, 'wildly successful' at the box office (Harmetz 1986: C21). The films were very different, but both engaged with subjects and provided cinematic experiences missing from mainstream media. *Shoah* consisted of nine hours of evasive, frustrating, gripping testimonies about the Holocaust; *Streetwise* drew viewers, through its *vérité*-style intimacy, into the marginal lives of homeless youths in Seattle.

The resurgence of theatrical documentary might be attributed to several factors: a rise in the number of cinemas capable of showing 16 mm films (though transfer to 35 mm would become the norm), the exploitation of urban markets and deployment of sophisticated 'niche' advertising campaigns (*Shoah* was promoted in cities with large Jewish populations, *The Times of Harvey Milk* [1984] was targeted at gay audiences) and shifts in audience tastes towards reality-based stories. Importantly, there was also greater interest in low-budget documentaries among distributors, who viewed them as lesser financial risks than big-budget features (Harmetz 1986: C21). During a period when cinema was dominated by 'corporate movie making' (*An Officer and a Gentleman* [1982], *Top Gun* [1986]) (Davies and Wells 2002: 4), documentaries were meeting changing expectations. Audiences seemed willing to accept – indeed were demanding – more fluid, unexpected, entertaining approaches to on-screen reality.

Subtle shifts in style and structure were becoming common. Suggesting the influence of innovative directors such as Werner Herzog (*Precautions Against Fanatics* [1969]), Michael Rubbo and Les Blank, filmmakers were disrupting traditional assumptions of authority and immediacy, instead playing with instability, irony and outright manipulation. Errol Morris's *Gates of Heaven* (1978) and *Vernon, Florida* (1981) and Ross McElwee's *Sherman's March* (1986), for example, drew out the comic potential embedded in documentary's pose of seriousness. *Gates of Heaven*, a tale of two pet cemeteries, derives its situational irony and impression of authenticity from highlighting rather than editing out 'bad takes' and outrageous comments delivered with forthright sincerity. Influenced by the ironic political critique and collage method of Emile de Antonio, Connie Field's *The Life and Times of Rosie the Riveter* (1980) encouraged audiences to laugh at the sexism of old promotional and documentary films, while offering a message of female empowerment. There *was* something funny about the earnestness of the documentaries that most Americans had grown up with in classrooms or obediently watched on educational television – and filmmakers were acknowledging it. These new documentaries permitted audiences to laugh at reality and, problematically in some cases, at other people: they were in this sense disruptive, liberating cinema experiences.

Following this trend, Michael Moore's *Roger and Me* (1989) injected humor into political documentary, a form better known for impassioned critique and moralizing. Moore's film both relies on and plays with embedded assumptions of documentary sobriety: this double-edged strategy is key to *Roger and Me*'s ability to surprise, amuse and inform all at once. As Moore stated: 'We violated the two rules of documentary filmmaking: our film is entertaining and people are going to see it' (quoted in Oberacker 2009: 1). But conventional assumptions weren't dismissed easily. *Roger and Me* was the most financially successful feature documentary ever released – but it wasn't, to many, a documentary at all. Touted for an Oscar, the Academy Awards committee summarily rejected it, citing concerns about verifiability and accurate sequencing. In the *New Yorker*, critic Pauline Kael derided the film as 'glib' and 'manipulative' (quoted in Bullert 1997: 157).

Moore's popular success signalled a commercial potential scarcely imagined a decade earlier. Documentary auteurs such as Morris, Moore, McElwee, Trinh T. Minh-ha and Barbara Hammer were building bodies of work at the same time that American 'indie' directors like Spike Lee, Jim Jarmusch and David Lynch were gaining prominence: together they signalled demands for alternatives to Hollywood's blockbuster mentality. For Chanan, around this time we might observe 'a crucial shift in the documentary idiom, almost an epistemological break, in which the old idea of objectivity is seen as naive and outmoded' (2007: 241). Documentaries were reflecting profound, popular shifts towards relativist views; they were becoming more idiosyncratic and less orthodox. Michael Renov has seen this movement as linked to changes in social attitudes where 'universalist' stories that once strove to articulate common interests were giving way to expressions of local knowledge that were openly subjective and could emphasize relative and contingent experiences (Renov 2004: 176).

Following from Renov, Chanan likens the objective and observational strategies of traditional documentaries to the universalizing meta-narratives, or 'grand narratives', that cultural theorist François Lyotard named as the western legacies of the Enlightenment (2007: 241). These key assumptions – such as progressive or linear history, the absolute knowledge of science and common human understanding – were at the core of western belief systems. As Jonathan Kahana sees it, the notion of a unified or holistic American nation – an ideal often invoked, for example, via direct cinema journalism – forms one such 'grand narrative'. In its explicit address to the national 'we', television journalism becomes 'an apparatus of a national-security state', relying on the documentary form as 'an instrument of truth' that projects common national interests (Kahana 2008: 298). Questions of what group precisely made up this 'we', and who was speaking to and for whom, were becoming vital and unavoidable. Writing in 1979, Lyotard saw the West's grand (or

'master') narratives as being thrown into question by a heightened awareness
– manifested in the kinds of representations cultures produced for and about
themselves – of difference, diversity and multiplicity. A proliferation of local
and personal perspectives – '*petit récits*' or micronarratives – were characteristic
of postmodern incursions into the modern era (Lyotard 1984 [1979]).

Shifts towards personalized, self-reflexive perspectives in cultural and
artistic production came amid wider investigations into the nature and fixity
of representation, and of the cultural currency and inherited faith in concepts
such as Truth and Reason. Truth (with a capital 'T') was gradually shifting
towards conceptions of truth as mediated and culturally constructed, as in
Friedrich Nietzsche's much-cited postulation: 'Truths are illusions which
we have forgotten are illusions' (1979 [1873]: 84). Writing in 1993 about the
postmodern turn in documentary, Linda Williams observed that 'many theorists do share a sense that the Enlightenment projects of truth and reason are
definitively over' (1993: 9). Although postmodern theory was at first couched
less in political than aesthetic terms, politicized accounts quickly took shape:
History was in a process of becoming histories (or 'herstories'), Society and
Culture were erupting into local communities and subcultures, Feminism
was giving way to feminisms, and both 'color blind' and fixed notions of race
were being disrupted by a critical focus on socially and culturally determined
ethnicities and mixed identities. As Andreas Huyssen suggested, postmodernity harbored the promise of 'a "post-white", "post-male", "post-humanist",
"post-Puritan" world' (1986: 194). The pluralization of truth suggested ways
of recognizing cultural and experiential diversity and difference.

Alongside this crisis of truth and legitimation, a crisis of representation
was grounded in questioning notions that textual interpretation was a unified
or easily systematized process. The task became to investigate the limits of
representations themselves rather than questing after certitudes once presumed embedded within them. Emphasis shifted towards the 'slipperiness'
of texts, stressing that texts might be polysemous in their multiple meanings
and polyvalent depending on the subject positions of readers, viewers and
listeners who engaged with them. In the context of ethnographic film, Karl G.
Heider referred to shifts towards polysemous and polyvalent readings as the
'*Rashomon*' effect' (1988: 73–81), based on Akira Kurosawa's *Rashomon* (1950).

In Kurosawa's film, four observer-participants of a single event (the rape
of a woman and murder of her husband) each relate different accounts based
on their own witnessing. The 'actual' event remains effectively constant but
appears to recede, and we are left only with the witnesses' (including the dead
man's) varying points of view. The process of narration, then, rather than
firming up or securing a truthful meaning, actually begins to destabilize any
sense of origin: people, so the film states, 'only remember what they want to
remember'. Key to the film's unsettling power is that none of the differing

narratives are lies, per se: each contains elements of fact grounded in a point of view; each professes to be true, yet none is authoritative. The critical task in *Rashomon* shifts from chiefly analyzing narrative meaning to analyzing the process of *narrativizing*: of unpacking how we make sense out of disparate, disorganized experiences of the world. But this approach comes with its own hazards. For Williams, a danger lies in producing a kind of *mise-en-abyme*: 'if representations, whether visual or verbal, no longer refer to a truth or referent "out there" [. . .] then we seem to be plunged into a permanent state of the self-reflexive crisis of representation. What was once a "mirror with a memory" can now only reflect another mirror' (1993: 9). Strategies for negotiating the potential pitfalls of representing such 'relative truths' are explored in the next section.

Of course any 'break' from tradition is usually gradual, and less than clean. In the case of US documentary, key assumptions were just beginning to be seriously challenged. Traditional techniques such as talking heads and interpretive voiceover still bestowed films with instant authority and self-evident veracity. Of these, Ken Burns's work – such as *The Statue of Liberty* (1985), *The Congress* (1988) and his enormously popular *The Civil War* (1990) – epitomizes an educational approach which imparts facts and certainties through accessible narratives. This is history retold through skillful lighting, pan and scan, and seamless editing that promotes unquestionably liberal, yet determinedly consensus, public opinion (Edgerton 2001: 3–6). The doctrine of direct cinema objectivity also persisted, remaining dominant in film schools right through the 1990s. Finally, among elite tiers of critics and practitioners (such as the Academy of Motion Picture Arts and Sciences), fixed conceptions of authenticity and accuracy still defined the privileged term 'documentary'. Critics of unconventional approaches like that of *Roger and Me* continued to invoke a gold standard of documentary objectivity; thus Moore's film was 'not a documentary' but merely represented the 'filmmaker's personal viewpoint' (quoted in Bullert 1997: 158). Rather than enacting an epistemological break, then, documentary filmmakers and audiences were (and are) in a process of negotiating with history, with remediation and with the form's multiple, inherited conventions. These negotiations were taking place at every level of production, distribution and reception. Through community access, university screenings and festivals, 'no-budget' documentaries were reaching new audiences. PBS, too, was playing a key role, initiating the hour-long public affairs program *Frontline* in 1983 and *P.O.V.* in 1988, the latter screening films such as *American Tongues* (1988) and *Who Killed Vincent Chin?* (1988). Moore, Morris and Jennie Livingston were undeniable box-office forces.

POSTMODERNITY AND 'NEW' DOCUMENTARY

As a mode grounded, often naively, in presumptions of factuality and reason, and in its appeal to 'epistephilia' (or pleasure in knowing) (Nichols 1991: 178), documentary became a fruitful if problematic site for investigating postmodern questions about truth and representation. Documentary's presumed immediacy – the 'directness' of direct cinema – was generally cast aside in favor of foregrounding the gaps between the filmic end-product and the raw material. Representation was seen as constituted by distances and approximations.

Many practitioners were already addressing these concerns, questioning (or in some cases merely ignoring) the impersonal and universalizing conventions of what Nichols labels the observational and expository modes (1991: 34–44), effecting a displacement of the seemingly neutral 'we' of documentary towards asserting the subjectivity of the 'I'. Andrew Noren's diary films of the mid-1960s were in the vanguard, while Ed Pincus explored processes of constructing a sense of self through film in *Diaries* (1971–6). Feminist documentary often focused on the intense social pressures of female self-making: the work of Liane Brandon (*Anything You Want to Be* [1971] and *Betty Tells Her Story* [1972]) highlighted the individual costs to women of patriarchal social expectations. Margie Keller's *Misconception* (1978), about childbirth, JoAnn Elam's *Rape* (1978) and Bonnie Klein's *Not a Love Story* (1981, made with the NFB) variously manifested filmmakers who constructed openly subjective points of view: feminist visions of interactive *vérité*. Some replicated *vérité*'s problematic elements. Klein's film shows the filmmaker successfully 'educating' a female stripper about the truth of her exploitation and, while it asserts a convincing feminist message about commodification of the female body, it never quite destabilizes power and knowledge hierarchies between director and subject.

Documentaries were linking testimony and performative self-making; here people were no longer just documenting the world but were 'constituting their own lives through the production and viewing of the videotape' (Jakobsen and Seckinger 1997: 151). This performativity ranged from Ross McElwee's low-key reflections to the over-the-top self-inventions of *Madonna: Truth or Dare* (Alek Keshishian, 1991). Obvious practical and stylistic differences aside, both films explore lives constituted for and through the camera. This 'I' was both filmic and 'actual': McElwee saw himself as 'creating a persona for the film that's based upon who I am, but it isn't exactly me' (MacDonald 1998: 23). McElwee, Moore, Nick Broomfield and others were stressing the 'I' of the presenter/director: the 'filmmaker-as-star syndrome' (Arthur 1998: 73; 2005: 21).

Amid these moves towards first-person subjectivity, representing history posed particular challenges. For Fredric Jameson, the task of historical reconstruction conjures up a hall of mirrors, with postmodern subjects 'con-demned' to seek out the past not through directly accessed events and facts, but through memories, mediated texts and representations. The past itself 'remains forever out of reach' (1996 [1983]: 194). Similarly, documentaries were drawing attention to their own unstable truth claims by focusing on an inability to fill the gaps in the historical record. Strongly influential were European films dealing with the Second World War, which offered formal expressions of the fragility of memory and the combined impossibility and urgency of regaining the past. Lanzmann's *Shoah* contains personal accounts and recollections but no historical footage of concentration camps, gesturing to the unrepresentable traumas of the Holocaust. Hans-Jürgen Syberberg's *Our Hitler* (1977) – like *Shoah* a mammoth project, running over six hours – is an ironic take on the historical documentary and its obsessions with Nazism, a narrative that 'has already been textualized over and over again' (Nichols 1991: 236).

Much discussion of postmodern documentary in the US has focused on Morris's breakthrough success, *The Thin Blue Line* (1988). Reflecting Morris's private detective experience, it reconstructs a recent history involving murder, imprisonment and a miscarriage of justice. Conflicting testimonials begin to build up '*Rashomon*-style' (Hinson 1988: D7) and seriousness overlaps with parody. Morris as documentary auteur presides over camerawork, lighting and a *mise-en-scène* that deliberately yet always approximately evoke *film noir*. Instead of being 'as unobtrusive as possible', Morris chose to be 'as obtru-sive as possible' (McEnteer 2006: 106). Direct cinema had largely banished non-diegetic music, but here a haunting Philip Glass score sustains a sense of urgency and uncertainty. The pastiche of old and current, fact and fantasy foregrounds the film's constructedness, yet Morris never fully suppresses the structure and appearance of traditional documentary. As Williams suggests, instead of 'careening between idealistic faith in documentary truth and cynical recourse to fiction', the film puts forward 'not an essence of truth but [. . .] a set of strategies designed to choose from among a horizon of relative and con-tingent truths' (1993: 14).

It is not that truth and fiction merely amount to the same thing, though *The Thin Blue Line* implies that some truths are truer than others and fictions contain necessary elements of truth. Truth and lies are no longer juxtaposed as polar opposites; fabrications, simulations and partial fictions that disguise and insulate traumatic events might be drawn upon in relation to other narratives to help reconstruct figurations of the past. The fragmentary nature of truth and witnessing is underscored when David Harris's confession is shown as a tape recording: a picture of 'a machine that records sound but not pictures'. Neither Harris nor Morris provides embodied 'visible evidence' before the camera (Michaels 1994: 50). The image and sound here slyly undercut, even

Figure 16. *The Thin Blue Line* (1988). American Playhouse. Courtesy of the British Film Institute.

while gesturing towards, the authority of both visual and acoustic technical reproduction.

The open questions of whether this film, or any film, can resolve the dilemmas it poses stymied some reviewers, who argued that Morris had 'hyped his material' and that his manipulations 'disqualified' the film as a 'factual document'. The smudging of fact and fiction seemed almost 'irresponsible' (Hinson 1988: D7). Still, the unorthodox approach of *The Thin Blue Line* would find itself incorporated into popular and even elite perceptions of documentary reality. Significantly, the Academy Awards again overlooked one of the year's most important films, though the Academy would later alter its biases (while retaining the term 'documentary', even with its mobile significations) in finally awarding Moore and Morris in 2003 and 2004, respectively.[1]

Albert Maysles bemoaned postmodern scepticism, stating that 'postmodernism has corrupted our confidence in gathering the truth' (Zuber 2007: 17). But, rather than undermining documentary altogether, postmodernity seemed to assert the resilience and flexibility of the 'hunger for documentary images of the real' (Williams 1993: 10). Filmmakers were revisiting and revising the playful exchanges between nonfiction and fiction, convention and experimentation, sobriety and humor that had marked nonfiction filmmaking before the documentary idea was distilled and institutionalized. Directly confronting documentary's burden of truth became an enabling factor posing creative possibilities for filmmakers such as Hammer, Riggs and Trinh, all of whom strove in different ways to expose and destabilize audience expectations.

Foregrounding avant-garde techniques and hybrid forms, Trinh's 1980s and 1990s work drew on feminist counter-cinema and Third Cinema political aesthetics to challenge popular assumptions. *Surname Viet Given Name Nam* (1989) is designed to undermine – through techniques such as staged readings by American-Vietnamese women masquerading as unrehearsed interviewees – the seeming transparency of documentary even while appearing to deploy its techniques. At the same time it poses questions about the fixity of identity and the stability of national and cultural borders. *Shoot for the Contents* (1991) also questions naturalized boundaries and viewing habits, elliptically addressing the Tiananmen Square massacre while drawing attention to the hierarchies of space, framing, focus and sound in documentary by homing in on images and noises usually forgotten in the background, the margins or off-screen. Hybrid approaches such as Trinh's not only suggest the emergence of 'post-documentary', but invoke documentary's (once) sublimated avant-garde histories and sensibilities. Such experiments invite us to break down oppositions such as documentary 'truth'/avant-garde 'fancy', hinting at an avant-garde that might be traced even through much of what is (often derisively) labeled 'Griersonian' documentary. As a concept, practice and kind of text consumed by audiences, the Griersonian approach was more formally flexible and experimental than many have allowed.[2]

As postmodern theory established itself, the notion that documentary films had to draw attention to their own constructedness and restricted points of view became almost de rigueur. Paul Arthur argued that 'the once-sacrosanct boundaries between [a documentary's] subjects and its processes are evaporating in the heat of a deconstructive gaze' (Arthur 1998: 73). Yet this strategy too could serve as a means to mask certain power hierarchies and presumptions of authority underlying the form. As Trinh argued in a biting critique:

> There is now a growing body of films in which the spectators see the narrator narrating, the filmmaker filming or directing [. . .] What is put forth as self-reflexivity here is no more than a small faction – the most conveniently visible one – of the many possibilities of uncovering the work of ideology that this 'science of the subject' can open into. (Trinh 1989: 147–8)

Indeed, many documentaries in the postmodern vein were shedding the presumed 'we' for the individuated 'I', yet leaving tendencies towards voyeurism and hierarchies of what Trinh calls 'us talking to us about them' relatively intact (1989: 134). Nick Broomfield's *Heidi Fleiss: Hollywood Madam* (1996) and *Fetishes* (1996) certainly follow this pattern, though by the time of

Aileen: Life and Death of a Serial Killer (2003) and *His Big White Self* (2006), Broomfield's on-screen relationship with his subjects and questions of who is controlling whom in producing 'truth' before the camera have become far murkier (and more interesting).

On the other side of the coin, documentaries that appeared to adhere more closely to convention still innovated in subtle ways and opened themselves to postmodern questions of identity, history and representation. Henry Hampton's PBS series *Eyes on the Prize* (1987) placed the Civil Rights Movement at the center of narratives of twentieth-century US history. Rather than focus on authoritative talking heads analyzing history from a distance, Hampton drew on a vast archive of testimony, photographs, protest songs, and amateur and news footage to weave together and 'reclaim' a compelling and often surprising narrative (Hadley 1999: 119). *Eyes on the Prize* appropriates and revises the conventions of the PBS educational format to confirm the centrality of 'minority' discourses of national history. Many films highlighting US ethnic diversity were becoming less focused on giving voice to marginal groups with the goal of assimilation into 'one nation', and were instead re-examining and relativizing constitutive elements of 'American' identities themselves, reframing concepts of national belonging as multiple and irreducible.

Working along related lines, Marlon Riggs's politicized history *Ethnic Notions* (1986) and its sequel *Color Adjustment* (1992) stick largely to a 'PBS-style' expository format, yet in meditating on racist artifacts commonly deemed too shameful for inclusion in the 'grand narrative' of US history, they push at the limits of historical representation. *Ethnic Notions* deals with 150 years of demeaning African American stereotypes, while *Color Adjustment* explores not only the suppression of African American themes and social concerns on US television (a key mediator of the 'American Dream') between the late 1940s and the 1980s, but also works to reveal how fantasies of homogeneity and conformity prop up the American ideal itself. Both films pose powerful critiques of 'melting pot' ideology, white privilege, commodity fetishism and class hierarchy. Moreover, as David Van Leer notes, *Ethnic Notions* is neither naive nor unselfconscious in terms of form. In the scene where the choreographer Leni Sloan re-enacts a blackface routine, an unsettling moment introduces a new perspective which interferes with Riggs's dominant presence as documentarian and source of evidence and argument. The 'self-conscious staging of the subjectivity of viewpoint' as Sloan constructs his blackface persona points to the staging of documentary authority in the rest of the film; it helps 'admit the fictiveness' of documentary realism rather than simply transpose a new documentary and historical 'truth' over a previous and outmoded one (Van Leer 1997: 164).

Documentary was, and is, a means for underrepresented groups to draw on presumptions of its evidential and heuristic authority. Documentary realities, while always constructs of some sort, draw on the camera's power as an 'indicative instrument'; they point to other realities and experiences of the world, relying on audiences to reinvest their own experiences of and in these realities (Perez 1998: 396). A number of films dealing with Native American issues suggest related strategies, including *More Than Bows and Arrows* (1978), narrated by M. Scott Momaday; Tom McCarthy's *Navajo Code Talkers* (1981), documenting Navajos who developed a communications code for the Marine Corps during the Second World War; *Broken Rainbow* (1985), revealing the political and corporate maneuvers behind the eviction of 10,000 Navajos from Hopi land; and Deborah Wallwork's *Warriors* (1987), which examines American Indian participation in the Vietnam War. While couched in relatively traditional formal approaches, these films effectively take up the task of reconfiguring received concepts of citizenship and what it means to be American.

Other films are sceptical about reclaiming any inclusive notions of Americanness, and aim more at issues of local community and cultural continuity. *Our Sacred Land* (1984), directed by Chris Spotted Eagle, focuses on Native American religious autonomy and the struggle of the Sioux to regain the Black Hills of South Dakota. Victor Masayesva's lyrical *Itam Hakim, Hopiit* (1984) explores myths, histories and oral traditions of the Hopi through a retelling of the life of Ross Macaya, one of the last members of the storytelling tradition. Such films aim towards at least two perhaps somewhat contradictory demands, expressing Indians' desires to 'remain distinct from the larger culture, to maintain a separate, coherent identity', and at the same time 'to invite others to view the world from [Indian] perspectives' (Leuthold 1994: 52). Assumptions about a homogeneous 'we' the people are replaced with an implicit message that no single ethnic or linguistic group can lay claim to US history or national character. This impels recognition of complex networks of local and cultural affiliations, interacting differentially with each other and with the nation. Americans on the fringes of the privileged establishment might be patriotic, others ambivalent about any presumed unified set of national beliefs, while still others might question the very legitimacy of 'America' itself. The melting pot gives way to the mosaic pattern of multiculturalism, where multiplicity is encompassed under a much more loosely defined umbrella term – 'America'.

Arthur Dong's adaptation of Allan Bérubé's *Coming Out Under Fire* (1994) and Christine Choy and Renee Tajima-Peña's *Who Killed Vincent Chin?* (1988) both place the idea of an inclusive America under scrutiny. Each reveals the paradoxes of being excluded while desiring to belong, of being marginalized even while striving after – and fighting to protect – the 'dream'. *Coming Out Under Fire* intensely criticizes the injustices and severe humiliations meted out to gay soldiers, forcing the question of why gay Americans should ever consider defending a nation that so actively excludes them. *Who Killed Vincent Chin?*

Figure 17. *Who Killed Vincent Chin?* (1988). Film News Now Foundation and WTVS Detroit. Courtesy of the filmmaker.

reconstructs the brutal murder of a Chinese-American engineer in Detroit. Chin is positioned as an assimilationist success story, yet – and the film never pretends to provide a comprehensive explanation – was beaten to death on the street just days before his wedding. Perhaps, many contended, this was because he was mistaken for Japanese, just as Japanese car manufacturers were being blamed for eclipsing the US industry and 'taking over American jobs'. At one level the film is a detective story, where extensive contextualization tries to fill in gaps not just about the murder, but about the disturbingly everyday facts of racist violence. The Chin case highlights the contradictions at the heart of American ideals of ethnic and cultural integration.

By juxtaposing narratives of victims and assailants – those of Chin's family and of his disturbingly blank and unrepentant killers – the film interweaves both parallel and strikingly divergent experiences of US identity and belonging. While Chin's mother often appears nearly mute, shaking with grief, one of Chin's killers, Ronald Ebens – an unemployed autoworker – invokes his own confused feelings of exclusion. He served in the army, yet his confidence in the American ideal has been undermined as the country now seems to say: 'we're against you'. We see the Chin controversy becoming a media event, and the film implicates media exploitation even while it reveals the Chin story as a galvanizing force for Asian American coalition-building and establishing links across different ethnic groups. One African American community leader is struck by parallels between the Asian American experience and a history of African American oppression, arguing that 'injustice is endemic in the American system'.

While containing few postmodern stylizations, *Who Killed Vincent Chin?* serves as a corrective to inherited myths of American unity and homogeneity and to any easy sense of patriotic belonging. The film's final, lingering close-up of Chin's bereft mother seems to pose unanswerable questions: the question of the film's title blurs into questions of whether America ever was, or ever can be, 'whole'. We are left to ponder whether an elusive idea of justice can set right histories of ethnic divisions and cultural miscomprehensions among various groups struggling to define and lay claim to 'American' identities.

Writing in 1984, Audre Lorde articulated questions of affiliation and separation, belonging and alienation, arguing for ways to negotiate differences that not only divided various groups from each other, but estranged individuals from their own multiple beliefs and histories:

> Certainly there are very real differences between us of race, age, and sex. But it is not those differences between us that are separating us. It is rather our refusal to recognize those differences, and to examine the distortions which result from our misnaming them and their effects upon human behavior and expectation. (1984: 115)

Lorde refused to deny, sublimate or simply relativize away human differences, while also critiquing the tradition of striving for a 'mythical norm' in US society. At the same time she deflected neo-conservative reductivisms, stating that 'the need for unity is often misnamed as a need for homogeneity' (1984: 119). The problem Lorde perceived was a fundamental lack of comprehension and respect across social, sexual, age and ethnic divides.[3] Documentaries such as *Tongues Untied*, which Jacquie Jones called 'possibly the most powerful examination of black sexual identity ever produced', formed part of efforts to negotiate these divides (Jones 1993: 256).

TONGUES UNTIED (1989)

Marlon T. Riggs's *Tongues Untied* echoes Lorde's demands to 'root out internalized patterns of oppression within ourselves' and assert the value and political urgency of recognizing multiple and irreducible identities (Lorde 1984: 123). In Riggs's case, this means determining his own relations to being black, male and gay in the US at a time when African American masculinity rarely, if ever, serves as a site for exploring issues of gender and sexuality (Blount

Figure 18. *Tongues Untied* (1989). Signifyin' Works. Image capture, Frameline DVD.

and Cunningham 1996: x). Black masculinity was effectively under attack at the time: black men were discussed in legitimate sociological circles as prone to criminality, lacking motivation and being weak fathers (myths explored in Marco Williams's *In Search of Our Fathers* [1992]).[4] Re-interpreting established belief systems is hardly a simple task, and the identity categories Riggs has to work with are rooted in preconceptions and stereotypes: identity itself is segmented into normative definitions that naturalize affiliations and encourage a sense of belonging (if you fit in) or impose exclusion and marginalization (if you don't).

This process is spelled out in one of *Tongues Untied*'s most directly autobiographical sequences, where Riggs describes growing up in Georgia. He speaks of being persistently 'cornered by identities I never wanted to claim'. Riggs looks into the camera, soliciting our attention through 'direct address' (Mercer 1993: 241), though his narrative is intermittently interrupted by close-ups. A shot of a young, black male's mouth that utters 'punk' is followed later by other mouths spitting out the words 'homo', 'faggot' and 'freak'. These acts of (re)naming usurp what Orlando Patterson has contended is 'the verbal sign of a person's whole identity, his being-in-the-world as a distinct person' (Patterson 1982: 54).[5] Homosexuality becomes an imposed, named identity, (mis)interpreted by others and labelled as an aberration. As Riggs speaks, another close-up of a mouth, now of a white male, cuts in with a further pariah status – 'mother fuckin' coon' – and yet another mouth reads out a slogan scrawled on his old school's wall: 'niggers, go home'. Riggs asserts that these hatreds aren't limited to simple oppositions, as he describes being considered 'uppity' by black schoolmates for attending classes aimed at 'the best and brightest'; another black mouth intones 'Uncle Tom'. As the epithets increase in frequency and speed, Riggs's image simultaneously retreats. Sheila Petty observes that 'the effect of the collision between angles is that of Riggs being crushed and pounded by the violence of the epithets' (1998: 421).

Riggs's early experiences are linked in later scenes to widespread social division and prejudice. We see church leaders referring to being gay as an 'abomination' while black activists dismiss homosexuality as 'selling out' the race. The conundrum of choosing from multiple identities and 'prioritizing' political and cultural loyalties is summed up by Riggs in a neat rephrasing of the Bible: 'How do you choose one eye over another?' Demands to 'confer one identity and erase another' operate at all levels of social expectation (for example, before 1997 the US census required respondents to identify them-selves under just one racial category) (see Hollinger 1995: 20). For Kendall Thomas, any choice between one's ethnic and/or sexual identities is 'forced, false, and ultimately fatal' – effectively a form of 'psychic suicide' (Thomas 1996: 61).

These autobiographical sequences indicate the multivalences of negative identities Riggs 'never wanted to claim'. They are culturally naturalized, stemming not just from white racism but from homophobia and what Lorde called internalized patterns of oppression in the black community as well. By the end of the earlier scene, Riggs temporarily retreats to silence, to presumed safety – though he is not safe. The dangers of being gay are underlined in the next scene, which begins with poetic imagery that rapidly becomes unsettling: 'summer full moon night, started with the rhetorical chant, "hey faggot" '. Inviting controversy at a time when hypermasculine hip hop and gangsta rap were grabbing media attention, the scene ends in the brutal beating of a black gay man at the hands of several black men. Just before the attack, the victim turns to look at the camera as if entreating for help, but a cut to another angle reveals the space already occupied by an attacker. There is no escape, and no 'kindness of brethren'. As Petty stresses, the careful cutting and compressing of filmic space signifies oppressions imposed by ideologies that strive to limit expressions of race and sexuality. The scene further links gay experience to black experience through the sense memory of threatened violence – both homophobic and racist. As Thomas notes: 'Gay and lesbian Americans of all colors and African Americans of every sexual orientation live with and under the knowledge that at any time, anywhere, we might be attacked for being gay or lesbian or bisexual, for being black, or for being both' (1996: 63).

Another identifying category that Riggs is impelled to negotiate in the film is HIV-positive status. Riggs was diagnosed in December 1988, midway through taping what he then expected would be a short video shown exclusively in gay venues. According to Havi Carel, illness imposes categories that 'other' you in the everyday world, where the ill person is treated from a 'third-person perspective' (2008: 13). In the 1980s, especially, HIV and AIDS hovered at the extremes of this othering process. As Max Navarre argued in 1987: 'As a person with AIDS, I can attest to the sense of diminishment at seeing and hearing myself constantly referred to as an AIDS victim, an AIDS sufferer, an AIDS case – as anything but what I am, a person with AIDS. I am a person with a condition. I am not that condition' (1988: 143). This social reductivism was compounded by the ways HIV was exploited by neo-conservative groups seeking to link homosexuality, promiscuity and degeneration. Jerry Falwell, founder of the Moral Majority, called HIV-related illness 'god's punishment'. AIDS first appeared in the press labelled as a 'gay plague', as if a form of divine retribution.[6]

Riggs underlines how gay men become compelled to internalize the alignment of sexual pleasure with fears of annihilation. In a love scene near the end of the film, the textures of skin and flesh are underscored by a heartbeat rhythm that, paradoxically, suggests mortality. This heartbeat punctuates the film, at times as a marker of life and sentience, at others 'a time bomb ticking in my blood' (Wallenberg 2004: 139). Just after it returns here, 'the resounding refrain of grown men in love' is subtly disrupted by the words 'now we think as we fuck'. The individual words of Essex Hemphill's poem 'Now We Think' run together as something like 'noweethikaweefuh', rendering the phrase obscure, a muffled return of the repressed that grows in volume and clarity. Robert LeBlanc stresses that the layering of image and sound in this scene aesthetically enacts the ways Riggs's film 'displaces' expectations: quite palpably, 'postmodern ways of representing the subject progress gradually into prominence in our film experience' (2009: 8). The scene further foregrounds the juxtaposition of body/mind, feeling/thinking, which parallels a range of responses potentially generated by the film. When I screened it in the early 1990s, the film elicited both emotional and physical responses from students, ranging from 'joy' to 'disgust'; others responded that the film 'made me think'.[7]

The fact of mortality comes to the fore in the next sequence, where a photo of Riggs appears among black men that have died: Joseph Beam, James McLaurin, artists, writers, drag performers and activists crowded among other anonymous faces. Riggs speeds up the montage until the images freeze on a photo of his own face, isolated in silence (we hardly register that the heartbeat has stopped). Connections between the 'suffering' of AIDS and a 'history of suffering' in the African American experience are again stressed (Wallenberg 2004: 139). But Riggs refuses 'victim' status; the heartbeat resumes as he invokes a history of African American political resistance. This film and its messages are resolutely not *his*, alone, but are polyvocal and transhistorical. The dissolves between Civil Rights marchers and men marching for the Minority Task Force on AIDS not only help to 'give the lie to the notion that black and gay identity are hostile to one another' (Thomas 1996: 61), they connect past political solidarities to ongoing struggles.

In spite of its autobiographical concerns, *Tongues Untied* didn't originate in Riggs insisting on articulating his own identity, though he ultimately determined it was his 'responsibility' to 'make that step in front of the camera' (Riggs 2008 [1991]). Riggs's hesitancy about producing a 'straight' autobiography is understandable, considering autobiography is 'customarily the genre in which dominant cultures first permit minorities to speak' (Van Leer 1997: 166). The film was inspired by the profusion of black men's cultural work going on around him, in particular the poetry of the 'Other Countries Workshop' in New York and collections produced by Beam and by the Gay Men's Press (Castro 2000). In the film, a poster for Isaac Julien's then recently released *Looking for Langston* (1989) is highlighted in the 'BGA'/Black Gay Activist's room, underscoring affiliations with queer filmmakers such as the UK-based Julien, Pratibha Parmar and the photographer Rotimi Fani-Kayode. Riggs later recalled: 'Taken as a group, we do not subscribe to notions of artistic effort for the sake of delighting the eye. Rather, our work addresses issues of identity, selfhood, and nationhood in an effort to interrogate received notions of who we are' (quoted in Castro 2000). The 'BGA' scene references this questioning of selfhood and nationhood by indicating wider synergies of black gay political work. The camera lingers over the political culture magazine *A Critique of America* (later called *Arete*), a t-shirt for the AIDS activist group ACT UP with the slogan 'silence = death', and a poster for the black gay publication *Blacklight*.

Essex Hemphill was a key collaborator, and his appearances and poetry are at the core of the film's emphasis on lyrical language and the rhythms and cadences of speech. The speech act – the nuances and shocks of language – is persistently twinned with its opposite, silence, which operates as a structuring motif in the film, stressing opposition and dialectical exchange between forms of liberation and oppression, openness and hiding in troubled 'safety'. Silence and its social and psychic effects are marked not only through language and its absence, but through image and absence: the bright pink ACT UP slogan against the black shirt, the black screen (which Chuck Kleinhans calls a 'black void') that frequently breaks into the visual field, juxtaposing invisibility with visibility (Kleinhans 1991: 110). For LeBlanc, when the film focuses on silence and absence as counterparts to presence, and on the margins or out-of-frame as opposed to the center, it betrays a postmodern scepticism and self-consciousness regarding 'transparent' representation. Rather than pointing to 'an imaginable moment of "completion" of the documentary's goal', absence and silence serve to posit 'an ultimate unrepresentability of certain events and subject positions' that are restricted by social expectations and responses (LeBlanc 2009: 2).

Tongues Untied openly wrestles with questions of representing the self and representing others, with ideas of belonging and exclusion, presence and absence. Though elements of traditional documentary are approximated and parodied, it seems clear that what Riggs wanted to express could never find voice – his tongue couldn't be 'untied' – through established filmic approaches. In her call to revaluate the norms and expectations of race, gender, class and age, Lorde argued that 'the master's tools will never dismantle the master's house' (1984: 123). In a similar sense Riggs dismisses the 'master's tools' while establishing a disruptive and deconstructive expository and aesthetic vehicle for a politicized subjective viewpoint. For Petty, 'the narrative premise of the video is very complex because Riggs negotiates, not within one cultural space, but four: black culture, white culture, gay culture, and black gay culture. This makes generalizations, either about his narrative structure, or his thematic material, almost impossible' (1998: 418). Yet this lack of homogeneity perhaps posed, and poses, an opportunity of sorts. It suggests that rather than appropriating or mimicking documentary authority to assert the truth of his experience, Riggs had to interrogate assumptions about the very production of truthful histories, in turn pointing towards the artificiality and inadequacy of linear narratives of US identity and history. There is little point, then, in a straightforward or sequential 'reading' of the film: our attempts to 'shoot for the contents' will be constantly deflected.

Riggs's filmic style is often jagged: fragmented by interruptions and seemingly empty shots and spaces – the 'dead spots' traditionally avoided by filmmakers (though taken up in avant-garde experiments such as Andy Warhol's *Sleep* [1963] and *Empire* [1964]) (Beattie 2008: 13–14). Unlike direct cinema, Riggs offers no illusion of immediacy or 'uncontrolled' reality; *Tongues Untied* is an exposed construct. Indeed, perhaps more precise than labelling Riggs's approach postmodern would be to say Riggs enacts a series of displacements of subjectivity and audience identification that reconstruct a *diasporic* sensibility.[8] Diaspora suggests nomadic exile, 'dispersal and reluctant scattering', yet is always ambivalently bound to questions of national belonging and 'home'. For Paul Gilroy, diaspora-identification 'exists outside of and sometimes in opposition to the political forms and codes of modern citizenship' (1994: 207). In other words, Riggs's African American ancestry forms part of the black Atlantic diaspora, yet his experience – with its complex affiliations and displacements on levels of ethnicity, gender and sexuality – renders any notion of 'return' to unity or 'home' an impossible illusion. At the same time the dominant conditions that determine belonging in 'America' induce other forms of exile and alienation from the self. Yet, Gilroy suggests, diaspora might also provoke new versions of and relations to national belonging, 'less through outmoded notions of fixity and place and more in terms of the ex-centric communicative circuitry that has enabled dispersed populations to converse, interact and even synchronize significant elements of their social and cultural lives' (Gilroy 1994: 211). In other words, diaspora as both a state of being and a concept can point to new ways of belonging that do not rely on traditional notions of citizenry and the nation-state – communities, affiliations and identities are formed through other cultural synergies and connections.

Riggs expresses the complexity and mobility of these synergies though variously structured and unstructured expressive modes. Dance in the film accents the importance of choreographed and creative movement, which becomes, as in the vogueing scenes, 'a form of resistance and community' (Castro 2000). Music expresses other forms of ambivalent longing through the elegiac use of Roberta Flack, Nina Simone, Billie Holiday and Steve Langley. Fittingly, Petty calls the film 'a symphony on race, culture, and sexuality' (1998: 418). Indeed, Riggs's diasporic style relies on impressions more than definitive facts and statements. The hypnotic, fraught movements of Riggs's body against the 'black void' early in the film, or the dazzling white fade after the film's opening black and white images: each leaves a momentary physical impression on the eye. Image, sound, words and movement in *Tongues Untied* tend to register as felt traces rather than as definitive assertions. Riggs refuses to enter into the public and academic competition for establishing the socio-logical 'truth' of black and/or gay life, but also doesn't retreat from political engagement. The film's formal approach is itself a bridging of political and aesthetic intervention.

Embedding his own voice and perspective amid a text that is insistently polyvocal, Riggs refuses the double bind of representation that would see a black gay director, due to a paucity of representation, having to appear as a delegate for the black, gay or black and gay communities as wholes. This latter situation suggests the 'burden of representation', according to Kobena Mercer, where the artistic production of minority individuals is harnessed to expectations to speak as 'representatives' for all in the marginalized com-munity (1994: 214). Riggs undermines expectations that his film might offer paradigmatic access to the black gay community, parodying institutional modes of address such as the ethnographic 'native informant' tradition. As Riggs and his friends demonstrate 'a basic lesson in snap!' sparring, a subtitle – 'courtesy of The Institute of Snap!thology' – indicates the filmed subjects' subcultural status to potentially curious onlookers. The subtitle follows the more traditionally rendered 'native informant' street interview with Master Snap! Grand Diva, slyly transforming the whole sequence into a mock-scientific investigation of what Paul Arthur calls the 'twin markers of blackness and homosexuality' (Arthur 1999: 281).[9] The gesture both implicates and undermines epistephilia: it snaps! the viewer and the documentary form itself.

A more ambiguous snap! at documentary convention occurs during Riggs's autobiographical reverie about a 'white boy' with 'grey-green eyes' and 'soft Tennessee drawl'. As Roberta Flack's mournful version of the English folk song 'The First Time Ever I Saw Your Face' plays, a photo floats out of the void. The photo's obvious 'blandness', the boy's awkward expression and outdated hairstyle all resist audience desires to identify or sympathize with Riggs's attraction, yet also underline the moment's 'air of tragic inevitability' (Van Leer 1997: 169). The video stylizations here imitate the 'pan and scan' approach of much PBS documentary – used by Riggs himself in *Ethnic Notions* – but the image doesn't impart evidence or bolster an argument. Rather than feeding epistephilia, the boy's image remains anonymous, a cipher that signifies memory as absence as much as presence.

The question of what fills the voids of identity and identification is partly addressed through Riggs's careful articulation, framing, positioning and lighting of the black male body in the film. Early on, in a gesture suggesting baptism and ritual transformation, he uncloaks his own body, revealing it to the camera's gaze. This exposure and vulnerability works as a counterpoint to the self-conscious distancing employed elsewhere in the film. The body is both performative and sentient, contested public 'territory' and sensual private experience. As Hemphill recites in the film, 'our lives tremble between pathos and seduction'. Scenes that suggest remoteness or parody are never far removed from those that evoke closeness and intimacy. The black male body as physical presence and as trope thus operates on a number of interrelated levels: the exposed body indicates the vulnerability of black and gay people to exposure in the world and in the media; the self-conscious manipulation of lighting and video exposures suggests the uneven social and psychic relations between whiteness and blackness, visibility and invisibility.

Relevant here are discussions that have theorized the haptic or tactile experience of the body in cinema, mapping complex relations between bodily representations and the filmgoer's multiple sensory responses. Jennifer Barker emphasizes sensory responses to film that range beyond the purely visual:

> Exploring cinema's tactility [. . .] opens up the possibility of cinema as an *intimate* experience and of our relationship with cinema as a *close* connection, rather than as a distant experience of observation, which the notion of cinema as a purely visual medium presumes. [. . .] We *share* things with it: texture, spatial orientation, comportment, rhythm, and vitality. (Barker 2009: 2)[10]

For David MacDougall, film might tap into ways in which we actively engage with physical objects; filmed bodies can be 'as much *projections* of our own bodies as independent of them' (2006: 21). Many New Queer documentaries of the late 1980s and 1990s work to heighten sensory relations between audiences and the cinematic body. As Riggs stated: 'I wanted to show how people touch, and the touching. I didn't want to show pornography. [. . .] I wanted to show two black men touching tenderly, romantically, sexually [. . .] an image that I had never seen and which would confirm an experience for a number of people' (quoted in Bullert 1997: 98). Like *Tongues Untied*, Barbara Hammer's *Nitrate Kisses* (1992) interweaves intimate footage with references to stereotyping and broader experiences of oppression: scenes of couples making love – lesbian, gay, white, black, interracial; some bodies shaven, pierced and tattooed – act as interruptions to a history of 'othering' queer sexuality. The very title, *Nitrate Kisses*, weds the realms of cinema artifice (silver nitrate) to the sensual.

The body's felt presence is also central to Tom Joslin, Mark Massi and Peter Friedman's *Silverlake Life: The View from Here* (1992), an intense portrayal of illness, AIDS and dying that engages with the endpoint of bodily sentience – the 'taboo' image of death. Like *Tongues*, the film aims to politicize private and subcultural experience through public acts of showing and speaking out (Lane 2002: 88). *Silverlake Life* works to conjure the body's felt presence by meditating on the sense of touch, on the feel and texture of flesh and skin. Indeed *Silverlake Life* starts here, gesturing to the audience's desire and inability to 'touch' the bodies on screen by invoking the memory of touching the sentient body of a person – here, a lover – now dead. The first words are from Mark Massi recalling his partner, Tom, through sense memory: 'The thing I remember most about Tom', Mark says, 'is what he feels like'. The use of the present tense is telling; it goes against the realization of absence, yet we might also recognize this leap of faith in our own experience. Only after meditating on touch does Mark consider the visual image of Tom, though now through a strangely moving anecdote about his dead body: 'It was scary to look at him, the first time after he died. And then I wanted to close his eyes, because it's strange to see a dead person staring, and I tried – just like in the movies – to close his eyes. But they popped back open. I said to Tom, I apologize, life isn't like the movies'. And though the movies are not quite like life, documentaries such as *Silverlake Life* work to 'point to a lived body occupying concrete space' (Sobchack 1999: 248), strikingly registering lived experiences and sensations.

Concluding *Tongues Untied*, nine title cards spell out the statement: 'Black men loving Black men is the revolutionary act'. While this might at first appear a denial of cross-ethnic relationships, a retreat to essentialism or an advocacy of 'black separatism', the words are not, in fact, Riggs's, but Joseph Beam's (Wallenberg 2004: 135; Van Leer 1997: 169). The quote is followed by a telling snap! cartoon, suggesting that even seemingly direct messages in Riggs's film are rarely direct. The words have already appeared earlier, emblazoned on the parade banner held by the Minority Task Force on AIDS. Riggs would later pluralize the interpretation of 'loving' in Beam's statement, beyond sexual and romantic connotations, to include 'friendship, community, family, and fraternity' (Van Leer 1997: 179; Simmons 1991: 194). In this sense, acts of black men loving black men are indeed crucial to establishing stable and mutually supportive relations in African American life. After the end titles, the words that close the film are: 'The nights are cold and silent, and the silence echoes with complicity'. The phrase challenges the audience to speak out, to create their 'revolutionary acts' or otherwise remain complicit in histories of denial and repression.

As Bullert points out, of all of the documentaries screened on the PBS *P.O.V.* series, none caused more public controversy than *Tongues Untied*. When it was broadcast in July of 1991, 110 of the 284 PBS stations that normally carried *P.O.V.* refused to air the film, leading to accusations from filmmakers and critics on the left of widespread media censorship. Most stations showed it late in the evening along with a 'viewer advisory' warning of 'explicit language and images', and it was condemned by conservative groups and politicians as 'obscene' and 'promoting a gay lifestyle' (Bullert 1997: 93). As a result of this small film, shot on video for roughly $40,000, Congress was pressed to cut off federal funds to public broadcasting. Part of the problem was that the film was seen as 'government funded': screened on PBS, with a small portion of the budget ($8,000) having come from National Endowment for the Arts funds (Bullert 1997: 99).

Among the African American community, concerns were raised about Riggs's 'negative' images, especially as this was the first *P.O.V.* program to feature an African American director. Though the National Black Programming Consortium (NBPC) had given *Tongues Untied* its documentary award in 1990, opinion remained divided. Founding director of the NBPC, Mable Haddock, recalled problems of homophobia in the black community: 'I've been a woman all my life. And black all my life, but when people found out I was supporting this program – I thought I knew hate, I thought I knew sexism and racism, but the hate – you could just feel it. It was palpable' (quoted in Bullert 1997: 101). Homophobia here is not characterized as merely an isolated prejudice; Haddock recognizes links to a history of sexual exploitation and stereotyping of the black community, and to a lack of open dialogue about sexuality, in particular homosexuality.

Riggs wanted *Tongues Untied* to 'start the dialogue' about black sexuality, but also to 'preserve our lives in a form that people can see and address, not only now, but in years to come. People will see there was a vibrant black gay community in these United States in 1989' (Simmons 1991: 193). These ambitions indicate impulses towards instruction and cultural preservation for which documentary is known, but turn them towards reframing and diversifying the idea of the nation itself, not only for the present but for a future that will one day be confronted by the absences of memory and history. The rendering of black history in the US has frequently involved a process of reinserting once-marginalized African American lives and experiences into a hegemonic narrative of US inclusiveness. More recently, through reality shows such as Bravo's *Queer Eye for the Straight Guy* (2003–7), the process of reinserting those historically 'edited out' of the grand American narrative has extended to reframing gay/queer identity as an example, par excellence, of the patriotic pleasures of consumerist and capitalist aspiration. If gayness and blackness were effectively 'erased' from history, Riggs was evidently less interested in battling this narrative than in remaking its very foundations, confounding its common terms of reference.

Riggs died in 1994 at the age of 37. His career spanned a period when essentialist definitions of 'race' were undergoing intense revaluation, when gay identity was engaging with broader notions of queer identities, and when HIV and AIDS were both repressing and radicalizing sexual attitudes. Though Riggs's work shares experimental aesthetic and political aims with postmodern-era directors like Morris, Riggs's layered – and what I have called diasporic – sensibility might be seen as 'more embodied than inscribed' (Gilroy 1994: 207). Riggs is distinctive in foregrounding a subjective point of view that articulates displacements while enacting new alignments and felt experiences. His films command attention because they still offer challenging points of view, problematizing reductive narratives of US identity and history.

On its own terms, *Tongues Untied* is a meditation on identities and their relations to larger imagined communities. With its television broadcast, it became something else entirely: a flashpoint for debates about special interests, funding for the arts, censorship versus freedom of expression, and moral standards (many objections came from politicians and religious figures who admitted they hadn't seen the film).

If, on the surface, at issue was the film's reliance on public money, a larger issue lay in the status of documentary itself, as a mode 'defined and applied in relation to a sense of the "Public"' and public interests (Corner 2002). Bullert concludes that the contested public spaces documentary can create are essential to democratic values: 'Not being able to hear the voices of talented independent filmmakers limits the public discussion of certain issues and the inclusion of certain viewpoints. This is at odds with the democratic principles on which the United States was founded' (1997: 190). Yet the relationship between democratic principles, freedom of the press, and access to media distribution channels has always been less than transparent. How can 'majority' and 'minority' interests ever be fairly represented in the media? How can marginal voices gain a public hearing and have access to spaces for self-expression?

Tongues Untied became an example of what Stuart Hall calls the 'double bind' of media power:

> The media cannot long retain their credibility with the public without giving some access to witnesses and accounts which lie outside the consensus. But the moment television does so, it immediately endangers itself with its critics, who attack broadcasting for unwittingly tipping the balance of public feeling against the political order. It opens itself to the strategies of both sides, which are struggling to win a hearing for their interpretations [. . .] This is broadcasting's double bind. (Hall 1988: 364)

This double bind persists, even as the ground shifts beneath documentary practices of production and distribution. Freedoms of expression face new challenges with increased media corporatization and reliance on market forces, yet possibilities for documentary action have also opened up through remediation in the form of cheaper digital equipment and the Internet.

By the 1990s documentary practice, distribution and reception had undergone sweeping changes, as had the media landscape as a whole. When media democratization movements such as guerrilla television and public access first arrived they propounded interventionist, even utopian, ideals, but the ability of alternative media to exert widespread social influence was, and remains, challenged by financial and distribution limitations. The appearance of satellite, cable and pay-per-view television seemed to offer the potential to enhance documentary's profile (the Discovery Channel, the most widely distributed cable network in the US, was launched in 1985). Cable promised new forms of televisual subjectivity, as viewers could 'actively seek out and select from a myriad of program choices', and independent producers hoped to connect with less visible and niche audiences that would have been almost impossible to reach through customary marketing techniques (Boddy 1990: 94). Yet in the midst of the cornucopia of choice, pushes for deregulation and major corporate mergers meant that the media came under the control of fewer and fewer global companies. Indeed, only about ten conglomerates now dominate the majority of US media production and dissemination.

On the big screen, documentary successes persisted through the 1990s (though dipping towards the end of the decade), helped by film festival exposure and specialist distributors like Fine Line and Miramax, subsidiaries of large interests such as Sony, Disney and New Line. Even mildly successful documentaries could yield a sought-after combination of high profit-to-cost ratios and award prestige for comparatively small investments in post-production and marketing. Steve James's *Hoop Dreams* (1994), an involving study of the struggles of two African American teenagers with aspirations to become world-class basketball players, garnered numerous awards (though controversially was denied an Oscar nomination) and surpassed the box office record set by *Roger and Me* a few years before. *Hoop Dreams* was later named by influential critic Roger Ebert as the best film of the year (and later, best of the decade), positioning documentary as a sophisticated and socially relevant alternative to big budget Hollywood fantasy.

New documentary auteurs such as Joe Berlinger and Bruce Sinofsky, who combined direct cinema with postmodern touches of narrative aporia, registered successes with *Brother's Keeper* (1992) and *Paradise Lost: The Child Murders at Robin Hood Hills* (1996). Cheryl Dunye's mockumentary *The Watermelon Woman* (1996) reconfigured issues of the archive and documentary truth in weaving together a fictional history of an elusive 1930s black Hollywood actress, at the same time engaging issues of black and lesbian representation and spectatorship. Documentary was not only financially viable and legitimate once again, but 'sexy'. Karen Cooper of New York's Film Forum, who in 1972 saw 'zero competition' for documentaries, proudly pointed out in a 1998 interview that nine of twelve films premiered at the theater during a six-month period that year were documentaries (Iseli 1998: 14).

Other financial successes ranged from biographical exposés such as *Crumb* (1995) and *Unzipped* (1995) to the queer cinema history *The Celluloid Closet* (1996). Major directors associated with fiction were drawn to the form: Spike Lee's *4 Little Girls* (1997) was conceived as a documentary because, Lee noted, only documentary could capture the complexity and human cost of the notorious bombing of the 16th Street Baptist Church, Birmingham, in 1963 (Susman 1997). But these high-profile films in many ways masked the larger picture of theatrical documentary's place in the transnational, corporate US film industry. Though a box office 'boom' was heralded in trade magazines, documentaries could not expand beyond the 'limited' (as opposed to 'nationwide') release category. Documentaries made up roughly 1 percent of US film earnings during this period, and even a significant hit like *Crumb* never played in more than sixty cinemas at the same time nationwide (when blockbusters such as *Batman Forever* [1995] were playing on nearly 3,000 screens). Moore's huge hit, *Bowling for Columbine* (2002), never played on more than 250 screens at one time.

Most smaller-scale documentary filmmakers were experiencing severe ideological and financial challenges. A hopeful development was the creation of the Independent Television Service (ITVS), established by an act of Congress in 1988 explicitly to encourage productions that 'take creative risks' and 'enrich the cultural landscape with the voices and visions of underrepresented communities' ('Mission Statement' 2010). But ITVS didn't end the conflict over public funding; in fact attacks on independent and political documentaries intensified. Controversy ensued over *Deadly Deception* (1991), a short film that juxtaposed the ideal worlds of advertisements for General Electric ('GE: We bring good things to life') with the lives ruined by GE's construction and testing of nuclear weapons. Attacked as a partisan misuse of public money, the film was denied a screening slot on PBS (which claimed a conflict of interest, as GE was a PBS underwriter). The British film *Damned in the USA* (1992) took up some of these issues – examining high-profile battles over public funding and censorship (in particular a landmark Cincinnati obscenity trial involving the exhibition of Robert Mapplethorpe photos) – and in turn was met with further controversy. The film's producers were sued by the Rev. Donald Wildmon, of the American Family Association, who wanted to bar the film's US release.

There was little relief from the ideological storm that was dubbed the 'culture wars'. Effectively the culmination of restrictions to public arts funding stretching back to the Reagan years, the culture wars were imbricated in larger battles over the definition and policing of American values and American identity: 'unity' versus diversity, cultural and ethnic homogeneity versus multicultural and multilingual networks. Documentary and public service television were on the front lines: in 1995, conservative Republican and Speaker of the House Newt Gingrich argued for the complete elimination of federal funding for public broadcasting. As Patricia Zimmermann argued at the decade's end: 'Documentary and public affairs programming are truly an endangered species' (2000: 25). Independent documentary was under 'siege': 'Congressional debates, political targeting by conservatives, geopolitical restructurings in the telecommunications sector, and new technologies have turned documentary into a bloody political battlefield where the casualties are mounting daily' (Zimmermann 2000: 12).

With the Telecommunications Act of 1996, regulations and centralized controls were severely curtailed. The premise of the Act was that market forces should be the guiding factors behind media and communication activities. Drafted amid pressures of powerful lobbies and corporate interests, the Act escalated the ongoing process of large corporations taking over smaller establishments, including community and local television, cable provision, newspapers and radio, leaving media ownership concentrated in the hands of a few companies such as Sony, Disney (owners of ABC and ESPN), and Time Warner (owners of CNN).[11] As Brian Winston puts it, the distinctly American sense of 'public service' was being absorbed into commercialism (Winston 2000: 45).

Still, there were what Zimmermann calls 'cracks' in corporate and government restrictions on independent production and distribution, some generated by the conglomerates themselves. These included funding from sources such as Time Warner's cable station HBO, which financed Lee's *4 Little Girls* and *When the Levees Broke* (2006). The *Independent Lens* series was launched by PBS in 1999, providing a platform for documentary features such as *The Weather Underground* (2002) and *Enron: The Smartest Guys in the Room* (2005). While most of these films take few formal risks, they draw on documentary traditions of engaging with questions of citizenship and social responsibility. Newer sites and forums, such as the Internet, remain crucial if the documentary form is to persist in some of its key functions: questioning received histories and ideologies, creating 'new social imaginaries' (Zimmermann 2000: 12).

NOTES

1. Controversial omissions from the best documentary Oscar nominations were *Shoah, Paris is Burning, Hoop Dreams, Roger and Me* and *The Thin Blue Line*, leading critics to argue that the Academy was not only narrow-minded about 'authenticity' but spurned commercially successful films. The outrage over *Hoop Dreams* led to changes in nomination practices. Moore was elected to the Academy Board of Governors (Documentary Branch) in 2010.
2. Coming from a different angle, Jeffrey Skoller has engaged with the social, political and historical value of the avant-garde (Skoller 2005).
3. More recently, theorists such as Chantal Mouffe have expanded on such observations about identity politics and multiculturalism. Mouffe cites a pluralist ideal of 'radical democracy' that creates a space where 'we acknowledge difference – the particular, the multiple, the heterogeneous' even across national boundaries (2005: 7).
4. See, for example, the widespread debates generated by Richard J. Herrnstein and Charles A. Murray in *The Bell Curve: Intelligence and Class Structure in American Life* (New York: Simon & Schuster, 1994), which suggested that 'both genes and environment' influenced intelligence, linking race to IQ and subsequent social success (see pp. 287, 292 and 311).
5. Patterson examines acts of renaming as part of a 'ritual of enslavement' (1982: 54).
6. In 1982–3, references to the 'gay plague' appeared in Philadelphia's *Daily News*, the *Toronto Star*, London's *Sun* and many other newspapers. See also Williams and Retter (2003: 162).
7. Student feedback to *Tongues Untied*, Freshman Summer Program, University of California, Los Angeles, August 1992.
8. See, for example, Mark A. Reid (ed.), 'African and Black Diaspora Film/Video', *Jump Cut*, 36 [special issue] (May 1991).
9. For further analysis see Becquer (1991: 6–17).
10. See also 'haptic visuality' in Marks (2000: xi).
11. In the US, data on market shares of media companies is forbidden from release into the public domain, therefore exact figures of who owns what and the relative power of each media organization is not clear.

CHAPTER 8

Media Wars: Documentary Dispersion

In a lengthy shot from Ross McElwee's *Six O'Clock News* (1996), the camera scans a bridge destroyed by a hurricane, panning the extent of the disaster, the media filming it, and the locals observing both them and it. In the shot, we are reminded that mediated realities are at the same time both packaged entertainments and 'real' experiences. As McElwee trails journalists that seek 'news' and 'stories' in lives devastated by natural disasters and traumatic events such as earthquakes, floods, hurricanes and murder, the film examines the blurred lines between first-hand experience and manufactured reality, closeness and distance. Ultimately, the different levels of filmic engagement with tragic events in *Six O'Clock News* create a kind of hall of mirrors: crews fabricating news out of disaster and trauma reflect and are filmed by the self-reflective documentarian chronicling his own version of events. Highlighting this interplay and blurring of documentary 'truth' and mainstream media 'infotainment', the film anticipates central questions facing documentary in the intensely mediatized world of the twenty-first century.

Representational and existential questions overlap in the film: how do we reach the 'true' experience of trauma beyond the anonymous media screen? How might the filmmaker make sense of a world rife with personal tragedy? McElwee reaches an 'epiphany', he states, when he befriends an earthquake survivor in Los Angeles called Salvador Peña, who suffered terrible injuries when trapped by a falling building. In spite of continuing debilitation and poverty, Peña remains stoic and deeply religious. When Peña signs a contract with the CBS docudrama *Rescue 911* to recreate his experience as reality television, he must pull out of the film – with McElwee's blessing – as financially and practically *Rescue 911* can do more for him than McElwee ever could. The film's positioning of direct experience against packaged news comes full circle as Peña's tragic experience, at least in some way, finds compensation in being transformed into commodified entertainment. The trajectories of Salvador's story – and of McElwee's, it turns out – come to pose questions about the state of documentary itself: whether developments such as reality television, tabloid news or the appropriation of documentary modes by mainstream fictions indicate the death of documentary, or its future.

The production of documentary reality in the twenty-first-century US faces serious challenges, magnified by a series of disasters and national crises that have seemed to defy representation. These events have reshaped the political spectrum and reconfigured conceptions of national identity and security on many fronts. Their abbreviated monikers – 9/11, Katrina, Afghanistan, Iraq, the recession – point to a vast archive of media discourse, political debate, social analysis and powerful emotional investment. They have been components, as well as what Slavoj Žižek calls 'symptoms', of a loss of confidence both in the unassailable might of the US and in presumptions of American exceptionalism. For Žižek, the symptom might describe critical events (Katrina, for example) that have been invested with profound cultural, historical, ideological and personal meanings. But this collective search for meaning and clear explanations for such events also 'obscures the terrifying impact of [the event's] presence', reflecting desires to both 'escape' and 'domesticate' the terrible thing itself, to mask the ways these events point to the actual precariousness of social and personal life. The symptom, therefore, both solicits and exceeds our ability to assimilate and come to terms with terrifying realities (Žižek 1989: 71).[1]

Documentaries have addressed these cultural 'symptoms' in both direct and indirect ways: some 'make sense' of the world by offering narrative coherence, interpretation and seeming solutions to dilemmas involving real people struggling in the midst of social crises both great and small. Others offer solace, identification and entertainment through formulaic solutions and forms of 'public therapy' (as in ABC's *Extreme Makeover: Home Edition* and *Wife Swap*): simplified personal transformations that might mask or defer more disturbing realities beyond our grasp. At other times documentaries, as seen in the previous chapter, mark the impossibility of desires for fuller explanation or completion, gesturing towards the unknown and ambivalent realms of experience. They can, Nichols notes, engage an 'awareness of the tension between representation and [. . .] magnitudes beyond representation' (1991: 233).

Production of this more complex picture of the world has come up against changing conceptions of private experience and public engagement. How can a documentary any longer claim to speak for a collective 'public'? If we can't presume the unity of a collective, then who do documentaries address, and to what ends? Ambiguities always present in the documentary form have surfaced with renewed force. Documentaries no longer have the luxury of implicit authority and transparency, they must succeed on numerous fronts: aligning with popular expectations of reality in representation, convincing through persuasive argument and evidence, winning over viewers with insightful and sometimes ironic acknowledgement of their own fabrications and limitations. Even then, success is hardly guaranteed.

This chapter will consider how documentaries have negotiated changing practices, markets and public expectations, while still attempting to represent and intervene in crises and shattering events that have marked twenty-first-century US life. I'll ultimately focus on one of these events, the Iraq War, which has produced a 'tide' of filmic responses since 2003 (Kahana 2008: 328). If this site of intense documentary work is any indication, it seems the key functions of the documentary form – in all its variety – still have potent cultural currency, particularly in the face of social and national crisis.

POST-DOCUMENTARY?

Recent years have witnessed a rapid expansion and dispersal of the functions of documentary, triggered by shifts in production contexts, technologies, channels of transmission and distribution, and public expectations. The range of approaches and styles encompassed by documentary is vast and, depending on how strictly one wants to define it, might include everything from reality television to home-made shorts on YouTube and Google Videos, or hybrid forms such as documentary musicals. In this case it would probably be easier to dispense with the term documentary and simply speak of an ongoing proliferation of nonfiction filmmaking – but as this book has argued, documentary has always been imbricated in a wider constellation of nonfiction film practices, and the boundaries between it and other kinds of films have long been less than clear. For example, documentary traditions have helped to inform and 'discipline' related activities such as amateur filmmaking, while these 'peripheral' forms and changing technologies have had profound effects on how people conceive, make and consume documentaries.

The term 'post-documentary' has been used to indicate the ways that perceptions of truth in documentary, along with the relative stability of 'documentary' as a descriptive term, have significantly shifted. Keith Beattie explains that post-documentary 'evokes a post-Griersonian documentary devoid of the authoritarian, expository positions which underpin the truth claims' of traditional approaches (2008: 151–2). Similarly Stella Bruzzi, while avoiding laying down strict categories or implying clean breaks from the past, invokes the term 'new documentary' to describe a form inflected by increasing attention to questions of its own mediation and the prevalent problematization of the 'real'. As a consequence, new documentary tends to foreground performativity rather than assuming transparency or applying solely to the task of essential truth telling (Bruzzi 2006: 9).

John Corner also stresses the performativity of post-documentary culture, which has seen a greater emphasis on 'documentary as diversion', or entertainment (Corner 2002, 2008). This has displaced – though not entirely replaced – documentary's core functions of encouraging democratic civic-mindedness, engaging in journalistic enquiry and interrogating dominant ideologies and naturalized viewpoints. Certainly after filmmakers like Michael Moore and Morgan Spurlock, documentary can no longer be seen simply as a discourse of sobriety. Performative and playful elements have always been present but were usually suppressed by more rigid and institutional definitions. Beattie highlights this long-standing, crucial but relatively under-examined function of documentary, noting that 'entertainment, fun and pleasure' – or what he calls 'documentary display' – can be viewed across a range of nonfiction modes, from early actualities and avant-garde experiments to rockumentaries and surfing films (2008: 5).

Clearly we are moving away from a time when documentary was primarily defined according to Griersonian notions of social instruction and authority, or determined by later perceptions of unvarnished directness and immediacy – yet we might not quite have arrived at a post-documentary moment, per se (indeed, Corner emphasizes the speculative and 'tongue in cheek' nature of the 'post-') (Corner 2008: 59). Critics such as Brian Winston have been key to ongoing revaluations of documentary as it continues to evolve, pointing to differences between post-Griersonian documentary and so-called post-documentary culture. Here documentary is viewed as always having been less stable than many theorists and advocates would have liked, and now might be seen as 'growing' to include docusoaps, reality television and hybrid forms such as docudrama. As Winston has suggested, 'we are [. . .] not living in a "post-documentary" era; we are, though, at a point when John Grierson's traditional definition ("the creative treatment of actuality") has clearly outlived its shelf-life' (Winston 2008a). As Winston stresses, much depends on how the documentary concept circulates in the public realm.

These shifting perceptions apply not just to documentary as a discursive mode, but to a whole range of media that serve the public. The forms and functions of these media are in a state of flux, and driven by increasingly market-centered forces. As Corner suggests, documentary's ongoing integrity as a concept and its place in public debate should be viewed against the reframing of the very notion of 'the public' itself. Changing ideas of citizenship and identities as 'public' subjects have

> very much to do with the [. . .] increasing emphasis on market systems, market values and the dynamics of production and consumption. These have generated a version of the 'popular' which is often in direct tension with notions of the 'the public'. [. . .] All media researchers know the

extent to which 'public service' broadcasting has been redefined and, in some countries, displaced both as a practice and as an aspiration, by these changes. (Corner 2002)

One of these countries, of course, is the US, where Patricia Zimmermann sees a link between a crisis in socially committed documentary, the erosion of public service ideals and a greater cultural and political emphasis on market forces. Here, 'the clear lines of distinction between public space and corporate space, between public affairs and private enterprise, between oppositional work and corporatist multiculturalism, between identity politics and niche marketing, between the nation and globe, have become murky' (2000: 50).

The satisfactions of participatory democracy no longer chiefly rely on identifying with a national collective. They might derive from posting on YouTube, twittering, blogging, engaging with – even shouting opinions at – the dramas of reality television, or voting for a contestant on *American Idol*. If an ideal of documentary as democracy in action has been seen as a means to define national values and priorities, to re-imagine the world and create spaces for public dissent and debate, then the new world order of dispersed, corporatized and commercialized notions of public participation and democratic access poses profound questions about the shape documentaries will take and what social functions they will serve.

Interestingly, while documentary has metamorphosed, it has also largely thrived amid this transforming public realm. What Linda Williams called the 'hunger for documentary images of the real' (1993: 10) seemed to vastly expand over the course of the 1990s and into the 2000s. From 1996 to 2002, an average of fifteen documentaries per year had a theatrical release; in 2003 and 2004, more than forty were being released to theaters each year. Newly formed distributors such as Magnolia were backing a range of projects. Domestic revenues for documentaries increased from $5 million in 2001 to $55 million in 2004, even leaving out the mammoth box-office takings of *Fahrenheit 9/11* ($119 million) (Arthur 2005: 18; Aufderheide 2005: 25). Some have argued that post-9/11 uncertainties instigated a renewed 'search for authenticity' and demand for stories that were 'genuine and real' (quoted in Arthur 2005: 19). For Paul Arthur, other factors should be recognized, such as the US population's established taste for reality television, which in a sense spilled over into theatrical markets. Films such as the highly successful *Capturing the Friedmans* (2003), marketed as a tell-all drama of a family haunted by repression and secrecy (with the tagline, 'who do you believe?'), deepened and complicated the kinds of television psychodramas refereed by the likes of Jerry Springer and Sally Jessy Raphael. When released on DVD, documentaries also made a comfortable 'fit' with small-screen viewing habits: indeed sales of documentary DVDs skyrocketed between 2001 and 2004 (Arthur 2005: 19).

Much documentary success of the 2000s has related to what Pat Aufderheide calls the 'high end market in documentary as artful entertainment'. At a time of widespread cynicism regarding corporate media, 'indie docs' have been groomed through film festival circuits, with public interest and anticipation built up through positive reviews (2005: 25). But the majority of documentary consumption takes place at the other end of the spectrum, through low-budget action and reality television programming. Highly formulaic structures and styles dominate this industrialized approach, resulting in 'low-cost, high-volume' documentaries. As a programmer for the History Channel stated: 'Our M.O. is clip, talking head, clip, talking head [. . .]. We do it because it works. If you want to do something else, tell us how it'll happen on a budget and why its better' (quoted in Aufderheide 2005: 26).

Even amid these commercialized, easily repeatable forms, more traditional documentary approaches are branching out to capture new audiences. Depending on one's perspective, reality television – with its fly-on-the-wall stylizations and reliable crisis structure – is either the monstrous child or most successful legacy of direct cinema. The customary addition of voiceover takes us back to documentary's explanatory and interpretive functions, though much voiceover has come to offer sarcastic or humorous observations instead of earnest contextualization and analysis. The elliptical style of postmodernism also has been absorbed into mainstream entertainments. Errol Morris's *film noir*ish penchant for forensic detail, dramatic re-enactments and hypnotic musical scoring has been adapted to serve cable television's 'true crime' shows such as *Serial Killers*, *The FBI Files* and *Crimes that Shook the World*. These series, while sensationally outlining facts and details, often leave larger questions of motivation, of why and how, unanswered, leaving viewers with an uneasy sense of postmodern indeterminacy.

Keeping in mind this potential range of current perceptions of documentary, I want to consider how 'serious' documentaries have attempted to come to terms with recent conceptual, stylistic and commercial turns while still engaging certain inherited social functions of documentary. Even after the ascendancy of postmodern irony and documentary as diversion, documentaries that recall the form's traditional functions do continue to retain a measure of cultural currency: commenting, interpreting and intervening at times of national crisis. The productive focus of recent documentary work on the war and occupation in Iraq is a measure of this persistent, if contested, 'faith' in the documentary form.

'WAR SHOWS'

It is important to remember that US documentaries dealing with the Iraq War have been produced under the shadow of representations both of the Vietnam War and of the previous Gulf War (1990–1). After Vietnam and, especially, the Gulf War, many critics were effectively writing off cinema's potential for critically engaging with war – for reversing or undermining an established symbiosis between war and US cinema that stretches back at least as far as 1898, when theaters boldly advertised their programs of Spanish-American War shorts as 'War Shows' (Kaplan 2002: 153).

As Harun Farocki's *Inextinguishable Fire* (Germany, 1969) set out to prove during the Vietnam War, electronically mediated versions of war's atrocities (in this case napalm burns) no longer seemed to have the power to shock viewers, who have been desensitized and thus 'close their eyes' to the sheer repetition of war imagery. Similarly, writing after the first Gulf War, Bernd Hüppauf argued that cinema had 'finally exhausted its critical potential' for dealing with war (1993: 41). Influenced by the theories of Paul Virilio and Jean Baudrillard, Hüppauf reiterated claims that the ever-proliferating mass reproduction of images meant that photographic representation had lost its power to persuade or invoke historical reality. With the dehumanized virtual realities that typified media images of the Gulf War ('surgical strikes', 'smart bombs', infrared guided missile footage, the eerie absence of human beings), war at a distance became a video game: fully technologized and remote from humanity. For Baudrillard, 'War, when it has been turned into information, ceases to be a realistic war and becomes a virtual war' (2001: 242). War became spectacle, a 'simulacrum of war' that, in public consciousness, 'did not take place' (232).

After the Gulf War, the possibility that moving images might be used as a tool for opposing powerful ideologies underpinning acts of war seemed to be receding, stacked against a growing consensus that the radical and counter-hegemonic potential of film had long ago dissipated. Anti-war cinema not only ran the risk of repeating 'exhausted' images, but, in its very invocation of war imagery (as in combat films such as *Full Metal Jacket* [1987] or *Saving Private Ryan* [1998]), of actually propagating patriotic and nationalist ideologies. For Hüppauf, it was no longer enough to practice a humanist montage that exhibited the effects of war – for example, that showed 'increasingly brutal war conditions [. . .] juxtaposing them with the [suffering] human face' (1993: 63). This approach suggested 'anachronistic' moral humanism that had lost its impact in the context of modern warfare and the 'structurally inhuman battlefield' (63). In this view, Robert Capa's war photographs, for example, or documentaries like *The Spanish Earth*, with its close-ups of dead children and the faces of young soldiers going to war, would have lost their ability to shock viewers into examining the consequences and casualties of war.

Figure 19. 'Target Iraq' graphic (2003).

History seemed to be repeating itself in 2003 in the run up to the Iraq War, with 'action' news broadcasts across the US rolling out colorful computer graphics, sound effects and slogans ('Target Iraq' on NBC; 'America's New War' on CNN). Twenty-four-hour commercial news was saturated by non-stop, up-to-the-minute reports, endless screen crawls and multiple televisual frames opening on to hyped-up (soon to be 'embedded') reporters, all providing the tense, carnivalesque atmosphere that has become almost de rigueur in US television news. The war hadn't yet started, but the story was already written. The blanket use of military personnel as key experts on networks such as CNN further reinforced, in Norman Solomon's words, 'a decidedly military mind set' even before war had been declared (2005: 124). Together, these suppressions and amplifications typify features of what Simon Dalby refers to as the dramatically successful tactics of 'tabloid imperialism' (2006: 304).

As has been widely observed, after the bombs began falling on Baghdad in March 2003, the Iraq War became television's sanitized war. There were few scenes of carnage on the streets. The Bush administration forbade broadcasting images of the coffins of returning dead soldiers, and the media complied. Embedded reporting was a tactic assuring media collusion with US military interests, where reporters could invoke Second World War-style heroics, while suppressing images of the dead and wounded. Dissent was silenced, as CBS news anchor Dan Rather recalled: 'There was a fear in every newsroom in America [. . .] fear of losing your job . . . the fear of being stuck with some label, unpatriotic or otherwise' (Pilger 2010: 7).

Yet the war also was met with a flurry of documentary production, determined to highlight mainstream media biases and elisions.[2] Robert Greenwald's *Uncovered: The Whole Truth About the Iraq War*, for example, was released in November 2003 via house parties and Internet publicity organized by the advocacy group MoveOn.org. Errol Morris's *The Fog of War* (2003), an extended interview with John F. Kennedy and Lyndon Johnson's Vietnam War czar Robert McNamara, was released six days after the capture of Saddam Hussein in December 2003 and spoke implicitly to the Iraq occupation (as Morris himself later stressed in his Academy Award acceptance speech). The following year saw films like Jehane Noujaim's *Control Room*, *Fahrenheit 9/11*, David O. Russell's (initially suppressed) *Soldiers Pay* and Petra Epperlein and Michael Tucker's *Gunner Palace*. Esteban Uyarra's *War Feels Like War*, screened on PBS – interestingly in light of Hüppauf's comments on the exhaustion of the war image of the suffering human face – eloquently employs close-ups to document the life-altering situations encountered by international journalists who refused to be 'embedded' according to the US military's demands. Many of these films, such as Greenwald's, draw on documentary mainstays of argument and persuasion; others, such as *Control Room*, draw on direct cinema.

As outlined in Chapter 5, war in film has harnessed powerful public sentiments, constructing potent rhetorical frameworks (as in Capra's *Why We Fight*) for conveying historical veracity and social urgency. Perhaps to avoid appearing manipulative, many Iraq War documentaries display an 'aesthetic of honesty' (Musser 2007: 15), minimizing excessive rhetorical and stylistic risks, relying instead on logic and reasoned argument. Some are accented with postmodern flourishes – as in Eugene Jarecki's response to Capra, *Why We Fight* (2005) or Greenwald's *Iraq For Sale: The War Profiteers* (2006) – but always towards establishing a more robust truth. Here, as Charles Musser suggests, documentaries mobilize a rhetorical structure where 'state' or 'official' truths are revealed as lies, as filmmakers 'penetrate the dissembling masks of public pronouncements and general knowledge that conceal or distort reality and so reveal what is hidden underneath' (2007: 12). Irrefutable evidence of this suppressed truth is provided through talking heads interviews, authoritative voiceovers and the recitation of facts, as in Charles Ferguson's forensic analysis of haphazard preparations for war, *No End in Sight* (2007). Still others recall the illustrated lecture, as in Loretta Alper and Jeremy Earp's study of the deceptive politics of launching wars, *War Made Easy* (2007, based on Norman Solomon's book). Fewer prominent films play a more dangerous game, blurring the lines between rationality, entertainment and sensation.

Documentaries dealing with critical issues such as military conflict tend to be restricted in their ability to play at the level of performativity and unstable truth claims. They risk opening themselves to the burden of proof and exceptional demands for verifiability and accountability. They wade into contested territories, deeply divided ideologies and allegiances. But perhaps most problematic is the way they must negotiate a prevailing public sense of irony and disengagement, where information has become unreliable disinformation or 'infotainment', where the 'real' has, paradoxically, retreated from perception with the ever-increasing proliferation of 'reality' images and 'live' feeds that take precedence on our multiple (television, computer, iPhone, BlackBerry) screens. Finally, documentaries dealing with the Iraq War have had to come to terms with the increasing tabloidization of television news and public information – and with this, the perceived instability of all media 'truth'. These are the networks of media oversaturation, 'voluntary' censorship and postmodern disengagement that Michael Moore entered into when making *Fahrenheit 9/11*, which is the focus of the next section.

John Corner suggests that 'the generous license accorded to the more diverting modes [of documentary] cannot, as yet, be simply transferred across to more serious kinds of documentary claims-making' (Corner 2002). Still, some filmmakers recently have attempted versions of this complex effort. The documentary musical *Soundtrack to War* (2005) by Australian filmmaker George Gittoes examines salient connections between war and mass media diversions, interweaving combat footage with dance, rap, heavy metal and the music video formats that dominate soldiers' amateur films posted on YouTube and elsewhere. At times the mood is meditative and unsettling, at others abandoned and entertaining. We discover that Gittoes's camera is just one lens on soldiers already flirting with media and celebrity culture. At one point when Gittoes asks for an interview, a soldier passes on the offer, muttering in the background, 'I've been interviewed by *Time*, *Newsweek*, *The New Yorker*, fuck it'. Similarly, *Fahrenheit 9/11* creates a dialogue with other modes of public information and popular entertainment (which includes Moore's own previous work), rather than retreating to the narrative and representational certainties of more traditional approaches.[3] Rather than aim for 'high-end' sobriety, Moore's film holds a mirror up to the media, taking a parodic stance that openly flirts with accusations of manipulation and falsification.

FAHRENHEIT 9/11 (2004)

The omnipresence of tabloid journalism and the media assault that accompanied the 'war footing' and 'war on terror' clearly influenced Michael Moore's decisions regarding how, stylistically and narratively, to approach the Iraq War. Appropriating its title from Ray Bradbury's classic dystopian novel

Fahrenheit 451 (1953), Moore implies the film will engage not just with the war, but with more general problems of censorship, propaganda and truth in representation. Yet while critical of the Iraq War and its pretexts, I would argue that the film ends up projecting ambiguous and perhaps contradictory conclusions about war as a mechanism of international policing and ideological influence. At the same time, *Fahrenheit 9/11* manages to capture a sense of the density, heterogeneity and instability of Americans' own national and patriotic self-perceptions.

Stella Bruzzi refers to *Fahrenheit 9/11* as 'quintessential cinema documentary' (2006: 177). Moore's film shows off the self-reflexive, performative and popular elements of new documentary, veering between subversive parodies of mainstream media and affective *cinéma vérité*. Cynthia Weber highlights the ways the film exemplifies 'vigilante journalism' (2006: 116). From the self-evident seriousness of PBS-style interviews to the superficiality of MTV and cheap wedding video effects: one could arguably refer to Moore's style as a form of political and pop-cultural bricolage (Scott 2007). In this sense, *Fahrenheit 9/11* is exemplary of the 'dialectical' tendencies that Bruzzi perceives in new documentary, which reveal 'the tensions between the documentary pursuit of the most authentic mode of factual representation and the impossibility of this aim' (2006: 7). But in content and style, I would suggest, the film gestures towards other realms of excess and undecidability – in particular towards the political aesthetics of surrealism. 'It is the excess of realism itself', suggests Nicholas Rombes, 'which creates the conditions for the revelation of absurdity that surrealism makes possible' (Rombes 2008).

Moore's film opens with fireworks etched against a night sky – a reference to the 'shock and awe' fire display that hit Baghdad starting on 20 March 2003 – and Moore's disembodied voice saying, 'Was it all just a dream?' After the camera pans down to Al Gore's Florida rally at the 2000 elections, Moore repeats the question: 'Was it a dream, or was it real?' These self-reflexive lines lend, before the fact, a certain irony to the flood of accusations regarding manipulation and fakery that followed the film's release. As Robert Brent Toplin notes, *Fahrenheit 9/11* quickly became recognized 'as an embarrassing example of over-the-top cinematic journalism, and Michael Moore has gained a reputation as an extremist and a propagandist'. Of these critics, Christopher Hitchens was one of the most outraged, calling the film 'a sinister exercise in moral frivolity, crudely disguised as an exercise in seriousness' (Toplin 2005: 8–10; Hitchens 2004). Yet, as Moore's ironic use of James Baker's comments on going to war asserts, perhaps 'all this talk about [he laughs] legitimacy is way overblown'. Indeed, perhaps a discussion of Moore's strategies should be couched in terms not just of whether the documentary makes stable truth claims, but of how the documentary attempts to cope with the truths and lies of going to war. The tactics of *Fahrenheit 9/11* in this sense fall somewhere closer to surrealist politics and the legacies of the avant-garde, as Moore's opening address about the slippage between dreams (and, one assumes, nightmares) and the conscious, 'rational' world begins to suggest.

Surrealism, after the First World War, developed a powerful anti-establishment rhetoric with regard to war. André Breton's observations of shell-shocked soldiers who believed war to be a sham, staged 'like some strange form of theatre', indicated ways of viewing war in terms of alternative realities (Breton 2006a [1918]: 204–5). In *Fahrenheit 9/11*, the theme of surreal spectacle and its ambiguous relation to the real extends to the 'domestic' or 'homeland' sphere as well, where the theatrics of live news coverage of election night (or, in NBC's slogan, 'Decision 2000') are underscored by Moore's addition of a *Beverly Hillbillies*-style banjo soundtrack. Surreal spectacle continues into the halls of Congress, where African American members of the House line up to decry the Supreme Court's decision to disallow an extended recount of votes in Florida. The scene ends with Congresswoman Maxine Waters's defiant exchange with the Chair of the proceedings, Senator Al Gore:

> *AG*: 'Is the objection in writing and signed by a member of the House and a Senator?'
> *MW*: 'The objection is in writing and I don't care that it is not signed by a member of the Senate.'
> *AG*: 'The Chair will advise that the rules do care' [laughter and applause from the floor].

Waters's passionate resistance (her voice breaks with emotion in the midst of her protest) contrasts with the political circus (underscored by the laughter from the floor, which borders on ridicule) breaking out around her. Gore's joke, too, is bounded by an ironic framework that verges on the unreal: not only is he the instrument of the very 'rules' that are in fact working against his interests (and possibly those of democracy), but he appears to be making light of it.

As if to underscore the emptying out of truth and justice, Moore returns to the Gore celebrations in Florida, but reverses the image, unfixing the bonds between history and the event, between representation and the 'reality' it represents. Just as surrealism, as in the documentary experiments of Vigo and Buñuel, attempted to harness film's oneiric 'power to disorient' (Breton 2006b [1951]: 786), Moore's film returns to the world of dreams: 'It turns out none of this was a dream, it's what really happened'. The authority of Moore's voiceover is itself rendered unstable in the face of the illusions, excesses and inversions of 'legitimacy' that have just been screened.

The opening credit sequence breaks quite late (ten minutes) into the film, disrupting the viewer's absorption into the story and drawing attention to the

Figure 20. *Fahrenheit 9/11* (2004). Dog Eat Dog Films. Courtesy of the British Film Institute.

process of viewing a filmic construct – and perhaps to the illusory power of cinema itself. The ensuing 'pre-roll' sequence documents the stage behind the stage, the 'off-camera' moments behind or edited out of the illusion: Bush administration officials preparing to be filmed. Recalling the documentary *Feed* (1992) about the New Hampshire primaries (featuring then-governor Bill Clinton), the images show us both 'the moments before an event of spectacle' and 'the technological conditions of its display', feeding scepticism about media authenticity while denying faith in political realities as unified or 'true' (Kahana 2008: 311, 316). *Fahrenheit 9/11*'s 'pre-roll' sequence is slowed down and further defamiliarized by Jeff Gibbs's hypnotic musical score, creating an aesthetic effect that underlines the abstraction and remoteness of the politicians on screen. The image of Paul Wolfowitz is especially memorable. 'Disgusting, and funny', Weber suggests (2006: 120), but also, as Wolfowitz wipes his comb back and forth across his tongue before combing his hair with it, oddly resembling another iconic figure: Flaherty's Nanook, performing a similar gesture with his 'walrus ivory' knife. Recalling the image of Nanook, too, is Wolfowitz's broad, uninhibited smile, which exudes uncanny brightness and clarity. The shot perhaps implicitly links the film to a wider network of unstable documentary images: here to Flaherty, the 'father' figure of American documentary, whose work has also been a flashpoint for accusations of fakery.

Moore's strategic usage of dialectical montage and self-reflexivity further recalls surrealism, which – as in Buñuel and Dalí's *Un Chien andalou* (1929) – drew attention to the 'rape and seduction of the viewer's vision' (Conley 2005: 197). Perhaps this rape and seduction is exemplified nowhere more than in war films, with their compelling mix of patriotic urgency and sensation. And it would be difficult to recall another 'iconic' image that has come closer to viewer rape and seduction than that of the endlessly repeated destruction of the Twin Towers.[4] Once again Moore reverses the natural order of things by refusing to privilege the visual: here sound upstages image. The technique is effective: the sound of the first plane emerging from silence and a black screen impels the audience, at the moment of impact, to imaginatively recreate the missing visuals. There is a brief instant, in Eisensteinian fashion, when the viewer 'sees' the anticipated image – so deeply ingrained are the links between the sounds of 9/11 and the apocalyptic visions that accompany them – before recognizing its absence. As Dalí wrote, the unconscious 'often confronts our consciousness with extreme cruelty' (2006 [1930]: 426).

The black screen is, effectively, the start of the narrative, which moves from the destruction of the Twin Towers towards the Iraq War and finally to the war's aftermath 'at home'. Efforts to subvert audience expectations continue: after one minute of black screen, the image fades to a woman's face, gazing upwards in shock. Slowly images merge with diegetic sound, which itself begins to ebb away, replaced by music. Human figures become more marginal as the visual field, previously suppressed, prevails. Here the film indulges in a series of (counter-intuitively) aesthetically rich images: slow motion ashes falling like snow on the city, papers blowing in the wind. The floating debris mirrors the final scenes of Antonioni's *Zabriskie Point* (1970), itself a poetic meditation on terrorism as social disenfranchisement and fatally confused political protest. The whole sequence recalls surrealism's objectives towards 'convulsive beauty' (quoted in Flitterman-Lewis 1996: 115).

With the sequence of Bush reading *The Pet Goat* to schoolchildren as the towers are hit, the film moves towards the familiar comic territory of Moore's previous work. Comedy and parody, too, engage with surrealism's legacy, where humor is linked to anger and subversion of a patriotic war footing. The humor was lost on the conservative radio commentator Rush Limbaugh, however, who referred to *Fahrenheit 9/11* as a 'pack of lies' (quoted in Toplin

2005: 8). Subsequent exposés such as Alan Peterson's *FahrenHYPE 9/11* (2004) portrayed the film as a dangerous web of deliberate misrepresentations. Yet Moore's parody consists far less of overt manipulation (such as Bush, Cheney, Rumsfeld and Blair photoshopped, with obvious sloppiness, on to the bodies of actors from the television western *Bonanza*) than of simply replaying US television news and found footage as it was broadcast. This practice of 'media piracy' (Zimmermann 2000: 186–7) has the effect of recontextualizing news images in order to defamiliarize the overly familiar. Newscasts branded with their 'War on Terror', 'America on Alert' and 'America Strikes Back' logos – explicitly transforming social crisis and national fear into commodity – fill the screen. We see stories about the terror threats posed by poison pens and model airplanes packed with explosives, and a sequence about a high-level terrorist alert for the town of Tappahannock, Virginia, rerun with little alteration. Such scenes encourage contemplation of the paranoia of the media world – reputedly the rational and objective reportage of the 'real' world – as a landscape of dreams and nightmares.

But even with its multi-layered bricolage and auteurist displays, Moore's film enacts a partial retreat from its manifestly subversive intentions. This becomes evident in Moore's self-projection as the prototypical American everyman, or 'Little Man' in baseball cap, t-shirt and baggy jeans (Rizzo 2006; Nolley 2005). Moore places himself prominently, like an oversized version of Chaplin's Little Tramp, at the center of the narrative and often at the center of the screen itself. For example, while the facts of Bush's tarnished military record and intimate relations with James R. Bath, who worked in a financial capacity for the bin Ladens, should not fail to convince (as drawn from the research of Craig Unger's *House of Bush, House of Saud* [2004]), the overstated manner in which Moore introduces them threatens their credibility. The sequence opens with a heroic, slow motion shot of Moore himself in profile, framed by an American flag and a captivated audience; a soothing piano score plays in the background. Moore stresses his popular influence: 'I called George W. Bush a deserter [. . .] in response, the White House released his military records'. The theme of cat and mouse enacted in *Roger and Me* returns here with force, leaving this scene's wider political implications subsumed to little man/big man personality clashes.

The scenes reconstructing the Bush/Bath case are intriguingly imaged through interwoven shots of appearing and disappearing textual evidence accompanied by a pulsating score reminiscent of *The Thin Blue Line*, but a striking difference from the latter is, once again, Moore's authoritative interpretation of events via the imposition of his voiceover. The omnipresent voice positions Moore as the figure of authority and audience identification, a 'US "we" that [. . .] is hyper-individualized and utterly collectivized at the same time', Weber notes. Moore generally fails 'to mouth the extremely complex and varied moral objections many Americans have to the Bush administration's security policies', and rather poses 'his own morally certain opposition to the moral certainty of the Bush administration' (Weber 2006: 124, 129). This tendency towards an oppositional framework – 'good' Moore/us versus 'bad' Bush/them – possibly limits the film's efforts to construct complex truths and produce a trenchant and more expansive political critique.

The appearance of Lila Lipscomb, for all her emotive screen presence, further generates a sense of ideological ambiguity. Lipscomb is positioned within Moore's diegesis not to critique patriotic war sentiments in favor of pacifism, but to reassert a more traditional sense of national identity amid an increasingly cynical and distrustful post-9/11 political climate. Moore frequently stresses that criticism of Bush and the Iraq War shouldn't be seen as an attack on the idea of nationalism: critiquing the patriotic 'we' would clearly alienate a substantial portion of his US audience. Lila never appears as anything less than a patriotic everywoman, though she is disillusioned with *this* war. We are led to believe that she might not be shocked by her loss in quite the same way had Iraq been a 'just' war. In interviews, Lipscomb's argument echoed Moore's, never interrogating the moral rightness of war, but focusing on the 'lies' uttered by politicians like Bush (Brockes 2004). Here *Fahrenheit 9/11* diverges from the radical anti-war stance of movements like surrealism, which 'eschewed any willingness to die for one's country' (Toohey 2007: 612).

In Lila's most affecting scene, she breaks down in front of the White House. Once a democratic symbol of openness and access to the supreme figure of national power, we see it barricaded with snipers patrolling the roof. As in the 'pre-roll' credit sequence, the image suggests leaders failing to serve the people: they are remote, self-protective, likely not to be trusted. Weber rightly suggests that the shift in focus to Lila, away from Moore, in many ways signals Moore's attempt to appropriate Lila's sympathetic yet authoritative voice as his own (2006: 128). Yet the shift is, significantly, also signaled by a stylistic move towards direct cinema. Unlike much of Moore's work, an ethic of relative non-interference takes over, indicating objectivity, embodied subjectivity and the '[film] material as evidence' (Winston 1988b: 26). Yet the embedding of direct cinema in *Fahrenheit 9/11* works quite differently from its application in other contexts. The audience relationship to Lila is one of 'knowing' her through Moore, and we always sense his proximity even in scenes where he isn't visible. Moreover, unlike direct cinema observation, the film's prevalent self-reflexivity positions viewers as active and vigilant to the manipulations of media representation. This cynical awareness instils a sense of having a savvy relationship to the recording apparatus. We might distrust politicians and the media, but Moore has also given us another vantage point in the film, one that allows us to discern when the camera has the power to reveal moments of 'truth'. This vantage point is created by juxtaposing images of obvious technical manipulation against revelatory moments (as in the 'pre-roll' sequence) that have been 'accidentally', and thus faithfully, inscribed by the apparatus.

Hence Lila's most affecting scene is marked by one of these 'accidents' of inscription: a woman breaks into the frame and states, 'this is all a stage'. We recognize our own media cynicism in this woman, so how can we, in effect, doubt the doubter? Yet, through Moore's careful juxtapositions and the stylistic shift to direct cinema, viewers are encouraged to mark the difference between media 'lies' and the documentary 'truth' of this moment. Since we intimately 'know' Lila and her story by this point, the woman's interruption suggests dramatic irony (as spectators, we know more than the doubting woman, therefore her behavior appears inappropriate). Lila, and presumably viewers, have been converted to Moore's 'truth': 'Ignorance', Lila states; 'people think they know, but they don't know. I thought I knew, but I didn't know.' In the figure of the doubting woman, confronting Lila in her moment of grief, Moore reveals a different, postmodern version of the interpellated subject: one no longer blinded by a faith in the national 'we' propagated by dominant ideology and the media, but a subject so desensitized and disaffected by media lies that she no longer recognizes the truth. Her appearance disavows any potentially lingering doubts about Lila's – and Moore's – moral integrity and authenticity.

A widely distributed publicity shot for *Bowling for Columbine* (2002) shows Moore with two objects, one slung over each shoulder: a gun and a camera. This juxtaposition not only underlines the film's subject matter, but suggests a project behind it: to use documentary as an idea-weapon, combating ingrained prejudices and corporate networks that support the US gun trade. But as in *Fahrenheit 9/11*, *Bowling for Columbine* ultimately reduces denser questions of cultural and psychic investment in violence to the realm of little people enacting victories against corporate interests (in *Bowling*, this involves successfully lobbying for the suspension of ammunition sales in Kmart). Similarly, many documentaries addressing the Iraq War avoid examining embedded, mythic structures of conquest and imperial 'right' that have underwritten support for military action. As Louis Menand argues, few films offer a denser reading of the 'intellectual investment' behind the war, and 'the intellectual investment in the Iraq War is much scarier than the financial involvement' (2004: 94).

For Weber, *Fahrenheit 9/11* offers no utopian vision, 'just a warning about our current and possibly future dystopia' (2006: 118). The same might be said of a number of Iraq War films, such as Jarecki's *Why We Fight*, which conveys a multi-layered, historical argument about the Iraq occupation as an inevitable outcome of the growth of the military industrial complex. Employing a thesis-driven approach, *Why We Fight* combines archival footage with interviews, compiling historical evidence to contest the insistence of Bush administration

Figure 21. *Bowling for Columbine* (2002). Dog Eat Dog Films. Courtesy of the Academy of Motion Picture Arts and Sciences.

officials that the US faces a 'new war' on terror, for which there is no relevant history or precedent.[5] Yet the film's critique of the military industries stops short of being pacifist or anti-nationalist, sidestepping accusations of anti- or un-Americanism. Such films (like Moore's) also sometimes hint at nostalgia for a 'better' America of just wars and honest industry. Nonetheless, they remain crucial for feeding public debate, generating forms of political belonging and responsibility, and fueling ongoing conversations that 'cut across boundaries of generations and geography' – in spaces ranging from cinemas, church halls, and house parties to the blogosphere (Aufderheide 2007a: 64).

THE REAL FACE OF OCCUPATION

While responses to the Iraq War by directors like Greenwald and Jarecki have critiqued the war 'at home', films engaging with those on the front lines tend to eschew the thesis and lecture formats in favor of more visceral, intimate and intensely subjective views of war. In the various video war diaries on YouTube, the lives of soldiers are relayed through short clips, including comedy sketches by bored soldiers stationed in armored vehicles and videos set to the music of bands like Slayer and Seether. Deborah Scranton's *The War Tapes* (2006) gathers up such video diary accounts to provide close-up views of soldiers in Iraq. Ellen Spiro and Phil Donohue's *Body of War* (2007) works to convey the personal costs of military conflict, foregrounding the soldier's traumatized body as the key trope for war. Errol Morris brought his auteur approach and interrotron interview device to *Standard Operating Procedure* (2008), chiefly a meditation on the ambiguities of photographic evidence (the Abu Ghraib torture images), with glimpses of some of the motives behind torture. At the other end of the spectrum of so-called grunt docs (Aufderheide 2007a: 59) are cable and Internet-streamed shows such as *Alpha Company: Iraq Diary* (the Military Channel), written and directed by former *Baywatch* director Gordon Forbes III. *Alpha Company: Iraq Diary* stresses action and machismo, pitching US troops squarely against 'the enemy' through a mixture of combat and patrol footage, high-energy music and sonorous voiceover. The collective 'you' is drawn directly into the frame, as in more traditional war propaganda.

Importantly, certain 'frontline' films have foregrounded not just soldiers, but the Iraqi people themselves. These are the Iraqis often seen in the margins of war films, portrayed in the media as 'good' allies or 'bad' insurgents, speaking untranslated in the background of journalists' diaries, crowding around cameras pointed from military vehicles, lying on the ground at the wrong end of a gun barrel, providing evidence of horrific injury or 'collateral damage'. Some of these 'learning-from-the-Iraqis-films' have had relatively high-profile releases, including James Longley's elegant and wrenching *Iraq in Fragments* (2006, made with HBO) (Aufderheide 2007a: 62). But generally, these films have had a harder time finding distribution and press attention, gaining audiences through alternative venues and Internet sites. Of these, Steve Connors and Molly Bingham's *Meeting Resistance* (2007) records personal testimonials of those labeled insurgents by the US military and media; Usama Alshaibi's *Nice Bombs* (2007) documents his cautiously optimistic 2004 return to Baghdad, which eventually he decides to flee. The film collective InCounter's *About Baghdad* (2004) is an account of the Iraqi writer and poet Sinan Antoon's explorations of tensions and fears in Baghdad during the summer of 2003, just after the fall of the Ba'ath regime.

A series of shorter documentaries have found limited distribution via the

Internet, film festivals and community and university screenings, for example: *500 Miles to Babylon* (David Martinez, 2006), the Al Qitaf Artistic Production *Testimonies from Fallujah* (Hamodi Jasim and Dahr Jamail, 2005), the anonymously made *Vietnam Street* (2004), *Terror* (Termite TV Collective, 2005) and Kareem Farooq, Molly Fink and Brian Drolet's *Globalization at Gunpoint: The Economics of Occupation* (2004). The latter was made with Deep Dish Satellite Network, an outgrowth of the video activist group Paper Tiger Television, established to gather and distribute community access work from around the US. Deep Dish also helped produce a film to which I'd like to briefly turn: *The Real Face of Occupation* (2004), a compilation documentary (included on the independently distributed DVD collection, *Shocking and Awful: A Grassroots Response to War and Occupation* [2004]) that draws on the footage of activist video groups like Democracy Now! and Occupation Watch.

The Real Face of Occupation at first appears to be a loose montage of harrowing clips drawn from found footage, documenting public addresses, protests, angry encounters, military aggression at checkpoints and the suffering inflicted by daily losses of life in Iraq. While the footage is drawn from various sources, the montage technique ultimately reveals underlying patterns. One sequence links a speech by the campaigner Yanar Mohammed of the Organization for Women's Freedom in Iraq to images of escalating tensions between US soldiers and women demonstrators in Baghdad during August 2003. These scenes move to seemingly unrelated night vision shots at a Baghdad checkpoint in July 2003, where US soldiers shout threats and profanities, aiming their rifles into a car in which a group of Iraqis are transporting an ill woman. The jarring scene cuts to an intense interview with a grieving family – father, brother, wife and children – of a man shot by US troops while waiting for a taxi (the military later claimed he had a pistol). The sequences seem to unfold randomly, documenting disparate locations and events through a variety of low-budget styles, but the juxtaposition of scenes indicates escalating tensions and lapses in communication, culminating in the eruption of violence and its devastating consequences. As opposed to the 'mathematical space emptied of human experience' (Hüppauf 1993: 74) that dominated images of the first Gulf War, Iraq War films often foreground embodied experience, the 'real face' of war, with images of conflict that have become 'highly subjective and chaotically intense' (Pisters 2010: 243).

In terms of production and distribution, films such as *The Real Face of Occupation* perpetuate not only the democratic ideals of community access, but recall aspects of activist documentary of the 1930s, emphasizing compilation reels rather than polished cinema products. The FPL, Belinda Baldwin and Robert Bahar argue, cemented a political documentary practice in the US that could 'bring marginal or invisible social identities to the forefront', challenging 'the commercial media's stranglehold over the American political agenda'.

Figure 22. *The Real Face of Occupation* (2004). Deep Dish TV. Image capture, Deep Dish TV DVD.

Indeed much recent activist documentary in the US, even with (or because of) digital cameras and the Internet, recalls versions of the ad hoc production and distribution techniques developed by the FPL (Baldwin and Bahar 2004: 12–16).

The work of organizations such as Deep Dish suggests that perhaps less depends upon producing a 'new aesthetic' (Hüppauf 1993: 76) to combat the distancing and dehumanizing of war's consequences than on the task of getting documentaries such as *The Real Face of Occupation* widely screened. For example, Adam Curtis's complex analysis of the 'war on terror', *The Power of Nightmares: The Rise of the Politics of Fear* (2004), while broadcast on BBC2 in Britain, was rejected by HBO and not commercially distributed in the US – though HBO's 'shock doc' that dealt with the occupation, *Baghdad E.R.* (2006), was shown as a lead-in to *The Sopranos*. Some of these films have been broadcast on PBS or can be accessed on Internet Archive or Google Videos, but most have had no mainstream network or theatrical distribution.

Here, especially with regard to access, the Internet plays a crucial role. Sites like WikiLeaks, in particular, have generated sensational debates relating to transparency, visual evidence and the role of documentary in shaping political views and national policy. In the WikiLeaks release of footage shot from an Apache helicopter gun-sight, entitled *Collateral Murder* (2010), we again witness the alignment of camera and weapon, revealing (as the film describes it) 'the indiscriminate slaying of over a dozen people in the Iraqi suburb of

New Baghdad', including two Reuters employees, along with two children seriously injured. Though drawing directly on military footage, the release was 'packaged' as a documentary, with two versions streamed online: one thirty-nine minutes and the other edited to seventeen minutes. The video's impact is enhanced by its status as a 'leaked' and authenticated military record, an 'accident' of technical inscription never meant for public view. As a result, we are aware as we watch that the deaths might 'never have taken place' were it not for the release of this video record. The film indicates WikiLeaks' attention to public paranoia about falsification and digital manipulation; thus any obvious interferences such as added voiceover are minimized, though it does contain subtitles and title cards of quotes, opinion and analysis, all framed by an unabashedly editorializing title. Some footage is slowed down to highlight the Reuters staff, and arrows point to details in the blurry images such as the men's camera equipment (referred to by soldiers on the radio track as weapons), the two injured children and dead bodies in the aftermath. There are also pointed repetitions, in particular the looped voices of soldiers who seem desperate to fire their weapons ('c'mon, let us shoot!'). They refer to the victims as 'dead bastards', congratulating themselves on 'good shootin' and laughing as a military vehicle drives over one of the victims' bodies. Their first person point of view recalls both video gaming and combat film, with the viewer engaged in the middle of the action, but here customary heroic identifications are reversed: we are locked into a viewpoint taking actions that arouse shock and repulsion. We witness close at hand the desubjectified and desensitized states of soldiers in combat mode, armed with sophisticated killing technology, and trained to use it.[6]

The New Yorker echoed WikiLeaks' Julian Assange's view that the video was 'a striking artifact – an unmediated representation of the ambiguities and cruelties of modern warfare' and an unsettling interrogation of the 'Rules of Engagement' (Khatchadourian 2010: 40). Fox News criticized the editing of the video, while US Defense Secretary Robert Gates complained that there was no 'context': 'there's no before and there's no after' (Stewart and Zabarenko 2010). *Collateral Murder* is not, however, unmediated 'pure' information: it makes use of the documentary form as a public mode for consuming factual material. It contains contextual analysis via title cards, quotes from witnesses and a three-minute introduction that includes 'after' images including the journalist Saeed Chmagh's grieving son, clutching a photograph of his dead father. The film's power to shock derives from its minimalism and its 'found' aesthetics that blur video gaming technology (on which soldiers are actually trained) with a visceral reality effect. Real-time footage shows the speed at which adrenaline-fueled desires to 'engage' can set in, how human beings in the wrong place at the wrong time are reduced to 'targets' and dispatched with a mixture of detachment and satisfaction in a job well done.

If another 'small war' – Vietnam – offers any precedent, together these films and videos of the Iraq War help us to track the development of war and its impact on national self-perceptions. Documentary's established functions of engaging with issues of social responsibility and citizenship, of questioning dominant ideologies and naturalized viewpoints and of creating public spheres and 'active interventions in public life' persist in this body of work (Aufderheide 2007a: 56). Documentary, Paula Rabinowitz notes, 'memorializes the present for the future' (2005: 31). If this is true, then documentaries dealing with the traumas of war and occupation address not only the present, but a future that will one day have to confront the gaps and silences of history and memory.

In *Notes of a Native Son* (1955), James Baldwin wrote: 'I love America more than any country in this world, and, exactly for this reason, I insist on the right to criticize her perpetually' (1984 [1955]: 9). Baldwin's critique was aimed at a future imagined nation – stronger, more equal, more just. A similar sentiment might be applied to recent documentaries such as *Fahrenheit 9/11*, which appeal to the idea of national regeneration through critique. They also imply, however, a stronger ambivalence about the future nation's capacity for generating a moral and just society. As Moore finally asks of those Americans who might be called on to defend a future America: 'Will they ever trust us again?' *The Real Face of Occupation* and *Collateral Murder* take far more pessimistic views of a nationalist agenda and the tunnel vision of naive or unquestioning nationalist thinking. Indeed, as Kahana has observed, much post-9/11 US documentary has noticeably moved away from applying social and political critique as a nation-building exercise towards asserting a greater sense of national indecision and incompleteness. Observing this contrast to the certainties and future imaginings that documentary once strove to produce, Kahana notes a contemporary 'foreshortening of the social horizon of documentary' (2008: 336).

The implications of this foreshortened social and historical perspective become more profound as the proliferation of reality images increases exponentially: we live amid an ever-increasing number of devices that reproduce, display and invite us to consume the real world. The realities they show us are often mundane or trivial, yet can also be heartbreaking or shocking: from comic stunts, dares and pet tricks to dramatic storms, floods and lives broken by war. These technologized realities flip by on our screens in numbers that would be staggering had they not become such common fixtures of modern life. Much nonfiction footage is consumed in isolated, decontextualized bites – fragments caught on image and sound recorders around the world. Yet to comprehend what they reveal is still not a simple process. If YouTube comments posted by viewers – a free-for-all forum for audience response –

provide any clue, these images cannot simply 'speak for themselves'. Take, for example, the many short films and images of the 2004 Indian Ocean tsunami, in which 230,000 people died. Whereas most YouTube viewers express pain or sorrow at the images, others actually joke about the staggering losses, label the images as 'fake' or even criticize the loss of life as stupidity. Clearly, such nonfiction images serve a variety of purposes across a vast number of sites. Just as clearly there remains a widespread lack of comprehension of the scale and impact – the magnitude – of events captured in fragments and streamed to global audiences.

For Nichols, this question of magnitude underlies the understanding, meaning and use of nonfiction images. The issue of magnitude 'involves a tension between the representation and the represented as experienced by the viewer' (1991: 232). Though we avidly consume and respond in various ways to technical reproductions of sounds and images of the world, we do not necessarily 'know' them, and simply being exposed to technologically reproduced realities does not necessarily add to our knowledge. Though we might engage in a 'visceral experience' of filmed reality, still that visceral experience 'must be rendered meaningful' (Nichols 1991: 232). In the case of extreme images such as those of war, natural disaster or other tragic events, there remain seemingly unbridgeable physical, temporal and technological gaps between those close to the tragedy and those viewing the events from a safe remove. For Nichols, 'the magnitudes opened up by a [film] text are not merely a matter of naming something of profound importance' – beyond this basic information, audiences need to be situated in positions where a received image or text can be endowed with 'subjective intensity'. Audiences develop an awareness of the meanings of filmed events through an awareness of a tension between what is represented and what this representation implies: those 'magnitudes beyond representation'. These palpable magnitudes include factors such as time, embodied subjectivity and histories and contexts that lie beyond the immediate frame (Nichols 1991: 232–3). Of course this process of endowing meaning and subjectivity to discrete fragments of filmed reality is complex, and can become a process of negotiation, contestation and, frequently, manipulation, as this book has hopefully made clear.

Transforming spectacles, sights, facts and information into forms of complex experience means linking them to magnitudes beyond the visible. This is the task – the ever receding horizon, perhaps – of the documentary form.

NOTES

1. On the 'symptom' as the collapse of the symbolic and 'real' of cultural events, see Žižek (1989: 11–54).
2. For an overview of Iraq War-related films, see Jaafar (2008: 16–22).
3. About seventeen shots from Gittoes's film were used in *Fahrenheit 9/11*.
4. On the 'iconic' image, see Bruzzi (2006: 21).
5. On the ahistoricism of the 'war on terror', see McAlister (2002).
6. Pisters cites John Protevi, who examines soldiers' training practices that induce desensitized states and reflexes for killing, including training on video gaming technology (2010: 243).

Bibliography

Aitken, Ian (1992) *Film and Reform: John Grierson and the Documentary Film Movement*. London: Routledge.

Alexander, William (1981) *Film on the Left: American Documentary Film from 1931 to 1942*. Princeton: Princeton University Press.

Allen, Robert and Gomery, Douglas (1985) *Film History: Theory and Practice*. New York: Knopf.

Altman, Rick (2006) 'From Lecturer's Prop to Industrial Product: The Early History of Travel Films', in Ruoff (ed.), pp. 61–76.

American Film Institute (2008) *AFI Catalog of Silent Films*. Online at: http://www.afi.com (accessed 15 August 2009).

Anderson, Benedict (1991) *Imagined Communities: Reflections on the Origins and Spread of Nationalism*. New York: Verso.

Anon. (1979) 'An Angry Film: *Native Land*' [1942], in Jacobs (ed.), pp. 200–1.

Anon. (1936) 'Cinema: Documented Dust', *Time*, 25 May, pp. 47–8.

Anon. (1948) 'Cinema: Old Master', *Time*, 20 September, pp. 94–6.

'Antarctica' (2009) IMAX Sydney. Online at: http://www.imax.com.au/films/film.asp?id=9 (accessed 15 June 2009).

Applebaum, Stanley (1980) *The Chicago World's Fair of 1893: A Photographic Record*. New York: Dover.

Armat, Thomas (1979) 'My Part in the Development of the Motion Picture Projector' [1935], in Raymond Fielding (ed.), *A Technological History of Motion Pictures and Television*. Berkeley: University of California Press, pp. 17–22.

Arthur, Paul (1998) 'Media Spectacle and the Tabloid Documentary', *Film Comment*, 34.1 (January): 74–80.

Arthur, Paul (1999) 'Springing Tired Chains: Experimental Film and Video', in Klotman and Cutler (eds), pp. 268–97.

Arthur, Paul (2005) 'Extreme Makeover: The Changing Face of Documentary', *Cineaste*, 30.3 (Summer): 18–23.

Atkins, Thomas R. (1976) *Frederick Wiseman*. New York: Simon & Schuster.

Aufderheide, Patricia (2005) 'The Changing Documentary Marketplace', *Cineaste*, 30.3 (Summer): 24–8.

Aufderheide, Patricia (2007a) 'My Country, Your Country: How Films about the Iraq War Construct Publics', *Framework*, 48.2 (Fall): 56–65.

Aufderheide, Patricia (2007b) *Documentary Film: A Very Short Introduction*. New York: Oxford University Press.

Aumont, Jacques (1987) *Montage Eisenstein*, trans. Lee Hildreth, Constance Penley and Andrew Ross. London: BFI.

Badger, Reid (1979) *The Great American Fair: The World's Columbian Exposition and American Culture*. Chicago: Nelson Hall.

Baldwin, Belinda and Bahar, Robert (2004) 'Docs that Make a Difference: The Politics of Political Documentaries', *International Documentary*, 23.3 (April): 12–16.

Baldwin, James (1984) *Notes of a Native Son* [1955]. Boston: Beacon.

Balio, Tino (ed.) (1993) *Grand Design: Hollywood as a Modern Business Enterprise, 1930–1939*. New York: Charles Scribner's.

Bancroft, Hubert Howe (1894) *The Book of the Fair; An Historical and Descriptive Presentation of the World's Science, Art and Industry, As Viewed through the Columbian Exposition at Chicago in 1893*. New York: Bancroft.

Barber, Theodore X. (1993) 'The Roots of Travel Cinema: John L. Stoddard, E. Burton Holmes and the Nineteenth-Century Illustrated Travel Lecture', *Film History*, 5.1: 68–84.

Barkawi, Tarak (2004) 'Globalization, Culture, and War: On the Popular Mediation of "Small Wars,"' *Cultural Critique*, 58 (Fall): 115–47.

Barker, Jennifer (2009) *The Tactile Eye: Touch and the Cinematic Experience*. Berkeley: University of California Press.

Barnouw, Erik (1964) 'Films of Social Comment', *Film Comment*, 2.1 (Winter): 16–17.

Barnouw, Erik (1983) *Documentary: A History of the Non-fiction Film* [1974]. New York: Oxford University Press.

Barsam, Richard Meran (1974) *Nonfiction Film: A Critical History*. London: George Allen & Unwin.

Barsam, Richard Meran (1988) *The Vision of Robert Flaherty: The Artist as Myth and Filmmaker*. Bloomington: Indiana University Press.

Barsam, Richard Meran (1992) *Nonfiction Film: A Critical History* [rev. edn]. Bloomington: Indiana University Press.

Barthes, Roland (1981) *Camera Lucida*, trans. Richard Howard. New York: Noonday.

Basinger, Jeanine (2003) *The World War II Combat Film: Anatomy of a Genre*. Middletown, CT: Wesleyan University Press.

Baudrillard, Jean (1983) 'The Ecstasy of Communication', trans. John Johnston, in Hal Foster (ed.), *The Anti-Aesthetic: Essays on Postmodern Culture*. Seattle, WA: Bay Press, pp. 126–34.

Baudrillard, Jean (2001) 'The Gulf War Did Not Take Place', in Mark Poster (ed.), *Jean Baudrillard, Selected Writings*. Cambridge: Polity, pp. 231–53.

Bazin, André (1967) *What Is Cinema?*, ed. and trans. Hugh Gray, 2 vols. Berkeley: University of California Press.

Bazin, André (1997) 'On *Why We Fight*: History, Documentation, and the Newsreel' [1946], in Bert Cardullo (ed.), *Bazin At Work: Major Essays and Reviews*, trans. Alain Piette. New York: Routledge.

Beam, Joseph (ed.) (1987) *In the Life: A Black Gay Anthology*. Boston: Alyson Books.

Beattie, Keith (2004) *Documentary Screens: Nonfiction Film and Television*. New York: Palgrave.

Beattie, Keith (2008) *Documentary Display: Re-Viewing Nonfiction Film and Video*. London: Wallflower.

Beckman, Karen (2003) *Vanishing Women: Magic, Film, and Feminism*. Durham, NC: Duke University Press.

Becquer, Marcos (1991) 'Snap!thology and other Discursive Practices in *Tongues Untied*', *Wide Angle*, 13.2 (April): 6–17.

Benelli, Dana (2006) 'Hollywood and the Attractions of the Travelogue', in Ruoff (ed.), pp. 177–94.

Benson, Thomas W. and Anderson, Carolyn (2002) *Reality Fictions: The Films of Frederick Wiseman*. Carbondale: Southern Illinois University Press.

Bercovitch, Sacvan (1993) *The Rites of Assent: Transformations in the Symbolic Construction of America*. New York: Routledge.

Berger, John (1980) *About Looking*. New York: Pantheon.

Betts, Ernest (1928) *Heraclitus, or The Future of Films*. New York: E. P. Dutton.

Betts, Raymond F. (2004) *A History of Popular Culture: More of Everything, Faster, and Brighter*. London: Routledge.

Bhabha, Homi K. (1994) *The Location of Culture*. New York: Routledge.

Blount, Marcellus, and Cunningham, George P. (eds) (1996) *Representing Black Men*. New York: Routledge.

Blue, James (1964) 'Thoughts on *Cinéma Vérité* and a Discussion with the Maysles Brothers', *Film Comment*, 2.4 (Fall): 22–30.

Bluem, A. William (1965) *Documentary in American Television: Form, Function, Method*. New York: Hastings House.

Boddy, William (1990) 'Alternative Television in the United States', *Screen*, 31.1: 91–101.

Boggs, Carl and Pollard, Tom (2007) *The Hollywood War Machine: U.S. Militarism and Popular Culture*. London: Paradigm.

Bolotin, Norman, and Laing, Christine (2002) *The World's Columbian Exposition: The World's Fair of 1893*. Champaign, IL: University of Illinois Press.

Bowser, Eileen (1990) *The Transformation of Cinema, 1907–1915*. Berkeley: University of California Press.

Boyle, Deirdre (1997) *Subject to Change: Guerrilla Television Revisited*. New York: Oxford University Press.

Boyle, Deidre (1998) 'Déjà New: 60s Vérité Meets the 90s', *Independent Film and Video Monthly*, 21.2 (March): 32–5.

Brakhage, Stan (1989) *Film at Wit's End: Eight Avant-Garde Filmmakers*. New York: McPherson.

Breton, André (2006a) 'Subject' [1918], in Matheson (ed.), pp. 204–5.

Breton, André (2006b) 'As in a Wood' [1951], in Matheson (ed.), pp. 786–92.

Brockes, Emma (2004) 'The Lie that Killed My Son', *The Guardian*, 8 July, G2, pp. 10–11.

Brown, Julie K. (1994) *Contesting Images: Photography and the World's Columbian Exposition*. Tucson, AZ: University of Arizona Press.

Brown, Simon (2009) 'Colouring the Nation: Spectacle, Reality and British Natural Colour in the Silent and Early Sound Era', *Film History*, 21.2: 139–49.

Brunius, Jacques B. (1948) 'Rise and Decline of an "Avant-Garde" (France 1919–32)', *Penguin Film Review*. London: Penguin, pp. 53–63.

Bruno, Giuliana (1993) *Street Walking on a Ruined Map: Cultural Theory and the City Films of Elvira Notari*. Princeton: Princeton University Press.

Bruno, Giuliana (2002) *Atlas of Emotion: Journeys in Art, Architecture, and Film*. London: Verso.

Bruzzi, Stella (2006) *New Documentary*. New York: Routledge.

Bullert, B. J. (1994) 'Anatomy of a Controversy: Public Television and the *Dark Circle* Case', *Wide Angle*, 16.1–2 (August): 6–39.

Bullert, B. J. (1997) *Public Television: Politics and the Battle Over Documentary Film*. New Brunswick, NJ: Rutgers University Press.

Burch, Noël (1981) 'Charles Baudelaire versus Doctor Frankestein', *Afterimage*, 8–9 (Spring): 4–21.

Burnett, Ron (1995) *Cultures of Vision: Images, Media, and the Imaginary*. Bloomington: Indiana University Press.

Burns, Jim (1998) 'Ben Maddow', *The Penniless Press*, 8. Online at: http://www. pennilesspress.co.uk/prose/ ben_maddow.htm (accessed 1 April 2010).

Byro. (1967) 'The Titicut Follies', *Variety*, 4 October, p. 12.

C. N. (1936) 'The World in Celluloid: Screen "Documents" and Their Aims', *John O'London's Weekly*, 34, 15 February, p. 763.

Campbell, Russell (1982) *Cinema Strikes Back: Radical Filmmaking in the United States 1930–1942*. Ann Arbor: UMI Research Press.

Campbell, Russell (1984) 'Radical Documentary in the United States, 1930–1942', in Waugh (ed.), pp. 69–88.

Campbell, Russell (1985) 'Radical Cinema in the 1930s: The Film and Photo League', in Peter Steven (ed.), *Jump Cut: Hollywood, Politics, and Counter-cinema*. Toronto: Between the Lines, pp. 123–33.

Campbell, Russell and Alexander, William (1977) 'Film and Photo League Filmography', *Jump Cut*, 14: 33–8.

Canby, Vincent (1969) 'Why, Even You and I Can Be Stars', *New York Times*, 27 April, p. C1.

Carel, Havi (2008) *Illness*. Durham: Acumen.

Carroll, Noël (1996) *Theorizing the Moving Image*. Cambridge: Cambridge University Press.

Castonguay, James (2006) 'The Spanish-American War in United States Media Culture', in Slocum (ed.), pp. 97–108.

Castro, Alex (2000) '*Tongues Untied*', *Senses of Cinema*, 6 (May). Online at: http://archive. sensesofcinema.com/contents/cteq/00/6/tongues.html (accessed 1 May 2009).

Chambers, John Whiteclay II (1996) '*All Quiet on the Western Front* (1930): The Antiwar Film and the Image of Modern War', in John Whiteclay Chambers II and David Culbert (eds), *World War II: Film and History*. New York: Oxford University Press, pp. 13–30.

Chanan, Michael (2007) *The Politics of Documentary*. London: BFI.

Chapman, William Ryan (1981) 'Ethnology in the Museum: A. H. L. F. Pitt-Rivers', DPhil thesis, University of Oxford. Online at: http://www.prm.ox.ac.uk/Kent/musantob/ 19anth.html (accessed 10 July 2009).

Cohn, Lawrence (1992) 'Truth Tellers Start to Tell Tales', *Variety*, 11 May, pp. 22, 54.

Committee on Un-American Activities, US House of Representatives (1948) *Citations by Official Government Agencies of Organizations and Publications Found to be Communist or Communist Fronts*, United States Government, 18 December.

Comolli, Jean-Louis (1994) 'Emergency Exit', *Dox*, 4 (Winter): 4–7.

Comolli, Jean-Louis and Narboni, Jean (1976) 'Cinema/Ideology/Criticism', in Bill Nichols (ed.), *Movies and Methods*, Vol. 1. Berkeley: University of California Press, pp. 22–30.

Conley, Tom (2005) '*Un Chien andalou*: A Rape of the Eye', in Geiger and Rutsky (eds), pp. 196–215.

Cook, David A. (2004) *A History of Narrative Film* [1981]. New York: W. W. Norton.

Corner, John (1996) *The Art of Record: A Critical Introduction to Documentary*. Manchester: Manchester University Press.

Corner, John (2002) 'Documentary in a Post-Documentary Culture? A Note on Forms and Their Functions'. Online at: http://www.lboro.ac.uk/research/changing.media/John%20 Corner%20paper.htm (accessed 5 April 2010).

Corner, John (2008) 'Performing the Real: Documentary Diversions', in Susan Murray and Laurie Ouellette (eds), *Reality TV: Remaking Television Culture*. New York: New York University Press, pp. 44–64.

Cowie, Elizabeth (1999) 'The Spectacle of Actuality', in Gaines and Renov (eds), pp. 19–45.
Crain, Mary Beth (1998) 'Forever Edie: *Grey Gardens*' Edie Beale', *L.A. Weekly*, 14 August, p. 43.
Cripps, Thomas and Culbert, David (1998) '*The Negro Soldier* (1944): Film Propaganda in Black and White', in Peter C. Rollins (ed.), *Hollywood as Historian: American Film in a Cultural Context*. Lexington: University Press of Kentucky, pp. 109–33.
Crowther, Bosley (1944) 'Vivid Film of Daylight Bomb Raid Depicts Daring of Our Air Forces', *New York Times*, 14 April, pp. 1, 3.
Culbert, David (ed.) (1990a) *Film and Propaganda in America, Vol. 2: World War II*. Westport, CT: Greenwood.
Culbert, David (ed.) (1990b) *Film and Propaganda in America, Vol. 3: World War II*. Westport, CT: Greenwood.
Culbert, David and Suid, Lawrence H. (eds) (1991) *Film and Propaganda in America, Vols. 4–5: 1945 and After*. Westport, CT: Greenwood.
Culbert, David Holbrook, Suid, Lawrence H. and Wood, Richard E. (eds) (1990) *Film and Propaganda in America, Vol. 1: World War I*. Westport, CT: Greenwood.
Curtin, Michael (1995) *Redeeming the Wasteland: Television Documentary and Cold War Politics*. New Brunswick, NJ: Rutgers University Press.
Dalby, Simon (2006) 'The Pentagon's New Imperial Cartography: Tabloid Realism and the War on Terror', in Derek Gregory and Allan Pred (eds), *Violent Geographies: Fear, Terror, and Political Violence*. New York: Routledge, pp. 295–308.
Dalí, Salvador (2006) 'The Moral Position of Surrealism' [1930], in Matheson (ed.), pp. 424–7.
Davidson, David (1981) 'Direct Cinema and Modernism: The Long Journey to *Grey Gardens*', *Journal of the University Film Association*, 33.1 (Winter): 3–13.
Davies, Philip John and Wells, Paul (eds) (2002) *American Film and Politics from Reagan to Bush Jr*. Manchester: Manchester University Press.
De Antonio, Emile (2000) 'Visions of Vietnam' [1974], in Douglas Kellner and Dan Streible (eds), *Emile de Antonio: A Reader*. Minneapolis: University of Minnesota Press, pp. 357–60.
'The Delhi Durbar' (1912) *New York Times*, 18 February, p. X9.
Denning, Michael (1997) *The Cultural Front: The Laboring of American Culture in the Twentieth Century*. London: Verso.
Denzin, Norman K. (1991) *Images of Postmodern Society: Social Theory and Contemporary Cinema*, London: Sage.
Denzin, Norman K. (1995) *The Cinematic Society: The Voyeur's Gaze*. London: Sage.
Dick, Bernard F. (1985) *The Star Spangled Screen: The American World War II Film*. Lexington: University Press of Kentucky.
'Dignity of Toil in Labor Films' (1936) *Mid-Week Pictorial*, 16 December. BFI clippings file, 'Documentary: 1930s'.
'Documentary' (1939) [review of Rotha, *Documentary Film*], *Manchester Guardian*, 6 June, p. 18.
'Documentary Film in Danger, Warns Rotha' (1947) *World's Press News*, 20 November. BFI clippings file, 'Documentary: 1940s'.
'Documentary Films in America: Demand for British Productions' (1939) *The Times* [London], 6 August, p. 32.
Doherty, Thomas (1993) *Projections of War: Hollywood, American Culture, and World War II*. New York: Columbia University Press.
Doherty, Thomas (1999) *Pre-Code Hollywood: Sex, Immorality, and Insurrection in American Cinema, 1930–1934*. New York: Columbia University Press.

Donald, James (1998) 'Introduction: Enthusiasms and Execrations', in Donald et al. (eds), pp. 28–35.

Donald, James, Friedberg, Anne and Marcus, Laura (eds) (1998) *Close Up, 1927–1933: Cinema and Modernism*. London: Cassell.

Drew, Robert (2008) Interview, special features, *Primary*, dir. Drew Associates [DVD], Docurama.

Dyer, Earle A. (1943) 'Another Government Film Experiment Ended', *Boxoffice*, 17 July, pp. 22, 25.

Edgerton, Gary R. (2001) *Ken Burns's America*. New York: Palgrave.

Eisenstein, Sergei (1949) *Film Form*, trans. Jay Leyda. New York: Harcourt Brace.

Ellis, Jack C. (1989) *The Documentary Idea: A Critical History of English-Language Documentary Film and Video*. Englewood Cliffs, NJ: Prentice Hall.

Ellis, Jack C. and McLane, Betsy A. (2005) *A New History of Documentary Film*. New York: Continuum.

Ellis, John (1977) 'Free Cinema', *1951–1976: BFI Productions*. London: BFI.

Ellis, Peter (1936) '*The Plow that Broke the Plains*', *New Theatre* (July): 18–19.

Elsaesser, Thomas (1996) 'Dada/Cinema?' in Kuenzli (ed.), pp. 13–27.

Elsten, Harold L. (1942) 'Mass Communications and American Democracy', in Douglas Waples (ed.), *Print, Radio, and Film in a Democracy*. Chicago: University of Chicago Press, pp. 3–14.

Engle, Harrison (1979) 'Thirty Years of Social Inquiry' [interview with Willard Van Dyke, 1965], in Jacobs (ed.), pp. 345–6.

Erish, Andrew (2006) 'Illegitimate Dad of "Kong,"' *Los Angeles Times*, 8 January, p. E6.

Fielding, Raymond (1972) *The American Newsreel, 1911–1967*. Norman: University of Oklahoma Press.

Fielding, Raymond (1978) *The March of Time, 1935–1951*. New York: Oxford University Press.

Fielding, Raymond (1983) 'Hales Tours: Ultrarealism in the Pre-1910 Motion Picture', in John L. Fell (ed.), *Film Before Griffith*. Berkeley: University of California Press, pp. 116–30.

Fielding, Raymond (2006) *The American Newsreel: A Complete History, 1911–1967*. Jefferson, NC: McFarland.

Findling, John E. (1994) *Chicago's Great World's Fairs*. Manchester: Manchester University Press.

Fischer, Lucy (1988) '*Sunset Blvd*: Fading Stars', in Janet Todd (ed.), *Women and Film*. New York: Holmes & Meier, pp. 97–113.

Flaherty, Robert J. (1926) 'The Handling of Motion Picture Film Under Various Climatic Conditions', *Transactions of the Society of Motion Picture Engineers*, 26 (May 3–6) . Online at: http://nimbus.ocis.temple.edu/~jruby/wava/Flaherty (accessed 12 July 2008).

Flaherty, Robert J. (1930) letter to Frances Flaherty, 3 February, box 2, Flaherty Papers, Butler Library, Columbia University.

Flitterman-Lewis, Sandy (1996) 'The Image and the Spark: Dulac and Artaud Reviewed', in Kuenzli (ed.), pp. 110–27.

Fraser, Nancy (1992) 'Rethinking the Public Sphere: A Contribution to the Critique of Actually Existing Democracy', in Craig Calhoun (ed.), *Habermas and the Public Sphere*. Cambridge, MA: MIT Press, pp. 109–42.

Freeman, Judi (1996) 'Bridging Purism and Surrealism: The Origins and Production of Fernand Léger's *Ballet Mécanique*', in Kuenzli (ed.), pp. 28–45.

Friedberg, Anne (1993) *Window Shopping: Cinema and the Postmodern*. Berkeley: University of California Press.

Friedberg, Anne (1995) 'Cinema and the Postmodern Condition', in Linda Williams (ed.), *Viewing Positions: Ways of Seeing Film*. New Brunswick, NJ: Rutgers University Press, pp. 59–86.

Friedman, Harry and Simons, Graham (2008) *Memphis Belle: Dispelling the Myths*. Peterborough: GMS Enterprises.

Froemke, Susan (2003) 'The Craft of Vérité', *Dox*, 45 (February): 8–9.

Froemke, Susan et al. (2001) Directors' commentary, special features, *Grey Gardens*, dir. David and Albert Maysles [DVD], Criterion.

Fuller, Linda K. (1994) *Community Television in the United States*. Westport, CT: Greenwood.

Gaines, Jane M. (2007a) 'Documentary Radicality', *Canadian Journal of Film Studies*, 16.1 (Spring): 5–24.

Gaines, Jane M. (2007b) 'The Production of Outrage: The Iraq War and the Radical Documentary Tradition', *Framework*, 48.2 (Fall): 36–55.

Gaines, Jane M. and Renov, Michael (eds) (1999) *Collecting Visible Evidence*. Minneapolis: University of Minnesota Press.

Garrett, Greg (1994) 'It's Everybody's War: Racism and the World War Two Documentary', *Journal of Popular Film and Television*, 22.2: 70–8.

Garroutte, Eva Marie (2003) *Real Indians: Identity and the Survival of Native America*. Berkeley: University of California Press.

Geiger, Jeffrey (1998) ' "The Camera and Man": Colonialism, Masculinity, and Documentary Fiction', *Third Text*, 44 (Spring): 3–21.

Geiger, Jeffrey (2005) '*Nanook of the North*: Fiction, Truth, and the Documentary Contract', in Geiger and Rutsky (eds), pp. 118–37.

Geiger, Jeffrey (2007) *Facing the Pacific: Polynesia and the U.S. Imperial Imagination*. Honolulu: University of Hawai'i Press.

Geiger, Jeffrey and Rutsky, R. L. (eds) (2005) *Film Analysis: A Norton Reader*. New York: W. W. Norton.

Gellner, Ernest (2006) *Nations and Nationalism* [1983]. Oxford: Blackwell.

Gilroy, Paul (1994) 'Diaspora', *Paragraph*, 17.3 (November): 207–12.

Gomery, Douglas (1992) *Shared Pleasures: A History of Movie Presentation in the United States*. Madison: University of Wisconsin Press.

Gorky, Maxim (1960) 'Review of the Lumiere Programme at the Nizhni-Novgorod Fair' [1896], in Jay Leyda (ed. and trans.) *Kino: A History of the Russian and Soviet Film*. London: Allen & Unwin, pp. 407–9.

Graham, Kathryn G. (2001) Interview with Edie Bouvier Beale and Albert Maysles [1976]. Special features, *Grey Gardens*, dir. David and Albert Maysles [DVD], Criterion.

Grant, Barry Keith (1998) 'Ethnography in the First Person: Frederick Wiseman's *Titicut Follies*', in Grant and Sloniowski (eds), pp. 238–53.

Grant, Barry Keith and Sloniowski, Jeannette (eds) (1998) *Documenting the Documentary: Close Readings of Documentary Film and Video*. Detroit: Wayne State University Press.

Grau, Robert (1912) *The Stage in the Twentieth Century*, Vol. 3. New York: Broadway Publishing.

Grierson, John (1946) 'First Principles of Documentary' [1932], in Hardy (ed.), pp. 78–89.

Grierson, John (1979) 'Flaherty's Poetic *Moana*' [1926], in Jacobs (ed.), pp. 25–6.

Griffith, Richard (1952) 'Documentary Film Since 1939: North and Latin America', in Rotha (1952), pp. 308–43.

Griffiths, Alison (2002) *Wondrous Difference: Cinema, Anthropology, and Turn-of-the-Century Visual Culture*. New York: Columbia University Press.

Guenette, Robert (1987) 'Oscar Winning Documentaries: Attention Must Be Paid', *Hollywood Reporter*, 17 March, pp. S26–S28.

Gunning, Tom (1990) 'The Cinema of Attractions: Early Film, Its Spectator and the Avant-Garde', in Thomas Elsaesser (ed.), *Early Cinema: Space, Frame, Narrative*. London: BFI, pp. 56–62.

Gunning, Tom (2002) 'Vienna Avant-Garde and Early Cinema'. Online at: http://www.sixpackfilm.com/archive (accessed 6 August 2010).

Gunning, Tom (2003) 'Never Seen This Picture Before: Muybridge in Multiplicity', in Prodger, pp. 222–72.

Gunning, Tom (2006) ' "The Whole World Within Reach": Travel Images Without Borders', in Ruoff (ed.), pp. 25–41.

Gunning, Tom (2009) 'Invisible Cities, Visible Cinema: Illuminating Shadows in Late Film Noir', *Comparative Critical Studies*, 6.3 (November): 319–32.

Hadley, Elizabeth Amelia (1999) '*Eyes on the Prize*: Reclaiming Black Images, Culture, and History', in Klotman and Cutler (eds), pp. 99–121.

Haggith, Toby (2005) 'Filming the Liberation of Bergen Belsen', in Haggith and Newman (eds), pp. 33–49.

Haggith, Toby and Newman, Joanna (eds) (2005) *Holocaust and the Moving Image: Representations in Film and Television Since 1933*. London: Wallflower.

Hall, Mordaunt (1933) '*Samarang*' [review], *New York Times*, 29 June, p. 22.

Hall, Stuart (1988) 'Media Power: The Double Bind', in Rosenthal (ed.), pp. 357–64.

Hall, Stuart (1996) 'Gramsci's Relevance for the Study of Race and Ethnicity', in David Morley and Kuan-Hsing Chen (eds), *Stuart Hall: Critical Dialogues in Cultural Studies*. London: Routledge, pp. 411–41.

Halleck, DeeDee (2002) *Hand-Held Visions: The Impossible Possibilities of Community Media*. New York: Fordham University Press.

Hamilton, Jim (1999) *The Writing 69th: Civilian War Correspondents Accompany a U.S. Bombing Raid*. Marshfield, MA: Green Harbor.

Hansen, Miriam (1994) *Babel to Babylon: Spectatorship in American Silent Film*. Cambridge, MA: Harvard University Press.

Hansen, Miriam (1995) 'America, Paris, the Alps: Kracauer (and Benjamin) on Cinema and Modernity', in Leo Charney and Vanessa R. Schwartz (eds), *Cinema and the Invention of Modern Life*. Berkeley: University of California Press, pp. 362–402.

Hardwicke, Leon (1944) 'Politics Blamed in Shelving of Soldier Movie', *Los Angeles Sentinel*, 30 March, p. 13.

Hardy, Forsyth (ed.) (1946) *Grierson on Documentary*. London: Collins.

Harmetz, Aljean (1986) 'Nonfiction is Surging in Movies', *New York Times*, 19 April, p. C21.

Harper, Kenn (2001) *Give Me My Father's Body: The Life of Minik, the New York Eskimo*. New York: Washington Square.

Haskell, Molly (1976) 'Whatever Happened to Baby Edie?' *Village Voice*, 1 March, p. 118.

Haynes, John (2007) 'Documentary as Social Justice Activism: The Textual and Political Strategies of Robert Greenwald and Brave New Films', *49th Parallel* 21 (Autumn): 1–16. Online at: http://www.49thparallel.bham.ac.uk/back/issue21/Haynes.pdf (accessed 10 July 2008).

Hayward, Susan (2005) *French National Cinema* [1993]. London: Routledge.

Heider, Karl G. (1988) 'The *Rashomon* Effect: When Ethnographers Disagree', *American Anthropologist*, 90.1 (March): 73–81.

Higson, Andrew (1995) *Waving the Flag: Constructing a National Cinema in Britain*. Oxford: Oxford University Press.

Hine, Lewis W. (1980) 'Social Photography: How the Camera May Help in the General
    Uplift' [1909], in Alan Trachtenberg (ed.), *Classic Essays on Photography*. New Haven, CT:
    Leete's Island Books, pp. 110–13.
Hinson, Hal (1988) '*The Thin Blue Line*' [review], *Washington Post*, 2 September, D7.
'History of the Reel World' (2008) Little Theatre website, Rochester, New York. Online at:
    http://www.thelittle.org/history.php (accessed 10 October 2008).
Hitchens, Christopher (2004) 'Unfairenheit 9/11: The Lies of Michael Moore', *Slate*, 21 June.
    Online at: http://www.slate.com/id/2102723 (accessed 15 January 2008).
Hockings, Paul (ed.) (1993) *Principles of Visual Anthropology*. The Hague: Mouton de
    Gruyter.
Hollinger, David (1995) *Postethnic America: Beyond Multiculturalism*. New York: Basic Books.
Hoorn, Frederick W. (1990) 'Memo for the Record, 21 December' [1942], in Culbert (ed.),
    Vol. 2, p. 377.
Horak, Jan-Christopher (1993) 'Avant-Garde Film', in Balio (ed.), pp. 387–404.
Horak, Jan-Christopher (ed.) (1995) *Lovers of Cinema: The First American Film Avant-Garde,
    1919–1945*. Madison: University of Wisconsin Press.
Huffman, Nicole (2001) 'New Frontiers in American Documentary Film: the 1930s'. Online
    at: http://xroads.virginia.edu/~ma01/Huffman/Frontier/frontier.html (accessed 1
    December 2008).
Hüppauf, Bernd (1993) 'Experiences of Modern Warfare and the Crisis of Representation',
    New German Critique, 59 (Spring–Summer): 41–76.
Hurwitz, Leo T. (1979) 'The Revolutionary Film – The Next Step' [1934], in Jacobs (ed.), pp.
    91–3.
Huston, John (1980) *An Open Book*. New York: Alfred A. Knopf.
Huyssen, Andreas (1986) *After the Great Divide: Modernism, Mass Culture, Postmodernism*.
    Bloomington: Indiana University Press.
Iseli, Christian (1998) 'Where Docs are Sexy', *Dox*, 18 (August): 14–16.
Ivens, Joris (1969) *The Camera and I*. Berlin: Seven Seas.
Ivens, Joris (1988) 'Reflections on the Avant-Garde Documentary' [1931], in Richard Abel
    (ed.), *French Film Theory and Criticism, 1907–1939: A History/Anthology*, Vol. 2. Princeton:
    Princeton University Press, pp. 78–80.
Jaafar, Ali (2008) 'Casualties of War', *Sight and Sound*, 18.2 (February): 16–22.
Jackson, Lynne (1987) 'The Production of George Stoney's *All My Babies: A Midwife's Own
    Story* (1952)', *Film History*, 1.4: 367–91.
Jacobs, Lewis (1947–8) 'Experimental Cinema in America' [Parts 1 and 2], *Hollywood
    Quarterly*, 3.2–3 (Winter and Spring): 111–24; 278–92.
Jacobs, Lewis (ed.) (1979) *The Documentary Tradition*. New York: W. W. Norton.
Jahusz, Alexandra (1999) 'They Said We Were Trying to Show Reality – All I Want to Show
    Is My Video: The Politics of the Realist Feminist Documentary', in Gaines and Renov
    (eds), pp. 190–215.
Jakobsen, Janet and Seckinger, Beverly (1997) 'Love, Death, and Videotape: *Silverlake Life*',
    in Chris Holmund and Cynthia Fuchs (eds), *Between the Sheets, In the Streets: Queer,
    Lesbian, and Gay Documentary*. Minneapolis: University of Minnesota Press, pp. 144–57.
James, David E. (2005) *The Most Typical Avant-Garde: History and Geography of Minor
    Cinemas in Los Angeles*. Berkeley: University of California Press.
James, David E. (2006) 'Film and War: Representing Vietnam', in Slocum (ed.), pp. 225–38.
Jameson, Fredric (1996) 'Postmodernism and Consumer Society' [1983], in John Belton (ed.),
    Movies and Mass Culture. New Brunswick, NJ: Rutgers University Press, pp. 185–202.
Johnson, Lyndon B. (1964) 'The Great Society' (22 May), *Humanities and Social Sciences*

Online. Online at: http://www.h-net.org/~hst306/documents/great.html (accessed 5 February 2010).

Johnston, Claire (1999) 'Women's Cinema as Counter-Cinema' [1973], in Sue Thornham (ed.), *Feminist Film Theory: A Reader*. Edinburgh: Edinburgh University Press, pp. 31–40.

Jones, D. B. (1988) 'The Canadian Film Board Unit B', in Rosenthal (ed.), pp. 133–47.

Jones, Jacquie (1993) 'The Construction of Black Sexuality', in Manthia Diawara (ed.), *Black American Cinema*. New York: Routledge, pp. 247–56.

Judovitz, Dalia (1996) 'Anemic Vision in Duchamp: Cinema as Readymade', in Kuenzli (ed.), pp. 46–57.

Kachru, Braj B., Kachru, Yamuna and Nelson, Cecil L. (2006) *The Handbook of World Englishes*. London: Blackwell.

Kahana, Jonathan (2008) *Intelligence Work: The Politics of American Documentary*. New York: Columbia University Press.

Kaplan, Amy (2002) *The Anarchy of Empire in the Making of U.S. Culture*. Cambridge, MA: Harvard University Press.

Kattelle, Alan D. (1986) 'The Evolution of Amateur Motion Picture Equipment, 1895–1965', *Journal of Film and Video*, 38 (Summer/Fall): 47–57.

Keil, Charlie (1998) 'American Documentary Finds Its Voice: Persuasion and Expression in *The Plow that Broke the Plains* and *The City*', in Grant and Sloniowski (eds), pp. 119–35.

Khatchadourian, Raffi (2010) 'No Secrets: Julian Assange's Mission for Total Transparency', *The New Yorker*, 7 June, pp. 40–51.

Kilborn, Richard (2003) *Staging the Real: Factual TV Programming in the Age of Big Brother*. Manchester: Manchester University Press.

Kirby, Lynne (1997) *Parallel Tracks: The Railroad and Silent Cinema*. Durham, NC: Duke University Press.

Kittler, Friedrich D. (1999) *Gramophone, Film, Typewriter*, trans. Geoffrey Winthrop-Young and Michael Wutz. Stanford: Stanford University Press.

Kleinhans, Chuck (1991) '*Ethnic Notions* and *Tongues Untied*: Mainstreams and Margins', *Jump Cut*, 36 (May): 108–11.

Klotman, Phyllis R. and Cutler, Janet K. (eds) (1999) *Struggles for Representation: African American Documentary Film and Video*. Bloomington: Indiana University Press.

Koppes, Clayton R. (1997) 'Regulating the Screen: The Office of War Information and the Production Code Administration', in Thomas Schatz (ed.), *Boom and Bust: The American Cinema in the 1940s*. New York: Charles Scribner's, pp. 262–84.

Koppes, Clayton R. and Black, Gregory D. (1988) *Hollywood Goes to War: How Politics, Profits, and Propaganda Shaped World War II Movies*. London: I. B. Tauris.

Koszarski, Richard (1990) *An Evening's Entertainment: The Age of the Silent Feature Picture, 1915–1928*. Berkeley: University of California Press.

Koszarski, Richard (2006) 'Nancy Naumburg: Vassar Revolutionary', *Film History*, 18.4: 374–5.

Kozloff, Sarah (2008) 'Wyler's Wars', *Film History*, 20.4: 456–73.

Kris, Ernst (1943) 'Some Problems of War Propaganda: A Note on Propaganda New and Old', *Psychoanalytic Quarterly*, 12.3: 381–99.

Krows, Arthur Edwin (1936) 'A Quarter-Century of Non-Theatrical Films', *Educational Screen*, 15.6 (June): 169–72.

Kuenzli, Rudolf E. (ed.) (1996) *Dada and Surrealist Film*. Cambridge, MA: MIT Press.

Lamb, Jonathan (ed.) (1994) *Eighteenth Century Life*, 18.3 (Special Issue) (November).

Lane, Jim (2002) *The Autobiographical Documentary in America*. Madison: University of Wisconsin Press.

Larson, Erik (2004) *The Devil in the White City: Murder, Magic, and Madness at the Fair that Changed America*. New York: Vintage.

Leacock, Richard (1990) 'Life on the Other Side of the Moon'. Online at: http://www.richardleackock.com/leackessays.html (accessed 1 July 2010).

Leacock, Richard (1997) 'A Search for the Feeling of Being There' (draft article) (20 May). Online at: http://www.richardleacock.com/leackessays.html (accessed 22 February 2009).

Leacock, Richard (2008) Interview [2000], special features, *Primary*, dir. Drew Associates [DVD], Docurama.

Leacock, Richard (2010) '*Crisis: Behind a Presidential Commitment*'. Online at: http://www.richardleackock.com (accessed 1 July 1010).

LeBlanc, Robert (2009) 'Representing Postmodernity and Marginality in Three Documentary Films', *Comparative Literature and Culture*, 11.2 (June): 1–10. Online at: http://docs.lib.purdue.edu/clcweb/vol11/iss2/12 (accessed 1 July 2010).

Leshne, Carla (2006) 'The Film & Photo League of San Francisco', *Film History*, 18.4: 360–73.

Leuthold, Steven M. (1994) 'Social Accountability and the Production of Native American Film and Video', *Wide Angle*, 16.1–2 (August): 41–59.

Leuthold, Steven M. (1997) 'Native American Documentary: An Emerging Genre?' *Film Criticism*, 22.1 (Fall): 74–90.

'Lewis Jacobs, 92, Writer and Teacher' (1997) Obituary, *New York Times*, 22 February, sec. 1, p. 28.

Lindqvist, Sven (2001) *A History of Bombing*. London: Granta.

Lorde, Audre (1984) 'Age, Race, Class, and Sex: Women Redefining Difference', *Sister Outsider: Essays and Speeches*. Berkeley: Crossing Press, pp. 114–23.

Lorentz, Pare (1975) *Lorentz on Film: Movies 1927 to 1941*. New York: Hopkinson & Blake.

Lorentz, Pare (1992) *FDR's Moviemaker*. Reno: University of Nevada Press.

Lorentz, Pare and Ernst, Morris L. (1930) *Censored: The Private Life of the Movie*. New York: Jonathan Cape.

Lott, Tommy Lee (1999) 'Documenting Social Issues: *Black Journal*, 1968–1970', in Klotman and Cutler (eds), pp. 71–98.

Low, Barbara (1998) 'Mind Growth or Mind Mechanization?' [1927], in Donald et al. (eds), pp. 247–9.

Lyotard, François (1984) *The Postmodern Condition: A Report on Knowledge* [1979], trans. Geoff Bennington and Brian Massumi. Manchester: Manchester University Press.

McAlister, Melani (2001) *Epic Encounters: Culture, Media, and U.S. Interests in the Middle East, 1945–2000*. Berkeley: University of California Press.

McAlister, Melani (2002) 'A Cultural History of War Without End', *Journal of American History*, 89.2: 439–55.

MacCannell, Dean (1999) *The Tourist: A New Theory of the Leisure Class* [1976]. Berkeley: University of California Press.

MacDonald, Scott (1998) 'Southern Exposure: An Interview with Ross McElwee', *Film Quarterly*, 49.4 (Summer): 13–23.

MacDonald, Scott (2003) *Cinema 16: Documents Toward a History of the Film Society*. Philadelphia: Temple University Press.

MacDougall, David (1995) 'The Subjective Voice in Ethnographic Film', in Leslie Devereaux and Roger Hillman (eds), *Fields of Vision: Essays in Film Studies, Visual Anthropology, and Photography*. Berkeley: University of California Press, pp. 217–55.

MacDougall, David (2006) *The Corporeal Image: Film, Ethnography, and the Senses*. Princeton: Princeton University Press.

McEnteer, James (2006) *Shooting the Truth: The Rise of American Political Documentaries.* Westport, CT: Praeger.

Mackenzie, Midge (2000) 'An Antiwar Message from the Army's Messenger', *New York Times*, 16 April, p. AR23.

McKernan, Luke (2006) 'The Delhi Durbar', *Charles Urban, Motion Picture Pioneer*. Online at: http://www.charlesurban.com/durbar_notices.htm (accessed 5 June 2009).

McKernan, Luke (2009) '"The Modern Elixir of Life": Kinemacolor, Royalty, and the Delhi Durbar', *Film History*, 21.2: 122–36.

McLane, Betsy A. (2007) 'The River Runs Through It: The Legacy of Pare Lorentz', *Documentary* (November–December): 81–6.

McLuhan, Marshall (1994) *Understanding Media: The Extensions of Man* [1964]. Boston: MIT Press.

Maloney, T. J. (ed.) (1936) *US Camera – 1936*. London: Newnes.

Maltby, Richard (2003) *Hollywood Cinema*. New York: Wiley-Blackwell.

Mamber, Stephen (1974) *Cinema Verite in America: Studies in Uncontrolled Documentary*. Cambridge, MA: MIT Press.

Marks, Laura U. (2000) *The Skin of Film: Intercultural Cinema, Embodiment, and the Senses*. Durham, NC: Duke University Press.

'The Martin and Osa Johnson Safari Museum' (2002). Online at: http://www.safarimuseum.com (accessed 5 July 2010).

Martinez, Elizabeth (1993) 'Beyond Black/White: The Racisms of Our Time', *Social Justice*, 20.1–2 (Spring–Summer): 1–8.

Matheson, Neil (ed.) (2006) *The Sources of Surrealism*. Aldershot: Ashgate.

Mathews, Jack (1985) 'Huston Documentaries: Only Following Orders', *Los Angeles Times*, 11 September, pp. 3, 6.

Mavor, Carol (1996) *Pleasures Taken: Performances of Sexuality and Loss in Victorian Photographs*. London: I. B. Tauris.

Maxwell, Anne (1999) *Colonial Photography and Exhibitions: Representations of the 'Native' and the Making of European Identities*. London: Cassell.

Mayne, Judith (1993) *Cinema and Spectatorship*. London: Routledge.

Maysles, Albert (2001) Interview with Albert Maysles, special features, *Grey Gardens*, dir. David and Albert Maysles [DVD], Criterion.

Maysles, Albert (2003) 'On Subjects and Truth', *Dox*, 45 (February): 7–8.

Menand, Louis (2004) 'Nanook and Me: *Fahrenheit 9/11* and the Documentary Tradition', *The New Yorker*, 9 August, pp. 90–4.

Mercer, Kobena (1993) 'Dark and Lovely Too: Black Gay Men in Independent Film', in Martha Gever, John Greyson and Pratibha Parmar (eds), *Queer Looks: Perspectives on Lesbian and Gay Film and Video*. London: Routledge, pp. 238–56.

Mercer, Kobena (1994) *Welcome to the Jungle: New Positions in Black Cultural Studies*. New York: Routledge.

Mertes, Cara (1998) 'And the Winner Isn't: Documentaries Lose Big on Oscar Night', *Independent Film and Video Monthly*, 21.5 (June): 7–9.

Metz, Christian (1983) *The Imaginary Signifier: Psychoanalysis and the Cinema*, trans. Celia Britton and Annwyl Williams. Bloomington: Indiana University Press.

Miall, Hugh (2007) *Emergent Conflict and Peaceful Change*. Basingstoke: Palgrave Macmillan.

Michaels, Lloyd (1994) '*The Thin Blue Line* and the Limits of Documentary', *Post Script*, 13.2 (Winter/Spring): 44–50.

Miller, Donald L. (2006) *Eighth Air Force: The American Bomber Crews in Britain*. London: Aurum.

Minow, Newton W. (1961) 'Television and the Public Interest (A Vast Wasteland)' (Speech to the National Association of Broadcasters, 9 May), *American Rhetoric*. Online at: http:// www.americanrhetoric.com/speeches/newtonminow.htm (accessed 1 February 2010).

'Mission Statement' (2010) ITVS, Corporation for Public Broadcasting. Online at: http:// www.itvs.org/about (accessed 1 November 2010).

Morin, Edgar (2003) 'Chronicle of a Film' [1960], in Rouch and Feld (ed. and trans.), pp. 229–65.

Moritz, William (1996) 'Americans in Paris: Man Ray and Dudley Murphy', in Horak (ed.), pp. 118–36.

Mouffe, Chantal (2005) *On the Political*. London: Routledge.

'Murmurs Against Overdose of War Subjects Increase' (1943) *Boxoffice*, 15 May, p. 19.

Murphy, William T. (1978) *Robert Flaherty: A Guide to References and Resources*. Boston: G. K. Hall.

Musser, Charles (1990a) *The Emergence of Cinema: The American Screen to 1907*. Berkeley: University of California Press.

Musser, Charles (1990b) 'The Travel Genre in 1903–1904: Moving Towards Fictional Narrative', in Thomas Elsaesser (ed.), *Early Cinema: Space, Frame, Narrative*. London: BFI, pp. 123–32.

Musser, Charles (2004) 'At the Beginning: Motion Picture Production, Representation and Ideology at the Edison and Lumière Companies', in Lee Grieveson and Peter Krämer (eds), *The Silent Cinema Reader*. London: Routledge, pp. 15–30.

Musser, Charles (2006) 'Introduction: Documentary Before Vérité', *Film History*, 18.4: 355–60.

Musser, Charles (2007) 'Film Truth in the Age of George W. Bush', *Framework*, 48.2 (Fall): 9–35.

Nasaw, David (1993) *Going Out: The Rise and Fall of Public Amusements*. Cambridge, MA: Harvard University Press.

Navarre, Max (1988) 'Fighting the Victim Label', in Douglas Crimp (ed.), *AIDS: Cultural Analysis, Cultural Activism*. Cambridge, MA: MIT Press, pp. 143–6.

Nichols, Bill (1980) *Newsreel: Documentary Filmmaking on the American Left*. New York: Arno.

Nichols, Bill (1981) *Ideology and the Image*. Bloomington: Indiana University Press.

Nichols, Bill (1991) *Representing Reality: Issues and Concepts in Documentary*. Bloomington: Indiana University Press.

Nichols, Bill (2001a) *Introduction to Documentary*. Bloomington: Indiana University Press.

Nichols, Bill (2001b) 'Documentary Film and the Modernist Avant-Garde', *Critical Inquiry*, 27.4 (Summer): 580–610.

Nichols, Bill (2005) '*Battleship Potemkin*: Film Form and Revolution', in Geiger and Rutsky (eds), pp. 158–77.

Nichols, Bill (2010) *Engaging Cinema: An Introduction to Film Studies*. New York: W. W. Norton.

Nietzsche, Friedrich (1979) 'On Truth and Lies in a Nonmoral Sense' [1873], in Daniel Breazeale (ed. and trans.), *Philosophy and Truth: Selections from Nietzsche's Notebooks of the Early 1870s*. Atlantic Highlands, NJ: Humanities Press, pp. 79–101.

Nilsen, Vladimir (1935) 'The Compositional Construction of the Shot', trans. Stephen Garry, *The Cinema as Graphic Art*. London: Newnes, pp. 116–19.

Nolley, Ken (2005) '*Fahrenheit 9/11*: Documentary, Truth-Telling, and Politics', *Film and History*, 35.2: 12–16.

Nugent, Frank S. (1984) 'Dragging *The River*' [1938], in Gene Brown (ed.), *The New York Times Encyclopedia of Film*. New York: Times Books.

O'Connell, P. J. (1992) *Robert Drew and the Development of Cinema Verite in America*. Carbondale: Southern Illinois University Press.

Oberacker, Jon S. (2009) *The People and Me: Michael Moore and the Politics of Political Documentary*. PhD dissertation, University of Massachusetts, Amherst.

Official Catalogue and Guidebook to the Pan-American Exposition (1901). Buffalo: Ahrhart.

Parks, Gordon (2005) *A Hungry Heart: A Memoir*. New York: Simon & Schuster.

Pattee, Fred Lewis (1930) *The New American Literature: 1890–1930*. New York: Century.

Patterson, Orlando (1982) *Slavery and Social Death: A Comparative Study*. Cambridge, MA: Harvard University Press.

Peary, Gerald (2004) Interview with Frederick Wiseman [March 1998]. Online at: http://www.geraldpeary.com/interviews/wxyz/wiseman.html (accessed 5 June 2009).

Pennington, Ron (1980) 'Huston's "Light" Cleared for Limited Screening After 35 Years', *Hollywood Reporter*, 16 December, pp. 1, 4.

Perez, Gilberto (1998) *The Material Ghost: Films and Their Medium*. Baltimore: Johns Hopkins University Press.

Petty, Sheila (1998) 'Silence and Its Opposite: Expressions of Race in *Tongues Untied*', in Grant and Sloniowski (eds), pp. 416–28.

Pierce, David (1992) 'Life With the Lions: Filming *Simba* with Martin and Osa Johnson in Africa' [press kit], *Simba, the King of the Beasts*, dir. Osa and Martin Johnson [DVD], Milestone Film and Video.

Pilger, John (2010) 'Why are Wars Not Being Reported Honestly?' *The Guardian*, 10 December, sec. G2, pp. 4–7.

Pisters, Patricia (2010) 'Logistics of Perception 2.0: Multiple Screen Aesthetics in Iraq War Films', *Film-Philosophy*, 14.1: 232–52.

Plant, Sadie (1992) *The Most Radical Gesture: The Situationist International in a Postmodern Age*. London: Routledge.

Plantinga, Carl (1997) *Rhetoric and Representation in Nonfiction Film*. Cambridge: Cambridge University Press.

Plantinga, Carl (2009) 'Documentary', in Paisley Livingston and Carl R. Plantinga (eds), *The Routledge Companion to Philosophy and Film*. London: Routledge, pp. 494–504.

Polan, Dana (2004) 'Stylistic Regularities (and Peculiarities) of the Hollywood World War II Propaganda Film', in Martin Kaplan and Johanna Blakley (eds), *Warner's War: Politics, Pop Culture and Propaganda in Wartime Hollywood*. Los Angeles: USC Norman Lear Center, pp. 38–47.

Pollack, Howard (1999) *Aaron Copland: The Life and Work of an Uncommon Man*. New York: Henry Holt.

Porton, Richard (2004) 'Weapons of Mass Instruction: Michael Moore's *Fahrenheit 9/11*', *Cineaste*, 29.4: 3–8.

Posner, Bruce (2005) 'Where the Buffalo Roamed . . . Relative Histories of an Early American Avant-Garde Film', in Bruce Posner (ed.), *Unseen Cinema: Early American Avant-Garde Film 1893–1941* [DVD]. Anthology Film Archives.

'*Prelude to War* shown to Public' (1943) *New York Times*, 14 May, p. 16.

Procter, John Robert (1972) 'Isolation or Imperialism' [1898], in Richard E. Welch (ed.), *Imperialists vs. Anti-imperialists: The Debate Over Expansionism in the 1890s*. Itsaca, IL: F. E. Peacock.

Prodger, Phillip (2003) *Time Stands Still: Muybridge and the Instantaneous Photography Movement*. Oxford: Oxford University Press.

Pryluck, Calvin (1976) 'Seeking the Longest Journey: A Conversation with Albert Maysles', *Journal of the University Film Association*, 28.2 (Spring): 9–16.

Rabiger, Michael (2004) *Directing the Documentary*. Amsterdam: Elsevier.

Rabinovitz, Lauren (1991) 'Temptations of Pleasure: Nickelodeons, Amusement Parks, and the Sights of Female Sexuality', *Camera Obscura*, 23 (Spring): 71–90.

Rabinovitz, Lauren (2006) 'From *Hale's Tours* to *Star Tours*: Virtual Voyages, Travel Ride Films, and the Delirium of the Hyper-real', in Ruoff (ed.), pp. 42–60.

Rabinowitz, Paula (1994) *They Must Be Represented: The Politics of Documentary*. London: Verso.

Rabinowitz, Paula (2005) 'The Political Documentary in America Today', *Cineaste*, 30.3 (Summer): 31.

Rafael, Vicente (2000) *White Love and Other Events in Filipino History*. Durham, NC: Duke University Press.

Ray, Robert B. (1985) *A Certain Tendency of the Hollywood Cinema, 1930–1980*. Princeton: Princeton University Press.

Reed, Christopher Robert (2000) *All the World is Here! The Black Presence at the White City*. Bloomington: Indiana University Press.

Renda, Mary A. (2001) *Taking Haiti: Military Occupation and the Culture of U.S. Imperialism, 1915–1940*. Chapel Hill, NC: University of North Carolina Press.

Renov, Michael (1988) *Hollywood's Wartime Woman: Representation and Ideology*. Ann Arbor: UMI Research Press.

Renov, Michael (1993) 'Towards a Poetics of Documentary', in Renov (ed.), pp. 12–36.

Renov, Michael (ed.) (1993) *Theorizing Documentary*. New York: Routledge.

Renov, Michael (1999) 'New Subjectivities: Documentary and Self-Representation in the Post-Verité Age', in Diane Waldman and Janet Walker (eds), *Feminism and Documentary*. Minneapolis: University of Minnesota Press.

Renov, Michael (2004) *The Subject of Documentary*. Minneapolis: University of Minnesota Press.

Renov, Michael and Suderburg, Erika (eds) (1996) *Resolutions: Contemporary Video Practices*. Minneapolis: University of Minnesota Press.

Reynolds, Charles (1979) 'Focus on Al Maysles' [1964], in Jacobs (ed.), pp. 400–5.

Rhodes, John David (2006) ' "Concentrated Ground": *Grey Gardens* and the Cinema of the Domestic', *Framework*, 47.1: 83–105.

Riggs, Marlon (1999) Interview [August 1990], in Klotman and Cutler (eds), pp. 376–83.

Riggs, Marlon (2008) Interview [*P.O.V.*, 1991], special features, *Tongues Untied*, dir. Marlon Riggs [DVD], Frameline.

Rizzo, Sergio (2006) 'Why Less is Still Moore: Celebrity and the Reactive Politics of *Fahrenheit 9/11*', *Film Quarterly*, 59.2: 32–9.

'Robert Hanson, Radio Operator and Last Survivor of the Memphis Belle' (2005) Obituary, *The Times* [London], 2 November, p. 66.

Robinson, David (1996) *From Peep Show to Palace: The Birth of American Film*. New York: Columbia University Press.

Rollins, Peter C. (1998) 'Ideology and Film Rhetoric: Three Documentaries', in Peter Rollins (ed.), *Hollywood as Historian: American Film in a Cultural Context*. Lexington: University Press of Kentucky, pp. 32–48.

Rombes, Nicholas (2008) 'Too Much Reality: Tracing New Wave Surrealism's Roots', *Solpix: Film and Fiction*. Online at: http://www.webdelsol.com/SolPix/sp-nicksurrel.htm (accessed 15 January 2008).

Rony, Fatimah Tobing (1996) *The Third Eye: Race, Cinema, and Ethnographic Spectacle*. Durham, NC: Duke University Press.

Roosevelt, Franklin D. with Rosenman, Samuel I. (1938) *The Public Papers and Addresses of Franklin D. Roosevelt, Vol. 1: 1928–1932*. New York: Random House.

Roscoe, Jane and Hight, Craig (2001) *Faking It: Mock-documentary and the Subversion of Actuality*. Manchester: Manchester University Press.

Rosen, Philip (1993) 'Document and Documentary: On the Persistence of Historical Concepts', in Renov (ed.), pp. 58–89.

Rosen, Philip (1996) 'Nation and Anti-Nation: Concepts of National Cinema in the "New" Media Era', *Diaspora*, 5.3: 375–402.

Rosenberg, Emily S. (1982) *Spreading the American Dream: American Economic and Cultural Expansion, 1890–1945*. New York: Hill & Wang.

Rosenthal, Alan (1971) *The New Documentary in Action: A Casebook in Filmmaking*. Berkeley: University of California Press.

Rosenthal, Alan (ed.) (1988) *New Challenges for Documentary*. Berkeley: University of California Press.

Rosenthal, Alan (2007) *Writing, Directing, and Producing Documentary Films and Videos*. Carbondale: Southern Illinois University Press.

Rosenzweig, Roy (1980) 'Working-Class Struggles in the Great Depression: The Film Record', *Film Library Quarterly*, 13.1: 5–14.

Ross, Steven J. (1998) *Working Class Hollywood: Silent Film and the Shaping of Class in America*. Princeton: Princeton University Press.

Rotha, Paul (1952) *Documentary Film* [1935]. London: Faber & Faber.

Rotha, Paul (1983) *Robert J. Flaherty: A Biography*. Philadelphia: University of Pennsylvania Press.

Rotha, Paul (1999) 'Some Principles of Documentary' [1935], in Duncan Petrie and Robert Kruger (eds), *A Paul Rotha Reader*. Exeter: University of Exeter Press, pp. 148–60.

Rothman, William (1996) 'Eternal Verités', in Charles Warren (ed.), *Beyond Document: Essays on Nonfiction Film*. Hanover, NH: University Press of New England, pp. 79–99.

Rothman, William (1998) 'The Filmmaker as Hunter: Robert Flaherty's *Nanook of the North*', in Grant and Sloniowski (eds), pp. 23–39.

Rouch, Jean and Feld, Steven (ed. and trans.) (2003) *Ciné-Ethnography*. Minneapolis: University of Minnesota Press.

Rowe, Jeremy (2002) 'A Photographic History of Arizona 1850–1920'. Online at: http://www.vintagephoto.com/reference/azphotohistory.htm (accessed 5 March 2010).

Rowe, John Carlos (1996) 'Eye-witness: Documentary Styles in the American Representations of Vietnam', *Cultural Critique*, 3 (Spring): 126–50.

Ruby, Jay (1988) 'The Image Mirrored: Reflexivity and the Documentary Film', in Rosenthal (ed.), pp. 64–77.

Ruby, Jay (2000) *Picturing Culture: Explorations of Film and Anthropology*. Chicago: University of Chicago Press.

'Rule Twelve: Special Rules for Documentary Awards' (2010) Academy of Motion Picture Arts and Sciences. Online at: http://www.oscars.org/awards/academyawards/rules/rule12.html (accessed 5 July 2010).

Ruoff, Jeffrey (ed.) (2006) *Virtual Voyages: Cinema and Travel*. Durham, NC: Duke University Press.

Ryan, Michael (1979) 'Militant Documentary: *Mai 68 par lui-même*', *Ciné-tracts*, 2.3/4 (Fall): 1–20.

Rydell, Robert W. (1984) *All the World's a Fair: Visions of Empire at American International Expositions, 1876–1916*. Chicago: University of Chicago Press.

Rydell, Robert W. (2000) 'World's Columbian Exposition', *The Electronic Encyclopedia of Chicago*. Chicago Historical Society. Online at: http://www.encyclopedia.chicagohistory.org/pages/1386.html (accessed 1 July 2008).

Rydell, Robert W. and Kroes, Rob (2005) *Buffalo Bill in Bologna: The Americanization of the World, 1869–1922*. Chicago: University of Chicago Press.

Sandburg, Carl (1921) 'The Cabinet of Dr. Caligari', *Chicago Daily News*, 12 May, p. 20.

Sapir, Edward (1966) 'Culture, Genuine and Spurious' [1924], in David G. Mandelbaum (ed.), *Culture, Language, and Personality: Selected Essays*. Berkeley: University of California Press, pp. 90–108.

Saunders, Dave (2007) *Direct Cinema: Observational Documentary and the Politics of the Sixties*. London: Wallflower.

Sbardellati, John (2008) 'Brassbound G-Men and Celluloid Reds: the FBI's Search for Communist Propaganda in Wartime Hollywood', *Film History*, 20.4: 412–36.

Schueller, Malini Johar (1998) *U.S. Orientalisms: Race, Nation, and Gender in Literature, 1790–1890*. Ann Arbor: University of Michigan Press.

Schulman, Bruce R. (1996) 'Interactive Guide to the World's Columbian Exposition'. Online at: http://users.vnet.net/schulman/Columbian/columbian.html (accessed 10 June 2008).

Schwartz, Vanessa R. (1995) 'Cinematic Spectatorship Before the Apparatus: The Public Taste for Reality in *Fin-de-Siècle* Paris', in Leo Charney and Vanessa R. Schwartz (eds), *Cinema and the Invention of Modern Life*. Berkeley: University of California Press, pp. 297–319.

Scott, Ian (2006) 'From Toscanini to Tennessee: Robert Riskin, the OWI and the Construction of American Propaganda in World War II', *Journal of American Studies*, 40.2: 347–66.

Scott, Karen (2007) '*Bowling for Columbine*: Postmodern *Cinéma Vérité*?' In the Picture: The Media Education Magazine. Online at: http://www.itpmag.demon.co.uk/Downloads/columbine.html (accessed 15 February 2008).

'Screen: Pictures of 1922' (1922) *New York Times*, 2 July, sec. 4, p. 3.

'The Screen' (1922) [review], *New York Times*, 12 June, p. 16.

Sebald, W. G. (2003) *On the Natural History of Destruction*. London: Hamish Hamilton.

Seltzer, Leo (1980) 'Documenting the Depression of the 1930s', *Film Library Quarterly*, 13.1: 15–22.

Shklovsky, Victor (1965) 'Art as Technique' [1917], in Lee T. Lemon and Marion J. Reis (eds), *Russian Formalist Criticism: Four Essays*. Lincoln, NE: University of Nebraska Press, pp. 3–24.

Shohat, Ella and Stam, Robert (1994) *Unthinking Eurocentrism: Multiculturalism and the Media*. New York: Routledge.

'Show Rainey's African Hunt' (1912) *New York Times*, 16 April, p. 13.

Simmons, Ron (1991) 'Tongues Untied: An Interview with Marlon Riggs', in Essex Hemphill (ed.), *Brother to Brother: New Writings by Black Gay Men*. Boston: Alyson Books, pp. 189–99.

Sklar, Robert (1994) *Movie-Made America: A Cultural History of American Movies*. New York: Vintage.

Skoller, Jeffrey (2005) *Shadows, Specters, Shards: Making History in Avant-garde Film*. Minneapolis: University of Minnesota Press.

Slocum, J. David (ed.) (2006) *Hollywood and War: The Film Reader*. London: Routledge.

Smith, Bernard (1992) *Imagining the Pacific: In the Wake of the Cook Voyages*. New Haven, CT: Yale University Press.

Smith, Valerie (1999) 'Discourses of Family in Black Documentary Film', in Klotman and Cutler (eds), pp. 250–67.

Snyder, Robert L. (1968) *Pare Lorentz and the Documentary Film*. Norman: University of Oklahoma Press.

Sobchack, Vivian (1999) 'Toward a Phenomenology of Nonfictional Film Experience', in Gaines and Renov (eds), pp. 241–54.

Sobchack, Vivian (2004) *Carnal Thoughts: Embodiment and Moving Image Culture.* Berkeley: University of California Press.

Solnit, Rebecca (2003) *River of Shadows: Eadweard Muybridge and the Technological Wild West.* New York: Viking.

Solomon, Norman (2005) *War Made Easy: How Presidents and Pundits Keep Spinning Us to Death.* Hoboken, NJ: Wiley.

Sontag, Susan (1991) 'Notes on Camp' [1964], in Sally Everett (ed.), *Art Theory and Criticism: An Anthology of Formalist, Avant-garde, Contextualist and Post-modernist Thought.* Jefferson, NC: McFarland, pp. 96–109.

Sorlin, Pierre (1994) 'War and Cinema: Interpreting a Relationship', *Historical Journal of Film, Radio, and Television*, 14.4: 357–366.

Springer, Claudia (1986) 'Military Propaganda: Defense Department Films from World War II and Vietnam', *Cultural Critique*, 3 (Spring): 151–67.

Stacey, Jackie (1991) 'Feminine Fascinations: Forms of Identification in Star–Audience Relations', in Christine Gledhill (ed.), *Stardom: The Industry of Desire.* London: Routledge, pp. 145–63.

Stange, Maren (1989) *Symbols of Ideal Life: Social Documentary Photography in America, 1890–1950.* Cambridge: Cambridge University Press.

Starr, Cecil (1954) 'The American Scene', *Saturday Review*, 9 January, pp. 44–6.

Stebbins, Robert (1936) 'Film Checklist', *New Theatre*, September, p. 34.

'Stefansson Off for Arctic Quest' (1913) *New York Times*, 26 May, p. 2.

'Stefansson Tells of White Eskimos' (1912) *New York Times*, 10 September , p. 5.

'Stefansson's Own Peril: Explorer Lessens Rescue Chances on Daring Ice Journey' (1914) *New York Times*, 14 September, p. 9.

Stein, Ellin (1984) 'Leaner Times for Documentarians', *New York Times*, 10 June, p. 25.

Steinmetz, George (2006) 'Drive By Shooting: Making a Documentary About Detroit', *Michigan Quarterly Review*, 45.3 (Summer): 491–513.

Stewart, Phil and Zabarenko, Deborah (2010) 'Gates Assails Internet Group Over Attack Video', *Reuters*, 13 April. Online at: http://www.reuters.com/article/ idUSTRE63C53M20100413 (accessed 5 August 2010).

Stocking, George (1968) *Race, Culture, and Evolution: Essays in the History of Anthropology.* Chicago: University of Chicago Press.

Stocking, George (ed.) (1989) *Romantic Motives: Essays on Anthropological Sensibility.* Madison: University of Wisconsin Press.

Stokes, Melvyn (2008) *D. W. Griffith's The Birth of a Nation: A History of the Most Controversial Motion Picture of All Time.* New York: Oxford University Press.

Stoney, George (2007) Interview, special features, *The Plow That Broke the Plains / The River*, dir. Pare Lorentz [DVD], Naxos.

Stott, William (1973) *Documentary Expression and Thirties America.* Oxford: Oxford University Press.

Strain, Ellen (2003) *Public Places, Private Journeys: Ethnography, Entertainment, and the Tourist Gaze.* New Brunswick, NJ: Rutgers University Press.

Stufkens, André (1999) 'The Song of Movement: Joris Ivens's First Films and the Cycle of the Avant-Garde', in Kees Bakker (ed.), *Joris Ivens and the Documentary Context.* Amsterdam: Amsterdam University Press, pp. 46–70.

Suárez, Juan A. (2002) 'City Space, Technology, Popular Culture: The Modernism of Paul Strand and Charles Sheeler's *Manhatta*', *Journal of American Studies*, 36.1: 85–106.

Susman, Gary (1997) 'The Director's Chair: Spike Lee' [interview], *Industry Central*. Online at: http://www.industrycentral.net/director_interviews/SL01.HTM (accessed 1 September 2009).

Sussex, Elizabeth (1975) *The Rise and Fall of British Documentary: The Story of the Film Movement Founded by John Grierson*. Berkeley: University of California Press.

Taylor, Philip M. (1994) 'War, Brutality, and the Documentary', *Dox*, 1 (Spring): 21–23.

'Tear Gas Routs Reds before White House' (1930) *New York Times*, 7 March, pp. 1–2.

'This Week's Playbills: Alaska-Siberia Pictures' (1912) *New York Times*, 26 May, p. X8.

'This Week's Playbills: Rainey Hunt Pictures' (1912) *New York Times*, 26 May, p. X8.

Thomas, Kendall (1996) ' "Ain't Nothing Like the Real Thing": Black Masculinity, Gay Sexuality, and the Jargon of Authenticity', in Blount and Cunningham (eds), pp. 55–72.

Thurber, John (2000) 'Lionel Rogosin: Made Films with Political Edge', Obituary, *Los Angeles Times*, 12 December, p. B6.

Tishkov, Valery (2000) 'Forget the "Nation": Post-nationalist Understanding of Nationalism', *Ethnic and Racial Studies*, 23.4: 625–50

Toohey, David (2007) 'Material Objects and Aura: Popular Images against and for War', *Review of Policy Research*, 24.6: 609–26.

Toplin, Robert Brent (2005) 'The Long Battle Over *Fahrenheit 9/11*: A Matter of Politics, Not Aesthetics', *Film and History*, 35.2: 8–10.

Triana-Toribio, Núria (2002) *Spanish National Cinema*. London: Routledge.

Trinh T. Minh-ha (1989) 'Outside In Inside Out', in Jim Pines and Paul Willemen (eds), *Questions of Third Cinema*. London: BFI, pp. 133–49.

Trinh T. Minh-ha (1990) 'Documentary Is/Not a Name', *October*, 52: 77–100.

Trinh T. Minh-ha (1992) *Framer Framed*. London: Routledge.

Tyler, Ralph W. (1942) 'Implications of Communications Research for the Public Schools', in Douglas Waples (ed.), *Print, Radio, and Film in a Democracy*. Chicago: University of Chicago Press, pp. 148–58.

Tyndall, Philip (2003) 'Melbourne Independent Filmmakers: Philip Tyndall'. Online at: http://www.innersense.com.au/mif/tyndall.html (accessed 1 June 2010).

Tzara, Tristan (1987) 'DADA Manifesto' [1918], in Mel Gordon (ed.), *DADA Performance*. New York: PAJ, p. 45.

Uricchio, William (1995) 'The City Viewed: The Films of Leyda, Browning, and Weinberg', in Horak (ed.), pp. 287–314.

Urry, John (1990) *The Tourist Gaze: Leisure and Travel in Contemporary Societies*. London: Sage.

Vaché, Jacques (2006) 'From *War Letters*' [1919], in Matheson (ed.), pp. 212–14.

Van Leer, David (1997) 'Visible Silence: Spectatorship in Black Gay and Lesbian Film', in Valerie Smith (ed.), *Representing Blackness: Issues in Film and Video*. New Brunswick, NJ: Rutgers University Press, pp. 157–82.

Vaughan, Dai (1999) *For Documentary: Twelve Essays*. Berkeley: University of California Press.

Vertov, Dziga (1984) *Kino-Eye: The Writings of Dziga Vertov*, ed. Annette Michelson, trans. Kevin O'Brien. Berkeley: University of California Press.

Virilio, Paul (1989) *War and Cinema: The Logistics of Perception*, trans. Patrick Camiller. New York: Verso.

Virilio, Paul (2002) *Desert Screens: War at the Speed of Light*, trans. Michael Degener. London: Athlone.

Vitali, Valentina and Willemen, Paul (eds) (2006) *Theorising National Cinema*. London: Palgrave.

Vogels, Jonathan B. (2005) *The Direct Cinema of David and Albert Maysles*. Carbondale: Southern Illinois University Press.

Waldman, Diane and Walker, Janet (eds) (1999) *Feminism and Documentary*. Minneapolis: University of Minnesota Press.

Wallenberg, Louise (2004) 'New Black Queer Cinema', in Michele Aaron (ed.), *New Queer Cinema: A Critical Reader*. Edinburgh: Edinburgh University Press, pp. 128–43.

Ward, Larry Wayne (1985) *The Motion Picture Goes to War: The US Government Film Effort During World War I*. Ann Arbor: UMI Research Press.

Ward, Paul (2005) *Documentary: The Margins of Reality*. London: Wallflower.

Wasson, Haidee (2005) *Museum Movies: The Museum of Modern Art and the Birth of Art Cinema*. Berkeley: University of California Press.

Watson, Mary Ann (1989) 'Adventures in Reporting: John Kennedy and the *Cinéma Vérité* Television Documentaries of Drew Associates', *Film and History*, 19.2 (May): 26–43.

Waugh, Thomas (1976) 'Beyond *Verité*: Emile de Antonio and the New Documentary of the 70s', *Jump Cut*, 10–11: 33–9.

Waugh, Thomas (1981) *Joris Ivens and the Evolution of the Radical Documentary, 1926–1946*. PhD dissertation, Columbia University.

Waugh, Thomas (ed.) (1984) *'Show Us Life': Toward a History and Aesthetics of the Committed Documentary*. Metuchen, NJ: Scarecrow.

Weber, Cynthia (2006). *'Fahrenheit 9/11*: The Temperature Where Morality Burns', *Journal of American Studies*, 40.1: 113–31.

Wehberg, Hilla (1938) 'Some Recent Developments in the Educational Film Field', *Journal of Educational Sociology*, 12.3 (November): 163–6.

West, Nancy Martha (2000) *Kodak and the Lens of Nostalgia*. Charlottesville, VA: University Press of Virginia.

Williams, Keith (2009) 'Victorian Cinematicity and H. G. Wells's Early Scientific Romances', *Comparative Critical Studies*, 6.3 (November): 347–60.

Williams, Linda (1981) 'Film Body: An Implantation of Perversions', *Ciné-tracts*, 3.4 (Winter): 19–36.

Williams, Linda (1993) 'Mirrors Without Memories: Truth, History, and the New Documentary', *Film Quarterly*, 46.3 (Spring): 9–21.

Williams, Walter L. and Retter, Yolanda (eds) (2003) *Gay and Lesbian Rights in the United States: A Documentary History*. Westport, CT: Greenwood.

Winkler, Allan M. (1978) *The Politics of Propaganda: The Office of War Information 1942–1945*. New Haven, CT: Yale University Press.

Winston, Brian (1986) *Misunderstanding Media*. London: Routledge.

Winston, Brian (1988a) 'Before Grierson, Before Flaherty: The Documentary Film in 1914', *Sight and Sound*, 57 (Autumn): 277–79.

Winston, Brian (1988b) 'Documentary: I Think We are in Trouble' [1978/79], in Rosenthal (ed.), pp. 21–33.

Winston, Brian (1995) *Claiming the Real: The Documentary Film Revisited*. London: BFI.

Winston, Brian (1998) *Media Technology and Society: From the Telegraph to the Internet*. London: Routledge.

Winston, Brian (2000) *Lies, Damn Lies and Documentaries*. London: BFI.

Winston, Brian (2008a) 'Documentary Now' [paper abstract], University of Dundee, 19 March. Online at: http://imaging.dundee.ac.uk/main/events/20080213213630 (accessed 15 July 2010).

Winston, Brian (2008b) *Claiming the Real II: Documentary, Grierson and Beyond*. London: BFI.

Wiseman, Frederick (1976) 'Reply to Elliot Richardson', in Atkins, pp. 69–73.

Wiseman, Frederick (1994) 'Editing as a Four Way Conversation', *Dox*, 1 (Spring): 4–6.

Wolfe, Charles (1993) 'The Poetics and Politics of Nonfiction: Documentary Film', in Balio (ed.), pp. 351–86.

Wolfe, Charles (1997) 'Historicizing the "Voice of God": The Place of Voice-over Commentary in Classical Documentary', *Film History*, 9.2: 149–67.

Wollen, Peter (1982) *Readings and Writings: Semiotic Counter-Strategies*. London: Verso.

Woodman, Sue (2002) 'Edith Bouvier Beale', Obituary, *The Guardian*, 9 February, p. 20.

Wrobel, David M. (1993) *The End of American Exceptionalism: Frontier Anxiety from the Old West to the New Deal*. Lawrence: University of Kansas Press.

Young, Colin (2003) 'Observational Cinema' [1974], in Paul Hockings (ed.), *Principles of Visual Anthropology*. The Hague: de Gruyter, pp. 99–114.

Zavattini, Cesare (1953) 'Some Ideas on the Cinema', *Sight and Sound*, 23.3 (October–December): 64–9.

Zimmermann, Patricia R. (1986) 'The Amateur, the Avant-garde, and Ideologies of Art', *Journal of Film and Video*, 38 (Summer/Fall): 63–85.

Zimmermann, Patricia R. (1995a) *Reel Families: A Social History of Amateur Film*. Bloomington: Indiana University Press.

Zimmermann, Patricia R. (1995b) 'Startling Angles: Amateur Film and the Early Avant-garde', in Horak (ed.), pp. 137–55.

Zimmermann, Patricia R. (2000) *States of Emergency: Documentaries, Wars, Democracies*. Minneapolis: University of Minnesota Press.

Žižek, Slavoj (1989) *The Sublime Object of Ideology*. London: Verso.

Zuber, Sharon (2007) 'The Force of Reality in Direct Cinema: An Interview with Albert Maysles', *Post Script*, 26.3 (Summer): 8–20.

Index